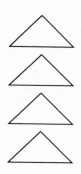

Nonprofit Organizations in a Market Economy

David C. Hammack

Dennis R. Young

Editors

Foreword by Reynold Levy

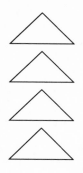

Nonprofit Organizations in a Market Economy

UNDERSTANDING NEW ROLES, ISSUES, AND TRENDS

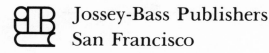

Jossey-Bass Publishers
San Francisco

Substantial discounts on bulk quantities of Jossey-Bass books are available to corporations, professional associations, and other organizations. For details and discount information, contact the special sales department at Jossey-Bass Inc., Publishers. (415) 433-1740; Fax (415) 433-0499.

For sales outside the United States, contact Maxwell Macmillan International Publishing Group, 866 Third Avenue, New York, New York 10022.

Manufactured in the United States of America

 The paper used in this book is acid-free and meets the State of California requirements for recycled paper (50 percent recycled waste, including 10 percent postconsumer waste), which are the strictest guidelines for recycled paper currently in use in the United States.

10% POST CONSUMER WASTE

The ink in this book is either soy- or vegetable-based and during the printing process emits fewer than half the volatile organic compounds (VOCs) emitted by petroleum-based ink.

Library of Congress Cataloging-in-Publication Data

Nonprofit organizations in a market economy : understanding new roles, issues, and trends / [editors], David C. Hammack, Dennis R. Young.
— 1st ed.
    p.   cm. — (A joint publication of the Jossey-Bass nonprofit sector series and the Jossey-Bass public administration series)
    Includes bibliographical references and index.
    ISBN 1-55542-540-2 (alk. paper)
    1. Nonprofit organizations—United States—Management.
I. Hammack, David C.   II. Young, Dennis R., date.   III. Series: The Jossey-Bass nonprofit sector series.   IV. Series: The Jossey-Bass public administration series.
HD62.6.N667   1993
658'.048—dc20   92-41367
                                                     CIP

FIRST EDITION
HB Printing   10 9 8 7 6 5 4 3 2 1   *Code 9343*

A joint publication in
THE JOSSEY-BASS
NONPROFIT SECTOR SERIES
and
THE JOSSEY-BASS
PUBLIC ADMINISTRATION SERIES

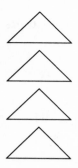

CONTENTS

**Part Three: Interfaces Between Nonprofit
Organizations and Business**

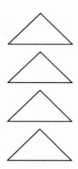

FOREWORD

Are you interested in purchasing a world map? How about a globe? If so, beware—nowadays, it is not easy to find one even reasonably accurate or up to date. The epochal events of the last few years have rapidly transformed the former U.S.S.R. into fifteen independent nations, jealously guarding their sovereignty and defending or redefining their borders. The identical process is well under way in Eastern Europe, including the former Czechoslovakia and Yugoslavia. Pity the mapmakers.

Less dramatically, to be sure, but no less significantly, the borders that once tidily separated governmental, for-profit, and nonprofit institutions are quickly vanishing. The cartographers who map these territories also confront a major challenge. Their representation of the third sector and its relationship to government and especially to business must keep pace with swiftly changing realities.

Vigorous and growing competition for customers between the third sector and business is one changing reality. From day care to foster care to nursing home services, from education to job training, and from the creation to the presentation of art, consumers can now choose between for-profit, governmental, and nonprofit providers.

Evolution is also evident in the deepening customer-supplier relationship between businesses and nonprofits. For enlightened businesses, nonprofit organizations are important sources of new ideas, of research and development, of goods and services, and of employees. Often they are also important customers. For nonprofits, business represents a large market to be tapped for multiple purposes: to garner earned and contributed income; to recruit board members and professional staff; to seek volunteer time, equipment, advertising, and marketing resources.

Beyond the growing competition and cooperation between business and nonprofits is the reality that they both must respond to increasingly similar environmental challenges, such as government regulation and taxation, growing demands from stakeholders for information and accountability, and the impact of rapid technological changes on markets and on management. To address these imperatives, it is critical that the two sectors share information and learn from each other.

Consider an illustration from the performing arts. In the aftermath of World War II, theater, music, and dance were largely the entrepreneurial province of businesspeople. They booked acts, marketed them, rented halls, and lived or died on box office income. These risk-taking impresarios are a vanishing species. Indeed, even the Shuberts and Nederlanders now depend on the creative product emerging from about fifty nonprofit regional theaters that did not exist forty years ago. And those theaters employ business techniques that would be familiar to any for-profit enterprise — advertising, direct mail and direct marketing, focus groups, quantitative consumer research, subscription campaigns, and competitive benchmarking.

The differences and commonalities among and between nonprofits and for-profits provide a rich source of inquiry. From their articulation, researchers, teachers, students, and practitioners can all benefit. To witness an anthology such as this emerge from the literature is therefore a delight.

Nonprofit Organizations in a Market Economy explores new territory and breaks new ground. Its contributors are cartographers quite as much as those who chart the rise and fall of nations. May their numbers multiply.

April 1993   Reynold Levy
                               Corporate vice president, AT&T
                               President, AT&T Foundation

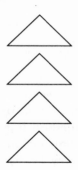

PREFACE

Private nonprofit organizations have sometimes been described as businesses with public missions. Their success is measured not in terms of how much money they make but in terms of how well they achieve the charitable or other public purposes for which they have been established. Accordingly, these organizations are commonly the beneficiaries of a variety of tax preferences and subsidies established by governments at all levels. Unlike governments, however, these organizations have no powers of their own to tax the citizenry or to build up unpaid debt. Like for-profit businesses, they must maintain their own viability by ensuring that revenues cover expenses. Whether they survive and do well depends largely on how effectively they participate in the marketplace. The purpose of this book is to explore the various ways in which nonprofit organizations participate in the market economy, and the issues and implications that derive from that participation.

Background and Scope of the Book

The subject of *Nonprofit Organizations in a Market Economy* is timely for three reasons. First, exploration of this topic helps to extend the boundaries of theory and expand our understanding of nonprofit organizations. The field of nonprofit organization research is a very young one: it began only in the early 1970s, when the Commission on Private Philanthropy and Public Needs, known as the Filer Commission, did the seminal work that helped precipitate the establishment of the sectorwide organization known as INDEPENDENT SECTOR and Yale University's Program on Non-Profit Organizations. Since then, a variety of economic theories have been developed to explain the presence of nonprofit organizations in a market economy and a democratic society. These theories have emphasized the place of nonprofits in areas of the economy where traditional business falls short in the quality of its services or where government fails to offer sufficient supply. While these theories have been critically important in extending our understanding of the nonprofit sector, they have emphasized the substitutive nature of nonprofit organizations—how nonprofits fill in when other institutions fail—not how nonprofits interact, combine, or work in tandem with other kinds of organizations in the economy. An exception is Lester Salamon's theory of third-party government, according to which nonprofit organizations function as contractual partners to government in the provision of public services. This book helps readers understand the other side of the coin—how nonprofits interact with business and how they compete and collaborate in the economic marketplace.

Another reason for the timeliness of this work is that markets have become increasingly important to the economy in the United States and in other countries over the last twenty years. Governments at all levels have been hampered by debt, tax-limitation movements, reductions in tax rates, and public skepticism about their effectiveness in delivering services. Privatization of public industries and contracting with private suppliers to provide publicly financed services have proceeded at a rapid pace. As government's role has receded, both for-profit and nonprofit organizations have come to play more prominent roles as suppliers of public and private services. As a result, markets have substantially replaced the halls of government as the forum in which the allocation and distribution of services and costs are determined and the needs of citizens are addressed.

Parallel developments can be seen in the United Kingdom and in other industrialized countries, too, as well as in the developing world. And of course in Eastern and Central Europe, just emerging from the fall of communism, newly forming democracies and market economies are struggling with many issues, including the role of nonprofit organizations in a market economy.

The third reason for the timeliness of this book is related to the first two. The speed with which markets have become more significant to the life of nonprofit organizations heightens the urgency for leaders, managers, and policy makers in all sectors to understand the role of nonprofits in markets and the issues and challenges resulting from that role. Whether the issue is competitive strategy, ethical practices, or adaptation of business management techniques, the business acumen of nonprofit leaders must be developed to adapt to the rough-and-tumble world of markets. Over the past decade, there has been a growing demand for sophisticated management education for nonprofit leaders and managers. Nonprofit management programs borrow substantially from methods used in the business sector, focusing on such subjects as marketing, entrepreneurship, and financial management, to give their constituents the tools and perspectives that they need to compete in the new market environment. However, an appreciation of how nonprofits operate in markets is a prerequisite to the proper application of those methods. Thus, the place of nonprofits in the market economy is no esoteric subject reserved for scholars and researchers but has important practical implications for those at the firing line in the nonprofit sector.

Audience

Nonprofit Organizations in a Market Economy should be of interest to a wide variety of practitioners and scholars. Lay leaders and top executives, program managers, human resource managers, and resource development professionals of nonprofit organizations — in health care, human services, education, the arts, trade associations, foundations, and many other fields — will find the market-related issues covered in this book to be timely and important.

Scholars and researchers interested in the nonprofit sector from the viewpoint of many different disciplines, including economics, history, political science, sociology, law, public policy, public administration, business and nonprofit management, and ethics, will be able to gain a contemporary understanding of nonprofit-market relationships. The subjects explored in this volume will help them shape their future research agendas. Graduate students intending to pursue nonprofit-sector careers in management, health care, social work, the arts, and other professions will find that the following chapters paint a candid picture of the current realities and the future environments of nonprofit work. Doctoral students in a variety of fields, including economics, political science, sociology, history, public policy, management, and ethics, will find many possibilities here for dissertation research.

Finally, the book should be of substantial import to policy makers in government and policy advocates in the nonprofit sector. There are many dimensions along which the changing market relationships of nonprofits require greater scrutiny by policy makers, including policies affecting competition, regulation, subsidy, and tax treatment of nonprofit organizations. All these are discussed from several different angles within the pages of this book.

Overview of the Contents

The chapter contributors grapple with a variety of issues associated with the participation of nonprofit organizations in a market economy. These include global issues, such as what role nonprofit organizations play in providing services within particular industries and how nonprofits compete with, combine, and facilitate the activities of for-profits in those industries. The

authors also address the participation of nonprofit organizations in the markets for the resources that they require to operate—notably, labor markets and capital markets. Finally, the
book focuses on the relationships between nonprofit organizations and business, asking how management practices and principles transfer between the sectors and how the two sectors use
each other in carrying out their respective agendas.

In the Introduction, the editors offer a historical and
theoretical overview of the development of the nonprofit sector
in the United States, emphasizing how constitutional issues have
helped shape the manner in which nonprofit organizations
participate in the market economy of this country. Part One
looks at the broad organizational and strategic issues associated
with nonprofit participation in markets. In Chapter One, Elinor
Ostrom and Gina Davis present a conceptual framework for
understanding the different roles that public and private organizations can play as they interface with one another in the
provision of public services. The choices available for organizing elementary and secondary education serve as illustration in
this chapter. In Chapter Two, Catherine C. Eckel and Richard
Steinberg analyze issues of competition and monopoly in nonprofit markets and the appropriateness of applying traditional
antitrust policy in this context. In Chapter Three, Louis Galambos describes, in broad historical terms, the role nonprofits have
played in the evolution of the market economy in the United
States. In Chapter Four, David B. Starkweather focuses on contemporary structural developments in the health care industry,
highlighting the intricate and complex ways in which nonprofits and for-profits have become intertwined. Then, in
Chapter Five, David Knoke examines the structural issues and
internal dynamics of trade associations, which serve as the nonprofit policy and service arms of both for-profit and nonprofit
industries.

Part Two studies the markets for resources that are critical
to the functioning of nonprofit organizations. In Chapter Six,
Anne E. Preston analyzes differences in compensation levels for
scientists and engineers in the for-profit and nonprofit sectors.
She discusses how those differences affect the ability of non-

profits to compete for professional talent. In Chapter Seven, Howard P. Tuckman describes the various strategies by which nonprofit organizations obtain capital and how these organizations compete in capital markets. In Chapter Eight, Lester M. Salamon focuses specifically on the investment practices of foundations, analyzing how these institutions manage their security portfolios in order to generate the investment returns required for charitable purposes. In Chapter Nine, Avner Ben-Ner outlines the reasons nonprofits barter for the resources they need instead of purchasing them in monetized markets and describes the circumstances under which bartering takes place. And in Chapter Ten, Robert F. Carbone reviews the ethical issues that arise as nonprofits operate in the context of the marketplace and employ marketplace practices to raise charitable resources.

Part Three examines specific interfaces between nonprofit organizations and profit-making business. In Chapter Eleven, David Billis offers a critical examination of the circumstances under which it is wise or inappropriate for business and nonprofit organizations to adopt each others' management practices. In Chapter Twelve, P. Michael Timpane documents the evolution of partnerships between schools and for-profit businesses and shows how nonprofit organizations facilitate such collaboration. In Chapter Thirteen, Richard R. Nelson examines how nonprofits are involved in the promulgation of innovations that spur the productivity of the business sector. And in Chapter Fourteen, Jagdish N. Sheth considers how marketing principles used in the business sector can be applied in the nonprofit context.

Finally, in the Conclusion, the editors review the findings of previous chapters and identify a number of important issues for future research. In this chapter, the market economy is characterized as a complex ecology in which nonprofit organizations occupy a variety of strategic niches, many of which are yet to be fully understood and appreciated.

Acknowledgments

Nonprofit Organizations in a Market Economy is the outcome of a national conference hosted by the Mandel Center for Nonprofit

Organizations at Case Western Reserve University in Cleveland, Ohio, in November 1991. (A list of conference participants appears in the Appendix.) The following funders are gratefully acknowledged for their support of the conference and the subsequent development of this volume: the Cleveland Foundation, the George Gund Foundation, the W.K. Kellogg Foundation, the Lilly Endowment, and an anonymous donor. The continuing support of the Mandel Center by the Mandel Associated Foundations and the Premier Industrial Foundation also helped make the conference and the development of the book possible. Finally, the Mandel Center wishes to thank the deans, faculty, and staff of its sponsoring schools for their help in hosting the conference: the Mandel School of Applied Social Sciences (Dean Richard Edwards), the School of Law (Dean Peter Gerhart), and the Weatherhead School of Management (Dean Scott Cowen).

April 1993   David C. Hammack
                                              Shaker Heights, Ohio

                                              Dennis R. Young
                                              Beachwood, Ohio

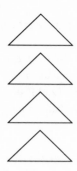

THE EDITORS

David C. Hammack is professor of history and chair of the Committee on the Master's of Nonprofit Organizations degree of the Mandel Center for Nonprofit Organizations at Case Western Reserve University. He received his B.A. degree (1963) in government from Harvard University, his Master of Arts in Teaching degree (1964) in social studies from Reed College, his M.A. degree (1967) in history from Columbia University, and his Ph.D. degree (1974) in history from Columbia University. He has held a Guggenheim Fellowship (1986–87) and has received grants from the American Council of Learned Societies (1988, 1989, 1990), the Russell Sage Foundation (1978, 1981), and the George Gund Foundation (1985). He is currently working on a study of the growth of the nonprofit sector in Cleveland, Ohio, with the help of a grant from Stern College at New York University, and is also compiling a reader on the political development of the nonprofit sector in the United States. Hammack is the author of *Power and Society: Greater New York at the Turn of the Century* (1982; paperback ed., 1987) and *The Russell Sage Foundation: Social Research and Social Action in America, 1907–1947* (1989). He has also authored many articles and reviews on the history of cities, education, and nonprofit organizations.

Dennis R. Young is governing director of the Mandel Center for Nonprofit Organizations and Mandel Professor of Nonprofit Management at Case Western Reserve University. He received his B.E. degree (1964) in electrical engineering from the City College of New York, his M.S. degree (1965) from Stanford University in electrical engineering, and his Ph.D. degree (1969) from Stanford University in engineering–economic systems. Young is author and editor of numerous papers and several books on public services, nonprofit organizations, and management, including *If Not For Profit, For What?* (1983), *Casebook of Management for Nonprofit Organizations* (1985), *Educating Managers of Nonprofit Organizations* (1988, with M. O'Neill), and *Governing, Leading, and Managing Nonprofit Organizations* (1992, with R. M. Hollister and V. A. Hodgkinson). Young is editor-in-chief of the journal *Nonprofit Management and Leadership.*

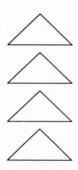

THE CONTRIBUTORS

Avner Ben-Ner teaches in the Industrial Relations Center at the University of Minnesota, Minneapolis St. Paul. He earned his B.A. degree (1975) in philosophy and economics at Ben Gurion University and his M.A. (1978) and Ph.D. (1981) degrees in economics at the State University of New York, Stony Brook. His research interests concern the structure and behavior of organizations from a comparative perspective. He is coeditor, with B. Gui, of *The Nonprofit Sector in the Mixed Economy* and coauthor, with J. M. Montias and E. Neuberger, of *Comparative Economics*, both forthcoming.

David Billis is founder and director of the Centre for Voluntary Organisation at the London School of Economics. He earned his B.Sci. degree (1956) in economics and his Ph.D. degree (1970) in government, both from the London School of Economics. He has more than twenty years' experience in teaching and research on the private, public, and nonprofit sectors and has acted as a consultant in Europe, Asia, and Africa. He is the author of numerous books and papers, the most recent of which is *Organising Public and Voluntary Agencies* (1992).

Robert F. Carbone recently retired from his position as professor of higher education at the University of Maryland, College Park. He received his B.S. degree (1953) in education from Eastern Montana College, his M. Ed. degree (1958) in teacher education from Emory University, and his Ph.D. degree (1961) in education from the University of Chicago. His teaching, research, and professional activities in recent years have focused on fundraising and philanthropy. He has served in several administrative positions, including dean of the College of Education at the University of Maryland from 1970 to 1973 and special assistant to the president of the University of Wisconsin from 1965 to 1970. Carbone is author of the book *Presidential Passages* (1981), and several monographs including *An Agenda for Research on Fund Raising* (1986), *Fund Raisers of Academe* (1987), *Fund Raising as a Profession* (1989), and *Becoming a Profession: Readings for Fund Raisers* (1990).

Gina Davis is a doctoral student in political science at Indiana University, where she has been a research assistant for the Workshop in Political Theory and Policy Analysis and associate instructor in the Department of Political Science. She earned her B.A. degree (1989) in journalism at Indiana University. Her dissertation will focus on alternative institutions for providing education in an urban context.

Catherine C. Eckel is associate professor and associate department head in the Department of Economics at Virginia Polytechnic Institute and State University. She received her B.S. degree (1977) from Virginia Commonwealth University in economics and her Ph.D. degree (1983) from the University of Virginia, also in economics. Her research is in applied microeconomics and economic policy, including privatization, antitrust regulation, experimental economics, and gender issues.

Louis Galambos is professor of history and editor of The Papers of Dwight David Eisenhower at The Johns Hopkins University. He earned his B.A. degree (1955) in history at Indiana University and his M.A. (1957) and Ph.D. (1960) degrees in history at Yale University. He has written extensively on United States business history, business-government relations, the rise of the modern bureaucratic state, and the political economy of institutional development in twentieth-century America. His books include *The Rise of the Corporate Commonwealth: United States Business and Public Policy in the Twentieth Century* (1986, with J. Pratt) and *America at Middle Age: A New History of the U.S. in the Twentieth Century* (1982). Galambos is past president of the Economic History Association and the Business History Conference.

David Knoke is professor of sociology at the University of Minnesota, where he was department chair from 1989 to 1992. He earned his B.A. degree (1969) in psychology and sociology at the University of Michigan, his M.A. degree (1970) in sociology at the University of Chicago, and his Ph.D. degree (1972) in sociology and social work at the University of Michigan. He was a Fulbright Senior Research Scholar at Kiel University in Germany in 1989 and a fellow at the Center for Advanced Study in the Behavioral Sciences at Stanford University in 1992–93. Knoke's books include *Organized for Action* (1981, with J. R. Wood), *The Organizational State* (1987, with E. O. Laumann), *Political Networks* (1990), *Organizing for Collective Action* (1990), and *Basic Social Statistics* (1991, with G. W. Bohrnstedt). His current research projects include investigating the human resource policies of U.S. organizations and comparing labor policy in the United States, Germany, and Japan.

Richard R. Nelson is professor of international and public affairs at Columbia University. He earned his B.A. degree (1952) in economics at Oberlin College and his Ph.D. degree (1956) at Yale University, also in economics. He was for many years a member of Yale's economics department and director of its Institute for Social and Policy Studies; he has also served as senior staff member of the Council of Economic Advisors and as economist at the RAND Corporation. His research has focused largely on the process of long-run economic change, with emphasis on technological advance and the evolution of economic institutions. He is the author of numerous books and papers, including *Technical Change and Economic Theory* (1988, with G. Dosi, C. Freeman, G. Silverberg, and L. Soete) and *National Innovation Systems: A Comparative Study* (forthcoming).

Elinor Ostrom is co-director of the Workshop in Political Theory and Policy Analysis and professor of political science at Indiana University. She earned her B.A. (1954) and Ph.D. (1965) degrees in political science at the University of California, Los Angeles. Her major academic interest is in the field of institutional analysis and design—the study of how rules-in-use affect the incentives facing individuals in particular settings, their behavior, and consequent outcomes. She has studied institutional arrangements related to metropolitan governance and natural resources in both the United States and the Third World. Her books include *Governing the Commons: The Evolution of Institutions for Collective Action* (1990), *Local Government in the United States* (1988, with V. Ostrom and R. Bish), *Strategies of Political Inquiry* (1982), and *Patterns of Metropolitan Police* (1978, with R. B. Parks and G. P. Whitaker).

Anne E. Preston is associate professor of economics at the W. A. Harriman School for Management and Policy at the State University of New York, Stony Brook. She earned her B.A. degree (1977) in economics at Princeton and her M.A. (1981) and Ph.D. (1983) degrees in economics at Harvard. She specializes in labor markets and industrial organization and has written extensively on the economics of the nonprofit sector. A large portion of her work focuses on the comparison of labor market and product market outcomes in the nonprofit and for-profit sectors. She is currently in the midst of a large project that investigates career paths of men and women in the sciences, math, and engineering.

Lester M. Salamon is professor of political science and policy studies at The Johns Hopkins University and director of The

Johns Hopkins Institute for Policy Studies. He earned his B.A. degree (1964) in economics and public policy at Princeton University, and his Ph.D. degree (1971) in government at Harvard University. He has served as director of the Center for Governance and Management Research and of the Nonprofit Sector Project at the Urban Institute in Washington, D.C.; deputy associate director for economic development of the U.S. Office of Management and Budget; and associate professor of policy sciences at Duke University. Salamon's most recent publications include *America's Nonprofit Sector: A Primer* (1992), *Government and the Third Sector: Emerging Relationships in Welfare States* (1992, with B. Gidron and R. Kramer), and *Human Capital and America's Future: An Economic Strategy for the 90s* (1991).

Jagdish N. Sheth is Charles H. Kellstadt Professor of Marketing in the Emory Business School, Emory University. He received his B.Com. degree (1960), with honors, from the University of Madras, and his M.B.A. (1962) and Ph.D. (1966) degrees in business administration from the University of Pittsburgh. Prior to his present position, Sheth was Robert E. Brooker Professor of Marketing at the University of Southern California, Walter H. Stellner Professor of Marketing at the University of Illinois, and a faculty member at Columbia University and the Massachusetts Institute of Technology. Sheth is nationally and internationally known for his scholarly contributions in the fields of marketing, customer satisfaction, global competition, and strategic thinking.

David B. Starkweather is professor of health services management at the University of California, Berkeley, where he holds faculty appointments in the School of Public Health and the School of Business Administration. He earned his A.B. degree (1955) at Bowdoin College, his M.S. degree (1966) at the School of Public Health and Administrative Medicine at Columbia Unviersity, and his Ph.D. degree (1968) in public health from the University of California, Los Angeles. Before joining the faculty in 1969 he was director of the Palo Alto–Stanford Hospital, a new nonprofit organization created to construct and operate a teaching hospital for the Stanford University School of Medicine and a community hospital for the city of Palo Alto. Starkweather is also a member of the College of Business, University of Colorado, and a visiting professor at Shanghai Medical University, People's Republic of China.

Richard Steinberg is associate professor of economics and philanthropic studies at Indiana University–Purdue University at Indianapolis. He received his S.B. degree (1977) in economics from the Massachusetts Institute of Technology and his Ph.D. degree (1984) from the University of Pennsylvania, also in economics. He serves as co-president of the Association for Research on Nonprofit Organizations and Voluntary Action and is deputy editor of the *Nonprofit and Voluntary Sector Quarterly*. His research concerns the economics of the nonprofit sector, including the "crowding out" of donations by government expenditures, the tax treatment of donations, the regulation of fundraising, and the regulation of commercial activities undertaken by nonprofits. He has published articles in several scholarly journals, including *The American Economic Review*, *RAND Journal of Economics*, and *Nonprofit Management and Leadership*.

P. Michael Timpane is president of Teachers College, Columbia University. He earned his B.A. degree (1956) in history and economics at Catholic University, his M.A. degree (1964) in history at Catholic University, and his Master's of Public Administration (1970) at Harvard University; he has also been awarded an honorary Litt.D. degree (1986) by Wagner College and an LL.D. degree (1991) by Catholic University. He has been deeply involved in school-business partnerships for the past fifteen years, working with the Carnegie Corporation of New York and the Committee for Economic Development. He served as director of the National Institute of Education under President Jimmy Carter from 1979 to 1981. He has published many articles and is the coauthor of *Business Impact on Education and Child Development Reform* (1991, with L. M. McNeill).

Howard P. Tuckman is distinguished professor of economics at Memphis State University and a consultant to many nonprofit, for-profit, and government agencies. He received his B.S. degree (1963) in industrial and labor relations from Cornell University and his M.S. (1967) and Ph.D. (1970) degrees in economics from the University of Wisconsin. He served as budget analyst in the federal Office of Management and Budget; as Brookings Economic Policy Fellow to the Secretary of Health, Education, and Welfare; and as executive director of the Florida Tax Reform Commission. He has also been a member of many nonprofit boards. The author of eight books and more than a hundred refereed journal articles, he has been particularly interested in high-level professional labor markets, salary structures, competitive strategies, and the financial position of for-profit and nonprofit organizations.

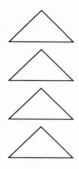

Perspectives on Nonprofits in the Marketplace

David C. Hammack
Dennis R. Young

Nonprofits in the marketplace? By definition, nonprofits exist for purposes other than profit making: they are prohibited from distributing profits to those who lead, control, or invest in them (the "nondistribution constraint"). In the U.S. context, non-profits enable citizens to take advantage of their First Amendment freedoms: to worship as they please and express their religious views through the arts, education, social services, and even medical activities; to live under a government that does not establish a religion; to hold, express, and publish through a free press the political, medical, social, educational, artistic, and other views that appeal to them; and to assemble as they will for the accomplishment of common purposes. U.S. nonprofits are wont to emphasize their "missions" and to state those missions in terms of ultimate values. Under the First Amendment, it might be said, nonprofits are the institutions through which Americans seek to create and maintain a marketplace of ideas and

1

beliefs and to manage the inevitable conflicts that arise in a diverse and expressive society.

Yet nonprofit organizations cannot exist without participating in the ordinary markets for goods and services, and in the United States, certain nonprofits play key roles in the organization of the markets themselves. Every nonprofit organization provides services of some kind, and a very few also produce goods, usually, as in the case of vocational training programs, as a by-product of a service activity. Every nonprofit buys many of the resources it must have to carry out its mission and must acquire other resources through what economists also conceptualize as markets: for charitable donations, for volunteers, and so on.

Nonprofits provide services in many different "markets." They sell many services directly to consumers. Often, their customers pay individually and directly: through tuition for education, admission fees for museums and artistic performances, dues for cultural and athletic centers, pew rents and annual pledges to religious congregations. Sometimes, the customers of nonprofits rely on indirect payments by "third-party" private or government insurance programs to cover fees, notably those charged for health care. Trade associations often provide services to organizations or groups of organizations—business firms, colleges, or local chambers of commerce—rather than to the ultimate consumers.

Nonprofits often provide services through the support of donors who intend to benefit or affect others, under arrangements that can also be conceived of as "markets." Government agencies, business firms, religious organizations, and individuals pay nonprofit organizations to provide counseling, job training, and social services. Government payments are sometimes designed to enable a nonprofit to provide a certain level or quantity of service, planned in advance; but often governments merely agree to pay on the basis of the actual number of clients served—an approach that is in part intended to create a conventional market in the services provided by nonprofits. Religious and cultural nonprofit organizations often provide services—ranging from the offering of prayers and the study of sacred texts to the performance of classical music and the display of modern art—without charge to all who seek them or at charges that do not cover the full cost, with the support of donations from those who are particularly committed to their activities. Through these and other arrangements, nonprofits in the United States engage extensively in the markets for ideas, beliefs, and values.

Nonprofits participate in more familiar markets when they set out to acquire the labor, capital, materials, and management skills that they must have to survive and carry out their missions. They purchase many of these resources in the same way that other economic agents do. But they also secure significant resources through venues not usually recognized as "markets," in which exchanges often involve resources other than money. These include markets for volunteers, in-kind goods and services, employee dedication, and charitable contributions. For example, religious and charitable nonprofits seek contributions from corporations, foundations, and individuals to build physical facilities, provide endowments, and cover operating expenses. In exchange, donors are assured that cherished beliefs will be upheld and valued needs will be served; donors may also receive recognition or other nonmaterial benefits as well. Mutual-benefit nonprofits enable their members to combine their efforts to achieve common goals and secure desired services; they often rely to a significant extent on contributions of labor and facilities.

The analysis of nonprofits in a market economy must thus consider three sorts of questions:

- How do nonprofit organizations acquire the resources necessary for survival and for the fulfillment of their missions? How do nonprofits behave—and how might they most effectively behave—as they participate in the markets for resources? The chapters in this book on the nonprofit labor market (Chapter Six), the capital market (Chapter Seven), investment returns (Chapter Eight), barter (Chapter Nine), and fundraising (Chapter Ten) deal with these questions.

- How are public policies designed for profit-making businesses applied to nonprofits that find themselves in the marketplace—and how *should* those policies be applied? Chapters Two, Three, Four, Five, and Thirteen address these questions.
- How should we understand the local, regional, national, and international ecologies—the numbers of and balances among nonprofit, profit-making, and governmental organizations? What are the conditions under which nonprofits thrive? Chapters One, Two, Three, Five, Eleven, Twelve, Thirteen, and Fourteen take up several of these questions.

All these questions are, in fact, closely related to one another. If it is to find its niche in the total ecology of organizations, each nonprofit must find customers, sponsors, or donors willing to support its production of services and must participate successfully in the relevant markets for labor (including donated or below-price labor), capital, and facilities. As it pursues strategies designed to find and hold its niche, each nonprofit not only must consider when to compete and when to cooperate with other organizations; it must also conduct itself in accordance with the laws and customs of the larger society. The aggregation of all nonprofit, government, and for-profit organizations, under the laws and customs of society and the general conditions of the environment, constitutes the total ecology of organizations that prevails at any given time. Like any other ecology, of course, the ecology of organizations is in constant flux as market conditions—and the social and political factors that shape markets—change.

It is well known that nonprofit organizations play key roles in American life and increasingly significant roles in many other nations (McCarthy, Hodgkinson, Sumariwalla, and Associates, 1992; Gidron, Kramer, and Salamon, 1992). In the United States, nonprofits account for about 7 percent of the gross domestic product and 10 percent of total employment (Hodgkinson and Associates, 1992). These organizations provide the lion's share of classical music, ballet and modern dance, and art and historical exhibitions; half or more of hospital care;

one-fifth of the places in colleges and universities; one-seventh of secondary education; two-thirds of day care; and a very large part of vocational training and family counseling (Rudney, 1987). In the United States, all religious organizations are non-profits. Mutual-benefit associations are also nonprofits in the United States, and they, too, play key roles in American society and politics: they include chambers of commerce and other trade associations, professional associations, interest groups ranging from the Sierra Club and the National Rifle Association to the right to life movement and the National Abortion Rights Action League, and self-help organizations ranging from small immigrant burial societies to very large mutual insurance companies and savings and loan associations (Simon, 1987).

In return for their acceptance of the nondistribution constraint under United States law, nonprofits are exempt from corporate income tax, and some are exempt from other federal, state, and local taxes. Tax provisions vary. Religious organizations are not required to register their existence or report on their activities to the Internal Revenue Service, nor must they pay Social Security taxes on their employees' salaries. On the other hand, governments are not allowed to provide religious organizations with funds or assistance, though they may contract with social service and health care organizations sponsored by religious groups. Charitable nonprofits exist to carry out special missions and to serve the public at large. For most of the twentieth century, those who contribute funds to them have been allowed, within limits, to deduct their contributions from their income when figuring their federal and state income taxes (Simon, 1987). In the past to a much greater extent than at present, charitable nonprofits also enjoyed important protections from lawsuits (Stevens, 1982). Foundations that maintain endowments and distribute funds to others come under a variety of special regulations. Mutual-benefit organizations enjoy certain tax exemptions, but not the deductability of contributions; labor unions and political parties each have their own special regulations; and mutual insurance companies and savings and loans are subject to tax and other regulations specific to their industries (Simon, 1987).

Institutional Failure Theories of Nonprofit Organizations

Economists have offered a variety of theories to explain why nonprofit organizations persist and even thrive in the organizational ecology of the United States and why they seem to be increasingly numerous in many parts of the world. In general, economists have assumed that the "natural" organization in the United States is profit making—that it is created to make profits by meeting a consumer demand, that it survives and grows if it is successful in meeting demand while keeping costs below revenues, and that if its revenues fail to cover its costs, it must go out of existence. In the economists' model, the market determines the fate of each individual organization and controls the overall mix of private organizations at any particular time. Economists go on to note that governments provide "public goods"—goods whose costs are the same whether they are enjoyed by one person or many and whose benefits cannot easily be restricted to those who pay for them. Examples include national defense; police and crime control; the criminal and civil courts; public health measures, ranging from clean water and sewerage to pollution control; radio and television broadcasts; and, under more generous definitions of public interest, education, transportation facilities, and parks and recreation.

As Hansmann (1987) has shown, economists have advanced four theories to account for the existence of nonprofit organizations in the market economy of the United States. First, Weisbrod (1974, 1977) and others argue that nonprofits produce *public goods* beyond those produced by governments, which are limited to the public goods that the "median voter" is willing to support.

Second, Arrow (1963), Nelson (1977), Nelson and Krashinsky (1973), Hansmann (1980), and others have argued that "nonprofits of all types typically arise in situations in which, owing either to the circumstances under which a service is purchased or consumed or to the nature of the service itself, consumers feel unable to evaluate accurately the quantity or the quality of the service a firm produces for them" (Hansmann, 1987, p. 29). Since these circumstances can give unfair advantages to for-profit producers of the service, consumers lack confidence in the arrangements that they are able to make with them. In view of this *contract failure*, they prefer to purchase medical, day-care, educational, public radio and television, and other services from nonprofits. For similar reasons, nonprofits encourage donations, thus increasing the variety of services available and reducing the costs that might otherwise be borne by taxpayers.

Third, Fama and Jensen (1983), Hansmann (1980), and others have suggested that various *government subsidies* — tax exemption, low postal rates, the ability to issue tax-exempt bonds, and favorable treatment under regulations governing taxation and other aspects of employment — help account for the presence of nonprofits in many fields.

Finally, Hansmann (1980), Ben-Ner (1986), and others point out that some nonprofits, especially mutual-benefit organizations that provide services solely to their members or supporters, seem to result not from contract failure or government subsidy but from a desire for *consumer control*, in the sense that members of a country club have an advantage over patrons of a commercial resort in securing the precise quality and cost they prefer — as well as in securing desirable fellow members.

These theories are sometimes stated in such a way as to imply that for the purposes of economic analysis, the "public" goods and services offered by for-profit, government, and nonprofit organizations are essentially homogeneous within general categories. Day-care service is day-care service, the assumption goes; while day-care service provided by one organization may be of higher quality than that provided by another, it is not *different* in any essential sense. But notions of what constitutes a "public good" vary more than many economists have acknowledged. The "median voter," "contract failure," and "consumer control" theories do, however, allow for a more sophisticated understanding: day care, schooling, or family counseling carried on under the "Catholic tradition," the "Orthodox Jewish tradition," the "Lutheran tradition," or the "Social Democrat tradition" may indeed include distinctive qualities that are very important to consumers. One cannot expect the "median voter" to be willing to pay for services desired by those who adhere to a minority religious or cultural tradition. Moreover, one might expect that those who share a common religious tradition will find it easier to share the information and values required to establish mutual trust and that they will value the ability to band together as consumers to control some of the services they need.

Whereas most economists have assumed that the "normal" organization in the United States is a profit-making business firm, political analysts such as Douglas (1987) have assumed that the logical alternative is government. Economists seek to explain the existence of nonprofits by reference to various "market failures." Douglas rejoins that nonprofits—at least those that can be described as public charities—also result from "government failure." Governments succeed, Douglas.argues, when they provide expensive public goods, such as national defense, public order, or clean water, that by their nature are enjoyed by all, whether they pay or not: using its coercive power to tax and to compel obedience, government, and only government, can solve the "free-rider" problem that arises when part of the community seeks to enjoy a general benefit without paying its fair share for it.

Douglas goes on to note, however, that "as soon as we invoke the coercive power of law. . . ordinary principles of democratic freedom and justice require restraints that are not applicable to a purely voluntary service" (1987, p. 46). Democratic governments are thus subject to what he calls the "categorical constraint" that the services they offer must be equitable, equal, uniform, and universal. He finds, in effect, a form of *government failure* when the categorical constraint, together with the "median voter," prevents government from offering diverse, experimental, or flexibly nonbureaucratic services.

Salamon (1987) has proposed that rather than considering either the profit-seeking business firm or government as the "normal" organization, we view the voluntary, charitable, nonprofit organization as the *"preferred mechanism* for providing collective goods" (p. 111). Thus he argues that Americans turn to government only in cases of *voluntary failure* or *philanthropic failure*. Salamon identifies four such failures: *philanthropic insuf-*

ficiency, which occurs when the "free-rider" problem cannot be solved through voluntary action; *philanthropic particularism*, which occurs when a voluntary organization serves only a part of the public — for example, members of its own religious group; *philanthropic paternalism*, which occurs when those who provide the resources exert excessive control; and *philanthropic amateurism*, which occurs when those who pay for a service insist that those who provide it be selected according to criteria other than professional excellence.

Constitutional Basis for Nonprofits in the United States

Like all other organizations, nonprofits are inescapably economic phenomena. But they are not *exclusively* economic phenomena. A brief foray into the historical development of some key constitutional and political characteristics of nonprofits in the United States can help show why Americans value nonprofits and why economic explanations for their existence and prominence are limited. Consideration of historical development can also make it clear why Americans care — and *ought* to care — about the economic health of their nonprofits.

Comparative studies of nonprofit organizations around the globe have just begun to appear, but if — as influential observers since Tocqueville ([1848] 1966) have uniformly asserted — nonprofits have been especially significant in the United States, that would seem to be due to basic constitutional and political decisions far more than to economic forces.

There is a good deal of historical evidence to support Salamon's suggestion (1987) that for Americans, private, voluntary organizations are the preferred providers of many social and cultural services. When Americans decided, in the years after the Revolution, that they disliked the idea of a powerful central government and that they were unwilling to pay high taxes at any level of government, they defined what was to be regarded as a "public good" much more narrowly than did Europeans — and they have maintained a narrower definition to this day. Many constitutional provisions, including federalism, the separation of powers, and the requirement that tax bills originate in the House of Representatives, were successfully designed to make it difficult to expand the role of the federal government.

When Americans further insisted, as a condition for the approval of the Constitution, on a First Amendment that forbids the government to give any church either the political privileges or the economic and moral support of "establishment," they eliminated the standard arrangements through which European nations — both before and after the Protestant Reformation and the Catholic Counter-Reformation — had used the state and the church together to support education, social services and poor relief, health care, and the arts. And when they went on to insist, also in the First Amendment, on guarantees for individual freedom of speech and of assembly, Americans laid the basis for the provision by private voluntary organizations of education, the arts, and much aid to the poor and health care.

Over the course of the nineteenth century, the power of private organizations in the United States grew stronger, most notably through the Supreme Court's endorsement of the integrity of corporate charters and the autonomy of corporate boards in the *Dartmouth College* case (Hall, 1987) and through the widespread adoption in the 1840s and 1850s of general incorporation laws in the states (Handlin and Handlin, 1947; Hartz, 1948). Despite the fact that it involved a nonprofit, the *Dartmouth College* case, like the general incorporation laws, benefited for-profit corporations as well as nonprofits. In addition, however, nineteenth-century nonprofits enjoyed expanding privileges, including reduced exposure to lawsuits, the power to acquire, retain, and increase endowments, and exemption from local and state as well as federal taxes.

Whatever the economic advantages of the nonprofit form, the political advantages have always been of primary importance to Americans. Indeed, political considerations, broadly conceived, have always been cited to justify the nonprofits' tax and other privileges. Above all, nonprofits made it possible to separate church and state. Nonprofits played and still play an essential part in the difficult effort to limit the political impact of America's remarkable religious diversity.

Nonprofits also make it possible for Americans to give concrete form to their rights of free speech. Through a nonprofit, it is possible to teach a very wide variety of political or scientific doctrines. It is possible to base a school, clinic, or antipoverty initiative on an idiosyncratic point of view that commands insufficient political support to influence a government-sponsored institution. And it is possible to found a museum, an academy of arts and sciences, or a cultural center whose purpose is to advance the values of a very specific national, ethnic, religious, or social group.

In the European tradition, as indeed in China and many other parts of the world, sovereignty — the ultimate legitimate power of a state — has almost always been seen as necessarily central and unified. The Constitution of the United States was remarkable in its time, and remains unusual to this day, for the ways in which it fractures sovereignty through the separation of powers and through federalism. With the *Dartmouth College* case, the Supreme Court fractured sovereignty yet again, by assigning what amount to inalienable basic rights to corporations.

In a fundamental sense, the constitutional fragmentation of sovereignty makes it possible for the United States to maintain and to some extent to manage its extraordinary religious, ideological, and ethnic diversity. Because they are allowed some fragments of the powers of sovereignty, nonprofits enable individual Americans to make manifest and to act on their rights to freedom of religion and freedom of speech. Because Americans are free to express their views through independent corporations that enjoy fragments of sovereign power, they can often avoid political conflict over absolutes. The fragmentation of sovereignty makes it easier to accommodate diverse views because it provides the constitutional basis for the "marketplace of ideas."

Recent developments in Yugoslavia, Czechoslovakia, and the former Soviet Union suggest some of the disadvantages of the traditional notion that sovereignty must necessarily be unified and central. These developments also suggest some of the advantages of the American fragmentation of sovereignty. In Central and Eastern Europe — as in Northern Ireland, central

and southeast Asia, and Quebec—members of ethnic and religious groups feel that they must control the central institutions
of the state in order to protect their most cherished cultural,
linguistic, and religious values. In the United States, by contrast,
ethnic, religious, and other groups can protect, preserve, and
advance their values through nonprofit organizations that are
independent of the state—and that the state is constitutionally
forbidden to control. In Yugoslavia, for example, Serbs feel that
they must control the state if they are to protect their language,
their literature, the knowledge of their history, and their religion; in the United States, Orthodox Serbs, Catholic Croats,
Muslims, and all other national and religious minorities are free
to establish language academies, schools, museums, homes for
orphans and the elderly, and so on—it is necessary only that
they muster the necessary resources.

The constitutional basis of nonprofits in the United States
has several implications for the analysis of their participation in
a market economy.

In the first place, in the United States, nonprofits exist not
simply to provide public goods, encourage donations, mitigate
contract failure, absorb subsidies, or empower private clubs.
Under the U.S. Constitution, nonprofits express fundamental
religious, cultural, or political values. They exist both because
the Constitution allows citizens the right to the free expression
of religious and other opinions and because it forbids the state
to establish any particular set of opinions. They provide Americans with the institutions essential to a market of ideas—and
they make it possible for the United States to maintain some
degree of domestic tranquility despite its extraordinary
diversity.

Nonprofits also exist because the American political tradition has generally opposed the level of taxation and government activity that is characteristic of European nations: they are
prominent in part because Americans have adopted a very
narrow definition of "public goods." Nonprofits do encourage
donations, reduce the incidence of contract failure, and allow
those who wish to do so to expand the definition and the
availability of public goods. But in the United States, even char-

itable nonprofits also express the beliefs, values, and opinions of those who support them.

For the purposes of economic analysis, an important consequence of the constitutional and political standing of nonprofits in the United States is that these organizations offer a very diverse array of services, within as well as among the many categories of services offered by nonprofits, categories that range from education, child care, family counseling, antipoverty organizing, and medical care to the presentation of concerts and exhibits. Within each major religious faith, for example, there are continual debates over the religious basis of family counseling or the role of religion in elementary, secondary, and collegiate education. Many ethnic groups maintain cultural centers, each using its own definition of *culture* and defining its own agenda. Even the homes for the elderly run by many ethnic and religious groups have their own characters. From this point of view, Americans utilize their ability to exert consumer control both to provide public goods that are favored by minorities and to resolve the potential conflicts inherent in situations of contract failure. But the term *consumer control* is not really adequate to describe the commitment to shared values and purposes and the concomitant mutual trust that can characterize the adherents to a religious sect or the commitment of those involved in a well-defined educational enterprise.

The essential diversity of American nonprofit organizations was perhaps more evident than it is now during the nineteenth century, when religious belief had a greater explicit impact on many aspects of life. Until the 1880s or later, it was quite generally believed that medical care and poor relief were best provided in a deeply religious context. Some relied chiefly on prayer to heal the sick; others, seeing that medicine had little to offer, believed that sickness should be treated as a prelude to death — and relied on their religious commitments for guidance in meeting the final crisis of life. Most leading thinkers on poverty either took literally the biblical saying "the poor ye shall always have with you" or optimistically believed that the best way to enable a poor person to escape poverty was to persuade him or her to adopt a firm religious faith and to follow a religious way of life.

The successes of scientific medicine and the popularity of "scientific" efforts to reduce poverty in the twentieth century have posed a formidable challenge to the health and welfare efforts organized by every religious tradition in the United States (Stevens, 1982; Rosner, 1982). Early in the twentieth century, business leaders, acting through private foundations, corporate donations, and Community Chest campaigns, began to limit their contributions to religious efforts in these fields and to direct funds toward nonsectarian hospitals and clinics, social service agencies, and universities. The New York School of Social Work and its counterparts in Chicago, Cleveland, and other cities began operations shortly after the turn of the century, providing "scientifically trained" social workers to replace the (sometimes overbearing, maternalistic, overzealous) "friendly visitors" sent out by many nineteenth-century religious congregations. Starting in 1909, the Carnegie Corporation offered pensions to professors who taught in nonsectarian colleges. In 1913, the most influential version of the Community Chest began raising funds for social service programs that were open to all. The community foundations that modeled themselves on the Cleveland Foundation, which dates from 1914, also limited their contributions to nonsectarian organizations (Hammack, 1989a, 1989b, 1987).

Secular, nonsectarian, and apparently nonideological organizations have proliferated throughout the twentieth century, especially in the fields of medicine and welfare. Yet religious and ideological issues have hardly disappeared, and many professedly "scientific" and nonsectarian organizations do in fact rely on deeply held beliefs of one kind or another.

All this makes the economic analysis of nonprofits in the American marketplace as important as it is difficult. A nonprofit is a peculiar sort of economic entity. And nonprofits are much more than economic entities. They enable Americans to express their opinions and to live by their religious beliefs — and they help Americans to manage their religious, cultural, and ethnic conflicts. Thus, there are constitutional and civic as well as

economic reasons to be concerned about the economic behavior and economic well-being of nonprofit organizations.

Contents of This Book

The chapters included in this book consider many of the issues
raised by the participation of nonprofits both in conventional
markets for resources and services and in the broader political
economy in which they are embedded.

The chapters in Part One, Market Strategy and Structure:
Nonprofits as Enterprises, concern the roles of competition and
cooperation among nonprofits and the place of nonprofits in
the U.S. ecology of organizations. From early in the nineteenth
century it has been possible for organizations to take form as
nonprofits, for-profit businesses, or government agencies. The
advocates of "choice" in the selection of schools have made the
question of organizational form a key issue in recent years, as
Elinor Ostrom and Gina Davis remind us in Chapter One. They
identify eleven problems in the provision and production of
education and suggest ways that these problems can be resolved.

Public policy in the United States assumes that a continuous state of competition prevails and should prevail among
individuals and firms in the marketplace. Nonprofits, however,
often seek to cooperate with one another as they endeavor to
meet common needs. As Catherine C. Eckel and Richard Steinberg point out in Chapter Two, prosecutors have recently argued — and courts have sometimes held — that antitrust laws apply to nonprofit corporations just as they apply to for-profit
firms (as, notably, in the "Ivy overlap" case involving consultation about financial aid awards to applicants to two or more
colleges that was decided against the Massachusetts Institute of
Technology in September 1992; DePalma, 1992).

Both profit-making and nonprofit firms do, however, le-
gitimately work to advance common interests through nonprofit associations. In Chapter Three, historian Louis Galambos
emphasizes the ways in which both kinds of firms have used
trade associations to advance their own interests and, in the
process, bring some order to key aspects of the American

economy in the twentieth century. But "order" is an elusive condition. In several fields, nonprofits have found themselves competing, directly or indirectly, with profit-seeking firms and, as a result, have had to confront difficult questions about the law and about appropriate behavior. Since the creation of the federal Medicare and Medicaid programs in the mid 1960s, the most important confrontations have occurred where the increased flow of money has put more at stake: in the health field. In Chapter Four, David B. Starkweather uses several detailed case studies to explore some of the rapidly evolving policy issues in this field, where serious questions have been raised about the rationale for the nonprofit status of some hospitals and other organizations. And in Chapter Five, David Knoke returns to trade associations, noting that whether they serve nonprofits or for-profits these associations are especially concerned with resource acquisition and allocation, authority, integration, and collective action.

The chapters in Part Two, Nonprofits in the Marketplace for Funding and Resources, emphasize the markets for labor and capital. The budgets of nonprofits suggest that labor, which accounts for nearly half of their total expenditures (Hodgkinson and Weitzman, 1989, p. 39), constitutes their most important resource. In Chapter Six, Anne E. Preston uses a detailed analysis of the market for scientists, engineers, and technical workers in the nonprofit and for-profit fields to raise a broad set of questions about the nature and effectiveness of the nonprofit labor market in general. In Chapter Seven, Howard P. Tuckman considers how and why nonprofit organizations obtain capital. Lester M. Salamon's Chapter Eight provides a benchmark assessment of the economic returns that private foundations have been securing on the financial capital they already possess.

In the face of financial stringency, nonprofits are often creative in the ways they secure the resources they need. In Chapter Nine, Avner Ben-Ner provides a thoughtful analysis of the observation that nonprofits rely on barter rather than money purchases more extensively than do profit-seeking firms. In the United States, most successful nonprofits also draw on the reservoir of goodwill "capital" that yields annual contributions from those who support their missions; in Chapter Ten, Robert F. Carbone considers a key aspect of this activity in his discussion of fundraising, ethics, and the marketplace.

The chapters included in Part Three, Interfaces Between Nonprofits and Business, consider a variety of issues that arise when we consider the behavior of nonprofit and profit-seeking organizations operating alongside one another. As the chapters by Galambos and Knoke in Part One emphasize, profit-seeking firms often work through nonprofits to express their views or achieve common purposes. In Chapter Eleven, David Billis discusses the benefits and hazards that arise in the exchange of ideas about management between profit-seeking and nonprofit organizations. In Chapter Twelve, P. Michael Timpane shows how business corporations in many U.S. cities are currently working through nonprofit intermediaries of one sort or another as they look for ways to help the public schools be more effective. Richard R. Nelson explores a still more specific topic, the role of the nonprofit research laboratory in promoting industrial innovation, in Chapter Thirteen. And in Chapter Fourteen, Jagdish N. Sheth argues that nonprofits can learn from the tactics of effective consumer-oriented profit-seeking firms. In these chapters, as throughout the book, we note the central place of nonprofits in the marketplaces for the exchange of ideas as well as goods and services.

In the Conclusion, Dennis R. Young and David C. Hammack review the arguments offered through the body of this book. They conclude with an extensive agenda of research questions raised by this first comprehensive survey of nonprofit organizations in the U.S. marketplace.

References

Arrow, K. "Uncertainty and the Welfare Economics of Medical Care." *American Economic Review*, 1963, *53*, 941–973.

Ben-Ner, A. "Nonprofit Organizations: Why Do They Exist in Market Economies?" In S. Rose-Ackerman (ed.), *The Economics of Nonprofit Institutions: Studies in Structure and Policy*. New York: Oxford University Press, 1986.

DePalma, A. "M.I.T. Ruled Guilty in Antitrust Case." *New York Times*, Sept. 3, 1992, pp. A1, A13.

Douglas, J. "Political Theories of Nonprofit Organization." In W. W. Powell (ed.), *The Nonprofit Sector: A Research Handbook*. New Haven, Conn.: Yale University Press, 1987.

Fama, E., and Jensen, M. "Agency Problems and Residual Claims." *Journal of Law and Economics*, 1983, *26*, 327–350.

Gidron, B., Kramer, R. M., and Salamon, L. M. (eds.). *Government and the Third Sector*. San Francisco: Jossey-Bass, 1992.

Hall, P. D. "A Historical Overview of the Private Nonprofit Sector." In W. W. Powell (ed.), *The Nonprofit Sector: A Research Handbook*. New Haven, Conn.: Yale University Press, 1987.

Hammack, D. C. "Philanthropy." In D. D. Van Tassel and J. Grabowski (eds.), *The Encyclopedia of Cleveland History*. Indianapolis: Indiana University Press, 1987.

Hammack, D. C. "Community Foundations: The Delicate Question of Purpose." In R. Magat (ed.), *An Agile Servant*. New York: Foundation Center, 1989a.

Hammack, D. C. "Private Organizations, Public Purposes: Nonprofits and their Archives." *Journal of American History*, 1989b, *76*, 181–191.

Handlin, O., and Handlin, M. F. *Commonwealth: A Study of the Role of Government in the American Economy: Massachusetts, 1774–1861*. New York: New York University Press, 1947.

Hansmann, H. "The Role of Nonprofit Enterprise." *Yale Law Journal*, 1980, *89*, 835–901.

Hansmann, H. "Economic Theories of Nonprofit Organizations." In W. W. Powell (ed.), *The Nonprofit Sector: A Research Handbook*. New Haven, Conn.: Yale University Press, 1987.

Hartz, L. *Economic Policy and Democratic Thought: Pennsylvania, 1776–1860*. Cambridge, Mass.: Harvard University Press, 1948.

Hodgkinson, V. A., and Weitzman, M. S. *Dimensions of the independent sector: A Statistical Profile*. Washington, D.C.: INDEPENDENT SECTOR, 1989.

Hodgkinson, V. A., and Associates. *The Nonprofit Almanac: Dimensions of the Independent Sector*. San Francisco: Jossey-Bass, 1992.

McCarthy, K. D., Hodgkinson, V. A., Sumariwalla, R. A., and

Associates. *The Nonprofit Sector in the Global Community*. San Francisco: Jossey-Bass, 1992.

Nelson, R. *The Moon and the Ghetto: An Essay on Public Policy Analysis*. New York: Norton, 1977.

Nelson, R., and Krashinsky, M. "Two Major Issues of Public Policy: Public Policy and Organization of Supply." In R. Nelson and D. Young (eds.), *Public Policy for Day Care of Young Children*. Lexington, Mass.: Heath, 1973.

Rosner, D. *A Once Charitable Enterprise: Hospitals and Health Care in Brooklyn and New York 1885–1915*. Cambridge, Mass.: Harvard University Press, 1982.

Rudney, G. "The Scope and Dimensions of Nonprofit Activity." In W. W. Powell (ed.), *The Nonprofit Sector: A Research Handbook*. New Haven, Conn.: Yale University Press, 1987.

Salamon, L. "Partners in Public Service: The Scope and Theory of Government-Nonprofit Relations." In W. W. Powell (ed.), *The Nonprofit Sector: A Research Handbook*. New Haven, Conn.: Yale University Press, 1987.

Simon, J. G. "The Tax Treatment of Nonprofit Organizations: A Review of Federal and State Policies." In W. W. Powell (ed.), *The Nonprofit Sector: A Research Handbook*. New Haven, Conn.: Yale University Press, 1987.

Stevens, R. "A Poor Sort of Memory: Voluntary Hospitals and Government Before the Depression." *Milbank Memorial Fund Quarterly/Health and Society*, 1982, *60*, 551–584.

de Tocqueville, A. *Democracy in America*. (G. Lawrence, trans.; J. P. Mayer, ed.) New York: HarperCollins, 1966. (Originally published 1848.)

Weisbrod, B. "Toward a Theory of the Voluntary Non-Profit Sector in a Three-Sector Economy." E. S. Phelps (ed.), *Altruism, Morality, and Economic Theory*. New York: Russell Sage Foundation, 1974.

Weisbrod, B. *The Voluntary Nonprofit Sector*. Lexington, Mass.: Lexington Books, 1977.

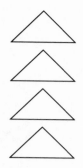

PART ONE

Market Strategy and Structure: Nonprofits as Enterprises

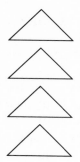

CHAPTER 1

Nonprofit Organizations as Alternatives and Complements in a Mixed Economy

Elinor Ostrom
Gina Davis

In a recent survey, *The Economics of Nonprofit Institutions*, Avner Ben-Ner (1986) asks an important question: "Why do nonprofit organizations exist in market economies?" Ben-Ner concludes by stating that "local public goods are the best candidates for provision by nonprofit organizations" (p. 109). Public goods are those that jointly affect a group of individuals and whose consumption by one person does not substantially reduce the availability of the good to others (Samuelson, 1954). In addition, it is difficult to exclude nonbeneficiaries from some benefits produced when public goods are provided.[1] Local public goods and services affect a subgroup of a population rather than all citizens living in a nation. Given heterogeneity of citizen preferences and demands, nonprofit organizations may facilitate the provision and production of a variety of collective goods to more homogeneous subgroups of diverse, larger populations.

Ben-Ner's conclusions are consistent with those of

Weisbrod (1988), Krashinsky (1986), and many others. These conclusions are based on an analysis of the types of information asymmetries that exist in the provision and production of many goods and services and the need for trust to be established between consumers and producers. With many goods and services, such as education and health care, the producers of the service possess more information about the quality of that service than do those who consume it. Most children and their parents are not as informed about the quality of their education as their teachers are at the time when they consume (or, better conceptualized, coproduce) education. Likewise, medical patients have considerably less knowledge regarding the diverse technical choices offered by health care providers than do their providers. Local, self-organized enterprises may offer better access than government to diverse, localized information, thereby overcoming some of the problems related to mixed goods such as education and health. Many advantages and disadvantages of various institutional types hinge on their success in coping with information problems (Weisbrod, 1988).

Nonprofit organizations have always been involved to a greater or lesser extent in the provision and production of primary and secondary education in the United States.[2] During the last half century, however, primary and secondary education has come to be provided primarily by public school districts. Further, many of these districts have undergone relatively massive consolidations during this era, and public schools are more likely to be part of a large bureaucratic system than to be independently organized, except in smaller suburban and rural communities.

The public school systems that have emerged from this consolidation process are currently the subject of considerable criticism and debate. The Carnegie Forum on Education and the Economy (1986) reports that urban school systems in the United States are marked by stifling bureaucracies, unmotivated students, and inadequate buildings and classrooms and that these schools function as "little more than human storehouses to keep young people off the streets" (Wilson, 1988). Violence against teachers and students in the schools has become almost routine.[3] Parents are taking their children out of public school systems and moving them to private schools. Poor academic performance by students is endemic. Many educators in the United States now argue that a culture of low expectations is fostered in many of the country's public schools. The 97,000 students in the Milwaukee public school system, for example, have a grade point average of 1.62 (D+); and almost half of the public school students drop out without graduating from high school (Fund, 1990). A University of Wisconsin survey showed in 1987 that 62 percent of Milwaukee teachers did not want their own children to attend the schools at which they taught. Nearly half the children of Milwaukee's public school teachers attend private schools — two times the average for all school-age children (Fund, 1990).

During the last decade, many reformers have called for a different set of institutional arrangements for providing local primary and secondary education. Proposals include moving closer to a private market solution by allowing for "educational choice" via pure privatization, vouchers, tax deductions or credits, contract services, and intradistrict, interdistrict, and statewide choice. The basic and common recommendation among policy proposals that fall within an "educational choice" category is that parents be given a greater degree of choice in the selection of their children's schools (Witte, 1990). Advocates of "market solutions" argue that students are the true clients of the educational system and that authorizing parents to choose schools for their children enables diverse demands to be met. A common theme among choice advocates is that choice means that schools will have to compete with one another for students.

Strong opposition is voiced against reliance primarily on market forces rather than governmental provision or regulation even when many of the schools in such a system are likely to be nonprofit organizations. Little is known about how educational levels would be affected in a universal market system or how current public school systems would evolve under market control (Tweedie, Riley, Chubb, and Moe, 1990). Most conceptualizations of the evolution of market-controlled schools assume that parents will choose schools for their children on the basis of such criteria as curricula, teacher competence, and facilities. However, critics of the "market solution" approach argue that parents might not behave as predicted—that is, we cannot be sure of what criteria parents will use to choose schools (Tweedie, Riley, Chubb, and Moe, 1990). Other critics argue that given that the U.S. public educational system has proved resistant to change, we cannot justify replacing it with a "nonsystem" that might be even less responsive to societal goals (Morganthau, 1990).

The current debate about the appropriate mix of institutional arrangements for primary and secondary education provides one highly relevant problem to be analyzed with tools that have been developed by institutional theorists for analyzing the relative capabilities and limits of diverse institutional arrangements. These tools can be used to analyze a variety of similar problems. We make occasional references to the problems associated with the organization of health services to further illustrate our method. In the first section of this chapter, tools developed by scholars engaged in institutional analysis and specifically in the analysis of public economies[4] will be used to identify eleven problems that may be exacerbated or ameliorated depending on the institutional regime used for provision and production of mixed goods such as educational and medical services. Six of these problems affect the provision of mixed goods, and five affect the production.

As we discuss in the next section, for each of the eleven problems, counteracting institutions can be proposed to reduce the potential costs involved in coping with a particular problem.[5] Private nonprofit organizations are frequently recommended as counteracting institutions that can reduce the potential costs of relying exclusively on governmental or private for-profit institutions. But in coping with one problem, counteracting institutions may create incentives that exacerbate other types of problems as "unintended consequences."

In the third section of the chapter, we examine how nonprofit organizations cope more or less effectively with the array of problems identified. This analysis helps to identify the likely trade-offs involved in relying on different types of institutional

regimes. Since all institutional arrangements cope more effectively with some problems than with others, policies relying
exclusively on any particular institutional panacea will fail in
some regards that citizens and officials feel are important. Different levels, types, and dimensions of "outputs" or results mean
that linear comparison between institutional types is highly
problematic.

In a federal system of governance, it is possible to experiment with a variety of different institutional regimes, and the
advantage of encouraging experimentation and learning from
experience is substantial. Reforms as experiments are the topic
of our conclusion. The recent emphasis on "choice" is indeed
encouraging, but a somewhat wider array of institutional
choices is possible than has recently been discussed.

Educational Problems and Counterproductive Behavior

Primary and secondary education is a complex service involving attributes associated with both private and public goods.[6]
Direct benefits of education involve changes in the skills and
knowledge of specific individuals. In regard to *direct* benefits,
education is not a public good — even a local public good. The
direct outcomes of education are immediately enjoyed by individual students, and students can be excluded from formal
educational facilities. All levels and types of education are,
indeed, provided through market exchanges in many countries
of the world. On the other hand, the *indirect* outcomes of education are the increased skills and capabilities of future generations of citizens and workers. An educated populace produces
many benefits for all members of society. Once the general level
of education in a society is increased, no one living in that
society can be excluded from these indirect benefits. Consequently, educational services cannot be fitted neatly into a
private-good-versus-public-good dichotomy: educational services are mixed goods. Many difficulties in designing effective
institutions are related to this fundamental complexity. Further,
the facilities constructed to produce education are jointly used

infrastructures and may even be used for other community services and entertainment.[7]

Similarly, while the direct benefits of an individual's investment in health care are private benefits from which others can be excluded, those direct benefits generate externalities. Immunization against infectious disease directly benefits consumers of that immunization but also generates a positive externality by limiting the spread of infectious disease to others. Likewise, while expenditures on prenatal care — a form of preventive care — offer private, direct benefits to the women receiving such care, one argument for encouraging and even subsidizing prenatal care is that expenditures on this and other types of preventive care can subsequently and significantly mitigate the need for future public expenditures for the care of unhealthy newborns. That is, there are both positive and negative externalities associated with health care — indicating the mixed (public and private) attributes of this good.

In studies of complex goods and local public economies, distinguishing the *provision* of a service from the *production* of it has been an essential step in understanding patterns of behavior and outcomes.[8] *Provision* refers to decisions made about: the kinds of goods and services to be provided; the quantity and quality of these goods and services; the degree to which private activities related to these goods and services are to be regulated; how the provision of these goods and services is to be financed; how the production of these goods and services is to be arranged; and how the performance of those who produce these goods and services is to be monitored. *Production* refers to "the more technical process of transforming inputs into outputs — making a product, or, in many cases, rendering a service" (Oakerson, 1987, p. 7).

In private for-profit exchanges, the distinction between provision and production is obvious. Individuals and households decide which goods and services they wish to provide for themselves and how to provide them. Owners and managers of firms decide how goods are going to be produced and made available to potential consumers. In the public or not-for-profit realm, however, the distinction is not so obvious. The same decision-making unit frequently undertakes both provision and production. The same unit of government, for example, may decide how much education to provide, for whom, who should pay for it, and how to monitor performance—all provision decisions. In addition, the same unit may decide where schools should be built, which teachers should be hired, what curricular materials should be included, and how many hours of instruction are needed—all production decisions. Similarly, a neighborhood school organized as a nonprofit enterprise might make both provision and production decisions without a clear demarkation between these analytically separate types of decisions. It is not, however, logically necessary that all aspects of both provision and production be handled by the same unit.

Once a collectivity (a unit of government or a nonprofit organization) has decided to provide a particular type of education, that collectivity must then decide whether it will produce educational services itself, mandate other enterprises to produce these services, encourage the production of education through financial incentives given to other enterprises, or contract with private or public agencies to set up a school, hire teachers, and teach students (Ostrom and Ostrom, 1978).

The Chain of Choices Involved in Educational Processes

Before one can successfully reform any system, one has to understand how the system operates. This involves learning how patterns of actions and outcomes are affected by incentives that are, in turn, generated by current institutions as these interact with the attributes of the goods and services involved. Simply understanding why current systems of education yield undesirable consequences is itself a considerable challenge, given the number of individuals who are involved in the complex processes of providing and producing education. Students, teachers, school administrators, legislators, parents, voters, and judges all make educational decisions. Individuals make such decisions on the basis of their beliefs, preferences, and time perspectives as they weigh perceived benefits and costs of each decision (V. Ostrom, 1990).

At the core of the process is a growing child who is confronted every day with a series of decisions that cumulatively affect the child's long-term future. The child is asked to invest time and effort in what is for many children a painful and unpleasant activity. Not only is acquiring skills and knowledge a difficult and, at times, frustrating task; it is one for which the child is constantly being judged and rewarded or sanctioned by teachers, friends, and parents. The child is making an investment decision under great uncertainty. Children are not expected to have the appropriate knowledge and time horizons to make "rational" investment decisions under uncertainty. Even adults often have difficulty making rational investment decisions in situations where uncertain results will not be felt for some years.

Because the key actor in the chain of decisions leading to the production of direct outcomes is not equipped to make rational investment decisions independently, adults are empowered to act as agents for the child. This is the first principal-agent problem involved in educational processes. The debates over educational institutions are largely related to the question of which adults in what positions should be empowered to act as the primary agents for children in regard to the children's education. In the institutional regimes designed by educational professionals and now in place in most U.S. urban areas, adults associated with state boards of education and consolidated school districts are assigned authority to act as agents for the children assigned to their jurisdictions. Unless parents opt out of the public educational system to select and pay for a private school, parental choice is limited to (1) housing decisions (involving high entry and exit costs); (2) voting decisions (which, as we discuss below, are not very effective in translating parents' concerns into educational outcomes); and (3) trying to help motivate their children and help them learn (which, in some schools, is strongly discouraged). It is feared that parents who have themselves been educationally disadvantaged will not serve as adequate agents for their children. School principals and teachers are also assigned a limited agency role with reference to students.

Because educational processes generate substantial indirect outcomes — externalities — affecting everyone in a society, a second principal-agent problem is also involved. Here the "principal" is a community and not a single child. Members of the community are benefited by an educated populace able to increase the wealth of the community and to participate effectively in civic affairs. Since education is costly, those paying taxes want education to be provided efficiently. A community of individuals, however, cannot take collective action to achieve indirect benefits without institutions that create agents authorized to act for the community. The same agents who are empowered to act for the child — with the exception of the parent — are also empowered to act for the community.

Education is not the only process that involves a large number of different individuals in an interdependent chain of choices. As Austrian economists (Hayek, 1945; Lachmann, 1978) and German theory-of-order (*ordnungstheorie*) economists (Eucken, 1951) long ago recognized, many products are produced as a result of a long chain of interdependent choices. Market mechanisms are amazingly effective in solving embedded coordination problems when most of the choices have large, immediate, and direct impacts on each participant and signal information and rewards consistent with each person's contribution to the overall outcome. No one need act as anyone else's agent when these conditions exist.

The chain of choices involved in educational processes, however, is not a straightforward coordination problem easily solved by the establishment of effective market institutions. The presence of two principal-agent relationships nested in the chain already signals the need for complex institutional designs involving efforts to generate information and incentives or payoffs to help increase the likelihood that agents effectively carry out the interests of their principals. Many of these choices in the educational chain will affect the structure of the chain itself as it unfolds through time. The consequences of individual choices may be only loosely connected to the individual chooser, even though the cumulative consequences for others may be of considerable magnitude. The alternatives available to children and their parents are strongly dependent on the choices made by many others at earlier junctures. Children and their parents may not have much impact on those earlier choices. All of these decisions can be made in regimes that generate various incentives leading to perverse rather than productive outcomes. Let us turn to an analysis of six problems occurring on the provision side and five on the production side of educational processes.

Institutional Incentives: Problems in the Provision of Education

Indirect Benefits, Nonexclusion, and Free Riding. Nonexcludability is cited by scholars as the hallmark of a good that must be publicly rather than privately provided. Whenever exclusion is costly, those wishing to receive benefits face a potential free-rider or collective-action problem (Olson, 1965). Individuals who gain from the indirect benefits (externalities) of an educational system, for example, may not wish to pay for these services, hoping that others will bear the burden. This is not to say that all individuals will free ride whenever they have the chance. Free-riding incentives are substantial enough in regard to education, however, that without counteracting institutions, the indirect benefits of education would be provided at a level that is far from optimal.

Several counteracting institutions can help beneficiaries to overcome free-rider incentives. A governmental unit organized at a local, regional, or national level taxes citizens to pay for educational services for all children of a particular age. Parents who pay tuition to a school can be given tax incentives or credits to encourage a higher level of investment in educational services without direct taxation. Private groups that can control their own membership, such as clubs, are also able to overcome some problems of collective action (Buchanan, 1965). Overcoming free-rider behavior dependent on strictly private institutions requires devising mechanisms that assure members that (1) the benefits they receive will be greater than their costs; (2) their contributions are necessary to the achievement of the collective benefit; and (3) most beneficiaries will contribute their share of needed inputs (Frohlich and Oppenheimer, 1971, 1974; Frohlich, Oppenheimer, and Young, 1971; E. Ostrom, 1990; Popkin, 1981).

Direct Benefits, Exclusion, and Equity. Given that the direct benefits of education are subject to exclusion, any institutional arrangement that relies primarily on private rather than public provision generates inequities over time. Children of poor families are unable to gain as good an education as their abilities warrant if their access to education is entirely determined by fees paid by their families. A strictly private market for education has extremely unattractive distributional consequences. Collecting taxes for education from a large taxing unit, however, does not ensure that educational services are made available in an equitable fashion. The distribution of access to educational services can easily be biased so that some individuals have many more opportunities than others.

In large-scale school districts, for example, new schools may be rapidly constructed in some neighborhoods in response to a growing population and only with considerable delay in neighborhoods serving poorer and less articulate families. Thus, while provision of education by large-scale governments has the surface appearance of solving distributional problems, detailed and careful analyses of the internal policies followed within particular school districts are needed before any confidence can be gained that equitable distribution has actually occurred (Levy, Meltsner, and Wildavsky, 1974).

The Public Fisc as a Common Pool and Rent Seeking. Assigning responsibility for the provision of education to a government reduces the opportunities for indirect beneficiaries to free ride and is presumed to solve the problem of inequitable distribution. Free riding on the part of beneficiaries, however, does not exhaust the opportunistic strategies that are potentially associated with the provision of educational services. Once a public fisc is used to provide any good or service, temptations to engage in rent seeking are generated. Rents are the profits earned by a holder of a property right that exceed the returns that could be obtained in a competitive market. Individuals may obtain rents simply because they are fortunate enough to hold property rights with special advantages. Rents may be created, however, by investing time and effort in seeking political advantages in the form of subsidies, contracts, increased salaries, or other forms of remuneration (Buchanan, Tollison, and Tullock, 1980; Krueger, 1974; Tollison, 1982).

The temptation to engage in rent-seeking activities and the likelihood of success for a well-organized activity are both enhanced when the source of the common fisc is large and distant. The larger the tax-collecting unit, the more public funds seem like "other people's money" and, thus, to be sought after rather than conserved and wisely expended. The effect of rent-seeking activities is frequently referred to as an "allocation" problem. Everyone wants more schools and more programs when the image is that whatever money is not spent in one location will be lost and spent somewhere else. The larger the unit providing the public fisc, the more likely that small and well-organized groups will successfully dominate expenditure decisions. Because the costs of such raids are thinly spread across a large group, the costs of information and organization to prevent rent-seeking activities are frequently so high that the collective-action problem involved in preventing these activities is insurmountable.

Educational officials face strong incentives to lobby for educational investments of greater scale and complexity (and, therefore, greater cost) than would be warranted by a more realistic prediction of the returns that can be expected from the investment. Special categories of potential consumers, such as the urban middle class, may stand to gain so much from educational services that they actively seek out public funds for projects, generating disproportionate benefits for these consumers.

The potential for rent seeking, then, raises questions regarding the incentives of district school board members elected by jurisdiction or ward and those elected at large. We expect rent seeking to at least be influenced by a school board member's own area of residence and tax district and the ability of certain smaller groups within a larger tax district to organize themselves and successfully influence school board members.

Measurement and Asymmetrical Information. Although the measurement of some attributes of virtually all goods is difficult, measuring the benefits produced by education presents numerous challenges to those responsible for provision and monitoring. Since the outcomes of education are difficult to measure, input measures are frequently used as proxies for outcomes. Such proxy measures as the money spent per pupil or the educational credentials of teachers are unreliable. High-paid, well-qualified teachers may not be able to overcome severe bureaucratic disincentives if they are placed in a working environment that is not conducive to the educational enterprise. Extensive research on factors that affect the quality of education has not established any regular relationship between increased levels of spending and improved performance (Cameron and Hurst, 1989; Chubb and Moe, 1990; Hanushek, 1981).

Once institutions to solve free-rider problems through coerced payments are developed, children may be assigned to schools through a process that involves little choice on the part of the student or parents. The absence of choice means that critical information about the preferences of beneficiaries is lost. (The producer of private goods, for example, obtains information about the preferences of consumers by measuring the choices that these consumers make in response to the particular goods made available.)

Not only is information about educational outcomes difficult to obtain in general, but there are severe asymmetries of information between consumers and producers. Deciding which school offers the best education for a particular student is similar to making an investment decision with considerable uncertainty about eventual returns. Some aspects of uncertainty are related to changes in exogenous factors, such as macroeconomic and technological trends. More relevant, however, is uncertainty about the quality of a particular school's services. Only after graduation does the family of a student ascertain how well the school helped the child to increase his or her knowledge and skills. That is, in the case of education, input measures are not nearly as useful or complete as output measures. Of course, parents and their children may be able to make some reasonable conclusions about knowledge and skill transfer prior to students' graduation: What career counseling is offered? Are homework assignments challenging? How often are parent-teacher conferences held? Similarly, we expect that some consumers of health care share relevant information about their experiences with doctors, clinics, and even medication.

In regard to strictly private goods and services, many counteracting institutions, such as brand names, warranties, and professional control of producers, have arisen to cope with similar problems of asymmetrical information (Akerlof, 1970). In regard to education, accrediting associations, professionalization of teachers, and governmental regulation are among the institutional arrangements that are used to help counteract the severe information and measurement problems (New England Association of Schools and Colleges, 1986; Orlans, 1975). In regard to health care, medical ratings, credentials of doctors, and government approval of medication for specific purposes offer information that can counteract asymmetries of information. While regulatory arrangements may enhance the overall performance of an educational or medical system, they tend to focus on inputs and processes rather than outcomes, and they may not effectively counteract the asymmetries of information involved in education or health care. Nonprofit organization is another counteracting institution that may offer more potential for evaluating performance on the basis of outputs as well as inputs.

Principal-Agent Relationships, Voting, and Agenda Control. Measurement problems also exacerbate the challenge of aggregating preferences whenever members of a community must rely on voting mechanisms as a key part of their decision-making arrangements. Except under extremely unusual circumstances, voting mechanisms do not automatically translate diverse citizen preferences into well-defined preference orders for a community (Arrow, 1951; McKelvey, 1976; Plott, 1967). Given the unpredictability that could result from a completely open agenda, most electoral processes are subject to considerable agenda control or even manipulaton to ensure a particular outcome (Kingdon, 1984; Shepsle, 1979). The difficulties of reaching agreements through the use of majority-rule voting mechanisms are exacerbated when there are many issues to be decided and when the community making the decision is heterogeneous (Bish, 1971). Further, if voters lack a sense of responsibility for their choices, they will invest little in searching for information about issues. If there is little chance of affecting the outcome or if a family does not plan to remain in a community for long, it is hard to develop a sense of responsibility.

In small groups, those affected may be able to discuss their preferences and constraints face to face and to reach a rough consensus. In larger groups, decision making is more formalized, with less reliance on reaching common agreement and more reliance on the use of majority-rule decision mechanisms to assign authority between winners and losers. The homogeneity of interests of those who jointly use a service facility also reduces the problems involved in using voting mechanisms to translate individual preferences into expressions of collective choice. The problems of unpredictability that can occur when heterogeneous preferences are present are reduced in more homogeneous groups.

Joint Use of Facilities and Potentials for Complementarity and Interference. Jointly used educational and medical facilities generate some services that are entirely subtractable on consumption by one user (for example, a face-to-face counseling session or use of a single highly technological piece of medical equipment); in other instances, consumption by one does not subtract from the availability to many others—at least up to a certain level of consumption (for example, listening to a teacher's instruction in a classroom or taking advantage of medical laboratory facilities). Unless effective rules are established, followed, and monitored to allocate fully subtractive services, some individuals will be able to obtain considerably more than others, leading to problems of under- and overuse and high levels of conflict. Even in cases where relatively nonsubtractive uses are made of the same facilities, the consumption behavior of some users may seriously interfere with consumption by others.

There are many studies that tell of the negative externalities of disruptive student behavior in the classroom. Students may withdraw from a school entirely because of their fear (and that of their parents) for their personal safety in the school building. School facilities present opportunities for many complementary activities. Bringing members of the community to a school to participate in civic and recreational events may increase citizens' interest in the school and the consequent level of resources made available to it. Thus, school facilities can be used to generate many mutually complementary services, but such use is extremely sensitive to the rules established to regulate it and the willingness of participants to follow reasonable rules.

Institutional Incentives: Problems in the Production of Education

The attributes discussed above concern the provision of education. Various attributes of the production of educational services also need to be taken into account in analyzing the patterns of behavior and outcomes achieved within different institutional regimes.

Uncertainty, Scale, and Scope. Many manufactured goods have well-known production functions, and decisions about how to produce these goods are relatively simple. Since education is a complex service lacking a well-specified production function, decisions about how to combine inputs—for example, capital facilities, teachers, students, books—so as to improve the educational skills of students are difficult to make and frequently require considerable context-specific information. Educational strategies that appear to work effectively in one setting frequently do not work in another. Since education is cumulative, teachers are rarely certain as to whether the strategies they adopt at one point in the process are effective in preparing students for later stages. The problem of uncertainty is exacerbated when teachers and administrators live far from the community in which they teach and rarely see students once they leave the classroom.

Educational facilities vary considerably in terms of the economies or diseconomies of scale involved in the original design and construction of the facility and its operation over the long run. Economies of scale mean that costs per unit of output are lower at higher levels of output. Economies of scope mean that costs per unit of output are lower when multiple services are produced together rather than separately. The presumption that economies of scale exist in almost all production processes is so widespread that many policy analysts have assumed substantial economies of scale in education.

In regard to primary education, little evidence exists that substantial economies of scale and scope are present. Personnel costs are the largest component of primary education, and diseconomies rather than economies of scale are most likely if a primary school gets too large. For secondary schools, on the other hand, the costs of scientific laboratories, auditoriums, and athletic facilities should theoretically be more efficiently spread over a moderate-sized student body than a very small one. But few studies have shown economies of scale even in regard to secondary education, and several studies have found the opposite: student performance declines as the size of the school district increases.[9]

When production is characterized by substantial economies of scale or scope, provision units do not have to be at the same scale as the production unit. To the extent, for example, that a particular type of education is characterized by economies of scale, a small-scale provision unit can arrange production with a large-scale public or private producer through a wide diversity of contractual arrangements. Is it also possible for large-scale provision units (national or state units of government, for instance) to arrange for production with small-scale production units? Different scales of production can be used for different types of educational services. Given that there are different scales of production for educational services, any educational system that relies on a single scale of production—

whether small or large—is unlikely to achieve the appropriate scale for producing most educational services.

Coproduction. Educational services cannot be produced by a school alone. The production of education requires the active participation of students and their parents (Parks and others, 1981; Percy, 1978; Whitaker, 1980). Educational inputs that are not under the direct control of a school include the time and effort that students spend in educational activities; the time and effort that a family spends in helping students to acquire basic skills or perform particular tasks; and the resources spent in acquiring a library collection, reference works, a typewriter or computer, and other materials that greatly enhance the ability of a student to do well in school.

Viewing the production of education as a process involving both the school, on the one hand, and the students and their families, on the other, as essential partners in a production process enables one to address questions somewhat differently than the more traditional view of looking at a school as the solitary producer. Since the famous Coleman report was issued during the mid 1960s (Coleman, 1966), hundreds of studies have been conducted of educational inputs and their relationship to educational achievement.[10] A consistent finding in this literature is that the family background of students strongly affects their performance. Students whose parents have higher levels of education and wealth consistently have higher achievement scores than students without these advantages. It was this finding that led many reformers to encourage busing as a method of bringing students from disadvantaged backgrounds into schools with students from advantaged backgrounds.

One apparent explanation for this consistent finding is that the social capital in the home of students from "advantaged" backgrounds leads the students themselves to be more active coproducers of their own education. "The homes of the best schools also are more likely to have parents who directly encourage their children to learn. Specifically, the families in the top schools monitor their children's schoolwork more attentively and maintain higher expectations for their achievement"

(Chubb and Moe, 1990, p. 109). In an extremely interesting analysis of the factors affecting student choices, Gambetta (1987) finds that children's time perspectives and the strength of their career ambitions strongly affect their dropping out or continuing in school and the type of higher education that they seek. Gambetta also finds that children whose parents have higher levels of education are more likely to persevere in school when others drop out. Thus, family background appears to work through its effect on the values, time perspectives, and career aspirations encouraged in the home, rather than as an element of a linear production function.

Team Production and Leadership. Not only students and their parents are essential parts of the educational process; so too are their teachers and the administrators of their schools. The way in which teachers and principals affect education, however, is somewhat different from what is represented in the traditional literature on the production function. In this academic tradition, it is the credentials of teachers that are represented as part of a linear, additive production function.[11] More recent educational research has shown, however, that it is not the simple presence of teachers with better credentials but rather how schools are internally organized that makes a big difference in educational performance (Chubb and Moe, 1990; Kolderie, 1988; but see also Witte, 1990). Schools that are led by principals who have considerable autonomy and can develop effective working teams are most likely to produce the kind of environment in which students make the most progress in terms of achievement scores.[12]

Asset Specificity. Much of the recent work by Williamson (1979, 1985) has analyzed the problem of asset specificity in the production of private goods. When the assets used in a production process are quite general and can easily be redeployed to other uses, there is little need for special governance arrangements. Owners of such general-purpose assets are willing to enter into a variety of exchange arrangements because they can easily seek alternatives if problems occur after original agreements are made. Thus, the presence of specific assets in a production process usually signals the need for carefully crafted counteracting institutions to avoid the higher costs and transaction failures that can easily result from their presence.

The assets used in producing education include both general-purpose assets that can be redeployed in other activities without cost and highly specific assets that would not easily be deployed in other activities. Schools are usually constructed in a way that limits their usefulness for other purposes. Thus, most schools must own and construct their own buildings rather than leasing space from a private owner. The capital required to construct a new building when school enrollments grow places heavy demands on new residential areas or areas that are changing from low-density to high-density use patterns.

Many regulations passed by state boards of education require highly specific types of training before individuals can qualify as teachers (Darlington and Berry, 1988). This tends to lock in those individuals who choose to obtain educational credentials, since these credentials do not generally prepare them for other kinds of careers. Further, these regulations tend to lock out others who might make highly motivated and well-trained teachers.

Clearly, medical services may require higher levels of asset specificity—specialized training of doctors, nurses, and other hospital staff—than education. However, overspecialization of these providers is, in part, responsible for high service fees designed to compensate providers for longer, more specialized training.

Regulation, Paper Pushing, and the Potential for Corruption. Not only can regulations increase the problems associated with asset specificity of educational inputs, but the imposition of many different requirements and the need for repeatedly filling out complex forms that affect future funding levels can generate highly counterproductive behavior. Given the difficulties of measuring performance and the importance of the many contextual factors discussed above, no standardized form can produce the relevant information to determine how well a particular school is performing. If funding formulas are based on certain data, school administrators who desire higher funding levels are strongly motivated to find means of increasing those figures that positively affect funding and decreasing those that negatively affect funding, whether or not the resultant actions actually improve performance.[13]

Nonprofit Organizations as Alternative Institutions

If educational processes involved only one of the eleven problems identified above, then the task of finding the best institutional arrangement for providing and producing primary and secondary education would be relatively simple. One would merely analyze the set of feasible institutional arrangements to determine their capability to counteract this difficulty and select the institutional arrangement that most effectively produced education while counteracting this problem. Given the diversity of problems, however, establishing institutions that effectively cope with one or more of them can easily produce incentives that exacerbate the others. The design of effective institutional regimes is, thus, more enigmatic than sometimes presented in the literature. Further, careful studies of the differences among government, nonprofit organizations, and profit-making enterprises in regard to all of these problems have not been undertaken.[14] It is possible, however, to rely on theoretical speculations and empirical research on some of the problems to conjecture about the likely effects of relying on nonprofit organizations in the production and provision of primary and secondary education.

On the production side, switching from large-scale governmental school systems to smaller, nonprofit organizations would ameliorate many problems. For example, nonprofit organizations are more likely to operate at the smaller scales of operation where the substantial diseconomies of scale currently generated by large school districts could be reduced. In addition, nonprofit schools might be willing to rent space in general-purpose buildings rather than investing in large physical structures that can be used only for educational enterprises,

potentially ameliorating some diseconomies of scope and ineffi-
ciencies of asset specificity. (In the following section, we discuss
the economies of scale in relation to authorizing producers of
education that are distinct from providers of education.)

Given a higher level of trust among parents, children,
teachers, and principals, one would expect to find reduced
uncertainty and higher levels of coproduction on the part of
children and team production on the part of teachers. A survey
of students in the three types of New York high schools included
in the study by Hill, Foster, and Gendler (1990, Table A.2) found
significant differences in the attitudes of students between the
regular public high schools, on the one hand, and both Catholic
schools and public schools that are allowed considerable autonomy to develop their own focus, on the other. In regard to
students, there were significant differences ($p < .001$) between
students in the regular public schools and the other two types of
schools in regard to:

- Feeling lucky to be able to go to their school
- Feeling safe in the halls of the school
- Feeling that school is a nice place to spend the day
- Feeling that regular attendance is important
- Respecting school and teachers
- Taking rules seriously
- Perceiving teachers as interested in students doing more
  than just passing a grade

These attitudinal differences translated into higher educational
performance as well. Students in the Catholic schools and the
focused and autonomous public schools had higher high school
graduation rates, were more likely to take SAT exams, and had
higher scores on those exams (Hill, Foster, and Gendler, 1990,
p. 32).

In the absence of large-scale bureaucratic constraints, one
can expect more innovative leadership among nonprofit organizations. The research on "school-based management" shows
that the key difference between "good" schools and "bad" schools
is usually the principals' and teachers' leadership abilities. One

also expects to find fewer problems associated with administrative paper pushing and red tape. Again, research shows that nonprofit organizations rely on much smaller administrative staff and fewer bureaucratic procedures. "The New York City central Catholic schools office, for example, manages the 12th largest school system in the United States with fewer than 30 employees" (Hill, Foster, and Gendler, 1990, p. 51).

We do not recommend reliance on nonprofit organizations as the *only* remedy to the ineffective school systems that currently operate in many American cities. The recent study by Hill, Foster, and Gendler (1990), which includes specialized *public* schools that have considerable autonomy, provides evidence that the performance of these schools comes close to equaling (and, in a few cases, excels) that of the Catholic schools with which they are paired. Among schools that are given considerable autonomy and encouraged to provide quality education to minority students, the operational differences between those that are run by large-scale religious orders and those that are part of large-scale public school districts are not as substantial as the terms *public* and *private* connote. Simply being private and not-for-profit or being public is not a sufficient attribute to determine the level of performance. The institutional contexts within which schools operate and the esprit and sense of community among teachers, pupils, and parents are also important factors that help any school, public or private, to perform better.

The picture is not quite as positive for nonprofit organizations on the provision side of education as it is on the production side. Relying on nonprofit organizations to provide primary and secondary schools could lead to their underprovision. Parents in middle-class and wealthier neighborhoods, who recognize the importance of education for their children as well as for all children in a society, would find it somewhat easier to overcome the problems of free riding and organize themselves to provide for a school. If, indeed, nonprofits have access to diverse, localized information, some of the problems of over- and underutilization of educational services can be eased. Further, nonprofit organizations that draw on a large religious community, such as Catholic schools, may provide high-quality education in neighborhoods that are not able to cover all costs. To be sure, energetic and entrepreneurial leaders, such as Marva Collins, founder of Chicago's Westside Preparatory School, would organize nonprofit schools in neighborhoods with fewer resources. Equitable availability of education to all children, however, would be at risk if nonprofit rather than governmental organizations were the only method of organizing for provision. The extent to which rent-seeking activities are less likely to be engaged in and to be successful where education is provided by nonprofits is unclear. Theoretically, if a nonprofit institution was the sole provider of education in a community—an unlikely prospect—the temptations associated with rent seeking would not be as great as they are under the present system, which frequently involves raiding a large, distant public fisc.

If parents participated in the governance of nonprofit organizations, they could well become more informed about what was going on in their children's schools than they are in regard to many of the schools serving urban neighborhoods today. In this way, nonprofits can serve as counteracting institutions. Some of the problems of coordination, interest articulation, and aggregation might also be reduced where nonprofits could be organized to accommodate sets of more distinct or more intense preferences. Discipline might also improve if a school did not have to retain a child who disrupted the educational experience of other children.

Nonprofit Organizations as Complementary Institutions

Rather than viewing nonprofits entirely as an exclusive alternative institutional arrangement to large-scale public schools, a more attractive option is to analyze the role that nonprofit organizations could play as complementary institutions in a multitier mixed public-private economy. If such a public-private economy were composed of large, medium, and small governmental units that undertook many of the provision activities and arranged for a mix of public and nonprofit organizations as producers, the overall mix of institutions could more substantially ameliorate problems on both the provision and the production sides. This would require careful disaggregation of provision and production units and explicit recognition of and attention to their often disparate economies of scale and scope in relation to different types of educational services. In this context, Salamon (1987) discusses the use of "third-party implementers" in an arrangement in which the domain of service delivery extends beyond different levels of government to include relationships between governments and private and nonprofit organizations.

Some of the voucher systems currently under consideration would in practice resemble multitiered, mixed-enterprise systems, since they would mean that a large-scale state-level government would be responsible for many aspects of provision, while parents would be able to choose from among a diversity of public and private schools including both for-profit and nonprofit enterprises. Many different types of voucher plans are possible. Citizens in Milwaukee, for example, recently instituted a reform agreement that allows 1,000 low-income students (students whose parents make less than $22,000 a year) to use state money ($2,500 per pupil) to attend private, nonsectarian schools. This institutional design explicitly requires public schools to directly compete with private schools but limits the number and type of students eligible. Vermont's voucher system permits towns that do not operate public schools—often rural areas—to pay their residents' tuition at secular, private schools. Many of the minority students attending Catholic schools in New York do so under a "partnership" system whereby their tuition is paid by the public school system.

Administratively less complex than voucher plans are those that allow all or part of the tuition or other costs of education for a student in a private or public school to be taken as a credit or itemized deduction on the parents' state income tax. Some initial experimentation with tax credits has been undertaken in Minnesota.

Reforms as Experiments in an Experimental Society

In addition to showing why current centralized solutions have failed on so many evaluative criteria, a public economy approach to the study of educational institutions opens up more than a single institutional alternative to the current system. The choice is not simply between government and markets. The key problem is making trade-offs among the potentials for perverse consequences that are associated with all institutional regimes. Further, the severity of these problems depends on the particular strategies adopted by specific individuals in historical settings. A community that has established high levels of trust and shared norms of responsible behavior may be able to successfully use a type of institutional arrangement whose implicit temptations would cause substantial harm to another community. Further, the consequences felt in one setting may be largely the result of the historical circumstances of that particular setting, so that the experiment could not simply be transferred to another setting with the expectation of similar outcomes.

Thus, rather than adopting any particular institutional regime as the panacea for solving educational problems, it is better to view all institutional reforms as experiments that can inform both participants and others about the array of consequences that they may produce. By learning from past experiments with a wide diversity of institutional forms, we can, as Weisbrod (1988, p. 167) contends, "take advantage of the unique role nonprofits can play in a mixed economy while avoiding their incursion into domains better served by private firms or governments."

Considerable theoretical and empirical research is needed. The institutional theories of the educational professionals and the advocates of parental choice posit simple relationships between a limited number of "causal" variables and "educational outcomes." Both lead to a recommendation for a "one best system." Empirical research has shown that these relationships are more complex than this and far from determinate. Future research could help identify how and why some institutions counteract incentives that lead to perverse outcomes while also creating other incentives with less desirable outcomes. Such research could then be used by citizens and public officials in the tough job of crafting specific institutions to fit particular settings. The presumption should not be that research will identify the optimal institution. Just as investment in education is done over the long term in highly uncertain cricumstances, investment in institutions also generates consequences that will not become evident for some time. As an investment decision made under extreme uncertainty, the choice of institutional regimes for the provision and production of primary and secondary education always involves risks of unforeseen circumstances and perverse incentives.

Relying on any single institutional model, whether central governmental control or nonprofit organization, produces far less information about alternatives and consequences than allowing multiple institutions to exist side by side. Enabling parents and other citizens greater opportunities to craft institutions themselves rather than limiting parental choice to options within institutions chosen for them may result in even better institutional regimes in the future than any conceived of by the professional educator or institutional analyst. Further, it is hard to imagine how a democratic regime can reproduce itself over time without citizens acquiring a first-hand understanding of the problems of governance.

Notes

1. See Ostrom and Ostrom (1978) for an analysis of the characteristics of public goods. See also Musgrave (1959).
2. In 1980, private schools accounted for nearly 10 percent of the elementary and secondary educational sector in terms of number of students and teachers and monetary resources spent. This translated into about five million students, 20,000 schools, and $4 million (Abramowitz and Stackhouse, 1980).
3. Martin (1990) reports that incidents of violence against teachers in New York City schools rose 39 percent during the first part of the 1990–91 school year, after a rise of 26 percent during the previous year, when 3,386 teachers were assaulted.
4. See, for example, Oakerson (1987); Oakerson, Parks, and Bell (1988); McDavid (1979); McIver (1978); Ostrom, Parks,

and Whitaker (1978); Ostrom, Schroeder, and Wynne (1993); Ostrom, Bish, and Ostrom (1988); Schneider (1989); and Stein (1982, 1990). See also the more general work of Commons (1957), North (1989), and Williamson (1979, 1985).

5. The concept of "counteracting" institutions is discussed in Akerlof (1970), where he is primarily concerned with the need for such institutions to ensure efficient provision of strictly private goods where asymmetries of information are involved. Akerlof discusses brand names, warranties, and coerced insurance systems as forms of counteracting institutions for the problems stemming from asymmetries of information.

6. This section draws in part on Davis and Ostrom (1991).

7. Ostrom, Schroeder, and Wynne (1993) provide an extensive analysis of various institutional incentives related to the provision and sustenance of infrastructures.

8. See Oakerson (1987); Ostrom, Parks, and Whitaker (1978); Ostrom, Tiebout, and Warren (1961).

9. See Gregory and Smith (1987), Kiesling (1967, 1968), Murnane (1981), Niskanen and Levy (1974), and Sher (1977). In Hanushek's (1981, p. 28) review of 130 studies, he concluded that Americans have been rather blindly "throwing money at schools": "The message, taken as a whole, is that the inputs on which schools tend to concentrate—and which lead to differences in expenditures—appear to have no consistent payoff in terms of higher student performance. The only thing we can say with any confidence is that 'improving' schools in the ways conventionally suggested will increase school costs."

10. See Hanushek (1986) for a review of many of these studies.

11. Alchian and Demsetz (1972) stress the difficulty of monitoring performance when production functions are interdependent and base their theory of the firm on "team" production functions.

12. See evidence summarized in Chubb and Moe (1990, chap. 3).

13. The incredibly perverse incentives related to pushing pa-

pers in the criminal justice system are brilliantly documented in a series of articles on "Justice in Distress" by
David Freed (1990).

14. One of the best studies examining the performance of
general-purpose public schools, focused and autonomous
public schools, and Catholic schools serving similar populations (minority students in New York City) demonstrates
that both the focused and autonomous public schools and
the Catholic schools produce an array of positive outcomes that far outstrip the performance of the regular
schools in that area (Hill, Foster, and Gendler, 1990).

References

Abramowitz, S., and Stackhouse, E. *The Private High School Today.*
Washington, D.C.: National Institute of Education, 1980.

Akerlof, G. "The Market for 'Lemons': Quality, Uncertainty and
the Market Mechanism." *Quarterly Journal of Economics*, 1970,
84, 487–500.

Alchian, A. A., and Demsetz, H. "Production, Information and
Economic Organization." *American Economic Review*, 1972,
62(5), 777–795.

Arrow, K. J. *Social Choice and Individual Values.* New York: Wiley,
1951.

Ben-Ner, A. "Nonprofit Organizations: Why Do They Exist in
Market Economies?" In S. Rose-Ackerman (ed.), *The Economics
of Nonprofit Institutions: Studies in Structure and Policy.* New York:
Oxford University Press, 1986.

Bish, R. L. *The Public Economy of Metropolitan Areas.* Chicago:
Markham, 1971.

Buchanan, J. M. "An Economic Theory of Clubs." *Economica*,
1965, *32*, 1–14.

Buchanan, J. M., Tollison, R. D., and Tullock, G. (eds.). *Toward a
Theory of the Rent-Seeking Society.* College Station: Texas A&M
University Press, 1980.

Cameron, J., and Hurst, P. (eds.). *International Handbook of Education Systems.* New York: Wiley, 1989.

Carnegie Forum on Education and the Economy. *A Nation Pre-*

pared: Teachers in the Twenty-First Century. New York: Carnegie Foundation, 1986.

Chubb, J., and Moe, T. *Politics, Markets, and America's Schools.* Washington, D.C.: Brookings Institution, 1990.

Coleman, J. S. *Equality of Educational Opportunity.* Washington, D.C.: U.S. Government Printing Office, 1966.

Commons, J. R. *Legal Foundations of Capitalism.* Madison: University of Wisconsin Press, 1957.

Darlington, L., and Berry, B. *The Evolution of Teacher Policy.* Santa Monica, Calif.: Rand Corporation, 1988.

Davis, G., and Ostrom, E. "A Public Economy Approach to Education: Choice and Co-Production." *International Political Science Review,* 1991, *12*(4), 313–335.

Eucken, W. *The Foundations of Economics.* Chicago: University of Chicago Press, 1951.

Freed, D. "Justice in Distress: The Devaluation of Crime in Los Angeles." *Los Angeles Times,* Dec. 16, 1990, pp. 15–22.

Frohlich, N., and Oppenheimer, J. A. "I Get By with a Little Help from My Friends." *World Politics,* 1971, *23*, 104–120.

Frohlich, N., and Oppenheimer, J. A. "The Carrot and the Stick: Optimal Program Mixes for Entrepreneurial Political Leaders." *Public Choice,* 1974, *19*, 43–61.

Frohlich, N., Oppenheimer, J. A., and Young, O. *Political Leadership and Collective Goods.* Princeton, N.J.: Princeton University Press, 1971.

Fund, J. H. "Milwaukee's Schools Open—to Competition." *Wall Street Journal,* Sept. 4, 1990, p. 1.

Gambetta, D. *Were They Pushed or Did They Jump? Individual Decision Mechanisms in Education.* Cambridge, England: Cambridge University Press, 1987.

Gregory, T. B., and Smith, G. R. *High Schools as Communities: A Small School Reconsidered.* Bloomington, Ind.: Phi Delta Kappa Educational Foundation, 1987.

Hanushek, E. A. "Throwing Money at Schools." *Journal of Policy Analysis and Management,* 1981, *1*, 19–41.

Hanushek, E. A. "The Economics of Schooling: Production and Efficiency in Public Schools." *Journal of Economic Literature,* 1986, *24*, 1141–1177.

Hayek, F. A. "The Use of Knowledge in Society." *American Economic Review*, 1945, *35*(4), 519–530.

Hill, P. T., Foster, G. E., and Gendler, T. *High Schools with Character*. Santa Monica, Calif.: Rand Corporation, 1990.

Kiesling, H. "Measuring a Local Government Service: A Study of School Districts in New York State." *Review of Economics and Statistics*, 1967, *49*(Aug.), 356–367.

Kiesling, H. *High School Size and Cost Factors*. Final Report for the U.S. Office of Education, Bureau of Research, Project no. 6-1590. Washington, D.C.: U.S. Department of Health, Education, and Welfare, 1968.

Kingdon, J. *Agendas, Alternatives, and Public Policies*. Boston: Little, Brown, 1984.

Kolderie, T. "School-Site Management: Rhetoric and Reality." Unpublished manuscript, Public Services Redesign Project, Humphrey Institute of Public Affairs, University of Minnesota, 1988.

Krashinsky, M. "Transaction Costs and a Theory of the Nonprofit Organization." In S. Rose-Ackerman (ed.), *The Economics of Nonprofit Institutions: Studies in Structure and Policy*. New York: Oxford University Press, 1986.

Krueger, A. O. "The Political Economy of the Rent-Seeking Society." *American Economic Review*, 1974, *64*, 291–301.

Lachmann, L. M. *Capital and Its Structure*. Kansas City: Sheed Andrews and McMeel, 1978.

Levy, F., Meltsner, A. J., and Wildavsky, A. *Urban Outcomes*. Berkeley: University of California Press, 1974.

McDavid, J. C. *Police Cooperation and Performance: The Greater St. Louis Interlocal Experience*. University Park: Pennsylvania State University Press, 1979.

McIver, J. P. "The Relationship Between Metropolitan Police Industry Structure and Interagency Assistance: A Preliminary Assessment." *Policy Studies Journal*, 1978, *7*(special issue), 406–413.

McKelvey, R. D. "Intransitivities in Multi-Dimensional Voting Models and Some Implications for Agenda Control." *Journal of Economic Theory*, 1976, *2*, 472–482.

Margolis, J. "A Comment on the Pure Theory of Public Expenditures." *Journal of Economics and Statistics*, 1955, *37*, 347–349.

Martin, D. "Violence Drives Teacher from Where He Belongs." *New York Times*, May 12, 1990, p. B1.

Morganthau, T. "The Future Is Now." *Newsweek*, Fall/Winter 1990, p. 78.

Murnane, R. J. "Interpreting the Evidence on School Effectiveness." *Teachers College Record*, 1981, *83*, 19–35.

Musgrave, R. A. *The Theory of Public Finance: A Study in Public Economy*. New York: McGraw-Hill, 1959.

New England Association of Schools and Colleges. *The First Hundred Years, 1885–1985*. Winchester, Mass.: New England Association of Schools and Colleges, 1986.

Niskanen, W. A., and Levy, M. *Cities and Schools: A Case for Community Government in California*. Berkeley: Graduate School of Public Policy, University of California, 1974.

North, D. C. "Institutions and Economic Growth: An Historical Introduction." *World Development*, 1989, *17*, 1319–1332.

Oakerson, R. J. *The Organization of Local Public Economies*. Washington, D.C.: U.S. Advisory Commission on Intergovernmental Relations, 1987.

Oakerson, R. J., Parks, R. B., and Bell, H. A. *Metropolitan Organization: The St. Louis Case*. Washington, D.C.: U.S. Advisory Commission on Intergovernmental Relations, 1988.

Olson, M. *The Logic of Collective Action: Public Goods and the Theory of Groups*. Cambridge, Mass.: Harvard University Press, 1965.

Orlans, H. *Private Accreditation and Public Eligibility*. Lexington, Mass.: Lexington Books, 1975.

Ostrom, E. *Governing the Commons: The Evolution of Institutions for Collective Action*. New York: Cambridge University Press, 1990.

Ostrom, E., Parks, R. B., and Whitaker, G. P. *Patterns of Metropolitan Policing*. New York: Ballinger, 1978.

Ostrom, E., Schroeder, L., and Wynne, S. *Institutional Incentives and Sustainable Development*. Boulder, Colo.: Westview Press, 1993.

Ostrom, V. "Problems of Cognition as a Challenge to Policy Analysts and Democratic Societies." *Journal of Theoretical Politics*, 1990, *2*(3), 243–262.

Ostrom, V., Bish, R., and Ostrom, E. *Local Government in the United States*. San Francisco: Institute for Contemporary Studies Press, 1988.

Ostrom, V., and Ostrom, E. "Public Goods and Public Choices." In E. S. Savas (ed.), *Alternatives for Delivering Public Services: Toward Improved Performance*. Boulder, Colo.: Westview Press, 1978.

Ostrom, V., Tiebout, C. M., and Warren, R. "The Organization of Government in Metropolitan Areas: A Theoretical Inquiry." *American Political Science Review*, 1961, *55*, 831–842.

Parks, R. B., and others. "Consumers as Coproducers of Public Services: Some Economic and Institutional Considerations." *Policy Studies Journal*, 1981, *9*, 1001–1011.

Percy, S. L. "Conceptualizing and Measuring of Citizen Co-production of Safety and Security." *Policy Studies Journal*, 1978, *7*, 486–492.

Plott, C. "A Notion of Equilibrium and Its Possibility Under Majority Rule." *American Economic Review*, 1967, *57*, 787–807.

Popkin, S. L. "Public Choice and Rural Development — Free Riders, Lemons, and Institutional Design." In C. S. Russell and N. K. Nicholson (eds.), *Public Choice and Rural Development*. Baltimore, Md.: Johns Hopkins University Press, 1981.

Salamon, L. M. "Of Market Failure, Voluntary Failure, and Third-Party Government: Toward a Theory of Government-Nonprofit Relations in the Modern Welfare State." *Journal of Voluntary Action Research*, 1987, *16*, 29–49.

Samuelson, P. "The Pure Theory of Public Expenditure." *Review of Economics and Statistics*, 1954, *36*, 387–389.

Schneider, M. *The Competitive City: The Political Economy of Suburbia*. Pittsburgh, Pa.: University of Pittsburgh Press, 1989.

Shepsle, K. "Institutional Arrangements and Equilibrium in Multidimensional Voting Models." *American Journal of Political Science*, 1979, *23*(1), 27–59.

Sher, J. P. *Education in Rural America: A Reassessment of Conventional Wisdom*. Boulder, Colo.: Westview Press, 1977.

Stein, R. "The Political Economy of Municipal Functional Assignment." *Social Science Quarterly*, 1982, *67*(3), 530–548.

Stein, R. *Urban Alternatives: Public and Private Markets in the Provi-*

sion of Local Services. Pittsburgh, Pa.: University of Pittsburgh Press, 1990.

Tollison, R. D. "Rent Seeking: A Survey." *Kyklos*, 1982, *35*(4), 575–602.

Tweedie, J., Riley, D. D., Chubb, T. E., and Moe, T. M. "Should Market Forces Control Educational Decision Making?" *American Political Science Review*, 1990, *84*, 549–568.

Weisbrod, B. A. *The Nonprofit Economy.* Cambridge, Mass.: Harvard University Press, 1988.

Whitaker, G. P. "Coproduction: Citizen Participation in Service Delivery." *Public Administration Review*, 1980, *40*, 240–246.

Williamson, O. E. "Transaction Cost Economics: The Governance of Contractual Relations." *Journal of Law and Economics*, 1979, *22*(2), 233–261.

Williamson, O. E. *The Economic Institutions of Capitalism: Firms, Markets, Relational Contracting.* New York: Free Press, 1985.

Wilson, D. "Math Centers Stress Tough Training." *New York Times*, Apr. 6, 1988.

Witte, J. F. "Understanding High School Achievement: After a Decade of Research, Do We Have Any Confident Policy Recommendations?" Paper presented at the annual meeting of the American Political Science Association, Aug. 30–Sept. 2, 1990.

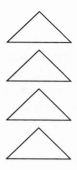

CHAPTER 2

Competition, Performance, and Public Policy Toward Nonprofits

Catherine C. Eckel
Richard Steinberg

The term *collusion* conjures images of backroom plots to injure the public for private gain; *cooperation* and *coordination* conjure images of noble and civilized ventures that help everyone. Despite the opposing implications of these loaded words, they could each be used to describe the same illegal acts under current antitrust laws. Firms might agree to "cooperate" by refraining from undercutting each other's prices; they might "coordinate" their market areas to avoid infringing on each other's territories. Both are illegal under current antitrust laws.

There are two types of legal standards for ascertaining whether antitrust laws have been violated. According to the

Note: Research for this chapter was supported by the Mandel Center for Nonprofit Organizations at Case Western Reserve University, for which the authors are eternally grateful. We acknowledge helpful suggestions from Okianer Christian Dark, Arthur Austin, Michael Krashinsky, Antony Dnes, Clark Kristensen, and the editors of this volume.

Sherman Anti-Trust Act of 1890, practices and agreements that constitute "contract[s or] combinations in restraint of trade" are illegal per se, regardless of whether such restraints are effective in restraining trade or whether they foster the public interest in any way. Antitrust law as construed by the courts is explicit on this point. A second category of practices or agreements falls under the "rule of reason"; that is, the courts examine the intent and effect of the agreement to determine guilt. Neither intent nor effect will be a successful defense in cases involving the per se restraint of trade or competition. Furthermore, the rule of reason does not permit questioning of the basic assumption that competition is "good." For example, in *National Society of Professional Engineers* v. *U.S.*, the Supreme Court considered the argument that competition would cause engineers to neglect safety in an effort to hold down costs. This argument was rejected as irrelevant and not evaluated on its merits, as the Court held that "The Rule of Reason does not support a defense based on the assumption that competition itself is unreasonable" [at 696].

In this chapter, we ask whether combinations in restraint of trade are necessarily harmful when they are carried on by organizations whose primary purpose is not trade. We find that "collusion" can be in the public interest under specified conditions and so hint that an amendment of the law might be in order. There has been little formal analysis of this essentially economic issue by economic scholars. Nonetheless, legal authorities aggressively pursue antitrust actions against a variety of nonprofit organizations. Lacking a sound intellectual foundation, the law proceeds by analogy. Thus, conventional economic wisdom indicates that monopolization of commercial markets by for-profit firms is harmful. It is not known whether, on balance, monopolization of commercial markets by nonprofits is harmful, but prosecutors focus on the commercial nature of many nonprofit activities to condemn by analogy.

We report our results from a formal economic model that highlights some of the trade-offs involved when authorities seek to block a merger between two nonprofit firms (Eckel and Steinberg, 1992). In our model, nonprofit mergers create the same social ills as for-profit mergers, but they also yield unique social benefits that may more than counterbalance the harmful effects. Although the model is specific to mergers, this insight also applies more generally. The same basic trade-off obtains when we evaluate collusion by nonprofit universities that supports need-based financial aid or when we assess United Way market restrictions that enhance fundraising efficiency.

In a number of recent cases, agencies of the U.S. government have sought to prevent mergers between nonprofit organizations. In two cases, the Justice Department moved to block the merger of nonprofit hospitals (*U.S. v. Carilion Health System and Community Hospital of Roanoke Valley* and *U.S. v. Rockford Memorial Corporation and the SwedishAmerican Corporation*). The Federal Trade Commission (FTC) has also moved against hospital mergers (*Adventist Health Systems/West; Ukiah Valley Medical Center v. FTC; FTC v. University Health, Inc.*). There appear to be unsettled issues of jurisdiction in cases involving mergers of nonprofits.

More than fifty-five private colleges and universities have been investigated by the Justice Department for collusion in the granting of financial aid (and, according to press reports that the department has neither confirmed nor denied, collusion in the setting of tuition and faculty salaries as well). Justice filed suit against nine universities on May 22, 1991 (*United States v. Brown, et al.*); the eight Ivy League defendants signed a consent decree, while the Massachusetts Institute of Technology lost at trial. Following Justice's example, a student filed a private antitrust suit (which provides for treble damages) against the Ivies, Wesleyan, Amherst, Williams, and Stanford (*Kingsepp v. Wesleyan, et al.*). The student alleges conspiracies with respect to both tuition rates and financial aid policies and has moved to certify a class of present and former students to join in the complaint.

Private antitrust actions have also been brought against local chapters of the United Way. For example, in the case of *Associated In-Group Donors v. United Way, Inc.*, plaintiffs alleged that the United Way of Los Angeles threatened to cut off funding of member agencies that accepted funds from a rival fundraising organization.

Although the practices challenged in *Brown* could be viewed as price fixing (an agreement on the discount to "list-price tuition" to be offered to common prospective customers), it could also be viewed as an agreement to charitably extend educational services to those who could not otherwise partake of them. If the Justice Department's logic prevails, this would constitute a precedent that could proscribe agreements by day-care centers, nursing homes, and other charities to use sliding-scale fee structures. Regardless of the ruling on price fixing or any other agreement between organizations, sliding-scale fees may be found by some future court to constitute illegal price discrimination under current antitrust statutes.

Finally, following earlier rulings against the National Collegiate Athletic Association (*National Collegiate Athletic Association* v. *Board of Regents of the University of Oklahoma*), the FTC challenged the agreement on broadcast rights between the College Football Association and ABC television (*In the Matter of College Football Association and Capital Cities ABC, Inc.*). The FTC argued that college sports are an essentially commercial venture wholly separable from the colleges' educational mission and that broadcasting contracts should thus be challenged under conventional antitrust holdings.

In the following sections, we review some of the economic concepts underlying our model; describe the model and present our major findings; and discuss some policy implications of the model and highlight facets of current controversies that it does not capture.

Economic Concepts Relevant to Market Competition Among Nonprofits

Monopoly, Duopoly, and Perfect Competition

Monopoly occurs when there is only one seller of a good or service and no potential rivals. That seller is free to pick any price and quantity combination that is acceptable to buyers. At the opposite extreme is perfect competition, where many sellers accept the price determined by the market as a whole and each decides on a quantity to produce. In between is duopoly (exactly two sellers) or, more generally, oligopoly (a few sellers).

Consumers' willingness to purchase is summarized by a demand curve. At each possible quantity, the height of the demand curve indicates the maximum price that consumers would be willing to pay to obtain one more unit of the good, which is also known as the consumers' "reservation price." For any given demand curve and market structure, it is a straightforward procedure to calculate the price and quantity decision that would maximize the firm's profits. (We use the Cournot-Nash procedure to calculate duopoly equilibrium. With this procedure, we find a set of quantities for the two firms such that each firm's quantity is the profit-maximizing response to the other firm's quantity, with prices set after quantity selection to exactly clear the market. This is a fairly standard approach but not the only way to go here. See, for example, Varian 1984, pp. 99–103.) Figure 2.1 provides an example of a demand curve (see Eckel and Steinberg, 1992). To keep the analysis simple, we assume that there are no production costs. As is always the case, monopolies produce a smaller quantity and charge a higher price. In this particular example, the monopoly output (Q_M) is half the competitive output (Q_C), and the duopoly output (Q_D) is two-thirds of Q_C.

Public Goods

Economists define public goods as goods whose consumption is nonrival — when one consumer enjoys the good, this does not in any way detract from the enjoyment that other consumers obtain from that good. My enjoyment of national defense does not make other citizens less secure; my reception of a television program does not impede reception by others; your reading of this chapter does not reduce the amusement and education that others could obtain from it. Public goods are the opposite of private goods, whose consumption is strictly rival. Cakes are private goods, for one cannot eat a cake and others have it too.

Public goods are of two types: excludable and nonexcludable. An excludable public good is one that it is feasible to keep some consumers from enjoying; nonexcludable public goods cannot be restricted to particular groups. The viewing of

Figure 2.1. Demand Curve for Monopoly, Duopoly,
and Perfect Competition.

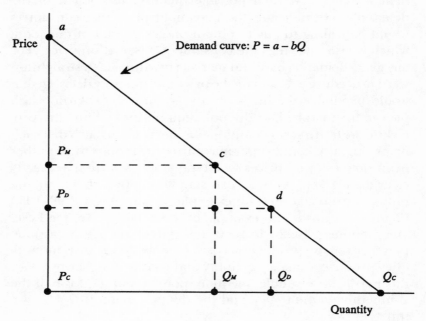

a movie is nonrival (up to the capacity of the theater) but is clearly excludable. A fireworks exhibition is both nonrival and nonexcludable. Either sort of public good is underprovided by markets that contain only for-profit firms. The reason is obvious for nonexcludable goods: the for-profit firm could not hope to collect any money if it could not restrict the benefits of its product to paying customers.

For-profit firms produce inadequate quantities of excludable public goods, and what is provided is not made available to as many people as it should be. From society's standpoint, once the good is produced, anyone who values it should be allowed to enjoy it. The benefits to paying customers are undiminished by extension of service to others, and yet the for-profit firm excludes some customers in order to maintain its price structure.

Nonprofit organizations commonly provide public goods. Medical research is certainly a public good, and both education and aid to the poor have some public good characteristics. Education helps society generally, because the benefits of an enlightened and literate citizenry redound to the entire electorate. Aid to the poor is a public good in a society of altruists, for when any person helps the impoverished, all other citizens who care about the poor are grateful.

Governments also provide these public goods. Coexistence is due to many factors. Weisbrod (1975) views nonprofits as satisfying leftover demands on the part of those who are dissatisfied with the level provided by government. Salamon (1987) reverses the picture, focusing on governmental provision as a response to inherent shortcomings of nonprofit organizations. Steinberg (1987) views the allocation decision as simultaneous, with neither sector reacting solely to a failure by the other. What is common to all these models is the implication that the combined provision of public goods by the public and private nonprofit sectors can be inadequate.

The cases where total spending on public goods is inadequate form the basis for the analysis in this chapter. We look at cases where profits from one market failure (monopoly) are used to correct another market failure (underprovision of public goods). This analysis makes sense only when public goods would otherwise be underprovided, so the possibility of overprovision forms an important caveat to our analysis.

Social Costs and Benefits

To evaluate the impact on social welfare of market structure or the provision of public goods, we employ the notion of "surplus" as a measure of welfare. For an individual, surplus is the difference between what she pays for a good and what she would have been willing to pay for it, or her "reservation price." If you could purchase a good for $5 that is worth $100 to you, your surplus from this transaction is $95. For a firm, surplus is the difference between what a good sells for and what it costs to produce: if there are no production costs (as in our example), it is simply

total revenue. Social surplus is the sum of producer and consumer surplus and is the yardstick for evaluating economic
outcomes.

Reservation prices are represented graphically by the
demand curve; consumer surpluses are areas underneath demand curves and above the price. Figure 2.2 illustrates the
reason for this. The height of the demand curve above a quantity
of 1 indicates the reservation price for the first unit. Subtracting
the actual price paid (p in Figure 2.2) gives the surplus from the
first unit. This surplus is numerically equal to the area of rectangle 1, because the rectangle has height equal to consumer
surplus and width equal to 1. The surplus for the second unit is
equal to the area of rectangle 2, and so forth, so that the total
consumer surplus is approximately equal to the area of triangle
abp in Figure 2.2. When there are no costs, producer surplus is
simply equilibrium price times quantity, which equals area $pbcd$
in Figure 2.2.

In Figure 2.1, consumer surplus for perfect competition
is equal to area aQ_CP_C, which also equals social surplus, because
producer surplus is zero. Monopoly has a smaller consumer
surplus (area acP_M) and a larger producer surplus (area
$P_McQ_MP_C$). Nonetheless, monopoly social surplus is smaller by
area cQ_CQ_M. In effect, part of the consumer's loss when going
from perfect competition to monopoly becomes the producer's
gain, and part simply vanishes. The part that vanishes, area
cQ_CQ_M, is known as the "deadweight loss" and measures the
social costs imposed by monopolies. Similar analysis indicates
that duopolies also impose social costs, with the duopoly deadweight loss equal to area dQ_CQ_D.

The trouble with markets that are not perfectly competitive is that output is restricted in them. Monopolies are
harmful not because they make high profits—profits can be
taxed away and redistributed to everyone else. Monopolies are
harmful because they reduce output below the optimal amount;
income tax policy can't fix that. Perfect competition is socially
optimal because it has the largest social surplus. Duopoly is
somewhat worse, and monopoly is much worse. So much for the
analysis of private goods provision by for-profit firms. However,

Figure 2.2. Measuring Consumer Surplus.

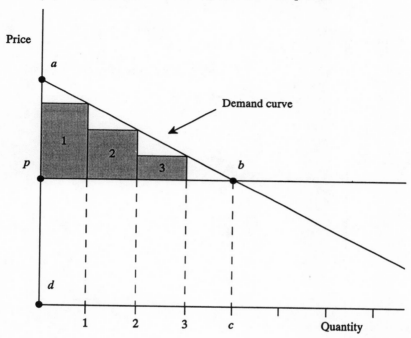

nonprofit organizations provide public goods as well, and we must also incorporate the surplus generated by these public goods.

The benefits of public good provision are shown graphically in Figure 2.3. Again, placing the quantity of the public good on the horizontal axis and the per-unit value of additional units of the public good on the vertical axis, we can construct the moral equivalent of a demand curve that measures the benefits from consuming one extra unit of the public good ("marginal social benefits," or MSB). However, in constructing the MSB curve, we must account for the fact that all consumers simultaneously benefit from each unit provided. This is done by adding together the reservation prices of all potential consumers and graphing this sum as the measure of marginal social value.

Figure 2.3. Consumer Surplus for a Public Good.

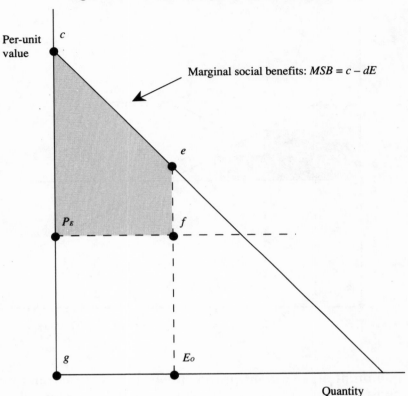

Once again, the area under this MSB curve up to the quantity provided (area ceE_0g in Figure 2.3) measures the total benefits accruing to all consumers when the quantity E_0 is provided. In our example, we assume that the public good can be purchased (by the government or nonprofit organization) from a perfectly competitive market at price P_E. Thus, social surplus (benefits net of costs) from public good provision is equal to the area of the trapezoid $cefP_E$.

The Model and Results

In our model, we assume that nonprofit organizations produce three distinct outputs: a private good, sold in order to obtain revenues to cross-subsidize the other two goods; "perqs," a composite private good provided to those in control of the organization at no cost to them; and a public good. All decisions are made in accord with the wishes of the person or group in control of the organization, which we shall refer to as "the manager." The manager has complete discretion over the allocation of the profits between perqs and public goods.

Although real-world interactions between duopolists unfold over time, we simplify by considering a "single-shot" analysis; that is, we imagine that the duopolists view their decisions on outputs as one-time-only choices made simultaneously by the two firms with due regard on the part of each firm to the likely behavior of its rival.

Nonprofit organizations can and often do earn profits (financial surpluses, increments to endowment, reserve funds, and so on), but, unlike for-profit firms, they cannot distribute these profits to shareholders or owners of the firm (the "nondistribution constraint"). Profits must be reinvested within the firm. In our model, this means that the monopoly profits are spent entirely on the combination of perqs and the public good. Although the ostensible purpose of the nondistribution constraint is to prevent excessive perqs, it is difficult to enforce proscriptions against excessive noncash benefits paid to managers. Thus, we do not constrain the nonprofit to devote all its surplus from sales to the provision of the public good.

Our model is similar to that of James (1983), who considers a nonprofit organization that sells two different goods, using profits from the sales of one good to "cross-subsidize" the price of the other good (so that the second good is sold below cost or given away). Our model differs from James's in that there are two cross-subsidized goods and one is explicitly public.

As James (1988) and , in a different setting, Preston (1988) have done, we include one additional feature, donations, to the model. We assume that donors care and are informed about the provision of public goods by each nonprofit firm and that they allocate donations among firms accordingly. Donations to any particular organization (net of fundraising expenditures) increase with that organization's spending on the public good. To a lesser extent, donations decrease with total public good expenditures by all firms. This latter effect is meant to capture the "commons" problem, highlighted in this context by Rose-Ackerman (1982a). That is, when one charity conducts a fundraising campaign, it makes it harder for other charities in related fields to raise funds, so that even after adjusting solicitation expenditures, net donations fall.

In Eckel and Steinberg (1992), we evaluate the different market structures by comparing their respective total social surpluses. We consider the consumer surplus derived from sales of the private good, the surplus from provision of the public good (including the manager's surplus from public good provision), and the surplus received by the manager from his or her expenditures on perqs; our findings are as follows:

1. Production and pricing of the private good by nonprofit firms is identical to production and pricing by for-profit firms.
2. Monopoly or duopoly may generate greater social surplus than perfect competition.
3. Duopoly may be worse than the other two alternatives.
4. Duopoly may be better than the other two alternatives.
5. Competition reduces the production of perqs.

We further consider each finding in turn.

1. Despite the fact that the firms we model are nonprofit organizations, they choose prices and quantities for the private good so as to maximize profits from sales of the good. Thus, nonprofit monopolies produce the same quantity as for-profit monopolies and charge the same price; nonprofit duopolies mimic for-profit duopolies. This is because profits are a means to accomplish managerial ends (public goods and perqs).

This result was properly anticipated by the courts. For example, the judge, in *Hospital Corporation of America* v. *FTC* observed that:

> The adoption of the nonprofit form does not change human nature [citation omitted], as the

courts have recognized in rejecting an implicit anti-trust exemption for nonprofit enterprises. [citation omitted]. . . Nonprofit status affects the method of financing the enterprise (substituting a combination of gift and debt financing for equity and debt financing) and the form in which profits. . . are distributed, and it may make management somewhat less beady-eyed in trying to control costs [citation omitted]. But no one has shown that it makes the enterprise unwilling to cooperate in reducing competition (some contrary evidence is presented in Hersch, 1984) — which most enterprises dislike and which nonprofit enterprises may dislike on ideological as well as selfish grounds [at 1390].

The judge in *Rockford Memorial* was even more explicit:

A not-for-profit company's fund balances, enlarged through monopoly profits, are a means to an end. The end may not be the personal wealth of the decisionmaker but could be for an objective held in nearly as great esteem. The not-for-profit decision-maker may desire more money for a new piece of equipment or to hire a new specialist or for a better office, salary or title, or just to keep the firm afloat in particularly lean or dangerous times. . . . Simply put, decisionmakers need not be solely interested in the attainment of profit to act anti-competitively [at 60, 543].

Although profits from sales are maximized, total firm profits are zero, because all net revenues from the private good are used to cross-subsidize the other two goods. This is unlike the case with for-profit firms.

2. It is possible that monopolies or duopolies generate greater total social surplus than does perfect competition. This is because a portion of the profits from one market failure (the lost surplus associated with imperfect competition) is used to

remedy another market failure (underprovision of public goods). In terms of Figures 2.1, 2.2, and 2.3, monopoly dominates perfect competition whenever the deadweight-loss triangle is smaller than the consumer-surplus trapezoid for the public good. Monopoly is more likely to dominate perfect competition when:

- The trapezoid is larger, as occurs when the value of the public good is large, governmental production of the good is low, and the cost of producing the good is low.
- The deadweight loss of monopoly is small, which, in turn, depends on the shape and location of the demand curve for the private good.
- The manager prefers to devote most of the financial surplus to the public good, rather than to perqs.
- There is a large "feedback effect" from public goods spending to donations. Donations increase when public goods spending increases. In turn, these added donations can be devoted to further public goods production. This is the feedback effect. There are both direct and indirect feedback effects. First, the added donations directly provide more resources to spend on the public good. Second, the feedback effect indirectly makes spending on the public good doubly attractive to the manager relative to spending on perqs.

Duopoly works in much the same way. Duopoly is likely to dominate perfect competition if the value of the public good is large, deadweight loss from the private good is small, feedback from one's own spending on the public good to one's own receipt of donations is large, and the manager allocates most of the profits from sales to the public good. One additional factor comes into play here: the commons problem. Because public good provision by one organization greatly reduces the other organization's ability to obtain donations, this will reduce total public good provision. If this effect is large enough, perfect competition will be the better alternative.

    3. Even in situations where duopoly is worse than perfect

competition, monopoly still may be best of all. This result is surprising, for among for-profits, perfect competition is always best, duopoly is always in the middle, and monopoly is always worst. If one could concoct a story whereby monopoly is best, one would expect the entire ordering to reverse; in contrast, we show that for nonprofit organizations, an "unnatural ordering" is possible.

The reason for this unnatural ordering is the commons problem. The commons problem reduces the ability of duopolists to provide the public good but does not affect the private good decision. The commons problem cancels some of the benefits from duopolies without reducing the social costs. It is possible for the public good surplus to dominate the deadweight loss for a monopoly while the deadweight loss dominates for a duopoly, resulting in an unnatural ordering.

What the policy impact of this result would be in a world of omniscient prosecutors and judges is clear. For duopoly industries where this unnatural ordering applied, any change would be advantageous. The government should not oppose a merger, but if a merger was not forthcoming, the government should seek to force divestiture. The policy impact is far less clear in practice, as discussed below.

4. Despite the commons problem, it is possible that duopoly is best of all. This is another sort of unnatural ordering, and when it occurs, omniscient prosecutors and judges should oppose both mergers and divestitures.

In monopoly or duopoly, profits are generated at the cost of a deadweight loss. The ratio of deadweight loss to profits is higher for monopoly. In our example, duopolies generate one dollar of deadweight loss for every four dollars of profit. In contrast, monopolies generate a dollar of deadweight loss for every two dollars of profit. For a given deadweight loss, duopolies can spend twice as much on the public good.

The situation is actually a bit more complicated than this, because donations are also devoted to purchases of the public good. The ratio of donations to deadweight loss may be larger or smaller for monopoly than for duopoly. This relationship is determined by the feedback from public goods purchases to donations, the dependence of public goods expenditures on sales of the private good, and the commons problem. These competing forces permit this sort of unnatural ordering, the sort of unnatural ordering discussed earlier, or the natural ordering. The various factors leading to alternative orderings can be summarized as follows:

Rank Ordering	*Factors Making This Ordering Likely*
Natural (perfect competition best, monopoly worst)	Underproduction of the private good creates large social costs (large deadweight losses).

Additional units of the public good bring small social benefits because:

- Government is already adequately providing the public good.
- The public good is not highly valued.

Nonprofit organizations produce a small quantity of public goods because:

- Nonprofit managers value perqs more highly than public good provision.
- Donors do not reward public good provision by significantly increasing their donations.

Inverse (monopoly best, perfect competition worst)

Underproduction of the private good creates small social costs.

Additional units of the public good bring large social benefits because:

- Government is constitutionally prohibited or otherwise restricted from providing an adequate quantity of public goods.
- The public good is highly valued.

Nonprofit organizations produce a large quantity of public goods because:

- Nonprofit managers value public good provision more highly than perqs.
- Public good provision is rewarded by increased donations (large feedback effect).
- The commons problem is moderate, so that duopolists do not simply steal donations from each other.

The monopoly is sufficiently more efficient than the duopoly in generating donations per unit of deadweight loss because the commons and net feedback effects are sufficiently large.

Unnatural, type 1 (monopoly best, duopoly worst)

The factors are similar to those for inverse ordering, except that the commons problem is very large.

Unnatural, type 2 (duopoly best, perfect competition worst)

The factors are similar to those for inverse ordering, except that the monopoly is not sufficiently more efficient (or is less efficient) in producing donations because the commons problem is small or nonexistent.

5. Increased competition reduces expenditures on perqs but has no clear effect on the ratio of perq to public good expenditure. Thus, if you consider perqs as a necessary cost of public good provision by nonprofits, competition is not unambiguously helpful.

Issues and Implications

Policy Implications of the Model

Nonprofit monopolies and duopolies can be socially beneficial if two prerequisites are met. First, nonprofits must provide a good or service with strong public good characteristics. If the nonprofit provides a mixed good with weaker public benefits (such as business education), there is less free riding and hence less need to supplement public good provision through monopoly profits. Second, governmental spending on the public good must be socially inadequate. This can happen for four reasons: the median voter may wish to see less provision than the mean beneficiary, the government may be prohibited from spending on the public good by statute or constitution (as in the case of religious monuments), the costs of government provision may be excessive, or the costs of government financing may be excessive.

It may be more expensive for government than for nonprofits to provide a public good for two reasons. First, there may be civil service rules, inefficient bureaucratic structures, or constraints that require all potential beneficiaries to be treated equally regardless of differences in the cost of serving them (see, for example, Salamon, 1987). Second, there may be production-side "economies of scope" that make it cheaper to produce the public good in combination with the marketed private good. For example, it is often cheaper to conduct medical research in a hospital than elsewhere, because in a hospital much of the medical overhead for research subjects is spread over the larger population of paying patients. At least in the United States, government is reluctant to produce private goods, as illustrated by the strength of the privatization movement in this country. Thus, any production-side economies of scope involving public goods must be realized in the private nonprofit sector.

Governmental provision may be inadequate because the cost of securing funds is high. In effect, it costs society twenty-five cents to raise a dollar in the form of duopoly profits, as noted above. Taxes also cause deadweight losses, and it is possible that the government would finance public goods with a particularly inefficient tax. Many regard the corporate income tax as one of the worst (for example, Ballard, Shoven, and Whalley, 1982, found that it costs society forty-nine cents in deadweight loss for each dollar raised), yet the 1986 tax reforms turned primarily to corporate tax increases to balance decreases in personal tax rates. To be fair, the 1986 reforms also reduced the deadweight loss associated with corporate taxation, but it remains high.

If governmental provision of public goods is inadequate for the first two reasons, then nonprofit monopoly power is a "second-best" corrective in the sense that political reforms could allow government to solve the problem without incurring monopoly's deadweight loss. If, however, governmental provision is inadequate because the costs of provision or financing are excessive, then nonprofit monopoly power may be the best solution.

Courts and prosecutors cannot act on possibilities; they must know whether particular monopolies are socially beneficial to decide how to act. However, as the courts have recognized when establishing "per se rules," judges and prosecutors are not particularly competent to weigh the claims of opposing lawyers and expert witnesses on the size of respective social surpluses. Expert witnesses themselves cannot testify with confidence because the respective surpluses can be estimated only with considerable uncertainty.

Policy makers should therefore strive for simple structural rules that resolve the burden of proof in favor of one party or the other. For example, Steinberg (1992) argues that the structure of a nonprofit's board of directors, as established in its articles of incorporation, could be used to establish legal presumption. Unlike for-profit boards, which have a clear incentive to utilize monopoly power to the detriment of consumers, *some* nonprofit boards are selected from and responsible to the patrons of the organization. If nonprofits that are legally controlled by the purchasers of the private good wish to merge and to raise private good prices, then there should be a presumption that the public good benefits outweigh the deadweight loss.

Policy Issues Not Addressed by Our Model

Our model does not directly address three issues that are important in the design of appropriate antitrust policy: price discrimination, asymmetrical information, and mixed-sector duopolies.

Price Discrimination. Price discrimination occurs when distinct customer groups are charged different prices or when the price depends on the quantity purchased. Our model does not allow for any form of price discrimination other than the implicit voluntary form (where a customer adds a donation to the purchase price). Yet price discrimination may form an important reason that nonprofit organizations exist and are advantageous. Hansmann (1981) and Ben-Ner (1986) each analyzed price discrimination by a monopoly nonprofit; it would be useful to examine duopoly price discrimination in these contexts.

In a sense, the *Brown* and *Kingsepp* cases are about price discrimination, for the suits in those cases alleged that the universities conspired to set the discount on list price (financial aid) to be offered to common customers. Thus, our model is clearly inadequate to weigh the competing claims in these cases. However, the basic trade-off in these cases is quite similar to the trade-off that we analyze—monopoly profits are needed to cross-subsidize the social benefit of need-blind access to higher education when governmental programs are insufficient for this purpose.

Asymmetrical Information. When the sellers know more about the quality or quantity of goods offered to buyers than the buyers do, this asymmetry can cause departures from social optimality in competitive markets. According to Hansmann (1980), one of the main reasons for the existence of nonprofit organizations is that they are less likely than for-profit organizations to take advantage of consumer ignorance in cases of asymmetrical information because the nondistribution constraint removes the incentive to cheat customers. Our model suggests a qualification to Hansmann's conclusion: managers may cheat customers in the sale of the private good in order to maximize profits that support expenditures on perqs and public goods.

However, Chillemi and Gui (1990) extend Hansmann's results in a different and relevant direction. They show that there are interactions between the price charged and the credibility of nonprofit firms in a competitive market. This suggests that monopoly and duopoly pricing may interact with product quality in nonprofit markets, a policy issue that our model does not address.

Mixed-Sector Duopolies. Sometimes, the competition is between nonprofit and for-profit firms. For example, in *Carilion*, the Justice Department objected to the merger of two nonprofit hospitals in a market where one for-profit hospital would remain. Although we have shown that nonprofit monopolists choose the same prices and quantities for the private good as would for-profit firms, the analysis is not complete in this setting, because nonprofit firms' tax and regulatory treatment is different from that of their for-profit rivals. Thus, the "unfair competition" controversy (Rose-Ackerman, 1982b; Steinberg, 1988) should be integrated with models of antitrust policy.

Conclusion

Because nonprofit organizations exist, in part, to cure market failures, the usual economic analysis of monopoly power is incomplete. When nonprofits devote financial surpluses to the provision of public goods, monopoly can be superior to perfect competition. Indeed, any social rank ordering of perfect competition, duopoly, and monopoly is consistent with our model when two additional complications are incorporated: the commons problem affecting donations and the differential ratios of profits to deadweight losses in the respective market equilibria. However, we have found no simple rule that would allow the judicial system to reliably determine the optimal market structure, and the types of judgments required are probably beyond judicial competence.

Nonprofit monopolies extend the tradition of the "robber barons" and other wealthy philanthropists of the late nineteenth and early twentieth centuries. Many prominent nonprofits bear the names of monopolists. The Rockefellers, Mellons, Carnegies, and Fords made their fortunes through monopoly power, and a portion of their riches became the Rockefeller, Mellon, Carnegie, and Ford Foundations, which have done much good. Indeed, this very book would not have appeared had it not been for the profits of the Mandel family. If the social benefits financed through, say, the Rockefeller Foundation outweigh the deadweight loss from the original monopolies, then the prosecution and court-ordered divestiture of the Standard Oil Company was harmful to society.

Like the robber barons, nonprofit monopolies act as quasi governments with managers or boards as benevolent dictators. These organizations can do good that outweighs the social costs that they impose. The high monopoly price that they charge for private goods is like a "tax" used to finance public purpose activities, no different from any other excise tax except that it is privately levied.

Robber barons and nonprofit monopolies are sometimes viewed as elitist and undemocratic. As they function as quasi governments, their funding priorities are established by a privileged elite whose benevolence we must trust; they are not answerable to a broadly constituted electorate. To some, this lack of accountability outweighs any possible social gain. But perhaps discipline for nonprofits comes from other sources. The choice of the nonprofit organizational form is itself a form of self-imposed discipline. Appointed boards also provide self-imposed discipline on the actions of the nonprofit. As we have seen in the recent fracas over the actions of the CEO of the United Way, press coverage can provide discipline. Finally, the market for the private good can impose some discipline, though indirectly. There is a wealth of evidence that consumers punish behavior that they consider unfair and that managers of firms avoid actions that consumers would think unfair (Kahneman, Knetsch and Thaler, 1986; Gorman and Kehr, 1992), and nonprofits are not immune to this market response.

Although nonprofit monopolies may restrict competition in a particular market, they may provide competition in the government sector. Democratic institutions leave too little room for the appropriate expression of minority interests. The legitimacy of these institutions is enhanced when a pluralistic system of powerful and independent "third-sector" organizations competes with and complements government activities. Pluralism also enhances innovation and efficiency, challenging both sectors to their finest efforts. Monopoly power by some third-sector organizations is itself a check and a balance, protecting against abuse of government's inherent monopoly power.

References

Ballard, C. L., Shoven, J. B., Whalley, J. *The Welfare Costs of Distortions in the United States Tax System: A General Equilibrium Approach.* Working Paper no. 1043, Cambridge, Mass.: National Bureau of Economic Research, 1982.

Ben-Ner, A. "Nonprofit Organizations: Why Do They Exist in Market Economies?" In S. Rose-Ackerman (ed.), *The Economics of Nonprofit Institutions: Studies in Structure and Policy.* New York: Oxford University Press, 1986.

Chillemi, O., and Gui, B. "Product Quality in Trust Type Nonprofits: An Expository Evaluation of Three Economic Models." In *Towards the 21st Century: Challenges for the Voluntary Sector.* Proceedings of the 1990 conference of the Association of Voluntary Action Scholars. London: 1990.

Eckel, C., and Steinberg, R. "A Robber-Baron Model of Nonprofit Monopoly." Working paper, Department of Economics, Indiana University–Purdue University, Indianapolis, 1992.

Gorman, R. F., and Kehr, J. B. "Fairness as a Constraint on Profit Seeking: Comment." *American Economic Review,* 1992, *82*(1), 355–358.

Hansmann, H. "The Role of Nonprofit Enterprise." *Yale Law Journal,* 1980, *89,* 835–901.

Hansmann, H. "Nonprofit Enterprise in the Performing Arts." *Bell Journal of Economics,* 1981, *12,* 341–361.

James, E. "How Nonprofits Grow: A Model." *Journal of Policy Analysis and Management,* 1983, *2,* 350–366.

Kahneman, D., Knetsch, J., and Thaler, R. "Fairness as a Constraint on Profit Seeking." *American Economic Review,* 1986, *76*(4), 728–741.

Preston, A. "The Nonprofit Firm: A Potential Solution to Inherent Market Failures." *Economic Inquiry,* 1988, *26,* 493–506.

Rose-Ackerman, S. "Charitable Giving and Excessive Fundraising." *Quarterly Journal of Economics,* 1982a, *97,* 193–212.

Rose-Ackerman, S. "Unfair Competition and Corporate Income Taxation." *Stanford Law Review*, 1982b, *34*, 1017–1139.

Salamon, L. "Of Market Failure, Voluntary Failure, and Third-Party Government: Toward a Theory of Government-Nonprofit Relations in the Modern Welfare State." *Journal of Voluntary Action Research*, 1987, *16*, 29–49.

Steinberg, R. "Voluntary Donations and Public Expenditures in a Federalist System." *American Economic Review*, 1987, 77, 24–36.

Steinberg, R. "Fairness and Efficiency in the Competition Between For-Profit and Nonprofit Firms." Working Paper no. 132, Program on Non-profit Organizations, Yale University, June 1988.

Steinberg, R. "How Should Antitrust Laws Apply to Nonprofit Organizations?" In D. R. Young, R. Hollister, and V. A. Hodgkinson (eds.), *Governing, Leading, and Managing Nonprofit Organizations: New Insights from Research and Practice*. San Francisco: Jossey-Bass, 1992.

Varian, H. R. *Microeconomic Analysis*. (2nd ed.) New York: W.W.Norton, 1984.

Weisbrod, B. "Toward a Theory of the Voluntary Nonprofit Sector in a Three-Sector Economy." In E. S. Phelps (ed.), *Altruism, Morality and Economic Theory*. New York: Russell Sage Foundaton, 1975.

Cases Cited

Adventist Health Systems/West, FTC Dkt. 9234 (issued Nov. 7, 1989).

Associated In-Group Donors v. *United Way, Inc.*, No. C. 23112 (Cal. Super. Ct. Los Angeles County, filed Mar. 28, 1978).

FTC v. *University Health, Inc.*, 1991-1 Trade Cases 69.444 (S.D. Ga.), reversed in part in *FTC* v. *University Health, Inc.*, 1991-1 Trade Cases 69.424 (11th Cir. 1991).

Hospital Corporation of America v. *FTC*, 807 F.2d 1381, 1386 (7th Cir. 1986).

In the Matter of College Football Association and Capital Cities ABC, Inc., FTC Dkt. 9242 (filed Sept. 5, 1990).

Kingsepp v. *Wesleyan, et al.*, Civil Action No. 89-6121 (S.D. N.Y. 1991).

National Collegiate Athletic Association v. *Board of Regents of the University of Oklahoma*, 468 U.S. 447 (1986).

National Society of Professional Engineers v. *U.S.*, 435 U.S. 679 (1978).

Ukiah Valley Medical Center v. *FTC*, 911 F.2d 261 (9th Cir. 1990).

U.S. v. *Brown, et al.*, Civil Action No. 91-3274 (E.D. Pa. 1991).

U.S. v. *Carilion Health System and Community Hospital of Roanoke Valley*, 707 F. Supp. 840 (W.D. Va. 1989).

U.S. v. *Rockford Memorial Corporation and the SwedishAmerican Corporation*, 1989-1 Trade Cases 68.462 (N.D. Ill. 1989).

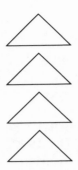

CHAPTER 3

Nonprofit Organizations and the Emergence of America's Corporate Commonwealth in the Twentieth Century

Louis Galambos

Most of us have had extensive personal experience with non-profit organizations—schools, hospitals, churches, museums, and professional groups—and few Americans would disagree, I believe, with the idea that their lives have been shaped to some considerable degree by those institutions and their values. Yet we give nonprofits, as such, little attention in our accounts of the history of the United States. I hope to correct that situation, and I would like to begin this task by looking briefly at two particular nonprofit organizations with which I have had some personal experiences. These were tiny, seemingly insignificant associations involved in the process of incipient professionalization.

The Business History Conference was involved in a sub-discipline, business history, that had grown like a little wart on one side of economic history. The Association for Documentary Editing was involved in a field that had barely taken shape as a distinct form of professional labor before the association was organized.

Both of these associations had a tough time in their early years. The work of the Business History Conference seemed irrelevant to the research being conducted by most of the practitioners in the larger discipline of economic history: in the post–World War II era, the front edge of the larger discipline was being shaped primarily by academicians trained in economics, not history. To scholars steeped in neoclassical theory, it was obvious that business organizations did not deserve histories: it was assumed that their internal development did not matter to the performance of the economy. Moreover, the Business History Conference did not even have control of the leading journal in business history; that journal was already being published by a prominent educational institution in Cambridge, Massachusetts. The organization could thus not control the information flow on its own self-defined intellectual turf. The Association for Documentary Editing had an even more serious case of the Rodney Dangerfield syndrome: "they couldn't get no respect" in any part of the academic world where they wanted jobs and status or in the foundation field where they wanted funding.

Now, some years later, I am happy to report that both groups are making it. The Business History Conference has in recent years benefited from a formidable intellectual and academic renaissance in the subdiscipline; people outside the sub-discipline — even those in much larger, more prestigious disciplines, such as economics — now actually pay attention to what business historians are saying! The Association for Documentary Editing has found a special niche between academia and the government funding agencies that support most of the documentary editing that takes place in the United States. Both organizations thus seem to have acquired semipermanent positions in the nation's vast array of nonprofit institutions.

As a result of their success in the early stages of professionalization, these organizations — however tiny and apparently powerless they are — deserve a place in the chronicles of what I believe to be the single most important change that has taken place in modern America. I refer, of course, to the astonishing organizational transformation of the past century. This transformation provides the historical context in which I am going to place these two little associations.

The Organizational Revolution, 1890–1940

Between 1890 and 1940, the United States experienced a profound organizational revolution that transformed the nation's political, economic, and social lives.[1] During those decades, there emerged three sets of new or newly transformed institutions: the modern administrative state; the modern corporation; and a complex array of nonprofit organizations that began in those years to redefine professional life, education, industrial labor, political relations, and the sources of status in the United States. All of these institutions were interwoven in complex ways. All of them were shaped by and had an impact on American values and ideologies. All of them from time to time competed for scarce resources and for political and social preference.

Why did that all-encompassing change take place? For every set of modern institutions that took shape during these decades, there is a different history, a different set of specific reasons why they evolved as they did. But when we look across all of them and ask ourselves why they changed or arose when they did, the most general explanation is still the one provided long ago by Adam Smith: the breadth of the market determined the degree of specialization (Smith, [1776] 1937, pp. 17–21).[2] In this case, too, the national dimensions of the market determined that many of these new institutions would be national in scope. In the United States in the latter part of the nineteenth century, the demand for organization was broadened dramatically by the development of transportation and communication systems, by the growth of cities, and by the tremendous increase in population that the country was experiencing as a result of immigration. The ability to supply organization was also changing, but the major shift appears to have been on the demand side.

Let us look first at the growth of the administrative state.

In the years following the Civil War, the United States was virtually a stateless nation, at least by comparison with most European countries. The government—local, state, or federal—did very little and appropriately had few permanent administrative agencies. As one distinguished scholar has pointed out, this was a government dominated by political parties and courts (Skowronek, 1982). This was not the case for long, however, after the railroad and telegraph tightened the links of commerce, after cities such as Chicago grew to a population of more than a million (1890), after eight million new Americans settled in this country between 1870 and 1890. Quickly, America began to construct an administrative state. Typically for the United States, it was (and still is today) a hodgepodge of local, state, and federal institutions. Also typically, it was a tribute to "ad hoc-ary," to an effort to solve each separate problem as it developed, with as little concern for consistency or order as the state and federal constitutions would allow.

With hindsight, we can discern two major patterns. First, there were increasing efforts, frequently led by reformers, to achieve through government a greater measure of either equity or security for some selected group or groups. Hence the creation of major elements of the regulatory state. Hence the development of the progressive income tax and of antitrust law. Hence the laws that regulated hours and working conditions, first for women and children, then for men in particular occupations.[3] Not all of those who desired or needed security were the "little people" of reform history: hence the banker-dominated Federal Reserve System and later the regulations that gave to a state-based cartel control of the price of one of the nation's most important sources of energy—oil (Kolko, 1963; Nash, 1968; Vietor, 1984). Second, while this transformation was taking place in U.S. government, the rise of the modern corporation was working a revolutionary change in the country's industrial economy.

These two phenomena have frequently been analyzed as if they had no relationship to one another, but actually the growth of the administrative state and the growth of the corporation were securely intertwined. Corporations were, after all, political creatures (Fligstein, 1990). They frequently found their interests at stake in the struggles over reform. It often behooved them to attempt to control legislation, administration, and adjudication in order to protect these interests. Their executives and managers were, moreover, as interested in security as were other Americans. When they sought too much of it through private means, in fact, they frequently found their very existence threatened by antitrust suits (Thorelli, 1955; Letwin, 1965; "The Sherman Act's First Century," 1989). One of the corporate responses to the need for security and control of the environment in the years following 1900 was to create new public relations and public affairs departments. These administrative innovations were products of the struggles of large private bureaucracies to develop better relationships with government and with a public that from time to time had a disconcerting tendency to change its elected officials and public policies (Raucher, 1968; Brooks, 1975).

While corporations perforce were concerned with security, they were the carriers of two other important values: efficiency and innovation. Companies that emphasized security to the exclusion of economies of scale, scope, and system were usually weeded out by competition during the first two decades following the great merger movement at the turn of the century (Chandler, 1990). Companies that were not mindful of their need to innovate over the long term soon found their positions of power eroded by more nimble competitors (Carlson, 1991; Tedlow, 1990; Graham, 1986). Among the institutional responses to the need for innovation was the industrial laboratory, which developed in the years after 1900 and became widespread in the industrial sector after 1920 (Reich, 1983). One of the aggregate measures of this transition was the increasing contribution to the growth of the U.S. economy made by productivity increases (Gallman, 1972; Abramovitz and David, 1973; Solow, 1957).

The third arena of institutional change during these years — the subject of this book, the nonprofit sector — is less well documented than the first two. Some might suggest that it is less studied because it had no independent existence, because it was merely a function of the other two sectors of institutional change. Others might contend that this is because it was inherently less important than the state or the corporation. I do not accept either line of reasoning. I think that the nonprofit sector has been less well studied because it did not fit either our dominant categories or theories of modernization or our historical syntheses. It did not fit in either progressive or revisionist history as a separate category because this historical construct was primarily concerned with one type of political change. It did not fit in neoclassical approaches to economic factors because institutions as such — including the corporation — did not until recently constitute a category for analysis in that paradigm.[4]

To a historian working in the organizational paradigm, however, the nonprofit sector plays a vital role in our history — including our economic history — and follows lines of development similar in many respects to the evolution of our modern governmental and corporate institutions. Nonprofit organizations experienced the same sort of explosive growth as did those institutions, starting at about the same time in the late nineteenth century. Nonprofits became carriers of the four dominant values we have mentioned: equity, security, efficiency, and innovation. In fact, we can use those four sets of values to categorize, for heuristic purposes, many of the vast number of new organizations that arose during this first stage of the organizational revolution.

When that revolution began, the United States was already populated with a deep, rich array of nonprofit organizations, many of which had as their primary role the expression of religious and aesthetic values. There were as well an incredible number of small local institutions that provided entertainment, reinforced the status system, and preserved a sense of community.[5] These clubs and their club cultures were important in a fast-growing, increasingly urban society, as were the religious and aesthetic institutions that tempered to some degree the materialism that pervaded nineteenth-century America. These organizations continued to play major roles in the United States in the twentieth century, and many of them influenced and were influenced by the four values that I have identified as central to the nation's organizational revolution. That was particularly true in the realm of reform, where American churches and church leaders made significant contributions to the effort to create a more equitable society (Hall, 1987).

But neither the religious nor the aesthetic nor the local social institutions were themselves prime movers in the nation's organizational transformation in the period between 1890 and 1940. They were more often the shaped than the shapers. They were frequently encroached upon and sometimes displaced by new regional and national organizations and were forced to accommodate to the new setting if they were to survive. Many did so successfully and today constitute an important element in our social and cultural life. But my focus is on the sources of change, and I trace these primarily to different sorts of organizations, such as the liberal or progressive interest groups taking shape at the turn of the century.

The reform-oriented nonprofits were primarily dedicated to the goals of achieving equity and security for those Americans who seemed in a market economy to have neither an opportunity to get ahead nor protection when things went wrong. It is instructive in this regard to read some of the literature of the early twentieth century—before there was a Social Security system, workers' compensation, or a minimum wage. "Our very first Christmas at Hull-House," reformer Jane Addams wrote, "when we as yet knew nothing of child labor, a number of little girls refused the candy which was offered them . . . , saying simply that they 'worked in a candy factory and could not bear the sight of it.' We discovered that for six weeks they had worked from seven in the morning until nine at night, and they were exhausted as well as satiated" (Addams, 1910).

Addams and thousands of other reformers organized, supported, or cooperated with nonprofits that created organizational networks and teams of experts bent on the ideological mission of changing these conditions by transforming U.S. government. To a substantial degree, they achieved their objectives during the years 1890 through 1940, developing in the United States the foundations of the liberal welfare state. Many of those objectives were achieved by way of regulation (McCraw, 1981; Galambos and Pratt, 1988). But even the regulations reflected the fact that institutional change was taking place because non-profit organizations were succeeding in changing people's attitudes toward what was correct behavior where equity and security were concerned. Thus, nonprofits played a vital role both in developing a new American culture and in creating the U.S. administrative state.

The reform nonprofits were, of course, part of a much broader movement that brought concepts such as security to the fore. Thus, the trade association movement of these years — a development that involved thousands of new organizations — had as a primary goal the provision of a degree of political and economic security for the associations' many business members (Steigerwalt, 1980; Galambos, 1966; Yamazaki and Miyamoto, 1988). While these associations also dealt with technical change and from time to time tried to promote innovation through cooperative means, the backbone of the trade association movement was the defensive effort to protect the interests of the associations' business members. Similarly, the labor movement of these years did much to protect the security of the labor elite, primarily but not exclusively the skilled workers (Montgomery, 1987; Tomlins, 1985). Labor unions are often excluded from discussions of nonprofits, but I do not understand how they differ from trade associations — which are included. I know that the Internal Revenue Service (IRS) does not allow trade unions to be classified as nonprofits, but even though the IRS may call a fish a bird, that does not mean that the fish can get out of the water, let alone fly. An expanded definition of *nonprofit* would include as well the political parties and all other nongovernmental bodies that do not operate for a profit. The historical study of nonprofits would, I think, be strengthened by this sort of definition.

Nor do I see that much difference among labor organizations, trade associations, and the sort of professional groups with which I began this chapter. They, too, protected their members' interests, some of them using licensing, some using other regulations to restrain competition. Even professional standards for training were a means of restricting entry—although they were, of course, always presented in public discourse as a means of protecting the public welfare (Abbott, 1988).

The professional nonprofits did many other things as well, and many of these organizations came to have a particularly close relationship to innovation. I refer especially to the groups in science and engineering during these years. They were experiencing rapid expansion and were fracturing into specialties and subdisciplines at a remarkable rate. Establishing close relationships with the foundations and the educational institutions that together provided a substantial part of the support available for scientific research in the years before World War II, these organizations published cutting-edge research, organized meetings at which innovative ideas could be discussed, and rewarded top performers with the symbols of social status that their employers frequently used as the justification for material rewards (Kohler, 1982; Oleson and Voss, 1979). As sociologist Talcott Parsons pointed out long ago, these professions built the concept of infinite progress into their value systems and sustained this idea through socialization and social control (Parsons, 1954). Indeed, few of the professions seem ever to have contemplated that progress in their discipline or subdiscipline might level off some day or might actually no longer be needed by society.[6]

Thus dedicated to progress, the professions provided people and ideas that accelerated innovation in the private and public sectors of society. They also promoted efficiency through standardization and the misnamed but nonetheless important "scientific management" movement (Chandler, 1977). The successful corporation stayed in touch with the professions relevant to its activities; some of the most important people in these corporations were the ones who worked the company's boundaries, harvesting new ideas and recruiting new professionals who could help the organization remain creative. This same function was being performed in the public sector—for example, in the U.S. Department of Agriculture, where the foundation was being laid in the years before World War II for the "green revolution" that would follow (Rossiter, 1979). If today we are able to supply food at affordable prices to many other countries of the world, it is largely because of the links that developed before 1940 between the new administrative state and the professions associated with the agricultural sciences.

By the time the United States entered World War II in 1941, the country had thus been reorganized. Local and regional institutions—including the religious and aesthetic nonprofits mentioned earlier—continued to play extremely important roles in American society. But now they were encased in and in many instances encroached upon by new functional and national organizations. U.S. politics had been transformed by an administrative state that controlled many activities previously left to the market to allocate and by an immense array of interest groups that were now performing some of the most important functions that political parties had performed during the previous century. As the relationships between interest groups and the administrative state solidified, various kinds of working relationships and alliances developed; they frequently became three-sided and have become commonly known as "triocracies" or "iron triangles." As these terms indicate, these alliances were often very durable, so resistant to change that they distress those who are studying American politics or trying to alter policy (Rourke, 1991; Galambos, 1982; Hansen, 1987). They involved the interest groups that wanted specific government programs, the agencies created to implement programs, and the congressional committees or subcommittees that oversaw these activities. The legislators received the support that they needed for reelection; the agencies got their programs refunded; the groups were rewarded with the specific programs that they sought to ensure that their members or clients would be protected or get a "fair shake."

These institutional changes embodied a new emphasis on security and equity. These values had certainly not replaced the central American value—materialism, or "making it"—but they had become substantially more important, as had efficiency and innovation, the key sources of the nation's economic growth in the twentieth century. The giant corporation had by this time reorganized the industrial economy, laying the foundation for the consumer society that would emerge in the 1940s to the chagrin of many intellectuals and to the delight of most Americans (Edsforth, 1987). This was a new society, in which nonprofits played a vital role and that nonprofits had done a great deal to shape.

The American Century, 1940–1970

The next three decades were kind to Americans and to this new set of institutions, including the nonprofits. World War II was expensive in terms of lives lost, but it forced the country to adopt policies that pulled the economy out of the Great Depression. It left the United States dominant in world markets and world politics. Prosperity encouraged rapid organizational growth in all three institutional sectors.

The administrative state was elaborated, acquiring new functions related to equity, security, and innovation. Let me mention only three major areas involving equity: civil rights for black Americans; equal rights for women; and the new concern for protecting the environment. The sources and sequences of change were different in these three sectors: in civil rights, traditional religious organizations and their leaders were dominant, while in the women's and environmental movements, new institutions, ideologies, and leaders were at the forefront of change. But all three movements produced similar results— revolutionary changes in the United States' postwar society. In all three, the direction of change, the pressure for change, and the continuing involvement needed to shape the administration of change came primarily from nonprofit organizations. Similarly in the realm of increased security, the extension of the social welfare system and of the currently troubled insurance system created for the financial sector were all to a considerable extent results of the activities of nonprofit groups working closely with relevant government agencies, themselves often promoters of change.

As different nonprofit groups succeeded in getting their programs implemented, they of course attached themselves to the new administrative state along the lines of the triocratic or iron-triangle alliances. These elaborate relationships continued to add a measure of stability to the state and to the nonprofits as well. Now, however, the political setting became even more complex. Swirling around the triocracies were growing numbers of experts and their related organizations—the "issue networks," so named because their members all shared an interest in and a technical grasp of a particular public issue (Heclo, 1978). Here, too, nonprofits had an important role to play. They provided most of the policy experts; they thus helped to staff the agencies and the legislative committees; when experts left these jobs, they frequently took their expertise to nonprofit groups interested in their policy arenas. Insofar as policy experts tended to be committed to particular ideological positions on the issues with which they dealt, the policy networks militated against political compromise and thus tended to stabilize the state, as did the interest-group alliances.

Perhaps the most surprising change during these years was the new role that the state took in encouraging innovation, and here, too, nonprofits played a central role. The successful wartime experience in combining educational institutions, professional expertise, and federally funded research and development encouraged the nation to experiment on a multibillion dollar level with a peacetime variant on this policy (Pinick and others, 1972). Nonprofit organizations and their members were at center stage in this grand national experiment, which produced such successes as the revitalized National Institutes of Health and such failures as the atomic energy program; the "pro-ministrative state" generated boondoggles as well as the breakthroughs that announced to the world that U.S. science and engineering had at last taken a position commensurate with the nation's economic standing (Shorter, 1987; Goodfield, 1991; Balogh, 1991a; McDougall, 1985). As the new network of private and public institutions took shape, it generated a new round of organizational experiments in the nonprofit sector: think tanks and related groups experienced a great expansion in numbers and influence.[7]

If any one organizational development characterized the

so-called American Century, however, it was the ascendancy of the U.S. corporation. During these years, the decentralized or multidivisional ("M-form") company became the standard structure for the U.S.-based multinational high-tech industrial firm. These were the firms that were the prime carriers for the values of efficiency and innovation. Run by professional managers, they were world leaders in the global economy. Decentralization enabled them to handle greater complexity—that is, more products and services—and to spread over broader geographical areas at home and abroad. Diversification became a common strategy, and there appeared for a time to be no limit to the size that these organizations could reach without becoming dysfunctional (Chandler, 1990).

What contribution did nonprofits make to these giant profit-making organizations and to the world economy that they were recasting? The professions provided the personnel that the companies needed to guide their expansion, the scientific and engineering disciplines that they drew on as they improved their services, products, and processes, and many of the managers who guided their internal development and external affairs. Those external relations were particularly important now, and nonprofits played a key role in ensuring that U.S. corporations would operate in relatively friendly political and social environments. No single company could afford to go it alone; all needed the appearance and sometimes the reality of widespread support.[8] By helping shape the external affairs and the growth paths of the M-form corporations, nonprofits and their members worked a decisive influence on the economic dimensions of the postwar world during the American Century.

The New Age of Global Competition, 1970 to the Present

Then, following a script provided long ago by the Bible and the Greek historians, America fell from grace. Just as the pride of the American Century became overbearing to its friends as well as its enemies, the United States experienced a series of depressing defeats. Abroad there was the Vietnam War, which the United States had lost by 1970, even though the final defeat did not come until 1975. And while the nation was suffering that agony, U.S. business was taking it on the nose overseas as well as in its own national market. Japanese and German competitors began to outproduce and outinnovate U.S. companies in a wide variety of industries. The U.S. economy was in disarray, beset by a high rate of inflation, astronomical interest rates, oil shocks, and a disconcerting long-term decline in the productivity increases that had become the nation's major source of growth (Galambos and Pratt, 1988).

Neither the private nor the public sector was producing the results Americans wanted, and in the 1970s in particular, their public leadership gave them cause for deep concern. Watergate and the revelations that ensued were deeply unsettling to a nation that had yet to become comfortable with its new administrative state. The defeat in Vietnam worked a similar influence, spreading gloom in a society beset by wrenching economic changes stemming from global competition.

In response to this new and challenging economic setting, the focus of political activity in the United States shifted decisively away from equity and security. Indeed, Americans began to dismantle parts of the regulatory system. We can stop for a moment and look at the deregulation movement, because it is an excellent guide to the change that had taken place in U.S. politics as a result of the organizational revolution and of the new role of nonprofits in the society. The initial impetus for change came not from a widespread discontent with regulation in industries such as air transportation but from experts, professional experts, who were concerned with the diseconomies and subsidies embodied in the regulatory system (Derthick and Quirk, 1985). In industry after industry, they found evidence that innovation had been discouraged by the lack of competition. Winning support from conservative as well as liberal leaders in the White House and then in Congress, they were able to turn the tide of change against the regulatory state (McCraw, 1984). The deregulation movement gradually picked up support from a wide range of nonprofits, from political action committees (PACs) representing interests that would benefit directly from new policies, and, of course, from the companies that stood to profit from deregulation. The relevant "issue networks" buzzed with activity as the movement accelerated.

The opposition to deregulation included significant numbers of those who would now be forced to confront the market without the protection of rate-of-return regulation. The lineups were interesting. They included labor unions as well as corporations. Wherever deregulation threatened to disrupt existing stability-oriented arrangements, triocratic politics came into play in an effort to prevent change (Derthick and Quirk, 1985, especially pp. 147–206). In some cases, even government regulatory agencies themselves were opposed to change when they saw their policy turf disappearing, replaced by the market.[9]

Other changes followed. Concerned about the costs of environmental programs and of further extensions of the welfare system, the nation's legislators and executives looked for new ways to improve the efficiency of the private sector instead of new programs along liberal-progressive lines. The structural side of antitrust policy was virtually abandoned. Now conservative nonprofits took the leadership role that liberal nonprofits had played in an earlier day. The ensuing struggles over environmental programs were especially fierce — and still are today. Each attempt to change an existing government program ran afoul of hedgerows of interest groups, triocratic alliances, and policy networks, which had by this time put down deep roots in and around the administrative state (Hays, 1987, especially pp. 491–543). These groups and their experts made particularly effective use of the courts to delay or prevent change. Nevertheless, in the years after 1970, the momentum clearly shifted in the government from a search for equity and security to a sometimes frantic search for efficiency and innovation.

As one might have predicted, the corporation has adjusted to this new competitive setting more quickly than has the state. Markets work faster than does the interest-group style of democracy in introducing change. By destaffing, by spinning off conglomerate activities, and by introducing new styles of labor relations, U.S. firms struggled through the 1980s to become more competitive (Galambos and Pratt, 1988, pp. 227–255). The search for competitive advantage has, of course, involved high-energy efforts to improve technology immediately and to develop public and private organizations capable of accelerating the pace of technical innovation over the long term. In pursuing these efforts, U.S. companies have been able to mine rich veins of information and personnel from the country's well-developed nonprofit professional sector. This is an asset that the nation did not lose during the American Century. If anything, it was strengthened during those years.

Nonprofits are thus playing a decisive role in the transition that the United States is now experiencing, just as they did in the previous two transitions. This volume asks "How will nonprofits compete and collaborate in a market economy?" My answer is "Look to their history." They have been competing and collaborating for the last century. In the last decade or so, we have witnessed some of the fiercest examples of competition and the most telling examples of coalition building in nonprofit history. This struggle is not nearly over. It will last through our lifetimes — and probably through the lifetimes of our great grandchildren.

Which brings me to my final point; and for that we must return to those two tiny professional associations with which I began this chapter. Now, I hope, we have a better context in which to fit their early struggles and recent successes. One of them, the Business History Conference, has made an intellectual contribution to the current transition. The research and writing of its members have largely (but not exclusively) been on the side of the recent changes in public policy; that is, on the side of the now dominant trend toward market forces. Business historians have provided a usable history for those who believe that during the past two centuries, U.S. companies have on balance done a good job of contributing to the nation's economic growth and its ability to provide the goods and services that its citizens need. In particular, the current generation of business historians has shown how giant vertical and horizontal combinations have achieved the economies of scale, scope, and system needed for them to be effective in a modern economic setting.[10]

The other group, the Association for Documentary Editing, has primarily (although, again, not exclusively) made historical contributions that support the other side of this political struggle over policy. Thus, the association has performed a different but equally important function. Moreover, the group and its practitioners, performing along typical triocratic lines, have in recent years helped to successfully fight off an effort to eliminate public support for the job of documenting the nation's past. Much of that documentation was of the sort that we need today. It reminds us that in our headlong rush to use market forces, we should not forget why Americans created an administrative state in the first place.[11] After all, market forces had produced the candy factory that employed little girls from seven in the morning until nine at night. People decided to change those conditions — and government seemed at that time to be the only effective way to achieve that objective.

The documentary projects thus remind us that the market has not been the only way to achieve our goals; democracy — interest-group democracy or otherwise — has been another significant way, and over the past century, U.S. society has voiced some powerful complaints about the outcomes that market forces yielded. We should remember those complaints today, just as we should bear in mind the benefits of a market economy. For those lessons in history, we can be grateful to nonprofits — institutions that have done much to shape America's corporate commonwealth in the past century.

Notes

1. For an excellent up-to-date critical review of the literature, see Balogh (1991b). My own contributions to this literature include Galambos (1970, 1983).
2. As Susan Helper (1991) correctly noted, Smith's analysis does not tell us what organizational form this division of labor will take; thus, the balance between public and private organizations will vary from society to society, even when they have similar divisions of labor.
3. These aspects of the modern state are treated at length in

most progressive or liberal histories of the United States in the twentieth century. A convenient guide to that synthesis is Hofstadter (1968). As centennials of the landmark measures occur, we can expect more reviews such as "The Sherman Act's First Century" (1989).

4. See the symposium on organizations and economics in the *Journal of Economic Perspectives* ("Organizations and Economics," 1991). As Susan Helper (1991) observed, economists have assumed that "all institutions . . . obey forces of supply and demand according to control over economic resources."

5. I am indebted to David C. Hammack for his perceptive comments on this aspect of the development of nonprofits. As he pointed out, we have such a vibrant nonprofit sector "because we decided, at the time of the American Revolution, to try to limit the state and to avoid an established church" (Hammack, 1991). Thus, long before the late nineteenth-century organizational transformation began, the United States was well populated with nonprofits expressing religious, cultural, and aesthetic values and functioning in many cases as private governments. (See also Hammack, 1989.)

6. Most surprising is the fact that historians, even the historiographers who chart the rise of the profession, seem not to contemplate an end point. Of late, there has been among historians some discussion of decline, but this is usually a consideration of quantitative measures of support, such as class enrollment, and not of the larger dimensions of the profession's role in society. Frequently, historians seem to think that any problems that exist stem from some failure in the audience.

7. The current edition of the *Research Centers Directory* (Hill, 1991) lists more than 12,000 university-related and other nonprofit research organizations.

8. Even AT&T, at that time the largest corporation in the world, needed support during the political-legal confrontations that led to its divestiture. See Temin and Galambos (1987).

9.   This happened to the Federal Communications Commission in the late stages of the divestiture settlement with AT&T, after the agency realized that it was losing its turf to a federal judge.

10.   The major work along these lines has been done by Alfred D. Chandler and his students and colleagues at the Harvard Graduate School of Business Administration. (In addition to the works by Chandler cited above, see Lazonick, 1990, pp. 35–64.)

11.   This generalization needs to be carefully qualified. The government agency involved and, indirectly, the association and its members have also provided support for, among others, organizing the papers of Dwight David Eisenhower. Eisenhower was certainly more friendly to the market than to the regulatory state. Still, I believe, a review of all these projects involving the last century of U.S. history would support my generalization.

References

Abbott, A. *The System of Professions: An Essay on the Division of Expert Labor*. Chicago: University of Chicago Press, 1988.

Abramovitz, M., and David, P. A. "Reinterpreting Economic Growth: Parables and Realities." *American Economic Review*, 1973, *63*, 438–439.

Addams, J. *Twenty Years at Hull-House*. New York: Macmillan, 1910.

Balogh, B. *Chain Reaction: Expert Debate and Public Participation in American Commercial Nuclear Power, 1945–1975*. New York: Cambridge University Press, 1991a.

Balogh, B. "Reorganizing the Organizational Synthesis: Federal Professional Relations in Modern America." *Studies in American Political Development*, 1991b, *5*(Spring), 119–172.

Brooks, J. *Telephone: The First Hundred Years*. New York: HarperCollins, 1975.

Carlson, W. B. *Innovation as a Social Process: Elihu Thomson and the Rise of General Electric, 1870–1900*. Cambridge, England: Cambridge University Press, 1991.

Chandler, A. D. *The Visible Hand: The Managerial Revolution in American Business.* Cambridge, Mass.: Harvard University Press, 1977.

Chandler, A. D. *Scale and Scope: The Dynamics of Industrial Capitalism.* Cambridge, Mass.: Harvard University Press, 1990.

Derthick, M., and Quirk, P. J. *The Politics of Deregulation.* Washington, D.C.: Brookings Institution, 1985.

Edsforth, R. *Class Conflict and Cultural Consensus: The Making of a Mass Consumer Society in Flint, Michigan.* New Brunswick, N.J.: Rutgers University Press, 1987.

Fligstein, N. *The Transformation of Corporate Control.* Cambridge, Mass.: Harvard University Press, 1990.

Galambos, L. *Competition & Cooperation: The Emergence of a National Trade Association.* Baltimore, Md.: Johns Hopkins University Press, 1966.

Galambos, L. "The Emerging Organizational Synthesis in Modern American History." *Business History Review,* 1970, *44*(Autumn), 279–290.

Galambos, L. *America at Middle Age: A New History of the U.S. in the Twentieth Century.* New York: McGraw-Hill, 1982.

Galambos, L. "Technology, Political Economy, and Professionalization: Central Themes of the Organizational Synthesis." *Business History Review,* 1983, *57*(Winter), 471–493.

Galambos, L., and Pratt, J. *The Rise of the Corporate Commonwealth: United States Business and Public Policy in the Twentieth Century.* New York: Basic Books, 1988.

Gallman, R. "The Pace and Pattern of American Economic Growth." In L. E. Davis and others, *American Economic Growth: An Economists' History of the United States.* New York: Harper-Collins, 1972.

Goodfield, J. *A Chance to Live.* New York: Macmillan, 1991.

Graham, M.B.W. *RCA and the VideoDisc: The Business of Research.* New York: Cambridge University Press, 1986.

Hall, P. D. "A Historical Overview of the Private Nonprofit Sector." In W. W. Powell (ed.), *The Nonprofit Sector: A Research Handbook.* New Haven, Conn.: Yale University Press, 1987.

Hammack, D. C. "Private Organizations, Public Purposes: Nonprofits and Their Archives." *Journal of American History*, 1989, *76*, 181–191.

Hammack, D. C. "Discussant Remarks." Presented at the conference on Nonprofit Organizations in a Market Economy, Case Western Reserve University, November 1991.

Hansen, J. M. "Choosing Sides: The Creation of an Agricultural Policy Network in Congress, 1919–1932." *Studies in American Political Development*, 1987, *2*, 183–229.

Hays, S. P. *Beauty, Health, and Permanence: Environmental Politics in the United States, 1955–1985*. New York: Cambridge University Press, 1987.

Heclo, H. "Issue Networks and the Executive Establishment." In A. King (ed.), *The New American Political System*. Washington, D.C.: American Enterprise Institute for Public Policy Research, 1978.

Helper, S. "Discussant Remarks." Presented at the conference on Nonprofit Organizations in a Market Economy, Case Western Reserve University, November 1991.

Hill, K. (ed.). *Research Centers Directory*. Detroit, Mich.: Gale Research Co., 1991.

Hofstadter, R. *The Progressive Historians: Turner, Beard, Parrington*. New York: Knopf, 1968.

Kohler, R. E. *From Medical Chemistry to Biochemistry*. New York: Cambridge University Press, 1982.

Kolko, G. *The Triumph of Conservatism: A Reinterpretation of American History, 1900–1916*. New York: Free Press, 1963.

Lazonick, W. "Organizational Capabilities in American Industry: The Rise and Decline of Managerial Capitalism." *Business and Economic History*, 1990, *19*, 35–64.

Letwin, W. *Law and Economic Policy in America: The Evolution of the Sherman Antitrust Act*. Chicago: University of Chicago Press, 1965.

McCraw, T. K. *Regulation in Perspective: Historical Essays*. Cambridge, Mass.: Harvard University Press, 1981.

McCraw, T. K. *Prophets of Regulation: Charles Francis Adams, Louis D. Brandeis, James M. Landis, Alfred E. Kahn*. Cambridge, Mass.: Harvard University Press, 1984.

McDougall, W. *The Heavens and the Earth: A Political History of the Space Age.* New York: Basic Books, 1985.

Montgomery, D. *The Fall of the House of Labor: The Workplace, the State, and American Labor Activism, 1865–1925.* New York: Cambridge University Press, 1987.

Nash, G. D. *United States Oil Policy, 1890–1964: Business and Government in Twentieth Century America.* Pittsburgh, Penn.: University of Pittsburgh Press, 1968.

Oleson, A., and Voss, J. (eds.). *The Organization of Knowledge in Modern America, 1860–1920.* Baltimore, Md.: Johns Hopkins University Press, 1979.

"Organizations and Economics." *Journal of Economic Perspectives,* 1991, 5(Spring), 15–110.

Parsons, T. *Essays in Sociological Theory.* New York: Free Press, 1954.

Pinick, J. L., and others (eds.). *The Politics of American Science, 1939 to the Present.* Skokie, Ill.: Rand McNally, 1972.

Raucher, A. R. *Public Relations and Business, 1900–1929.* Baltimore, Md.: Johns Hopkins University Press, 1968.

Reich, L. S. *The Making of American Industrial Research: Science and Business at GE and Bell, 1876–1926.* New York: Cambridge University Press, 1983.

Rossiter, M. W. "The Organization of the Agricultural Sciences." In A. Oleson and J. Voss (eds.), *The Organization of Knowledge.* Baltimore, Md.: Johns Hopkins University Press, 1979.

Rourke, F. E. "American Bureaucracy in a Changing Political Setting." *Journal of Public Administration Research and Theory,* 1991, *1,* 111–129.

"The Sherman Act's First Century: A Historical Perspective." *Iowa Law Review,* 1989, *74*(entire issue 5).

Shorter, E. *The Health Century.* New York: Doubleday, 1987.

Skowronek, S. *Building a New American State: The Expansion of National Administrative Capacities, 1877–1920.* New York: Cambridge University Press, 1982.

Smith, A. *An Inquiry into the Nature and Causes of the Wealth of Nations.* New York: Modern Library, 1937. (Originally published 1776.)

Solow, R. M. "Technical Change and the Aggregate Production Function." *Review of Economics and Statistics*, 1957, *39*(Aug.), 312–320.

Steigerwalt, A. K. "Organized Business Groups." In G. Porter (ed.), *Encyclopedia of American Economic History*. Vol. 2. New York: Scribner, 1980.

Tedlow, R. S. *New and Improved: The Story of Mass Marketing in America*. New York: Basic Books, 1990.

Temin, P., and Galambos, L. *The Fall of the Bell System*. New York: Cambridge University Press, 1987.

Thorelli, H. *The Federal Antitrust Policy: Origination of an American Tradition*. Baltimore, Md.: Johns Hopkins University Press, 1955.

Tomlins, C. L. *The State and the Unions: Labor Relations, Law, and the Organized Labor Movement in America, 1880–1960*. New York: Cambridge University Press, 1985.

Vietor, R.H.K. *Energy Policy in America Since 1945: A Study in Business-Government Relations*. New York: Cambridge University Press, 1984.

Yamazaki, H., and Miyamoto, M. (eds.). *Trade Associations in Business History*. Tokyo: University of Tokyo Press, 1988.

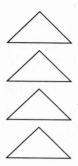

CHAPTER 4

Profit Making by Nonprofit Hospitals

David B. Starkweather

The last decade has witnessed a rise in profit-making activity by nonprofit hospitals. This is for two main reasons. First, during this time, the health field was massively altered from one supervised by government through regulation to one guided by the silent hand of the competitive marketplace. This flowed from the "deregulation years" of the Reagan administration. Economists saw this shift as bringing rationality and discipline to a health care system that had otherwise resisted control and efficiency. The business motive, operating in competitive markets, was viewed as the best way to meet human needs in a health care economy of limited resources.

Thus, it is no longer the case that hospitals are measured by the service they render to their communities. Increasingly, they are measured by their bottom lines. After all, hospitals that do not attend to their financial requirements will cease to exist and therefore will not serve any future public interest. Many community hospitals now operate by the dictum "No margin, no mission."

Second, while most hospitals are nonprofit entities, they operate in partnership with doctors, and the practice of medicine is a business. Medicine has undergone a transformation away from a profession with a clear service orientation. The code of ethics of the American Medical Association, adopted in 1912, asserted that the principal objective of doctors should be the service they render to humanity; and that financial gain should be a subordinate consideration. This principle was dropped in 1957. Since then, and particularly in the last decade, a business orientation has developed. Patients visiting their doctor are likely to walk through doors marked "Dr. Goodcare, A Professional Corporation." Advertising is no longer considered unethical and is, in fact, common. This change is carefully documented in Paul Starr's Pulitzer Prize–winning book *The Social Transformation of American Medicine*. Starr (1982) documents the "corporatization of medicine." His definition of American medicine is broad; it includes all of the profit and nonprofit institutions in the field as well as the medical profession.

Thus, both the conduct of hospitals and the practice of medicine have moved toward a business orientation. Further, the interaction and interrelationship between these two parties — always complex and subtle — have become laced with market and economic incentives and imbued with the profit motive.

The relationship between physicians and hospitals is one of exchange and mutual dependence. Physicians' power in this exchange comes from their control of patients and their decisions as to which hospitals to admit their patients to and what services to order for them. The power of hospitals stems from their provision of technology and services to physicians, without which they could not practice medicine. Recently, this relationship has become both more collaborative and more competitive. Physicians have undertaken enterprises previously regarded as the affair of hospitals, such as physician-owned outpatient surgery centers. Likewise, hospitals have constructed urgent care centers and outpatient clinics that were previously assumed to be the prerogative of doctors. But physicians and hospitals have also collaborated. The prime example is the joint venture between nonprofit hospitals and groups of physicians.

All of this has blurred the lines between the practice of medicine and the conduct of hospitals. It has also blurred the lines between the not-for-profit and the for-profit behaviors of these parties. In one decade, the entire realm of medical care delivery has become known as an "industry."

Given these developments, why do profit-seeking hospitals retain their nonprofit status? What are the advantages? Obviously, nonprofits pay few or no taxes. Equally obviously, they may be the recipients of gifts from people or corporations that can make charitable deductions on their income taxes. In decades past, this was of major benefit to hospitals: large proportions of their capital requirements and sometimes their operating deficits were met by donated funds. A related advantage is the ability to receive government grants that are restricted to nonprofit or government entities. Many hospitals were built with federal and state government grants obtained under the Hill-Burton Program.

Not so obvious is the fourth advantage: access to tax-exempt capital financing. Federal and state laws permit hospitals to issue tax-exempt bonds through local or state governments. This allows hospitals to borrow money at substantially lower rates than offered by lending institutions, because bondholders need not pay taxes on the bond interest income. Tax-exempt bonds currently provide approximately 80 percent of all capital funds for hospitals.

These are the four major advantages. Minor advantages include possible exemption from federal antitrust laws administered by the department of Justice and the Federal Trade Commission, the right under certain circumstances to seize land by eminent domain, and, in a few states, the ability to hire physicians without offending corporate practice laws.

The word *profit* is used loosely. The accounting definition is "excess of revenue over expenses." Terms used interchangeably are *net income* and *earnings*. In a for-profit company, this excess or net income is subject to income tax. Any earnings that are retained or distributed to stockholders as dividends are applied after profit taxes have been paid. But it can be shown that nonprofit hospitals must also make profits in order to meet their full financial requirements and perpetuate themselves (Young, 1983).

Any organization that wishes to continue in business when the economy is inflating must have an excess of revenue over expenses in order to replace its assets. This is because fixed assets are recorded and depreciated at their historical values rather than their current or replacement values. Thus, a long-term asset can cost two or three times as much to replace as is shown on a firm's balance sheet. Even if an organization funds all the depreciation "earned" by these assets, there will be insufficient funds at replacement time. The nonprofit hospital has only three ways to make up this substantial difference: (1) seek grants or donations, an uncertain and insufficient source in present times; (2) borrow money, creating high and expensive debt levels; and (3) generate equity internally.

A hospital's equity should increase in amounts that match inflation. Barring philanthropy and grants, the only source of equity buildup is retained earnings, and the only source of retained earnings is profit. Working capital requirements also increase in an inflationary economy. Grants and donations are not likely to be made for this purpose, and it is imprudent to cover this increase with long-term debt. Again, the only practical source of this funding is net income.

While the amount of surplus needed for these two purposes can be accurately calculated, there has been little recognition of the difference between "prudent profit" needed for these purposes and "excess profit." Yet there is no doubt that nonprofits need profits. The president of the Healthcare Financial Management Association defends the right of tax-exempt hospitals to generate profits as long as these funds are channeled toward the hospital's charitable purposes. "Not for profit means not for private profit. Most people don't understand this, and hospitals need to clarify why they need to realize a profit and how these dollars are reinvested in the community" (Lumsdon, 1991, p. 27).

Calculating profit is complicated by the fact that hospitals often operate on the basis of fund accounting. This means that they have two or more sets of books, one of which is designed to permanently segregate funds designated for new or replacement plant and equipment. These monies cannot be commingled with operating funds. Some hospitals, however, do not so segregate such funds, which means that investment income from those funds must be considered a contribution to operating profit. Prince conducted a study that reconciled these practices (Prince, 1991). In a representative sample of nonprofit hospitals in the United States, he found the mean operating margins of 225 church-owned hospitals for the three-year period ending in 1988 to be 3.0 percent for hospitals with restricted funds and 3.3 percent for those without restricted funds. The comparable figures for 874 nonreligious community hospitals were 2.66 and 2.93 percent. We do not know from this study whether some hospitals greatly exceeded these figures, but as a whole, these profit margins are not excessive. Indeed, they are below what would meet full financial requirements. Hospital profit margins have declined since 1988 ("Hospitals Report . . . ," 1991).

There is an emerging body of research and literature on the subject of the business behavior of nonprofit hospitals (Powell, 1987). One approach focuses on mission and governance. This approach is often historical in nature and examines changes in mission in the context of private volunteerism as an American value and tradition (Seay and Vladeck, 1988). Another approach is financial or economic, looking at profits, prices, and costs. Comparisons are made between nonprofit and for-profit hospitals (Hollingsworth and Hollingsworth, 1987; Marmor and others, 1987). Variations in amounts of uncompensated care are analyzed (Lewin and others, 1988; Sofaer, Rundall, and Zeller, 1990), and the amounts of charity care are compared to the "tax subsidy" provided by relief from corporate income taxes (Herzlinger and Krasker, 1987; General Accounting Office, 1990). A third approach, drawn from the field of tax law, concentrates on laws relating to eleemosynary corporations and the appropriateness of these laws (Clark, 1980; Hansmann, 1981; Simpson and Strum, 1991).

We will take yet another approach here, one that focuses on the behavior of the firm. Hospitals are organizations struggling to do something new in response to a changed environment. They do so by creating new organizational forms and by changing their behavior. These efforts are constrained by the laws of federal and state governments as interpreted by lawyers and adjudicated by courts. So we have a set of natural experiments in organizational change in the context of social control and societal norms.

A more specific statement of this model is shown in Figure 4.1. The altered environments of competitive markets affect hospitals by inducing a change in strategy. Strategies are influenced by mission and goals as well, but the reverse is also the case. These organizations then undertake an examination of their structures to determine fit with the changed environment. Corporate forms are often changed: we see corporate restructuring and joint venturing. This yields organizational performance, stated in terms of financial results, services offered, and charitable care rendered. Finally, performance influences the environment, that is, new laws and regulations for control of nonprofit hospitals.

Strategies and Structures

Having briefly described the altered environment of the 1980s, we can now turn to the three principal strategies and structures by which nonprofit hospitals pursue profits: direct profit making without any special corporate form; the pursuit of profits through for-profit corporations that are subsidiaries of nonprofit entities, commonly called "corporate restructuring"; and

Figure 4.1. The Business Behavior of Nonprofit Hospitals.

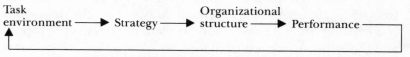

Source: Adapted from Shortell, Morrison, and Robbins, 1985.

the pursuit of profits through joint ventures between nonprofit hospitals and physicians.

Direct Profit Making by Nonprofit Hospitals

The definition of charitable activity by hospitals stems from English common law relating to the concepts of private volunteerism vis-à-vis the role of government. The "law of charity" specified that the funds of private nonprofit social agencies must be used for certain specific charitable purposes that would otherwise be carried out by government. In the case of hospitals, that purpose was defined as the direct rendering of charitable care. This meant that hospitals had to document specific amounts of charitable care and specific charitable practices, such as the volunteering of time by the doctors of these hospitals to provide care to the poor. Thus, in 1956, the Internal Revenue Service (IRS) issued a ruling that a nonprofit hospital "must be operated to the extent of its financial ability for those not able to pay for the services rendered and not exclusively for those that are able and expected to pay" (Rev. Rule 56-185).

In 1965, government entered into hospital financing in a large way through the Medicare and Medicaid programs. Up to half of the total revenue of most nonprofit hospitals now comes from government. With the advent of these programs, it became, to use the phrase of one IRS officer, "hard to find an indigent patient" (*Eastern Kentucky Welfare Rights Organization* v. *Simon*, at pp. 1288–1289). (This was an exaggeration then, as it is now.) In 1969, the IRS changed the rules for defining tax exemption to hold that the provision of health care services — the relief of suffering, rather than the relief of poverty — was a charitable act in its own right, a definition not unlike that applied to private schools. This relieved hospitals of the obligation to provide direct charitable care in order to maintain tax exemption.

Specifically, the "community benefit" standard of the 1969 ruling exempted a hospital if "it promotes the health of a sufficiently broad class of persons such that it benefits the community as a whole, even if the class of beneficiaries does not include all members of the community" (Rev. Rule 69-545). The IRS decided that a hospital provides adequate community benefit when it (1) operates a full-time emergency department available to all persons and (2) furnishes services to Medicare and Medicaid beneficiaries. In 1983, the IRS modified this ruling to allow continued exemption for hospitals that lack emergency rooms if a state health planning agency has judged an emergency department unnecessary because it duplicates facilities adequately provided by other institutions in the community (Rev. Rule 83-157).

There are other limitations on tax-exempt hospitals, such as the prohibition of political activity. However, the most important limitation is the prohibition of private inurement: any unreasonable transfer of the assets of the charitable organization to a private party. The test of private inurement is a fuzzy one. What is "reasonable"? Is rent-free space in hospital facilities for a physician who will refer patients to the hospital reasonable? How about guaranteed income for a young physician who promises to start her practice at the hospital, with no recovery of funds? According to R. L. Clarke, the test of reasonableness has become whether the activity "enhances the ability of the charity to advance its charitable purpose" (Lumsdon, 1991), and under this dictum, significant amounts of hospital dollars can be given over to profit-making activities.

Against this legal history, notably the elimination of the requirement to show specific relief of poverty, the behavior of nonprofit hospitals has moved toward the dual strategy of eliminating services that do not make money and inaugurating services that do. This has led some observers to conclude that the distinction between profit and nonprofit hospitals has narrowed beyond recognition (Relman, 1991) and has led others to challenge the continued tax exemption of hospitals (Herzlinger and Krasker, 1987; Henry, 1991).

An example of the elimination of "losing" services by hospitals is the closure of emergency rooms. Hospital emergency rooms have traditionally been the places where all people in the community could receive immediate care regardless of their ability to pay. Historically, the great bulk of direct charity care by hospitals has been rendered in emergency rooms or has been rendered to inpatients who were hospitalized from emergency rooms. For a variety of reasons, hospitals continued to provide emergency services even after the 1983 IRS ruling eliminating the obligation to provide such services in order to maintain tax exemption. For many hospitals, emergency service was a "loss leader": a major source of inpatient referrals. Up to 30 or 40 percent of a hospital's admissions might come through the emergency room. For a few, state laws mandated the offering of emergency services as a condition of obtaining a hospital license. Many continued emergency services because of their community service mission.

Some hospitals, while continuing their emergency services, started to transfer emergency patients who could not pay for their care to other community or government hospitals. But this practice caused hospitals engaging in it to receive enormous amounts of bad press for "dumping" patients (Simpson and Strum, 1991) and led state Medicaid administrators to begin withholding Medicaid reimbursements from them (Dallek and Waxman, 1986). As a result, many of these hospitals decided to shut down their emergency services—not because state health planning agencies found them unneeded but in order to discourage indigent patients from presenting themselves for treatment. They calculated that the costs of providing uncompensated care in the emergency room and in the inpatient beds filled through the emergency room were not compensated for by the business of paying patients who also came to the emergency room. It is significant that this is the kind of calculation made by these charitable institutions: a straight business cost-benefit analysis. It is also significant that they ignored the IRS rulings of 1969 and 1983 concerning the offering of emergency services as justification of tax exemption (Melnick, 1989)—and so did the IRS (J. B. Simpson, personal communication, November 9, 1991).

Another area where hospitals have eliminated unprofitable services is inpatient pediatric care, where declining profitability is responsible for the steady decline in number of pediatric beds. Pediatric inpatients are typically seriously ill and use more hospital resources, particularly nursing time, than adult patients. This means that hospitals must either charge more for pediatric care than for adult care—more than the traffic will bear—or subsidize pediatric care with adult care revenue. One study of pediatric care in teaching hospitals determined that 34 percent of pediatric nursing care is borne by adult patients (National Association of Children's Hospitals and Related Institutions, 1989). But hospitals with pediatric units compete with those that do not, and they cannot compete in adult care services with the financial burden of subsidized pediatrics. So many have closed their pediatric units. Between 1984 and 1988, there was a loss of 5,500 pediatric beds, or 15 percent of the nation's service capacity (Koska, 1989). In short, we can see that the character of a hospital and its performance can change through time by the elimination of services that lose money and retention or initiation of activities that make money.

Another method by which nonprofit hospitals undertake direct profit making is through "unrelated business activity"—business activity that falls outside the main scope of the hospital's charitable purpose. The unrelated activity may be taxed while the hospital conducting the business remains tax exempt. There are two IRS rules that define the type and amount of unrelated business activity allowed. The first is the "nexus" rule. Under this rule, if a hospital owned a medical office building and rented space to physicians, the operations of the medical office building would not be taxed if a nexus could be shown between the operation of the medical office building and the conduct of the main charitable purpose of the hospital (Henry, 1991). This could readily be documented, as physicians using the office building would usually practice at the hospital. The second rule applies to business ventures that are obviously unrelated, such as an off-site automobile dealership operated by a hospital. In such a case, the hospital would be taxed for these business activities while maintaining its tax exemption for its principal purposes, so long as the sum of these activities is judged an "insubstantial part" of the hospital's overall operations (Henry, 1991). Apparently, anything that creates more than 20 percent of a hospital's total revenue is considered substantial and may lead a hospital's overall tax exemption to be reviewed.

Review is even more likely if the IRS has received a complaint from a taxable business in the hospital's community claiming unfair competition.

In general, the definition of *related activity* is becoming tighter. For example, hospital pharmacies may refill prescriptions that originated in the hospital or in the hospital's outpatient department without incurring tax liability, but if they refill prescriptions that were originated off site, they must pay taxes on the income received from this activity. Even so, "A hospital is unlikely to lose its federal tax exempt status because of excessive unrelated activity" (Henry, 1991, p. 32).

The third way in which nonprofit hospitals become directly involved in profit-making activities is through mergers and consolidations. Starkweather and Carman (1987) followed three communities in California that were chosen to represent varying degrees of market development and competitiveness. In the most competitive community, a metropolitan area in northern California, they observed interorganizational strategies on the part of hospitals that led to a rapid restructuring of the entire health care market. In 1981, the community had had fourteen independent and freestanding hospitals, each attempting to compete with all others. Four years later, these had been replaced by four multihospital systems: one formed between a medical school and a county facility, another among three Catholic facilities, a third among four community hospitals, and a fourth between two hospitals previously owned and operated by a large health maintenance organization (HMO). This constituted a market restructuring from monopolistic competition to oligopoly.

What triggered this phenomenon was a set of strategic calculations made by one of the community hospitals. This hospital performed a "portfolio analysis" of all its "products" and, using the two criteria of "business strength" and "market attractiveness," made heavy investments in certain winners and "deselected" certain losers. The hospital then divided the metropolitan area into numerous submarkets and determined through patient origin statistics what combination of hospitals would yield a domination in each of these submarkets of at least

25 percent of hospital patients. The calculations yielded a set of merger partners for that hospital that would optimize market dominance in the largest number of submarkets. The hospital then approached the other institutions. There was a quick merger of three hospitals; the other mergers in the community followed in response to this first set.

What stimulated these mergers was market forces — the wish to control or dominate the market. In order to take the steps that it did, the original hospital had to become more business oriented than it could be under the goals and missions of its prior eighty-five-year history. With the primary mission of the "relief of poverty," the hospital had seen approximately 45 percent of its patients unable to pay their full bills. In a remarkable case of goal displacement, it abandoned its commitment to these patients by intentionally failing to contract with the state of California for the care of Medicaid patients. It could now deny admission to Medicaid patients. This also had the effect of excluding physicians whose practices consisted primarily of Medicaid patients. The hospital's patient care volume immediately shrank to almost half its former level. In the words of its chief executive, the institution was now "lean and mean" and able to successfully compete in the new environment.

We see in this example both the source and the sequence of organizational change. Deregulation evoked formation of a competitive market. Hospitals developed new strategies in response. To pursue these strategies, they changed their goals from a mission orientation to a margin orientation. One strategy was to merge in order to better control the market; this was corporate restructuring — profit-making behavior by nonprofits.

Not all hospitals abandoned their charitable mission. Starkweather and Carman (1987; Starkweather, 1990) studied a Catholic hospital whose religious order stipulated that no less than 25 percent of the hospital's margin be spent on charity care and that it must be spent locally or else the religious order would confiscate 25 percent and use it to provide charity care elsewhere. The hospital management feared that the hospital would not be able to successfully compete with those that did not provide charity care and that its future survival in this highly competitive community was in jeopardy.

The last type of direct profit making by nonprofit hospitals involves what might be considered the nonprofit's last act, sale to a for-profit enterprise. It has recently been common among HMOs to convert to for-profit status. The reason for this is the need for investor capital. The following describes a typical sequence:

The HMO was originally organized on a nonprofit basis, perhaps as a subsidiary of a nonprofit hospital or a nonprofit health insurance plan. (In the late 1970s and early 1980s, the federal government provided grants designed to encourage the development of health maintenance organizations.) Following a period of planning and development, the HMO started enrolling members. After two or three years of operation and an enrollment of perhaps 5,000 to 8,000, managers of the HMO realized that it needed to grow more quickly. With so few members, it could easily be wiped out if one member had gigantic medical care costs. In addition, market and competitive conditions were such that it needed a larger share of its market in order to survive. It was felt that an HMO needed 25,000 to 30,000 members in order to be viable. The HMO could not grow at the rate required without new capital. Its nonprofit status meant that it could neither acquire investment capital nor borrow enough to finance the needed growth. Thus, it converted to for-profit status.

Conversion to for-profit status raised two important issues for HMOs. The first issue was valuation of the corporation at the time of conversion: should it be according to book value or market value? A number of state corporation commissioners ruled that the conversion must take place at market value. This eliminated so-called two-stage conversions, in which an initial conversion to for-profit status was arranged at book value, leaving a small amount available for charity, followed by a second conversion when the corporation was sold again, yielding a greater profit for its new owners. We see here the profit motive at work in an organization originally chartered as a not-for-profit entity. Again, the founding goals had been abandoned.

The second issue was whether the proceeds of sale could go to a charity closely related to the HMO operation or must go to an unrelated charity. State corporation commissioners had seen a number of cases in which the monies derived from the sale of a hospital were placed in a newly created foundation controlled by the hospital's new owners and the for-profit hospital and new foundation then applied the "charitable funds" exclusively to the reduction of bad debts at the for-profit hospital. Therefore, commissioners often ruled that sale proceeds must go to a charitable organization unrelated to the original corporation or to the new owners.

As we have seen, nonprofit hospitals undertake a variety of profit-making activities undertaken directly by nonprofit hospitals. The hospitals are motivated by the desire to use profits to maintain or advance the nonprofit entity in an environment suddenly restructured as a competitive market. This environment is profit-oriented by its very nature. After all, how is success in a competitive market defined but by the making of money for the corporation? It is not surprising that nonprofit hospitals have been inventive and creative in their responses.

There are, however, several constraints on these kinds of activity. First, hospitals that engage in them may lose their nonprofit status through regulations issued by the Internal Revenue Service that specify that the unrelated profit-making tail may not wag the nonprofit dog. Second, hospitals must pay taxes on their unrelated business activity. Third, they may lose their access to tax-exempt bonds. Fourth, they may be required to pay certain taxes on their entire operation. Court cases and legislative acts in Utah, Colorado, Vermont, Pennsylvania, and elsewhere have challenged hospitals for insufficient charity and required that they pay local property taxes (Henry, 1991). Fifth, they face the risk of state action against "excess profits," such as a Nevada law imposing a tax on nonprofit profits in excess of a certain percentage or a California law providing exemption from property taxes only to nonprofit corporations whose profits are below a certain percentage (Simpson and Strum, 1991). More than a dozen states are now considering one or another of these provisions.

These risks could be avoided if hospitals returned to the mission uniformly subscribed to before the changes in federal laws of the late 1960s: the direct relief of poverty. But this return is very difficult when hospitals are operating in competitive markets.

Profit-making Subsidiaries

A nonprofit corporation may have a subsidiary corporation that is for-profit. (The reverse is illegal, because this could yield gains from the nonprofit entity for the private owners of the for-profit enterprise.) The common method among hospitals for establishing for-profit subsidiaries is a process called "corporate restructuring." Typically, a single nonprofit hospital creates a parent holding company. This parent, in turn, retains the original hospital as a subsidiary and also creates other subsidiaries. In the early 1980s, these additional subsidiaries were usually other hospitals; this is how multihospital systems were formed. Later in the 1980s, subsidiary corporations were formed to pursue other lines of business, such as construction and operation of ambulatory surgery facilities, magnetic resonating imaging facilities, and urgent care centers.

Between 1980 and 1985, 35 percent of U.S. hospitals went through some form of corporate restructuring. The larger its size, the more likely was a hospital to restructure: 55 percent of all hospitals with more than 300 beds did so. Other factors also affected the likelihood of restructuring. For example, more church-owned hospitals (53 percent) than secular not-for-profits (42 percent) restructured, 36 percent of investor-owned hospitals restructured, while only 10 percent of government hospitals did so (Alexander and Orlikoff, 1987). We do not know what proportion of these restructurings originally included for-profit subsidiaries; some did, but most did not. However, it is clear that for-profit subsidiaries were added to holding company structures in subsequent years.

An example provides a sense of the magnitude and extent of this restructuring. In 1980, a hospital in northern California that we shall call "Center Hospital" created a parent holding company with two subsidiaries—the original hospital and a subsidiary to operate four nursing homes that had been sold to the hospital under favorable terms. The parent company then also acquired a small hospital in a neighboring community that was about to close. Center Hospital operated the facility for a while as a rehabilitation hospital; then the parent company sold it to a group of primary care doctors who pledged to refer their patients to Center Hospital. Center Hospital and another, nearby community hospital together formed a health maintenance organization, and the two hospitals then merged. Following this, Center Hospital's parent corporation merged with a Sacramento-based health care system that operated four hospitals (three of which were transferred to a Catholic hospital system just prior to the merger) and many nursing homes. There followed a period of vertical diversification and expansion into a large commercial referral laboratory, a visiting nurse association, several sports medicine clinics, an urgent care center, an ambulatory surgery facility, three magnetic imaging resonating services, a CT scanning service, a home infusion therapy service, a home oxygen service, a durable medical equipment supply company, a nurse registry, two physician corporations designed to contract with payers for medical care, part interest in another HMO, three more long-term-care-facility corporations, a breast screening center, and two ambulatory care clinics (one located in a shopping center). There was then a merger with a large children's hospital in San Francisco, followed by the "decoupling" of the Sacramento health system, followed by the decoupling of the children's hospital in San Francisco, followed most recently by a merger with another five-hospital system which had just merged with the children's hospital recently decoupled! In the course of a decade, more than fifty different subsidiary corporations, including seven for-profit subsidiaries and thirteen joint ventures, were involved in the "Center family of companies." The overall enterprise was generating somewhat over $400 million in gross revenues.

In the holding comapny–subsidiary arrangement, the parent corporation controls the subsidiary primarily through appointment of the subsidiary's directors. The subsidiary is the operating entity. Sometimes the parent is the sole corporate member of the subsidiary. Sometimes the subsidiary has a management contract with the parent corporation or with the original hospital to run its entire operation. Proceeds of subsidiaries are transferred to the parent. If the subsidiary is a for-profit corporation, this transfer usually takes the form of a stock dividend.

A number of different strategies are used by hospitals in establishing for-profit subsidiaries. One of these is "unrelated passive investment." Here, the for-profit activity is completely unrelated to the hospital's sphere of activity; its sole purpose is to produce income for the nonprofit entity. It is passive because the health care corporation has little or nothing to do with the operation of the for-profit activity. Starkweather and Carman (1987) studied a Catholic hospital that owned a printing company that produced approximately a half million dollars per year for the hospital. A Baptist hospital in Georgia owns a commercial bank. A hospital's parent corporation in St. Louis owns an airline.

Another strategy is "passive investment, cost reducing." Here, the subsidiary performs some instrumental function for the hospital, which acquires it as the result of a "make-or-buy" decision: the hospital (or group of hospitals) acquires the facility because it can thus obtain its services at a lower cost than it would if it had to buy them elsewhere. The relationship is passive, however, in that the directors and managers of the hospital do not assume the running of the subsidiary activity. Examples of such subsidiaries include a group purchasing corporation that arranges volume purchases of pharmaceuticals and supplies and an insurance company that provides malpractice or public liability insurance at lower costs than would otherwise be available.

Still another strategy is "active investment, revenue producing." Here, the hospital is intimately involved in the development and operation of the subsidiary activity because this activity is in the health field and is related to the hospital's main purposes and goals. The strategy is either to make a direct profit on the activity, as is the case with a sports medicine clinic, or to obtain a market share or referral source for other hospital services, such as a home health service, that will indirectly be profitable. Frequently, it is unclear which of these strategies is behind a hospital's money-making motives since at the outset it is difficult to determine what the profit level or market penetration might be.

In 1988, the American Hospital Association conducted a survey of various diversification efforts of U.S. hospitals (Alexander, 1990). Seven different diversification strategies were found to be turning profits at the majority of the hospitals surveyed: freestanding outpatient surgery programs, freestanding diagnostic centers, inpatient rehabilitation centers, outpatient psychiatric centers, women's medicine programs, industrial medical clinics, and substance abuse treatment centers. "Industrial medical clinics are probably the big winners this year," reported Barry Moore, the survey director. "More than 50 percent of the hospital respondents which had industrial medical clinics reported profitability that had increased over the prior year" (Sabatino, 1989, p. 28).

The survey found that preferred provider organizations represented the strategy most likely to break even or to lose money. This is an example of continuing an investment in an activity that does not make money in itself but will bring patients to the hospital for other profits. The only diversification strategy that lost money at the majority of hospitals where it had been implemented was a "wellness/health" program. The survey director reported that "wellness/health promotion programs are a financial drain on hospitals but build up good will in the community and ultimately benefit a hospital. Many hospitals view wellness/health promotion programs as loss leaders" (Sabatino, 1989, p. 28).

There are also arrangements that include taxable corporations that are not strictly subsidiaries. For example, the Scott-White Clinic in Temple, Texas, comprises three parallel entities. The hospital is a nonprofit corporation. The clinic, a large group practice of physicians, is an unincorporated association; its operation is similar to that of a professional partnership, but it is not a subsidiary of the hospital. The clinic has a contract with the hospital that provides that clinic monies left over after bonuses are paid to physicians are turned over to the hospital; the clinic thus pays no taxes. The third organization, also not a subsidiary, is organized as a membership corporation — a health maintenance organization. Its corporate form means that any residual profits after the payment of property taxes are returned to the health plan members (Grant, 1984).

Joint Ventures

In contrast to the holding company–subsidiary arrangement, a hospital joint venture usually involves a partnership between a nonprofit hospital and a profit-seeking entity, such as a collective of physicians drawn from the hospital's medical staff. These joint ventures have a variety of purposes, including expansion of business opportunities and revenue; attraction of equity capital; expansion of medical and hospital services; development of incentives to increase hospital admissions or referrals to ancillary services; and recruitment and retention of physicians.

Legal Forms

There are two forms of joint ventures between hospitals and doctors, both involving the creation of a new legal entity (Rosenfield, 1984): the corporate model and the limited partnership. With the corporate model, a new corporation, jointly owned by the hospital and physician investors, is formed to undertake a venture. Because it is partially owned by private individuals, it must be organized as a for-profit entity. The corporation is capitalized through the sale of stock to the hospital and physician investors. The percentage of stock ownership is negotiated in advance, as are the rights and obligations of shareholders. The joint venture corporation acts through a board of directors elected by the stockholders according to procedures laid out in the corporation's bylaws. Typically, the board contracts for its management with the hospital. Also, if it is a corporation that develops professional services, it contracts with its physician investors for these services. It might also lease space from the hospital or from a corporation of physicians that owns a medical office building.

The corporate form has the advantage of limiting the liability of its owners and directors. Further, the appointment of a board means that there is a group of committed and skilled directors paying attention to the business of the corporation. Operating through a corporation that is distinct from the hospital provides the venture activity exemption from licensure and certification requirements. This is particularly important in states that have certificate-of-need laws that limit what hospitals can do in their service areas; these laws are circumvented when the activity is undertaken by a nonhospital entity. A disadvantage of the corporate form for its investors is the possibility of double taxation on joint venture profits—taxation on both corporate profits and dividends. The corporate form also limits tax credits and income deductions for physician investors.

The other joint venture form, the limited partnership, is a hybrid of a general partnership and a corporation. The limited partnership resembles a corporation in that the limited partners are not held liable for losses or liabilities of the joint venture in excess of their investment. It resembles a general partnership in that its investors can take full advantage of carefully structured tax shelters, tax credits, and income tax deductions generated by assets acquired by the partnership. Each limited partnership must have at least one general partner, which is usually a hospital or its parent holding company. The general partner does not enjoy limited liability and is exclusively responsible for the management of the venture. The limited partners, usually physicians, are investors only; they may not participate in day-to-day management.

Types of Joint Venture

In recent years, the most common type of joint venture has been the ancillary service venture, in which a hospital and a group of physicians join to develop and operate a magnetic resonating imaging center, ambulatory surgery center, or urgent care clinic (Mancino, 1984). The purposes of these joint endeavors are all business-related: to obtain capital funds from new sources (physician investors), to maintain or increase physician-patient referrals, to improve market share, to meet the competition in the marketplace for ancillary services, and to combine the skills and expertise of the venture participants.

The second most common type of joint venture is the creation of an entity that contracts with third-party payers: health insurance companies, large employers, preferred provider organizations, and health maintenance organizations. These ventures have some drawbacks. They bind the participating physicians to a form of contracted medical care that may be less lucrative than fee-for-service medicine. And while the large contracts provide hospitals with increased patient admissions, the price of this business is reduced hospital charges. For both partners, there is a danger of violation of antitrust and private inurement provisions.

The third most common type of joint venture is one in which a hospital joins with physicians to construct a medical office building, often on space leased from the hospital. This obtains capital for the building and gives physicians rental space that is convenient and accessible to the hospital. It also provides the hospital, formally or informally, with patient referrals from the physicians leasing space in the office building. This kind of joint venture has become less common since the enactment in 1989 of a federal law that exposes such joint ventures to charges of fraud and abuse if the office building lease rates are not consistent with fair market value, are not negotiated as arm's-length transactions, and are calculated to take into account the volume of physician referrals to the hospital (McIlrath, 1991).

A fourth kind of venture does not involve physicians. With this arrangement, sometimes called a "specialty venture," the hospital enters into a joint venture with a specialized firm set up to provide psychiatric services, chemical dependency treatment, or rehabilitation. The specialty company leases hospital space and operates the service. It often provides its own physicians or at least its own medical director, while other employees are on the hospital's payroll. Profits are shared between the specialty company and the hospital.

Constraints on Profit Making

There are two major constraints on profit making through joint ventures: the issue of private inurement and the issue of physician ownership of medical businesses to which they refer patients.

Private Inurement. Prior to 1979, it was the position of the Internal Revenue Service that participation by a nonprofit hospital in a joint venture would per se jeopardize its tax exemption, because the charitable organization had no right to enter into such forms of business venture with taxable parties (Bromberg, 1986). The legal basis for this position was that the sharing of profits and losses from the joint venture was equivalent to the sharing of profits and losses of the tax-exempt organization and would thus constitute inurement — a device by which some portion of a charitable organization's earnings or assets are used for the benefit of private persons without adequate compensation or in a manner that does not further the organization's charitable purposes.

In 1979, the IRS relaxed its objection; it stated that such participation as a general partner would not automatically result in denial of tax exemption. Instead, the IRS would examine the facts and circumstances of each arrangement to determine its effect on exemption. The legal basis for the IRS's concern shifted. It was no longer as concerned with private inurement as it was with the conflict between (1) the hospital's fiduciary responsibility to maximize profits for the limited partners, in its capacity as general partner, and (2) the hospital's obligation to further its tax-exempt purposes in relation to the joint venture. This is a special concern when the limited partners of the joint venture are hospital trustees.

In its examination of various joint ventures, the IRS has developed the "two-part test" (Bromberg, 1986). The first part of the test is whether the arrangement furthers the hospital's tax-exempt purposes. For example, a joint venture that provided a new community health care service would not jeopardize a hospital's tax exemption. The second part is whether the arrangement takes away the hospital's ability to operate exclusively for tax-exempt purposes. This, in turn, depends on whether there has been any private inurement to the benefit of the nonexempt joint venture and whether such benefit derived by the joint venture is merely incidental to the achievement of the hospital's public purposes. The factors that have been judged to be nonincidental include a disproportionate allocation of profits and losses, the making of commercially unreasonable loans, sale or lease of services or facilities by the hospital to the joint venture at less than fair market value, and purchase or lease of services by the joint venture from other corporations at more than fair market value.

Finally, there is the question discussed previously of whether joint venture income to the hospital is itself taxed as "unrelated business income." Under the "convenience rule," a determination is made of whether the activity of the joint venture is carried out primarily to serve the convenience of the hospital's patients. If the activity provides services to people who would otherwise be classified as patients of the hospital, income received by the hospital from the joint venture is not taxed. There is also a determination of whether the activity of the joint venture is "substantially related" to the tax-exempt functions of the hospital.

In short, there is no outright prohibition on profit making by nonprofit hospitals through joint ventures. Instead, the questions are to whom the profits flow and whether the money-making activity has any relationship to the hospital's charitable purposes. And unrelated activities are not prohibited; they are simply taxed. Under these circumstances, it still may be worth the hospital's while to undertake the activity.

Physician Ownership. The second set of constraints does not rest on the hospital but on its partnering physicians. The issue here has two parts: is it unethical for a physician to own part of a joint venture to which he or she can refer patients? And is it illegal?

The code of ethics of the American Medical Association (AMA) expects physicians to put their patients' interests before their own. But there is no prohibition of physician ownership of medical services. Thus, with or without a joint venture, it is not unethical for physicians to own laboratories, radiology centers, nursing homes, and so on. In late 1991, a study ordered by the Florida legislature showed that the prices charged by laboratories, imaging centers, and physical therapy clinics owned by physicians were higher than those charged by nonphysician facilities and that physician referral rates to the operations that they owned were higher (Pear, 1991).

Following quickly on the release of this study, the AMA warned doctors to be alert to possible conflicts of interest when they refer patients to laboratories and other businesses owned by them. But the association stopped short of telling physicians not to send patients to such businesses. The AMA defended physician ownership, saying that doctors' investments have "indisputably benefited patients" by making services available that might not otherwise be so. The association told physicians that profits must be "commensurate with the risk taken, and must not be linked to the number of patients they refer" (Pear, 1991, p. 3).

There has been much controversy on the matter. In 1980, Arnold Relman, then editor of the *New England Journal of Medicine*, launched an attack on the "medical industrial complex" and argued that ". . . practicing physicians should derive no financial benefit from the health care market except from their own professional services" (Relman, 1980, p. 967). Many physicians have followed this dictum and have not invested in enterprises to which they could refer patients. This has limited some hospital joint ventures with physicians, particularly those aimed at attracting physician-invested capital or enhancing physician referrals.

A second attack on physician ownership comes from state and federal law. Starting in the mid 1980s, numerous states passed disclosure laws requiring physicians who own portions of businesses to which they refer patients to advise their patients of that fact by notices posted in their medical offices. Other states passed laws prohibiting any ownership above a certain percentage. The general theory was that a minor investment by a physician, say less than 5 percent, does not constitute sufficient incentive to alter the physician's referral patterns, while larger amounts would change behavior.

Then, in 1987, Representative Fortney Stark (now chair of the Health Subcommittee of the House Ways and Means Committee) introduced legislation to prohibit most forms of physician ownership of medical businesses whose success or failure could be influenced by referral practices. Stark's legislation was modified and incorporated into the Omnibus Budget Reconciliation Act of 1989. This law prohibits physicians from sending patients to clinical laboratories in which they have an economic interest and imposes reporting requirements. All health care entities receiving Medicare or Medicaid payments must report to the federal government all services provided as well as the names of physicians who have a financial interest in the entity (Group on Government Affairs, n.d.).

The federal government then issued revised regulations dealing with fraud and abuse in the care of Medicare and Medicaid patients. These regulations stipulate that the investment terms offered to physician investors in joint ventures cannot be based on past or expected referrals, nor can those physicians be required to make referrals in order to continue as investors. No joint venture may encourage "passive" physician investors to make referrals, nor can payments to physician investors be based on referrals (Andersen, 1992), and physician investors may not be loaned funds by joint ventures.

Joint venturing by hospitals with physicians has lent impetus to the long-standing criticism that hospitals act to benefit their physicians rather than their community. Herzlinger and Krasker (1987) report on research that concluded that nonprofit hospitals operate primarily to benefit their profit-making physicians and that hospital decision making is unduly influenced by these physicians. They assert that this behavior does not warrant continued tax exemption and argue that for-profit hospitals yield greater social benefit because they pay taxes.

The Policy Debate

An equation has been struck between the social benefits provided by nonprofit hospitals, measured by amounts of charity care provided, and the social subsidy provided nonprofit hospitals through tax exemption: the former had better exceed the latter, or continued tax exemption is in jeopardy. Congress is considering laws that either eliminate tax exemption for hospitals participating in these kinds of profit-making activity or require payment of surcharges as if nonprofits were organized to make money (Kuchler, 1992). In addition, there are numerous proposals to limit the availability of tax-exempt bonds to nonprofit hospitals.

In May 1990, the House Select Committee on Aging held a hearing on the extent of charity care provided by tax-exempt hospitals. At these hearings, a General Accounting Office (GAO) report was released that was critical of many not-for-profit hospitals (General Accounting Office, 1990). The GAO had conducted a nationwide survey and also analyzed data from California, Florida, Iowa, Michigan, and New York to assess the distribution of uncompensated care (including charity care and bad-debt expenses) among hospitals. The GAO concluded that (1) government hospitals provide a disproportionately high amount of uncompensated care; (2) large urban teaching hospitals furnish higher shares of uncompensated care than do other nonprofits; (3) nonprofit hospitals with the highest profit margins provide the least uncompensated care: (4) the strategic goals of nonprofits are similar to those of for-profits, focusing on increasing market share rather than on fulfilling community need; and (5) many service activities of nonprofit hospitals are indistinguishable from those of for-profit hospitals. (This last finding is at odds with an Institute of Medicine study at mid-decade that identified a substantial list of health care services provided by voluntary hospitals with far greater frequency than by for-profit hospitals; Gray, 1991.) Significantly, the GAO found that between 43 percent (New York) and 71 percent (California) of nonprofit hospitals in the five states studied provided less charity care than the estimated value of their federal and state tax exemptions. The GAO report concluded that an insufficient link existed between charitable tax status and service to the poor for the nation's nonprofit hospitals. The report suggested three alternative standards: (1) a minimum level of care provided to Medicaid patients; (2) a minimum level of free care provided to the poor; and (3) a minimum level of efforts to improve the health status of underserved portions of the community.

The chair of the House Select Committee on Aging then proposed a bill that would require each tax-exempt hospital to provide charity care equaling at least 50 percent of the value of its tax exemption, to provide additional uncompensated community benefits totalling 35 percent of the value, and to provide written justification of how it benefited the community in ways that for-profit hospitals do not (Lumsdon, 1991).

Herzlinger proposes requiring nonprofit hospitals to devote at least half of their annual profit to the care of people unable to pay for it and prohibiting the use of any bad debt in calculating that amount. "Every business in the United States has bad debt. This label is given to people who can afford to pay but who choose not to do so. But that does not mean that business should be reimbursed by the government for the expenses" (Lumsdon, 1991, pp. 27–28). Herzlinger would have this 50 percent charity tax set aside in a pool for indigent care. She would also require hospitals to report their volumes of charity care to the press, governing bodies, and so on, with the amounts "valued at the cost of care and not arbitrarily inflated by exaggerated charges" (p. 28).

One bill introduced in Congress would restrict access to tax-exempt bond financing by hospitals with insufficient proportions of Medicare and Medicaid patients; another would restrict the use of tax-exempt bonds to health care facilities with Medicaid participation agreements (Henry, 1991). This would effectively limit tax-exempt bonding to hospitals providing charity care, since government reimbursement for care of Medicaid beneficiaries is well below cost.

Quite another approach is emerging from the voluntary sector, rooted in the traditions of private certification and accreditation of U.S. hospitals. A Hospital Community Benefits

Standards Program is now being demonstrated and tested in forty-nine hospitals (Hospital Community Benefit Standards Program, n.d.). It is likely to become available to all hospitals through a process similar to that of the Joint Commission on Accreditation of Health Care Organizations. The program establishes four community benefit standards, including one that delineates hospitals' obligations to relieve poverty. A certified hospital is expected to have projects and services for its community in each of three areas: (1) improving health status; (2) addressing the health problems of minorities, the poor, and other medically underserved populations; and (3) containing the growth of community health care costs. The standard further provides that "In meeting its community's health care needs, a hospital should take steps to assure adequate access to patient care services for all persons, regardless of their financial status. . . . [S]uch services are viewed as basic to a hospital's patient care mission rather than as part of its community benefit program. The justification for such thinking is evidenced by the need for hospitals and their communities to make special efforts to address the health problems of the disadvantaged that go far beyond the provision of uncompensated care" (p. 5).

It is unclear which, if any, of the congressional proposals will become law and how far the voluntary Community Benefit Standards Program will spread. But discussion of the issues has caused hospital boards and managements to rethink the fundamental purposes of their institutions. This has been worthwhile in itself. At the root of the debate is the large and fundamental societal problem of approximately forty million U.S. citizens without insurance or other means of access to medical care. The provision of charitable care by the country's 3,200 tax-exempt hospitals constitutes an important response to this problem. Excess profit making by hospitals and forgone tax revenues to governments are peripheral issues. The central issue is the same one that was present at the founding of the U.S. hospital system: whether relief from government taxes should be conditioned on the private relief of poverty.

Summary

For more than a decade, we have witnessed the emergence of competitive health care markets, brought on by the deregulation that followed the 1960s and 1970s, when government regulation failed to check rapidly rising health care costs. Hospitals started to compete for patients, first with services and then with prices. The impact of competition was accentuated by dramatic declines in hospital utilization resulting from shifts in medical care to ambulatory settings and the rise of health maintenance organizations and diagnostic-related-group (DRG) prospective payment. Admission rates and lengths of stays declined such that hospitals previously operating at 80 to 85 percent capacity are now operating at 45 or 50 precent, leaving unused and unnecessary beds.

Operating under the original dictum of "relief of poverty," some nonprofit hospitals developed heavy loads of charitable care while others experienced light loads. These differences were due partly to the socioeconomic profiles of their patients and partly to hospital policy. With the rise of competition, these hospitals found themselves competing in the same markets. But they were on "uneven playing fields." Those hospitals relieving high amounts of poverty had to subsidize this care through charges to full-paying patients. The higher prices charged by these hospitals drove patients away to lower-priced competitors that were not burdened by charitable care.

The high-burden hospitals followed the lead of their low-burden competitors by eliminating services associated with charity care and substituting or adding profit-making ventures. Through corporate restructuring, parent holding companies were created that were nonprofit in charter but did not uphold the traditions of community service and charitable care of their originating hospitals. Instead, these holding companies were novel entities that usually adopted bottom-line orientations. To this was added joint venturing, which was patently commercial and placed hospitals in dubious relationships with their doctors. All of this has attracted the close scrutiny of tax authorities and the wrathful attention of Congress.

In late 1991, Arnold Relman provided a ten-year review of his earlier depiction of the "medical industrial complex." "What I had not fully appreciated in 1980 was that the pressures on voluntary hospitals would lead many to behave just like their investor-owned competitors. . . . The result of all this has been a gradual shift in the focus of our voluntary hospital system. . . . Decisions about the allocation of hospital resources, the creation of new facilities, or the elimination of existing ones are now based more on what is likely to be profitable than on the priorities of community health needs. . . . In any case, we are witnessing a pervasive change in the ethos of the voluntary hospital system from that of a social service to that of a business" (Relman, 1991, p. 856).

References

Alexander, J. A. "Diversification Behavior of Multi-Hospital Systems: Patterns of Change, 1983–1985." *Hospital and Health Services Administration*, 1990, *35*(1), 83–102.

Alexander, J. A., and Orlikoff, J. E. "Hospital Corporate Restructuring Gains Widespread Acceptance." *Trustee*, Jan. 1987, pp. 16–18.

Andersen, A., and Company. *Washington Healthcare Newsletter*, May 1992, pp. 3, 4.

Bromberg, R. S. "Can a Joint Venture Threaten the Hospital's Tax Exempt Status?" *Healthcare Financial Management*, Dec. 1986, pp. 76–78, 82–86.

Clark, R. C. "Does the Nonprofit Form Fit the Hospital Industry?" *Harvard Law Review*, May 1980, *92*.

Dallek, J. M., and Waxman, R. "Patient Dumping: A Crisis in Emergency Medical Care for the Indigent." *Clearinghouse Review*, 1986, *19*, 1413–1414.

Eastern Kentucky Welfare Rights Organization v. *Simon*, 506 F.2d 1288–89 (D.C. Cir. 1974).

General Accounting Office. *Nonprofit Hospitals: Better Standards Needed for Tax Exemption*. Report to the Chairman, Select Committee on Aging, U.S. House of Representatives. GAO publication no. HRD 90-84. Washington, D.C.: U.S. Government Printing Office, 1990.

Grant, P. N. "Joint Ventures in Health Care." Unpublished manuscript, Health Policy Institute, University of California, Berkeley, 1984.

Gray, B. H. *The Profit Motive and Patient Care: The Changing Accountability of Doctors and Hospitals*. Cambridge, Mass.: Harvard University Press, 1991.

Group on Government Affairs, American Medical Association. "Medicare/Medicaid Restrictions on Ownership/Investment/ Referrals by Physicians to Health Care Facilities." Unpublished memorandum, Group on Government Affairs, American Medical Association, n.d.

Hansmann, H. "The Role of Nonprofit Enterprise." *Yale Law Journal*, April 1980, pp. 835–901.

Henry, W. "Tax Exempt Challenge Warrants Hospitals' Attention." *Health Care Financial Management*, Jan. 1991, 30–32, 36–38.

Herzlinger, R. E., and Krasker, W. S. "Who Profits from Nonprofits?" *Harvard Business Review*, Jan.–Feb. 1987, pp. 93–106.

Hollingsworth, R., and Hollingsworth, E. J. *Controversy About American Hospitals: Funding, Ownership, and Performance*. Washington, D.C.: American Enterprise Institute, 1987.

Hospital Community Benefit Standards Program. *A New Certification Program for Hospitals That Meet High Standards of Community Service*. New York: Hospital Community Benefit Standards Program, New York University, n.d.

"Hospitals Report Mixed Results in 1990." *Healthcare Financial Management*, Nov. 1991, pp. 16, 18.

Koska, M. T. "Community Hospitals Swallow Pediatric Losses." *Hospitals*, Jan. 5, 1989, p. 31.

Kuchler, J. A. "Tax-Exempt Yardstick: Defining the Measurement." *Healthcare Financial Management*, Feb. 1992, pp. 21–32.

Lewin, L. S., and others. "Setting the Record Straight: The Provision of Uncompensated Care by Nonprofit Hospitals." *New England Journal of Medicine*, 1988, *318*, 1212–1215.

Lumsdon, K. "Pressure Growing in the Fight to Stay Tax Exempt." *Health Care Financial Management*, Jan. 1991, p. 21–28.

McIlrath, S. "New Safe Harbor Rules Narrow." *American Medical News*, Aug. 12, 1991, pp. 1, 33–35.

Mancino, D. M. "Hospital-Physician Joint Ventures: Some Critical Considerations." *Hospital Progress*, Jan. 1984, pp. 30–35.

Marmor, T. R., and others. "Nonprofit Organizations and Health Care." In W. W. Powell (ed.), *The Nonprofit Sector: A Research Handbook*. New Haven, Conn.: Yale University Press, 1987.

Melnick, G. "Uncompensated Emergency Care in Hospital Markets in Los Angeles County." *American Journal of Public Health*, 1989, *79*, 514.

National Association of Children's Hospitals and Related Institutions, unpublished manuscript, 1989.

Pear, R. "Doctors Warned on Conflict of Interest." *New York Times*, Sept. 4, 1991, p. 3.

Powell, W. W. (ed.). *The Nonprofit Sector: A Research Handbook*. New Haven, Conn.: Yale University Press, 1987.

Prince, T. R. "Assessing Financial Outcomes of Nonprofit Community Hospitals." *Hospital and Health Services Administration*, 1991, *36*(3), 331–349.

Relman, A. S. "The New Medical Industrial Complex." *New England Journal of Medicine*, 1980, *303*, 963–970.

Relman, A. S. "Dealing with Conflicts of Interest." *New England Journal of Medicine*, 1985, *313*, 749–751.

Relman, A. S. "Shattuck Lecture: Health Care Industry: Where Is It Taking Us?" *New England Journal of Medicine*, 1991, *325*(12), 854–859.

Rev. Rule 56-185, 1956, C.B. 202.

Rev. Rule 69-545, 1969-2, C.B. 117.

Rev. Rule 83-157, 1983-2, C.B. 94.

Rosenfield, R. H. "Market Forces Set Off Skyrocketing Interest in Hospital-Doctor Ventures." *Modern Healthcare*, May 1, 1984, pp. 70–74.

Sabatino, F. "The Diversification Success Story Continues: Survey." *Hospitals*, Jan. 5, 1989, p. 28.

Seay, J. D., and Vladeck, B. (eds.). *In Sickness and in Health: The*

Mission of Voluntary Health Care Institutions. New York: McGraw-Hill, 1988.

Shortell, S., Morrison, E. M., and Robbins, S. "Strategy Making in Health Care Organizations: A Framework and Agenda for Research." *Medical Care Review,* 1985, *42*(2), 219–266.

Simpson, J. B., and Strum, S. D. "How Good a Samaritan? Federal Income Tax Exemption for Charitable Hospitals Reconsidered." *University of Puget Sound Law Review,* Spring 1991, pp. 633–670.

Sofaer, S., Rundall, T. G., and Zeller, W. L. "Restrictive Reimbursement and Uncompensated Care in California Hospitals, 1981–1986." *Hospital and Health Services Administration,* 1990, *35*(2), 189–206.

Starkweather, D. B. "Competition, Integration, Diversification: Seven Hospitals of Growthville, U.S.A." *Journal of Health Administration Education,* 1990, *8*(4), 519–570.

Starkweather, D. B., and Carman, J. M. "Horizontal and Vertical Concentrations in the Evolution of Hospital Competition." In R. M. Scheffler and L. F. Rossiter (eds.), *Advances in Health Economics and Health Services Research.* Vol. 7: *Mergers in Health Care, the Performance of Multi-Institutional Organizations.* Greenwich, Conn.: JAI Press, 1987.

Starr, P. *The Social Transformation of American Medicine.* New York: Basic Books, 1982.

Washington Report, Sept. 6, 1991.

Young, D. W. "Nonprofits Need Surplus Too." *Hospital Financial Management,* July 1983, pp. 124–131.

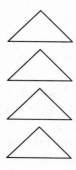

CHAPTER 5

Trade Associations in the American Political Economy

David Knoke

In one form or another, trade associations of profit-making businesses have been active in the United States since its earliest days. A 1799 strike by journeyman shoemakers in Philadelphia was opposed by the Society of Cordwainers, a "protective association" of employers organized the decade before (Commons, 1909). Regional and national "trade associations" consisting solely of nonprofit organizations—such as the United Way, the YMCA, and the Boy Scouts—began to emerge about a century

Note: Research grants from the National Science Foundation (SES82-16927 and SES85-08051) were essential for the data collection for this chapter. The assistance of Richard Adams, Lois Kelly, and the Center for Survey Research at Indiana University, Kathryn Cirksena, field director, is gratefully acknowledged. Howard E. Aldrich's and David F. Gillespie's contributions to this chapter are appreciated. I especially thank Dennis R. Young for his encouragement and many helpful suggestions, which improved the quality of the analyses.

later (Hopkins, 1951; United Way of America, 1977). The key role that business associations play in the functioning of the market economy has long been appreciated by scholars. But in their efforts to facilitate the work of business and industries, the for-profit trade associations also affect the work of non-profit organizations. By examining business trade associations' structures and activities, we can better understand the internal dynamics of trade associations in general and begin to comprehend the even wider interplay between nonprofit organizations and the operations of the market economy.

What Are Trade Associations?

Trade associations are membership organizations whose members are organizations operating in a specific economic sector "that represent their members' political and economic preferences, although at times they also act as vehicles for governments to implement public policies" (Aldrich and Staber, 1988, p. 112). Some analysts distinguish between employer associations, which specialize in representing their members' relationships with organized labor, and trade associations, which represent their members' other economic interests, such as subsidies, tariffs, patents, and taxation (Windmuller, 1984, pp. 8–9). However, this distinction is more relevant in other countries than in the United States, where the full spectrum of economic, labor relations, and political issues of an industrial sector are often handled by a single association. Indeed, the broader focuses and longer duration of trade associations set them apart from such narrowly based social formations as single-purpose coalitions, informal market cartels, business political action committees (PACs), and corporate governmental affairs offices.

Trade associations constitute "the largest important unit of political activity" in the U.S. business sector (Vogel, 1978, p. 67). They also perform numerous nonpolitical service functions for their members, including such services as "advice and assistance on accounting practices, advertising, product standardization, trade statistics, employee relations, and the like" (Schlozman and Tierney, 1986, p. 41; see also Levitan and

Cooper, 1984, pp. 45–46; Schneiberg and Hollingsworth, 1990, p. 323). Other service functions may include public relations and advertising, research on technical developments and economic conditions, setting industry quality and certification standards, labor power management, and administration of pension and insurance programs. Although industrywide collective bargaining with labor unions was often an important historical factor in forming employers' associations, many firms reject association bargaining as unnecessary or a violation of antitrust regulations (Derber, 1984, pp. 93–97, 110). More often, industries create a distinct entity for collective bargaining, such as the Bituminous Coal Operators Association, which may or may not offer other trade association services. Corporatist arrangements, which bring labor and business into direct negotiations on a broad spectrum of economic issues, are much more prevalent in Europe than in the United States (Salisbury, 1979; Berger, 1981; Streeck and Schmitter, 1985; Cox and O'Sullivan, 1988).

Nonprofit associations typically emerge to supplement or displace market and state regulation as interorganizational coordination and governance mechanisms. They seek to perform public tasks delegated to them by the state, to fulfill tasks not attempted by the state or the for-profit sector, or to influence the direction of public policy (Hall, 1987). Most nonprofit and voluntary organizations concentrate their efforts on local community issues, even when they are chapters of national organizations, such as the American Red Cross and the Girl Scouts of the U.S.A. (Young, 1989). Still, the nonprofit sector has achieved some significant presence at the national level, through central headquarters that represent broader concerns of their member organizations. The American Council on Education, the American Federation of Arts, and the Child Welfare League of America exemplify national groups that promote the interests of organizations operating outside the market economy. Nonprofit trade associations engage in a variety of service functions for their member organizations that are indistinguishable from those of their for-profit counterparts, such as information, training, technical assistance, pension and insurance programs, and lobbying support (Adler, 1988; Smucker, 1991).

An inherent tension between internal (member servicing) and external (lobbying, public relations) applications of limited organizational resources is shared by all types of membership associations. In Mancur Olson's renowned hypothesis (1965), public goods—those from whose enjoyment noncontributors cannot be excluded—are poor inducements for potential supporters of collective activities. Instead, "selective incentives," whose receipt is contingent on the payment of dues, are allegedly necessary to ensure adequate resource contributions. Collective actions that produce public goods for the organization's members and nonmembers alike—for example, the American Hospital Association's successful resistance of federal cost-containment regulations—must inevitably be a by-product of an organization's primary focus on satisfying its members' service demands (Olson, 1965, pp. 132–138).

Empirical support for Olson's hypothesis is weak (Marwell and Ames, 1979; Knoke and Wright-Isak, 1982). As inducements to join and remain in a voluntary organization, lobbying activities may prove as powerful as direct services to members. Marsh (1976) found that member firms of the Confederation of British Industry made little use of that association's services yet asserted that they received greater public goods benefits than did nonmembers. A survey of five trade and occupational associations' members showed that "economic services have greater inducement value than politics," but "the motivational role of lobbying and feelings of responsibility are not at all insignificant" (Moe, 1980, p. 209). For many members, "Politics plays a pivotal role in their decision to maintain membership" (p. 218). Confronted with a hypothetical trade-off, members of associations with substantial political goals emphasized the greater importance of lobbying than of direct services (Knoke, 1990, pp. 133–135). These findings suggest that, although trade associations apply substantial resources to provide selective member benefits, a portion can be allocated to collective action efforts that will also be attractive to members.

In their dual emphases on member services and political influence over governmental policies, trade associations resemble many kinds of associations and interest groups whose members are individuals (Knoke, 1986). But trade associations differ most importantly in being more "minimalist" than other organizations, in the sense that very little capital and labor is required to create and maintain them. Trade associations can more readily adapt to abrupt resource changes in their environments than can their nonprofit or profit-making members (Halliday, Powell, and Granfors, 1987). Hence, many trade associations can sustain themselves on relatively narrow and specialized membership bases, which would be jeopardized by efforts to recruit members with more diverse interests. Very few "peak associations," which claim to represent broad economic or nonprofit sectors, can be found in the United States. There are only about forty for-profit peak groups, including the National Association of Manufacturers (NAM), the U.S. Chamber of Commece, and the National Federation of Independent Business (NFIB). An unknown but probably smaller number of peak nonprofit trade associations have emerged, for example, the INDEPENDENT SECTOR and the National Health Council.

Also intriguing are hybrid organizations that combine nonprofit, corporate, and government agencies to deal with common problems, for example, the Consumer Federation of America, the Council on Foundations, and the National Association of Health Data Organizations. These heterogeneous entities must constantly grapple with the need to reconcile divergent ideological and substantive concerns among large and small members, public and private auspices, or traditional and technologically innovative organizations. Such internal divisions induce high membership turnover rates in peak associations and the founding of new specialist trade organizations to represent distinctive views (Moe, 1980, pp. 191–199; Levitan and Cooper, 1984, pp. 13–17). Both for-profit and nonprofit trade associations purchase organizational stability and cohesion through specialization, implied in the proliferation of such narrow groups as the National Neighborhood Coalition, the

Congress of National Black Churches, and the Public Services Satellite Consortium.

Because so little empirical research about nonprofit trade associations has been done, the remainder of this chapter examines the available historical and contemporary evidence about national for-profit trade associations. Whether and how they differ in structures and functions from labor unions, professional societies, recreational clubs, philanthropic organizations, and public interest groups (PIGs) is a central theme. At relevant points, I discuss the implications of the findings for nonprofit trade associations, and I suggest fruitful directions for future research on this important sector.

The Growth of For-Profit Trade Associations

The few nineteenth-century for-profit trade associations pursued an offensive strategy of improving the market conditions faced by their member firms, particularly by fostering mutual agreements on competition and the suppression of organized labor (Windmuller, 1984). The takeoff phase in employers' associations came around the turn of the twentieth century, as national markets replaced local and regional enclaves. The destructive consequences of unbridled big business competition grew increasingly evident. Because strong central state institutions did not precede the rise of big capital (McCraw, 1984), collective efforts at stabilizing cutthroat competition among firms fell largely to these emergent employers' associations. At the same time, a revitalized labor union movement strove to force one company after another to engage in industrywide collective bargaining (Bonnett, 1922, 1956). Large economic, political and organizational forces compelled a transformation of an earlier era's "dinner-club" cartels and trusts into hard-nosed business-service associations staffed by professionals skilled in technical matters (Galambos, 1988). As Figures 5.1 and 5.2 show, annual foundings of new employers' associations increased the population from fewer than 200 national organizations in 1900 to more than 1,500 by 1950. Thereafter, rising

Figure 5.1. Number of Foundings and Dissolutions per Year, 1900–1982.

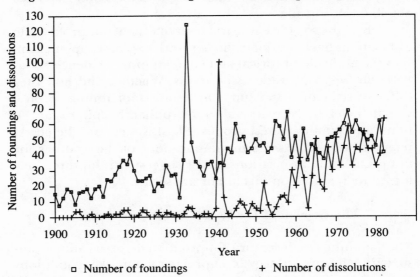

Source: Aldrich and Staber, 1988. Used by permission of Harper-Collins Publishers.

rates of mergers, acquisitions, and dissolutions gradually brought the population into equilibrium, at a "carrying capacity" of about 2,200 national for-profit trade associations by the 1970s (Aldrich and Staber, 1988, pp. 123–124).

Aldrich and his colleagues' analyses of for-profit trade association formations, mergers, and disbandings over the twentieth century leave little doubt that aggregate population rates responded to industrial differentiation and the resource niches available to specialists (Aldrich, Staber, Zimmer, and Beggs, 1990a, 1990b; Aldrich and Staber, 1988; Staber and Aldrich, 1983; Staber, 1987). A "logic of membership" appeared partly responsible for this dynamic. Business trade associations depend much more on their members for resources than do nonprofit and citizens' organizations, which often receive external support from wealthy donors, foundations, and even governments (Walker, 1983). Hence, they must be particularly respon-

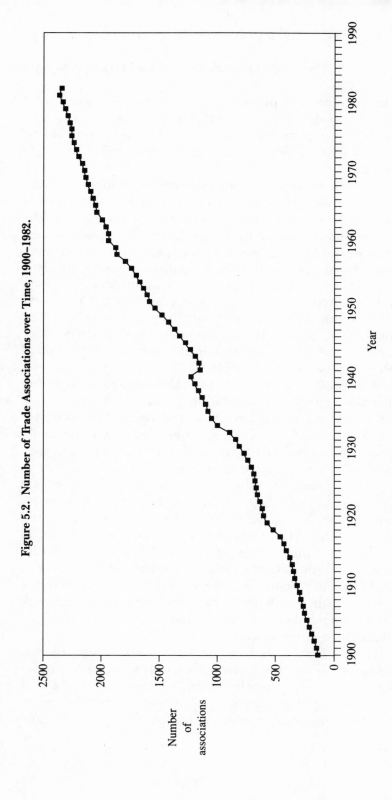

Figure 5.2. Number of Trade Associations over Time, 1900–1982.

Source: Aldrich and Staber, 1988. Used by permission of HarperCollins Publishers.

sive to current and prospective members' economic and political interests. Progressive industrial innovation and division of labor create an inexorable conflict of viewpoints among businesses that cannot be easily accommodated in a single organization.

The U.S. trade association population proliferated as the national economic structure grew more complex at the turn of the century. New organizations emerged to fill niches created by industrial differentiation, with these specialist associations exhibiting greater internal member homogeneity than their predecessors. I hypothesize that the formation of nonprofit trade associations depends less on marketplace differentiation than on the sustained business profits and government tax largesse from which donations and grants are derived. Thus, the takeoff period for nonprofit trade associations probably occurred after the end of the Great Depression and during the sustained economic boom following World War II.

A parallel "logic of influence" also seemed to drive for-profit trade association population growth. State policies toward business may compel firms to band together for collective action to compete for government concessions and direct subsidies and to combat the negative effects of legislative and judicial actions. Although state intervention is more extensive in European corporatist political economies, notable federal efforts to coordinate U.S. production and distribution occurred during both world wars and with the brief National Industrial Recovery Act (NIRA) of the early New Deal (McQuaid, 1982, pp. 26–29). But only the latter event produced a statistically significant increase in the rate of national trade association foundings (Aldrich, Zimmer, Staber, and Beggs, 1990b). And despite the enormous upsurge in federal regulatory actions beginning in the 1970s, the number of for-profit trade associations stabilized and actually declined modestly.

Further investigation of association disbandings revealed a tendency to survive the infancy years, only to face a rising rate of dissolution with increasing maturity. Lobbying the federal government may divert resources that would otherwise be applied to meeting member demands for special services. Organizations with diverse member interests and those with ties to other employer associations had lower disbanding rates, suggesting that longevity may be enhanced when economic and political stresses drive firms to act collectively and force them "to set their parochial preferences aside" (Aldrich, Staber, Zimmer, and Beggs, 1990a, p. 48). The nonprofit trade association population may have received its greatest boost under the Reagan-Bush administrations' impetus toward privatizing many public and welfare services. The recent phenomenon of hybrid associations combining nonprofit, corporate, and government agencies — such as the Crime Prevention Coalition (creators of McGruff the Crime Dog) — undoubtedly reflects exigencies of an era of fiscal limits.

Aldrich and his colleagues' analyses were premised on an assumption that employer organizations are equivalent units in a homogeneous population whose dynamics operate uniformly over time. Such uniformity across many decades seems implausible, given the huge historical changes outlined above. For example, the specific members of a given trade association change over time as these organizations are born, expand, merge, and die in response to their own environmental dynamics. The internal composition of an apparently stable trade association may change radically in a few years, thereby altering its structure, purposes, and activities. Thus, a trade association population whose members consist of many small associations undoubtedly has a different impact on its members from that of a population consisting of only a few large organizations.

Aldrich and his colleagues' failure to uncover significant effects of federal government regulations on aggregated population dynamics does not mean that such environmental conditions are entirely inconsequential. Rather, their main effects may operate primarily at the intra-associational and interorganizational levels of analysis, rather than at the population level. To understand the dramatic developments in for-profit trade association political activity in recent years, a historical overview of major transformations in national policy making is indispensable.

Transformations of the Pressure-Group System

For the first two-thirds of the twentieth century, businesses allegedly enjoyed a privileged position in the U.S. political economy (Lindblom, 1977, p. 175). Politicians saw their own electoral fates as heavily intertwined with business decisions — a rising standard of living, full employment, productivity gains, plant investments, low inflation, high tax receipts, and technological advances were important to their chances of reelection. The vulnerability of the economy to unhealthy business performance induced a pro-business deference among politicians eager to reap credit with their constituents by supporting expansionary economic policies. This intimate interdependence of government and economy was neatly captured in "Engine Charlie" Wilson's famous statement to the Senate Armed Services Committee, "What's good for the country is good for General Motors, and what's good for General Motors is good for the country." Cozy "iron triangles" consisting of specific industries, regulatory agencies, and congressional oversight committees concocted mutually beneficial policy decisions out of sight of and thus out of the mind of the general public (Gais, Peterson, and Walker, 1984). Likewise, Marxists criticized an excessive catering by public policy makers to a skittish "business climate" (Block, 1977).

The prevailing consensus among capitalists, politicians, and the general public was that business should run its affairs as it saw fit, with minimal government intervention. Prior to the 1960s, corporations and firms saw little need for political efforts to achieve individual or collective advantages (Wilson, 1990, p. 30). Business associations could concentrate on their member-servicing functions to the neglect of political activities. An influential study of foreign trade politics in the 1950s depicted business lobbying as underfinanced, poorly staffed, and incompetent (Bauer, de Sola Pool, and Dexter, 1963). NAM and the U.S. Chamber of Commerce vied for the role of preeminent voice of American business in the executive and legislative councils. Their strident conservatism often led them to advocate extreme policy positions that reduced their credibility and effectiveness with governmental officials (Gable, 1953). But the limited intrusion of government in the economy, even after the New Deal, meant that inept business advocates did little harm.

Within less than two decades, these moribund business pressure groups were transformed beyond recognition by political upheavals that precipitated a remarkable resurgence in their political effectiveness. The origin of this revolution lay in a strong swing of the political pendulum in the liberal direction, which permitted passage of antibusiness, pro-social legislation during the 1960s and early 1970s. In the immediate post–World War II era, the general public gave business high marks for its economic accomplishments but remained suspicious of "excessive" profits, industrial concentration, and undue political influence at the expense of the public (Lipset and Schneider, 1983, pp. 163–198). Public opinion poll expressions of antibusiness sentiments constituted a fairly stable minority at around 39–42 percent until 1967, when a steep rise began that brought them to an all-time high of 67 percent by 1981 (p. 33). This decline of public confidence in business leadership was part of a deepening distrust of *all* American institutions, including labor unions and the government. The origins of a sea change in public sentiments were many and complex — the endless Vietnam debacle and obstreperous protests by racial, environmental, consumer, and women's social movements — and efforts to disentangle them would take us too far afield. But the consequence of rising institutional disillusion was a general repudiation of business's privileged position in the political system (Vogel, 1989, p. 35). The Great Society's civil rights and poverty amelioration legislation, passed by swollen Democratic congressional majorities, launched greatly expanded federal intervention into and regulation of the economy. New "maximum-feasible" citizen-participation provisions empowered the formerly disenfranchised to confront and challenge policy makers (Berry, 1984, p. 31). The business community, so long complacent at having things its own way with little effort, found itself on the defensive along many fronts.

The high tide line of liberal activist success was reached in 1970. An onslaught of socially conscious legislation and regulation caught business with its lobbies down: the Federal Trade Commission's ban on television and radio advertising of cigarettes; the creation of the Environmental Protection Agency, the Occupational Safety and Health Administration, and the Consumer Product Safety Commission; and the strengthening of the Clean Air Act. In a final insult, John Gardner, a former Republican cabinet member in the Johnson administration, founded Common Cause as a citizens' lobby to push for further restrictions on private sector privileges (McFarland, 1984). The Nixon administration, despite its conservative rhetoric, proved neither a steadfast nor an effective ally of business (Vogel, 1989, p. 90), and it was ultimately decimated by the Watergate scandal. Further inroads occurred in post-Watergate reforms of congressional procedures that broke the conservative committee chairs' dominance (Mann and Ornstein, 1979). Ironically, the federal election campaign financing reforms, which were intended to reduce the influence of fat-cat contributors, ultimately paved the way for corporate and trade association political action committees to channel large sums to politicians desperate to cover the escalating costs of reelection in a television age (Sabato, 1984; Stern, 1988; Loomis, 1988). Neither unions nor public interest groups could match the deep pockets into which business groups dug to support their favored candidates, especially incumbents with proven track records of sponsoring pro-business legislation.

Faced with these cumulative governmental intrusions into domains in which it had regarded itself as sovereign, the business community rallied for a counterattack. Before his appointment to the Supreme Court, Lewis Powell wrote a confidential memo in 1970 to the U.S. Chamber of Commerce outlining aggressive political actions, bold media campaigns, and substantial internal reorganization of the chamber (Levitan and Cooper, 1984, p. 20; Vogel, 1989, p. 57). A multifaceted mobilization of political resources began to revitalize business's influence (Pertschuk, 1982, pp. 47–68). Hundreds of for-profit trade associations flocked to the nation's capital to monitor and intervene in the political scene (Berry, 1984, pp. 20–23; Vogel, 1989, pp. 197–198). Between 1,700 and 2,000 associations of all kinds, employing many thousands of lobbyists, made Washington their headquarters (Berry, 1984, p. 20; Schlozman, 1984).

Individual corporations also increasingly set up their own government affairs operations or hired Washington representatives to plead their cases with public officials (Salisbury, 1984; Heinz, Laumann, Salisbury, and Nelson, 1990). The Business Roundtable was formed in 1972 to give a united voice to the CEOs of the 200 largest business firms, while the NAM finally registered as an official lobbyist with Congress in 1975. The politicized business associations began applying the same sophisticated tactics as used by their liberal adversaries to influence the policy decisions of judicial, legislative, and executive branch agencies. The most commonly used influence techniques were contacting government officials to present views, testifying at formal hearings, presenting research results, and mounting grass-roots lobbying efforts by stimulating constituents' letters and phone calls to their senators and representatives. Less frequently used tactics included talking to the media, contributing money and labor to electoral campaigns, litigating, and running advertisements about organizational positions (Schlozman and Tierney, 1986, pp. 150–151; Wilson, 1990, pp. 53–64).

Business interests finally scored victories in 1978 by blocking a consumer protection agency, labor-law reforms, and Federal Trade Commission regulatory proposals (Pertschuk, 1982, pp. 69–117). With the subsequent presidential elections of Ronald Reagan and George Bush, both ideologically committed to "getting government off our backs," businesspeople could finally feel that they had reversed the tide of federal economic intrusion sponsored by their labor and public interest group opponents. Although the 1970s and 1980s saw increased involvement by both corporations and trade associations in public policy making, their influence was muted whenever disagreements arose among their members over specific goals (Vogel, 1989, pp. 283–289). The legacy of the current era is that many for-profit trade associations are now much better equipped to react politically whenever perceived threats to the economic interests of their member firms arise.

The nonprofit trade associations' role in this picture is

still unclear, for the history of their participation remains to be written. Most obviously, these organizations' fates were bound up in the political-economic transformations that affected how they acquire the resources necessary for their survival and prosperity. Thus, health and social welfare association budgets are shaped by tax-code provisions on charitable deductions by persons and corporations. Environmental and consumer advocacy groups' effectiveness varies with their difficulty in qualifying for tax-exempt status. Universities' and schools' enrollments are driven by tax allocations and student loan guarantee programs. With such enormous stakes at risk, the nonprofit sector could not sit idly by while the corporations and social movement organizations slugged it out. Competition for slices of the shrinking public pie forced the nonprofits to abandon any pretense of aloof purity and to immerse themselves in hard political struggle. Uncovering how they learned collectively to pool resources in local, state, regional, and national trade associations to influence the public policies affecting their members is a fascinating project awaiting historians.

Research Questions

Although both for-profit and nonprofit trade associations have dramatically increased their visible political participation on the U.S. national stage, the extent to which such prominent actors as the National Association of Manufacturers and the INDEPENDENT SECTOR exemplify the larger population remains unknown. With few exceptions (for eample, Staber, 1987; Young and Sleeper, 1987), most evidence comes not from representative samples but from case studies of particular organizations and events whose generalizability is doubtful. Few systematic analyses have been made of the organizational and environmental factors that affect trade association behavior. Fortunately, a recent survey of all U.S. national associations included sufficiently large numbers of organizations to permit quantitative contrasts both among several types of organizations and within the business trade association subsample itself.

Among the basic research questions addressed below are

how for-profit trade associations compare to labor unions, professional societies, and other interest organizations. Do these types differ on such dimensions as membership size, resources, expenditures, formal administrative and governance structures, and collective decision making? In what ways do the goals sought by business associations — particularly services targeted directly to members and policy-influencing actions targeted at government officials — differ from the aims of the other kinds of associations? Have for-profit trade associations developed greater capacities than other organizations to pursue their political agendas, and do they more frequently mobilize their members for political ends? Or are they primarily internally oriented around providing essential services to their constituent members?

Within the heterogeneous business association population, what internal and environmental factors discriminate their relative emphases on member-servicing and political-influence goals? Do diverse goals, organizational characteristics, and environmental conditions jointly explain the development of political capacity, the assertion of public policy preferences, and the mobilization of associations' members? I offer answers to these questions after describing the data and measures in the following section.

Data

Data to examine the preceding research questions are taken from the National Association Study (NAS), a stratified sample of all U.S. national associations and random samples of members of three types of organizations (Knoke, 1990, pp. 68–72). Because no membership samples were drawn from the 109 for-profit trade associations in the first sample, analyses reported below are confined to information collected at the organizational level.

Three compendiums were used in 1983 to compile a master list of all national mass-membership associations in the United States (Colgate and Fowler, 1983; Colgate and Evans, 1981; Akey, 1983). Organizations were classifed into five strata:

business trade associations, professional societies, labor unions, recreational associations, and a residual category. On the basis of directory information about their annual budgets, the trade, professional, and recreational categories were each subdivided into small and large sizes, with the former having about a fifth to a third of each type. After duplicates, nonassociations, and defunct groups were eliminated, approximately 13,000 organizations remained in the population. Random samples of 50 to 60 organizations were drawn from each of the eight sampling strata. In January and February 1984, hour-long computer-assisted telephone interviews (CATI) were conducted with an executive director or chief elected official for each organization. Interviews were completed with 459 informants, for an overall response rate of 92.7 percent.

The 3,503 U.S. national trade associations were classified into 790 large (annual budgets of $250,000 or more) and 2,713 small (annual budgets of less than $250,000) organizations. (This cut point was chosen to produce a 25:75 split, thus enabling equal subsamples to be drawn from both the large- and small-organization strata.) A total of sixty interviews were completed with informants from the large organizations and forty-nine with informants from the small organizations, for respective response rates of 98 and 91 percent (Knoke, 1990, p. 71). In analyses reported below, these two strata are first examined separately in comparison to the other kinds of organizations. Then the 109 business trade associations are combined into a single sample, with each organization weighted to reflect its stratum's relative proportions in the population of all for-profit trade associations (that is, the weighted sample contains 27 large and 82 small organizations).

Association Structures and Processes

Some answers to the question of how for-profit trade associations compare to other organizations can be found in Table 5.1, which compares the mean characteristics of large and small trade associations to those of labor unions, professional societies, and other associations (the combined recreational and residual strata). The correlation ratios (eta-square) indicate how strongly each association attribute varies across the five organizational types; their significance is assessed with either a chi-square test (for categoric attributes) or an F-test (for continuous measures).

A basic feature of any organization is its scale of operations, captured by such dimensions as membership size, resources, and formal structure. In comparing trade association membership sizes to other organizations' sizes, an immediate difficulty is how to count the number of members. Labor unions, professional societies, and other associations typically enroll individuals as members, and some memberships may reach into the millions. Most trade associations restrict their memberships to formal organizations (firms) in a specific industry and hence have numerically far fewer members. Even more complicated are organizations that include both individual and organizational membership categories. Indeed, in the NAS sample, 59 percent of the 109 for-profit trade associations allow only organizational members, 32 percent have both organizational and individual members, and 9 percent consist only of individuals (many of whom are owners of small businesses, such as cattle ranchers). How to conceptualize equivalence in membership size across these associations is unclear. The first row in Table 5.1 shows the mean membership size when each organization and individual is counted as a single member. Both of the trade association categories clearly have the smallest average memberships (3,313 and 524). If only organizational members are included, the means are much smaller yet: 1,077 and 265 organizational members for the large and small associations, respectively. Trade associations appear to be tiny organizations when placed next to labor unions and other associations, which both average more than 100,000 individual members. However, association size is so heterogeneous within each of the five categories that these impressive differences are not statistically significant, as shown by an eta-square of only .08.

Also impressive is the range in scope of operations that is reflected in annual revenues. The large trade associations more closely resemble the labor unions, although their $4.4 million

Table 5.1. Characteristics of American Associations (Means).

Characteristic	Large trade (n = 60)	Small trade (n = 49)	Labor union (n = 60)	Professional society (n = 110)	Other association (n = 182)	Eta
Membership size	3,313	524	152,658	5,575	105,296	.08
Annual revenues ($000)	$4,447	$206	$14,411	$716	$1,048	.31[a]
Percentage of revenues from member dues	50.9	65.7	82.7	58.9	63.4	.26[a]
Percentage of revenues from services, sales	36.2	18.4	2.8	23.2	16.8	.29[a]
Age (years old in 1983)	46.8	31.0	60.3	36.5	34.1	.33[a]
Number of local chapters, branches	16.3	4.4	247.3	21.6	46.0	.47[a]
Number of paid staff	41.3	3.5	115.8	8.1	7.5	.34[a]
Percentage highly bureaucratized	86.7	30.6	78.3	38.4	32.7	.40[a]
Number of standing committees	18.4	5.1	5.4	8.6	4.9	.27[a]
Percentage in which board elects president	50.8	49.0	5.0	18.4	36.7	.35[a]
Percentage in which board influence exceeds members' influence	45.0	50.0	20.8	47.1	55.0	.24[a]
Percentage in which convention makes many policies	21.4	31.1	69.5	46.6	37.3	.25[a]
Percentage turnout for elections	46.0	60.3	69.3	40.9	37.7	.36[a]

[a]$p < .001$.

income is still $10 million dollars less than that of an average union. Small trade associations command less than $250,000 in annual revenues, far less than any other type. However, the annual per capita resources available to for-profit trade associations are considerably higher: $1,342 for large and $393 for small association members, compared to $128 for professional societies, $94 for unions, and a mere $10 for other association members. Income sources are notably differentiated: large trade associations depend less than others on their members and more on the sale of services and merchandise, while the small trade association revenue streams are similar to those of other associations. Perhaps the average younger age (in 1983) of both these latter types accounts for their greater dependence on member dues, although the far older labor unions also rely much more on their members' dues.

The formal organizational structures of these national associations disclose a clear divergence between the large and small trade associations. Administratively, the large trade associations have several times more state and local chapters or branches, far more paid staff, and more bureaucratization (three or more hierarchical levels or horizontal departments) than their smaller brethren. Although both kinds of for-profit trade associations have fewer subnational units than other kinds of organizations, the large trade associations are a notable outlier in their greater number of standing committees for conducting organizational affairs. They also resemble labor unions in their substantial bureaucratization.

For-profit trade associations tend to exhibit fewer aspects of democratic governance than do other organizations, again notably in contrast to the labor unions. Boards of directors elect the president or chairperson much more often in business associations than in other associations, which give their members that franchise. Business association conventions are less likely to make many policy decisions than are the mass membership meetings of other organizations. Half the informants from both kinds of for-profit trade associations rated their boards' influence over policy matters much higher than their members' influence, similar to evaluations in professional so-

cieties and other associations but much higher than the labor
union informants' judgments. Only the mean rates of membership voting in association elections show both business associations falling between the extremes. But because trade
association boards exercise greater control over many decisions,
electoral participation has smaller impact than among other
organizations.

In summary, U.S. national for-profit trade associations
constitute a structurally distinct organizational form. Composed predominantly of organizational rather than individual
members, they have smaller membership sizes, more financial
resources per member, and more restricted member involvement in internal governance. The large trade associations are
substantially more administratively complex, closely resem-
bling national labor unions on those dimensions.

Organizational Goals

Informants were presented with eight possible goals and asked
whether their associations considered each to be "major, moderate, minor, or not a goal." Table 5.2 shows the percentages of the
five association types reporting each to be a major goal, as well
as the mean number of major goals held by each type. Large and
small trade associations differ by more than 10 percent on three
of the eight goals: large trade associations are more likely than
smaller ones to stress improving their members' incomes and
economic conditions, seeking to change societal values and
beliefs, and attempting to influence governmental policy decisions. They consistently agree that conducting research and
education (the most important goal for small trade associations)
and raising member firms' status and prestige are important
objectives. But both types express little concern about members'
social and recreational lives, their cultural or artistic experiences (what these conditions would mean for business firms is
difficult to comprehend), or nonmembers' situations. Large
business associations resemble national labor unions in their
much higher emphasis than other organizations place on both
improving economic conditions and influencing public pol-

icies. Unions pursue a wide range of organizational goals, averaging 3.32 important goals, compared to 2.63 and 2.47 for large trade associations and professional societies, respectively. Small trade and other associations both sustain a much narrower scope of interests (fewer than two major goals on average).

In the analyses described below, only the goals of improving economic conditions and influencing public policies are examined further. Not only are they the most important concerns of the major for-profit trade associations, but they correspond most closely to the conceptual distinction between member servicing and lobbying. Within resource constraints, organizations may be forced to choose one or the other objective rather than attempting to pursue both simultaneously. Indeed, within the pooled sample of U.S. for-profit trade associations, only 39 percent reported that both improved conditions and policy influence were major goals. Approximately one-fifth stated that only economic conditions were a major concern, another fifth reported only policy influence as paramount, and the remaining fifth described neither goal as major. Factors that account for these differential emphases are examined below.

Political Capacity and Member Mobilization

Associations may translate their concerns about governmental policies into a variety of actions. Two important measures of political potential are an organization's *political capacity* — specific mechanisms for monitoring and intervening in the policy-making process — and efforts at *mobilizing members* to bring influence to bear on public officials. Table 5.3 displays the distributions within organizational types for both the individual items and the means of these two scales. The political capacity scale simply counts the number of components present in an organization. The four items making up the member mobilization scale were each measured by four ordinal categories, from "regularly" (4) to "never" (1). Table 5.3 reports the percentage of associations that regularly or sometimes mobilize members for each action and the average organizational scores

Table 5.2. Major Goals of American Associations (Percentages and Means).

Organizational goals	Large trade (n = 60)	Small trade (n = 49)	Labor union (n = 60)	Professional society (n = 110)	Other association (n = 182)	Eta
Improve incomes, economic conditions	56.7%	34.7%	95.0%	13.2%	5.7%	.67[a]
Influence government's policy decisions	56.7%	30.6%	62.7%	36.3%	16.9%	.44[a]
Conduct research, member education	53.3%	44.9%	29.3%	60.4%	45.4%	.14[b]
Raise member status, prestige	43.3%	36.7%	74.1%	40.9%	15.7%	.44[a]
Change larger society's values, beliefs	30.5%	16.3%	27.6%	39.2%	24.0%	.21[a]
Affect nonmembers' lives	23.3%	18.4%	32.2%	49.3%	28.4%	.17[a]
Develop social, recreational lives	0.0%	0.0%	8.5%	3.3%	24.8%	.39[a]
Enhance cultural, artistic lives	0.0%	6.1%	8.5%	6.8%	21.5%	.29[a]
Mean number of major goals	2.63	1.88	3.32	2.47	1.82	.34[a]

[a]$p < .001$.
[b]$p < .05$.

on the four-point scale for all four items (see Knoke, 1990, pp. 195–201, for details on both scales).

Labor unions have developed substantially more political capacity than other kinds of associations. In particular, they are more likely to have their own lobbyists and political action committees. Large for-profit trade associations do not lag very far behind, particularly in legal counsel (in-house lawyers and lawyers on retainer), technical data staff, and policy monitors. The smaller trade associations have fewer resources to sustain elaborate political capacity, and hence they resemble the less politically engaged professional and other associations. A similar differential between unions and other associations exists in mobilizing members for collective action. Unions are far more likely to deploy their members to assist candidates in elections and to picket or demonstrate (activities refined through application in strikes). They more frequently stimulate their members to write letters to newspapers and magazines on behalf of union interests. Only the large trade associations come close to matching unions in their use of members to contact public officials on policy matters. In contrast to higher business association political capacity, they are almost indistinguishable from other kinds of associations in member mobilization activity.

In the following analyses, only the for-profit trade association subsample in the NAS is examined. The two sampling strata were pooled and weighted to represent their frequencies in the total population (25 percent large associations, 75 percent small associations). Thus, the effects of explanatory variables examined in these analyses can be generalized to the entire population of U.S. business associations in the mid 1980s.

As reported above, the relative emphases on income and political (lobbying) goals vary among for-profit trade associations. But which organizational characteristics contribute to this variation has not been previously investigated. Table 5.4 shows the results of a multiple discriminant analysis in which four groups combining high and low income and political goals are predicted as functions of six characteristics: organizational age; level of bureaucratization; annual revenues (logged value); whether federal government actions "make it much more diffi-

Table 5.3. Political Actions of American Associations (Percentages and Means).

Political actions	Large trade (n = 60)	Small trade (n = 49)	Labor union (n = 60)	Professional society (n = 110)	Other association (n = 182)	Eta
Political capacity						
Policy monitors	96.7%	67.3%	96.7%	75.7%	53.4%	.34[a]
Lawyers on retainer	83.3%	57.1%	70.0%	37.2%	19.1%	.43[a]
Public relations unit	78.3%	61.2%	74.6%	47.5%	51.0%	.21[a]
Technical data staff	76.7%	34.7%	71.7%	26.4%	33.0%	.34[a]
Congressional mobilization program	65.0%	28.6%	76.3%	25.9%	17.4%	.44[a]
Washington office	63.3%	20.4%	61.7%	22.4%	8.8%	.45[a]
Lobbyists	43.3%	10.2%	70.0%	10.0%	8.2%	.54[a]
In-house lawyers	41.7%	16.3%	55.9%	15.4%	9.0%	.40[a]
Political action committee	35.0%	6.1%	62.7%	4.4%	3.6%	.59[a]
Scale mean	5.83	3.02	6.35	2.65	2.03	.62[a]
Mobilizing members						
To contact officials	70.0%	32.6%	86.5%	45.3%	24.1%	.43[a]
To write letters to media	28.4%	20.4%	62.7%	35.1%	34.4%	.32[a]
To work for candidates	10.0%	2.0%	54.2%	2.7%	3.5%	.58[a]
To demonstrate and picket	0.0%	4.1%	71.2%	0.8%	5.6%	.72[a]
Scale mean	1.83	1.51	2.86	1.60	1.53	.62[a]

[a]$p < .001$.

Table 5.4. Discriminant Analysis of Trade Association Political and Income Goals.

Discriminating variables	Function one	Function two	Function three
Standardized canonical discriminant function coefficients			
Federal government an obstacle	.76	.34	−.19
Annual revenue (log)	.70	−.40	−.46
Association age	−.07	−.83	.07
Number of member service staff	−.07	.40	−.28
Leaders have policy discretion	−.13	.46	.32
Bureaucratic structure	.02	.17	1.15
Functions evaluated at group means (group centroids)			
Low political and low income goals	−.63	.71	−.11
Low political and high income goals	−.59	−.70	−.28
High political and low income goals	−.26	−.18	.52
High political and high income goals	.73	.03	−.07
Canonical correlation	.53	.42	.27
Percentage of variance	57.80	31.20	11.10
Probability level	.00	.00	.13

cult to achieve our goals"; the number of staff providing direct services to members; and whether "members give leader great discretion to make policy." A discriminant analysis weights and linearly combines the predictor variables so that the groups are forced to be as statistically distinct as possible. The standardized coefficients for a discriminant function can be interpreted as partial regression coefficients that show the net effect of that variable on a particular group function (Kerlinger and Pedhazur, 1973, p. 337). The group centroids are the mean discriminant scores for each group on the respective functions; they express the relationship among the dependent groups and each function.

The three discriminant functions reveal distinct configurations of variables predicting each goal combination. In the first function, business associations expressing both high member income and high lobbying goals are contrasted with all other combinations. These organizations have large annual revenues and consider the federal government an obstacle to achieving their objectives. In the second function, associations with both low income and low political goals are contrasted mainly with organizations holding only high income goals. These former associations are younger and less wealthy but give their leaders policy discretion and have substantial staff devoted to member services. Finally, the third function discriminates those associations having high political and low income goals from all others. These organizations have low annual revenues but are very heavily bureaucratized.

Although these patterns come from cross-sectional data, they suggest a possible developmental sequence of for-profit trade association goals: when they are young and poor, associations concentrate on their members' interest in income goals to the exclusion of lobbying goals. In order for a poor association to promote exclusively political goals, formal bureaucratic structure can compensate for a lack of financial resources. As organizations obtain more resources, they are able not only to continue promoting their members' income goals but also to take on lobbying goals if the government is seen as an obstacle to accomplishing their purposes. Confirming that such developmental expansion of objectives actually occurs would require a study of for-profit trade associations over their life cycles.

Organizational goals are important in explaining which business associations develop greater political capacity and mobilize their members for political ends. The regression equations in Table 5.5 treat political capacity as prior to and thus a factor in an organization's attempted member mobilization. In the first column, association political capacity is enhanced by larger annual incomes, greater bureaucratization, a larger proportion of income from members, and greater emphases on both lobbying goals and member income goals (although the latter measure has the weakest standardized effect). That is, both structural and financial resources exert positive effects on the development of substantial internal units for political action, net of collective objectives. In the second column, only political capacity and the income and lobbying goals significantly raise member mobilization. Thus, all the financial and structural

Table 5.5. Regression Analysis of Trade Association Political Actions (Standardized Coefficients).

Independent variables	Dependent variables	
	Political capacity	Members mobilized
Annual revenue (log)	.38[a]	− .08
Bureaucratic structure	.28[b]	.03
Percentage of revenue from members	.19[b]	.03
Political goal	.22[b]	.36[a]
Income goal	.14[c]	.29[a]
Political capacity	—	.29[b]
Multiple R^2	.509[a]	.415[a]

[a]$p < .001$.
[b]$p < .01$.
[c]$p < .05$.

effects on member mobilization are indirect, through their fostering of greater latent capacity to act. Although greater political capacity leads to greater mobilization efforts, the income and lobbying goals are about equally important in promoting greater business association political activation.

Conclusion

Two major trends are apparent from a review of for-profit trade association history. At the population level, an initial period of rapid growth, stimulated by proliferation of differentiated and specialized economic niches, was followed by the present era of stability. Barring an unforeseeable shift in sustaining resources, the national population seems likely to remain at around 2,000 associations. At the organizational level, business associations grew increasingly sophisticated in their ability to monitor and intervene in the political arenas where so many key public policies have important consequences for their members. Employer associations resemble other interest groups in their reaction to changing institutional rules for shaping the enormous volume of legislation, regulation, and legal precedent issuing from the national government over the past generation. Fewer and fewer groups claiming to serve their memberships' interests can afford to forgo some form of involvement in lobbying for favorable treatment by public officials.

Despite the pressing necessity for political activism, fewer than half the national for-profit trade associations asserted a high interest in both economic services for members and public policy influence goals. Youth and its accompanying lack of resources prevent many from pursuing both agendas, although bureaucratic internal structure may compensate enough for some trade groups to specialize in lobbying to the exclusion of member services. To seek both economic and political goals, business associations must acquire substantial resources and sufficient motivation from perceptions that the federal government's policies present obstacles to the organization's goal achievement. Large revenues, particularly from members, and bureaucratic internal structures are first translated into greater political capacity: larger staffs to monitor developments, technical and legal expertise, programs to mobilize members for political influence campaigns. Once in place, such political capacity and high organizational emphasis on economic and political goals are the key factors in collective efforts to contact public officials and agitate through the media on behalf of the association's policy objectives.

To increase our understanding of general trade association dynamics, particularly the interplay of member demands for services and the collective interest in public goods, a broader spectrum of research focused on comparing nonprofit and for-profit trade association members should be conducted. As with many types of organizations, "the vitality and effectiveness of most [trade] associations seem to depend on the strength of membership interest and participation" (Derber, 1984, p. 111). But as organizations of organizations, trade associations may exhibit internal dynamics vastly different from those of associations whose members are individuals. The fact that funding and participation in governance tend to be proportional to the size of member firms initially skews domination toward the larger members. If evidence from other types of associations is any

clue, the exclusion of small members from meaningful governance leads to their detachment and eventual departure to form
more specialized associations focused on their unique concerns. Research that examines how communication networks
and resource contributions operate inside trade associations
would go a long way toward clarifying how intra-associational
political processes operate to strengthen or weaken associational political economies (Knoke, 1990, pp. 85–117).

A close examination of national or regional nonprofit
trade associations reveals a substantial variety of formal governance structures (Young, 1989). At one extreme are associations
whose members are highly differentiated organizations of all
sizes and shapes, such as the American Hospital Association and
the American Symphony Orchestra League, whose only common bond is that they operate in the same industry. Further
along the spectrum are associations, such as the United Way of
America, whose member organizations follow a common model
of operation and share a common credo but remain fully autonomous and locally self-governing. Further still along the spectrum are organizations, such as the Girl Scouts, whose local
member councils are individually incorporated and self-
governing but are chartered by the national organization and
required to adhere to uniform standards of operation. And at
the extreme are organizations, such as the American Cancer
Society, whose affiliate chapters are not separately incorporated
and operate essentially as branch offices of the national
organization.

Research on these highly differentiated structures among
nonprofit trade associations offers unique opportunities for
extending our meager knowledge about trade association behavior, which is largely confined to for-profit organizations. For
example, the nonprofit sector is a good place to test a generalization of the hypothesis that bureaucratized trade associations
place greater emphasis on public policy goals than on their
obligation to provide member services. Given the great variation in centralized versus decentralized governance structures
among nonprofit trade associations, one might expect the char-

tered forms to stress lobbying objectives and the decentralized forms to pursue member-servicing objectives.

Another area for comparative inquiry is the behavior of affiliate members in relation to the trade association's central office. Important questions include how each component contributes to the growth or consolidation of the organization and how the association's structure influences its mode of growth and change. For example, the history of many nonprofit associations reflects the discovery of common needs among similar but unaffiliated organizations in different locales. At one time, the YMCAs in different cities discovered their shared roots and mutual needs and banded together to form a national association (Hopkins, 1951; Zald, 1970). This member-driven expansion dynamic seems to recur frequently among nonprofit trade associations that construct "federated" governance forms, "characterized by autonomous local member organizations that share a common purpose, mission, and history and that have joined together under the auspices of a national organization that articulates this mission at the national level and provides leadership for the movement" (Young, 1989, p. 104). In contrast, more centralized or "corporate" structures, such as that of the Boy Scouts, tend to originate from national centers that stimulate new membership and facilitate association growth by extending the franchise into areas where there are no current members. In effect, the national organization "owns" and controls the branch units. This center-driven expansion dynamic would appear to result in different growth patterns among corporate associations than among the member-driven scenarios characterizing federated organizations. These patterns may also exist among for-profit trade associations, though perhaps in weaker form. Thus, they offer yet another insight into how the nonprofit trade association facilitates, extends, and reshapes the operations of the market economy.

Finally, note that the term *franchise* was used purposely above to refer to the operations of some national nonprofit associations. Some research scholars (Young, 1989, 1992) have begun to draw this parallel between the two sectors, although debate rages over how extensively the franchise model applies in the nonprofit sector. For example, Oster (1992) examined various ways that national nonprofits tax their local subsidiaries for services rendered and attempt to restrict these affiliates' territorial operations. Some of the same motivations behind for-profit franchising seem to drive nonprofit associations: promotion of a uniform, wholesome image so that customers get what they expect no matter where they go; simplification and codification of production processes so that recruiting and training new entrepreneurs and attracting working capital are easier; and division of the market into exclusive geographical areas with noncompeting market shares. Some questions remain unanswered: To what extent is the franchise system an extension of the trade association phenomenon? When do trade associations become so specialized that they become essentially franchiselike systems? And, even more broadly, where do trade associations leave off and more integrated industrial structures begin? The study of trade associations in both the for-profit and nonprofit sectors attests to the fact that, in terms of its basic constituent organizational structures, the market economy is indeed complex and the boundaries between the two sectors even more blurred than most discerning scholars have observed to date.

References

Adler, M. W. "Relations in Governmental and Nonprofit Organizations." In T. D. Connors (ed.), *The Nonprofit Organization Handbook*. (2nd ed.) New York: McGraw-Hill, 1988.

Akey, D. (ed.). *Encyclopedia of Associations*. (18th ed.) Detroit, Mich.: Gale Research, 1983.

Aldrich, H. E., and Staber, U. H. "Organizing Business Interests: Patterns of Trade Association Foundings, Transformations, and Death." In G. Carroll (ed.), *Ecological Models of Organizations*. New York: Ballinger, 1988.

Aldrich, H. E., Staber, U., Zimmer, C., and Beggs, J. J. "Minimalism and Organizational Mortality: Patterns of Disbanding Among U.S. Trade Associations, 1900–1983." In J. V. Singh (ed.), *Organizational Evolution: New Directions*. Newbury Park, Calif.: Sage, 1990a.

Aldrich, H. E., Zimmer, C. R., Staber, U. H., and Beggs, J. J. "Trade Association Foundings in the 20th Century." Paper presented at the meeting of the American Sociological Association, Washington, D.C., Aug. 1990b.

Bauer, R., de Sola Pool, I., and Dexter, L. A. *American Business and Public Policy: The Politics of Foreign Trade*. New York: Atherton Press, 1963.

Berger, S. D. (ed.). *Organizing Interests in Western Europe: Pluralism, Corporatism, and the Transformation of Politics*. Cambridge, England: Cambridge University Press, 1981.

Berry, J. M. *The Interest Group Society*. Boston: Little, Brown, 1984.

Block, F. "The Ruling Class Does Not Rule: Notes on the Marxist Theory of the State." *Socialist Revolution*, 1977, *33*, 6–27.

Bonnett, C. E. *Employers' Associations in the United States: A Study of Typical Associations*. New York: Macmillan, 1922.

Bonnett, C. E. *History of Employers' Associations in the United States*. New York: Vantage Press, 1956.

Colgate, C., Jr., and Evans, L. (eds.). *National Recreational, Sporting and Hobby Organizations of the United States*. (3rd ed.) Washington, D.C.: Columbia Books, 1981.

Colgate, C., Jr., and Fowler, R. L. (eds.). *National Trade and Professional Associations of the United States*. (18th ed.) Washington, D.C.: Columbia Books, 1983.

Commons, J. R. "American Shoemakers, 1648–1895." *Quarterly Journal of Economics*, 1909, *24*, 39–84.

Cox, A., and O'Sullivan, N. (eds.). *The Corporate State: Corporatism and the State Tradition in Western Europe*. Aldershot, Hants, England, and Brookfield, Vt.: Edward Elgar, 1988.

Derber, M. "Employers Associations in the United States." In J. P. Windmuller and A. Gladstone (eds.), *Employers Associations and Industrial Relations: A Comparative Study*. Oxford, England: Clarendon, 1984.

Gable, R. W. "NAM: Influential Lobby or Kiss of Death?" *Journal of Politics*, 1953, *15*, 254–273.

Gais, T. L., Peterson, M. A., and Walker, J. L. "Interest Groups, Iron Triangles, and Representative Institutions in American

National Government." *British Journal of Political Science*, 1984, *14*, 161–185.

Galambos, L. "The American Trade Association Movement Revisited." In H. Yamazaki and M. Miyamoto (eds.), *Trade Associations in Business History*. Tokyo: University of Tokyo Press, 1988.

Hall, P. D. "A Historical Overview of the Private Nonprofit Sector." In W. W. Powell (ed.), *The Nonprofit Sector: A Research Handbook*. New Haven, Conn.: Yale University Press, 1987.

Halliday, T. C., Powell, M. J., and Granfors, M. W. "Minimalist Organizations: Vital Events in State Bar Associations, 1870–1930." *American Sociological Review*, 1987, *52*, 456–471.

Heinz, J. P., Laumann, E. O., Salisbury, R. H., and Nelson, R. L. "Inner Circles or Hollow Cores? Elite Networks in National Policy Systems." *Journal of Politics*, 1990, *52*, 356–390.

Hopkins, C. H. *History of the Y.M.C.A. in North America*. Association Press, 1951.

Kerlinger, F. N., and Pedhazur, E. J. *Multiple Regression in Behavioral Research*. New York: Holt, Rinehart & Winston, 1973.

Knoke, D. "Associations and Interest Groups." *Annual Review of Sociology*, 1986, 12, 1–21.

Knoke, D. *Organizing for Collective Action: The Political Economies of Associations*. New York: Aldine de Gruyter, 1990.

Knoke, D., and Wright-Isak, C. "Individual Motives and Organizational Incentive Systems." *Research in the Sociology of Organizations*, 1982, *1*, 209–254.

Levitan, S. A., and Cooper, M. R. *Business Lobbies: The Public Good and the Bottom Line*. Baltimore, Md.: Johns Hopkins University Press, 1984.

Lindblom, C. E. *Politics and Markets*. New York: Basic Books, 1977.

Lipset, S. M., and Schneider, W. *The Confidence Gap: Business, Labor, and Government in the Public Mind*. New York: Free Press, 1983.

Loomis, B. *The New American Politician: Ambition, Entrepreneurship, and the Changing Face of Political Life*. New York: Basic Books, 1988.

McCraw, T. K. "Business and Government: The Origins of the

Adversary Relationship." *California Management Review*, 1984, *26*, 33–52.

McFarland, A. S. *Common Cause*. Chatham, N.J.: Chatham House, 1984.

McQuaid, K. *Big Business and Presidential Power*. New York: Morrow, 1982.

Mann, T., and Ornstein, N. *The New Congress*. Washington, D.C.: American Enterprise Institute, 1979.

Marsh, D. "On Joining Interest Groups: An Empirical Consideration of the Work of Mancur Olson, Jr." *British Journal of Political Science*, 1976, *6*, 257–271.

Marwell, G., and Ames, R. E. "Experiments on the Provision of Public Goods. I. Resources, Interest, Group Size, and the Free Rider Problem." *American Journal of Sociology*, 1979, *84*, 1335–1360.

Moe, T. *The Organization of Interests: Incentives and the Internal Dynamics of Political Interest Groups*. Chicago: University of Chicago Press, 1980.

Olson, M., Jr. *The Logic of Collective Action: Public Goods and the Theory of Groups*. Cambridge, Mass.: Harvard University Press, 1965.

Oster, S. M. "Nonprofit Organizations as Franchise Operations." *Nonprofit Management and Leadership*, 1992, *2*, 223–238.

Pertschuk, M. *Revolt Against Regulation: The Rise and Pause of the Consumer Movement*. Berkeley: University of California Press, 1982.

Sabato, L. J. *PAC Power: Inside the World of Political Action Committees*. New York: W.W.Norton, 1984.

Salisbury, R. H. "Why No Corporatism in America?" In P. C. Schmitter and G. Lehmbruch (eds.), *Trends Toward Corporatist Intermediation*. Newbury Park, Calif.: Sage, 1979.

Salisbury, R. H. "Interest Representation: The Dominance of Institutions." *American Political Science Review*, 1984, *78*, 64–76.

Schlozman, K. L. "What Accent the Heavenly Chorus? Political Equality in the American Pressure System." *Journal of Politics* 1984, *46*, 1006–1032.

Schlozman, K. L., and Tierney, J. T. *Organized Interests and American Democracy*. New York: HarperCollins, 1986.

Schneiberg, M., and Hollingsworth, J. R. "Can Transaction Cost Economics Explain Trade Associations?" In A. Mashiko, B. Gustafsson, and O. Williamson (eds.), *The Firm as a Nexus of Treaties*. Newbury Park, Calif.: Sage, 1990.

Smucker, B. *The Nonprofit Lobbying Guide: Advocating Your Cause and Getting Results*. San Francisco: Jossey-Bass, 1991.

Staber, U. H. "Corporatism and the Governance Structure of American Trade Associations." *Political Studies*, 1987, *35*, 278–288.

Staber, U., and Aldrich, H. "Trade Association Stability and Public Policy." In R. Hall and R. Quinn (eds.), *Organizational Theory and Public Policy*. Newbury Park, Calif.: Sage, 1983.

Stern, P. M. *The Best Congress Money Can Buy*. New York: Pantheon, 1988.

Streeck, W., and Schmitter, P. C. (eds.). *Private Interest Government: Beyond Market and State*. Newbury Park, Calif.: Sage, 1985.

United Way of America. *People and Events: History of the United Way*. Alexandria, Va.: United Way of America, 1977.

Vogel, D. "Why Businessmen Distrust Their State: The Political Consciousness of American Corporate Executives." *British Journal of Political Science*, 1978, *8*, 45–78.

Vogel, D. *Fluctuating Fortunes: The Political Power of Business in America*. New York: Basic Books, 1989.

Walker, J. L. "The Origins and Maintenance of Interest Groups in America." *American Political Science Review*, 1983, 77, 390–406.

Wilson, G. *Interest Groups*. Oxford, England: Basil Blackwell, 1990.

Windmuller, J. P. "Employer Associations in Comparative Perspective: Organization, Structure, and Administration." In J. P. Windmuller and A. Gladstone (eds.), *Employers Associations and Industrial Relations: A Comparative Study*. Oxford, England: Clarendon, 1984.

Young, D. R. "Local Autonomy in a Franchise Age: Structural Change in National Voluntary Associations." *Nonprofit and Voluntary Sector Quarterly*, 1989, *18*(2), 101–117.

Young, D. R. "An Interview with Peter F. Drucker: Part Two." *Nonprofit Management and Leadership*, 1992, *2*, 295–301.

Young, D. R., and Sleeper, S. *National Associations and Strategic Planning: Results of a Survey.* Stony Brook: Harriman School, State University of New York, 1987.

Zald, M. N. *Organizational Change: The Political Economy of the YMCA.* Chicago: University of Chicago Press, 1970.

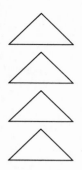

PART TWO

Nonprofits in the Marketplace for Marketplace for Funding and Resources

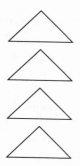

CHAPTER 6

The Market for Human Resources: Comparing Professional Career Paths in the Public, Private, and Nonprofit Sectors

Anne E. Preston

The 1980s were years of institutional change as governments at all levels worked to balance their budgets and nonprofit organizations tightened their belts in response to large cuts in government grants. While a complete analysis of how these changes affected the employees in the nonprofit, for-profit, and government sectors is impossible because of a lack of necessary data, this chapter, which compares career patterns of scientists and engineers in the three sectors during the 1980s, presents a piece of the puzzle.

Unlike studies comparing nonprofit and for-profit employees during the 1970s and early 1980s, which used cross-sectional data, this study uses longitudinal data tracking labor market experiences of scientists and engineers from 1982 to 1989. With these data, I build on the previous studies, which documented relatively low salaries of nonprofit employees, in several ways (see, for example, Mirvis and Hackett, 1983;

Weisbrod, 1983; Preston, 1989). First, I estimate changes in sectoral salary differentials and sectoral salary growth over time, an especially important task given the changes in the fiscal environments facing the three sectors in the 1980s. Equally important, however, I also estimate the extent of sectoral and labor market mobility of nonprofit employees over the period. Finally, I determine whether the low wages paid in the nonprofit sector lead to sectoral exit.

The focus on scientists and engineers, a relatively small and distinct group within the nonprofit labor force, has some important advantages. Scientists and engineers make up a professional work force that has significant job opportunities in all three sectors. In private businesses, scientists and engineers are involved primarily in the direct production process and in research and development. In the government sector, scientists and engineers are employed within all levels of government, in organizations ranging from federal agencies such as the Department of Defense, to state and local colleges and universities, to community hospitals. Similarly, nonprofit organizations employing scientists and engineers encompass private universities and colleges, nonprofit health institutions, and nonprofit research laboratories.

There is an important intersection of the set of government institutions and the set of nonprofit institutions employing scientists and engineers: both sectors include hospitals, colleges, and universities. In 1983, government employees made up just over 60 percent of the scientists and engineers employed in hospitals and postsecondary educational institutions. However, during the 1980s, there was a general retrenchment of the public sector. By 1991, the percentage of scientists and engineers who were employed by government had fallen to 48 percent, and nonprofit scientists and engineers outnumbered government scientists and engineers in these industries.

Because of the wide range of opportunities afforded scientists and engineers, their labor market experiences are probably most relevant to health care employees, since the health care industry houses significant numbers of nonprofit, government, and for-profit organizations. On the other hand, their experiences may be very different from the labor market experiences of social or religious workers or arts organization employees, whose opportunities are generally limited to the nonprofit and, possibly, the government sectors. However, employees of health care institutions make up more than 45 percent of all nonprofit paid employees (Hodgkinson and Weitzman, 1989). Therefore, increased knowledge of the labor market experiences of nonprofit employees who have job opportunities in other sectors is valuable to both scholars and practitioners in the nonprofit sector.

Data for the Study

The data set used to study career patterns of scientists and engineers in the three sectors is the National Science Foundation's Survey of Natural and Social Scientists and Engineers (SSE) (U.S. Bureau of the Census, 1989). The survey, first conducted in 1982 and subsequently in 1984, 1986, and 1989, was sent to a stratified systematic sample of respondents to the 1980 census. Since the census does not directly identify scientists and engineers, the SSE sampled those 1980 census respondents who were employed in one of several occupations related to science and engineering, had four or more years of education (two or more if the occupation was engineering), and were either employed, experienced unemployed, or not in the labor force but had worked in the last five years in an occupation related to science or engineering.

More than 88,000 individuals responded to the 1982 survey, and 69.7 percent of these respondents were employed as scientists or engineers in 1982. Respondents who were American citizens employed in civilian science or engineering jobs in 1982 form the sample that will be analyzed in the remainder of this chapter. For the initial 1982 wave of the SSE, this sample consists of 52,807 scientists and engineers. Information on respondents includes education, training, job characteristics, and job history.

The identification of sectoral affiliation of employer is generated from the question "Which category best describes the type of organization of this job (principal employment)?" Categories assigned a nonprofit status are junior college, two-year college, or technical institute; medical school; four-year college or university other than medical school; hospital or clinic; and nonprofit organization other than hospital or educational institution. There are also categories for federal, state, and local government. However, federal, state, and local government universities and hospitals are likely to be classified as universities or hospitals rather than government organizations. Similarly, for-profit hospitals are likely to be classified as hospitals rather than business or industry. Because for-profit hospitals rarely have a research or teaching component, the number of scientists employed by for-profit hospitals is likely to be small.

The following list shows the percentage of scientists and engineers working in each sector in 1982:

I.	Total nonprofit		16.29
	A.	Total educational	9.99
		1. Junior college	1.61
		2. Four-year college or university	8.38
	B.	Total health-related	3.65
		1. Medical school	1.32
		2. Hospital or clinic	2.33
	C.	Other nonprofit organization	2.65
II.	Business or industry		60.45
III.	Total government		18.53
	A.	Federal	10.69
	B.	State	4.24
	C.	Total local	3.60
		1. Elementary and secondary school systems	1.07
		2. Other local	2.53
IV.	Other, including self-employed		4.72

As the list shows, a majority of scientists and engineers were employed in the private business sector. Of the 16.29 percent of scientists and engineers employed in the nonprofit sector, more than 60 percent were employed by educational institutions, roughly 20 percent by health-related firms, and 16 percent by other types of nonprofit organizations. The government sector employed 18.5 percent of the scientists and engineers working in science or engineering jobs in 1982, and the federal government was the largest government employer.

The group of nonprofit scientists and engineers is contaminated by the unavoidable inclusion of government employees. Estimates from the 1983 Current Population Survey (CPS) reveal that 61.4 percent of scientists and engineers employed in hospitals and postsecondary educational institutions were employed by the government (U.S. Bureau of the Census, 1983). Therefore, roughly 50 percent of the "nonprofit" employees are government workers. However, the extent of contamination differs by industry. In particular, according to the 1983 CPS data, only 26 percent of the scientists and engineers employed in postsecondary education worked for a private institution. And within educational institutions, the percentage of scientists and engineers employed by the government was highest for two-year colleges and technical schools and lowest for four-year colleges and universities. Within the hospital industry, 63 percent of the scientists and engineers were employed in private institutions. By definition, 100 percent of the scientists and engineers employed in the category "nonprofit institutions other than hospitals or educational institutions" were nonprofit employees.

This contamination is likely to blur any distinct sectoral patterns that exist. Any significant differences in sectoral employment that are revealed by these data are likely to underestimate the magnitude of the true differences. However, in order to ensure the validity of the results, the majority of the following analyses are performed on the sample of scientists and engineers employed in the contaminated "nonprofit" sector and on the sample of scientists and engineers employed in the smaller set of "nonprofit organizations other than hospitals or educational institutions." The sectoral differences uncovered tend to be most distinct for the scientists and engineers employed in the smaller generic nonprofit sector.

Table 6.1 presents descriptive statistics on the scientists and engineers by sector of employer in 1982. These statistics reveal that the sectoral differences in labor force characteristics of scientists and engineers are similar to the sectoral differences for all professional employees documented in previous labor market studies (see Preston, 1990, 1991). Furthermore, more detailed statistics, displayed only for selected characteristics below, reveal that these patterns are not driven by the characteristics of employees in nonprofit organizations contaminated with public and for-profit employees. Rather, distinct characteristics of the nonprofit scientists and engineers extend uniformly to scientists and engineers employed by health-related, educational, and generic nonprofit organizations.

Consistent with economywide comparisons revealing that nonprofit employees have 1.55 more years of education than for-profit employees (Preston, 1990), the nonprofit scientist or engineer has a significantly higher level of education than his or her counterparts in the government and for-profit sectors. Within the nonprofit sector, the nonprofit scientists and engineers employed in colleges or universities have the highest level of education; however, nonprofit scientists and engineers in health organizations and in the generic nonprofit organizations also have significantly higher levels of education than their public or for-profit counterparts.

The difference in the gender composition of the nonprofit work force (72 percent female in 1985) and the for-profit work force (56 percent female in 1985) extends to the current sample of scientists and engineers. Furthermore, the percentage of scientists and engineers who are women in each of the three nonprofit groups—educational (26.8 percent), health-related (46.8 percent), and generic (32.7 percent)—is significantly higher than the percentage of women employed in for-profit or government organizations. As in economywide comparisons, the percentage of managers in the nonprofit sector is significantly lower than the percentage of managers in the other two sectors. Furthermore, work activities in the nonprofit sector differ from work activities in the for-profit sector. Scientists and engineers in the nonprofit sector are significantly more likely to teach and to perform basic research than scientists and engineers in the government and for-profit sectors. Finally, salaries of nonprofit employees are significantly lower than salaries of

**Table 6.1. Average Values of Selected Characteristics of
Private Nonprofit, Private For-Profit, and Government Employees
Working in Science and Engineering in 1982.**

	Nonprofit (N = 8,525)	For-profit (N = 30,642)	Government (N = 9,695)
1. Age	41.4	39.3	40.1
	(10.3)	(10.3)	(9.6)
2. Percentage female	32.7	13.8	20.7
3. Percentage never married	16.1	13.3	14.4
4. Percentage with dependent under 5 years of age	20.3	25.7	24.1
5. Years of education after high school	7.5	4.9	5.5
	(2.4)	(2.0)	(2.1)
6. Percentage part-time	10.5	1.1	2.3
7. Percentage working in:			
a. Natural sciences	53.7	21.5	38.2
b. Engineering	15.6	76.4	47.8
c. Social sciences	30.7	2.2	14.3
8. Percentage whose primary work is:			
a. Management	15.4	26.8	31.3
b. Teaching	42.4	0.1	3.4
c. Applied research	8.9	5.5	11.3
d. Basic research	12.5	0.7	3.9
e. Development	2.2	17.4	7.9
9. Percentage paid with federal government funds	34.5	20.7	76.5
10. Annual salary	$27,996.60	$34,625.00	$29,497.50
	(15,055.4)	(13,163.8)	(10,632.0)

Note: For all characteristics, the nonprofit mean is significantly different from both the for-profit mean and the government mean at the 0.1 level.
Numbers in parentheses represent standard deviations.

for-profit or government employees. Within the nonprofit sector, salaries of scientists and engineers employed in the generic
nonprofit organizations are lower than salaries of scientists and
engineers employed in health or educational organizations.

These statistics, however, also point out one important
difference between scientists and engineers and the typical nonprofit professional. Science and engineering occupations are
male-dominated, while the professional occupations in the gen-

eral nonprofit sector tend to be female-dominated. According to the SSE data, only 33 percent of the scientists and engineers employed in the nonprofit sector are female. In contrast, data from the 1985 Current Population Survey reveal that 65.8 percent of professionals in the nonprofit sector are female. Still, the nonprofit scientist or engineer is much more likely to be female than the scientist or engineer employed in the government or for-profit sector.

Sectoral Wage Differences in 1982 and 1989

In order to make more accurate estimates of sectoral salary differentials in 1982, I estimated a cross-sectional salary equation for the sample of respondents to the 1982 survey. The dependent variable is the natural logarithm of the weekly salary. Independent variables include dummy variables for gender, race, marital status, and presence of children under age five in the household. Job characteristics are described with a set of dummy variables representing employment in a management job, occupational affiliation with engineering, occupational affiliation with natural sciences, and federal financing of the respondent's job. Human capital variables include years of post–high school education, years of professional work experience, and dummy variables representing participation in an employer-sponsored training program and participation in another type of training program. Finally, the sectoral variables include a dummy variable for private sector employment, a dummy variable for government employment and a dummy variable for "other" sectors, which include self-employment and employment outside the private, nonprofit, and government sectors defined earlier.

The log salary equation was estimated for all full-time employees and for the two subsamples of full-time employees with five or fewer years of professional experience and full-time employees with more than five years of professional work experience. The results are presented in Table 6.2. In 1982, nonprofit scientists and engineers earned salaries 3.4 percent lower than comparable government employees and 17.8 percent lower than

**Table 6.2. Sectoral Salary Differentials in 1982 and 1989
(Full-Time Survey Respondents).**

	1982	1989
Total sample		
1. Nonprofit/government	− 0.034[a]	0.103[a]
	(0.008)	(0.010)
2. Nonprofit/for-profit	− 0.178[a]	− 0.127[a]
	(0.008)	(0.009)
N	29,427	16,824
Five years or less of experience		
3. Nonprofit/government	− 0.103[a]	0.088[a]
	(0.021)	(0.027)
4. Nonprofit/for-profit	− 0.264[a]	− 0.149[a]
	(0.019)	(0.024)
N	4,996	2,490
More than five years of experience		
5. Nonprofit/government	− 0.016[b]	0.107[a]
	(0.009)	(0.011)
6. Nonprofit/for-profit	− 0.163[a]	− 0.124[a]
	(0.008)	(0.010)
N	24,431	14,334

[a]The coefficient is significant at the .01 level.
[b]The coefficient is significant at the .10 level.

comparable for-profit employees. When the sample is broken down by years of professional experience in the labor force, nonprofit scientists and engineers with five or fewer years of professional experience suffer much more severe wage losses relative to the other two sectors than their more experienced nonprofit counterparts. Nonprofit scientists and engineers with more than five years of professional experience earn salaries 1.6 percent lower and 16.3 percent lower than their government and for-profit counterparts, respectively. However, the nonprofit employees with five or fewer years of work experience earn salaries 10.3 percent lower than comparably inexperienced government scientists and engineers. Furthermore, this same group of nonprofit employees experiences salaries that are 26.4 less than those of comparable for-profit employees.

In keeping with the descriptive statistics, more detailed regression results reveal that the generic nonprofit employees received the lowest wages of all the nonprofit employees in 1982. Therefore, the inclusion of government employees in the educational and health-related nonprofits may be masking the true magnitudes of the observed patterns.

> *Conclusion 1:* In 1982, scientists and engineers in the nonprofit sector, like other nonprofit professionals, received relatively low pay compared to for-profit scientists and engineers and, to some degree, government scientists and engineers. The pay differential for nonprofit scientists and engineers was greatest for the least experienced employees. Within the nonprofit sector, generic nonprofit employees received lower pay than employees in health care or education.

Comparable cross-sectional salary equations for 1989 were estimated for individuals who responded to the 1989 survey. A dummy variable representing employment outside science and engineering was included in this equation, since some of the 1982 respondents had left the science and engineering professions by 1989. The coefficients on the sectoral dummy variables are presented in Table 6.2. According to these estimates, the nonprofit/government differential became positive over the period, and by 1989, nonprofit scientists and engineers earned salaries 10 percent higher than their government counterparts. The nonprofit/for-profit differential shrank from -0.178 to -0.127. These changes in the salary differentials over the seven-year period remained consistent in the two cohorts of respondents who had five or fewer years of professional experience in 1982 (twelve or fewer years in 1989) and who had more than five years of professional experience in 1982. However, while the nonprofit/for-profit differential fell by more than eleven percentage points in the sample of respondents with five or fewer years of experience in 1982, this same differential fell by less than four percentage points in the more experienced sample. Within both subsamples, however, the estimated 1982 non-profit/for-profit salary differential is significantly different from the estimated 1989 salary differential. Again, more detailed regression results reveal that, among the nonprofit scientists and engineers, the greatest relative change in salaries occurred for the generic nonprofit employees.

The change in nonprofit salaries relative to government and for-profit salaries is not necessarily evidence of a change in the relative earnings of nonprofit scientists and engineers over the seven-year period. This change consists of three major components: differing wage distributions of employees entering the sectors, differing wage distributions of employees leaving the sectors, and differences in relative salary growth between sectors. Since the survey follows an initial sample of working scientists and engineers in 1982 and does not add any new scientists and engineers over time, labor force entrants are not captured. The only type of sectoral entry that I can capture is entry due to sectoral switching. While I do not analyze the characteristics of entrants to each sector in relation to incumbents, I do control for the effects of sectoral entry on estimated wage differentials in my discussion below, when I constrain the sample of 1989 scientists and engineers to scientists and engineers who remained employed in the same sector between 1982 and 1989. The remainder of this chapter, therefore, generally focuses on sectoral exit rates and levels of salary growth and their effects on the estimated salary differentials.

Exit and Estimated Salary Differentials

Given the nature of the longitudinal survey, there are several types of exit that can affect the estimated wage differentials: employment exit, sectoral exit, and survey exit.

Employment Exit

Table 6.3 gives rates of exit from employment by sector for individuals initially working in science and engineering jobs in 1982 who remained in the survey through 1989. Nonprofit

Table 6.3. Percentage of 1982 Scientists and Engineers who Left
Employment by 1989 by Reason for Departure and Sector.

	Nonprofit	For-profit	Government
1. Total sample	3.38[a][b]	4.69	2.81
a. Unemployment	0.79[a]	2.24	1.07
b. Family reasons	0.54[c]	0.62	0.34
c. Other reasons[d]	2.07	1.83	1.40

[a]The nonprofit mean is significantly different from the for-profit
mean at the .05 level.

[b]The nonprofit mean is significantly different from the government
mean at the .05 level.

[c]The percentage of nonprofit employees out of the labor force is
significantly different from the percentage of government employees out of
the labor force at the .01 level.

[d]The sample does not include scientists and engineers who retired.

employees were more likely than for-profit employees but less
likely than government employees to remain employed. A disaggregation of exit rates according to the three categories of
reasons—unemployment, family reasons, and other reasons—
gives more information on sectoral differences in exit behavior.
Nonprofit employees were less likely to become unemployed
than employees in the other two sectors. However, they were
more likely than employees in the other two sectors to leave the
labor force.

In order to get more precise estimates of employment exit
that control for personal and occupational characteristics, I use
a Cox proportional hazards model to estimate a competing risk
model of employment exit. The dependent variable is time until
exit from employment. Exit can take two forms: unemployment
or leaving the labor force. The covariates, some of which vary
with time, include a set of personal characteristics, a set of job
and occupational characteristics, and a set of sectoral characteristics. (See Preston, 1992, for a more complete explanation of
the theoretical model underlying this empirical model of occupational exit.)

The employee characteristic covariates give information
on demographics, human capital accumulation, quality of the

match between the individual's skills and the skills required by the occupation, and family characteristics. Years of post–high school education and dummy variables representing race and sex are included in the specification. In addition, to more fully describe human capital, I include a dummy variable representing participation in employer-sponsored training programs during the two-year period immediately prior to potential exit. The deviation between actual salary and predicted salary, generated from a log salary equation estimated for the sample of all working scientists and engineers in the time immediately prior to possible exit, measures the quality of the occupational match.

Family characteristics are expected to affect exit, particularly for women. Therefore, the equations for the hazard of exit from employment include dummy variables representing being married, spouse being present, and dependents under five living with the respondent during the period prior to the exit decision.

Occupational categories identified within the survey correspond closely to twenty-eight academic fields, such as biology, chemistry, and economics. Differences in skill depreciation rates and financial opportunities across fields may be particularly important determinants of exit. Financial opportunities are measured by the growth in doctoral salary levels by field over the two-year period immediately prior to potential exit (National Science Foundation, 1977–1986).

Skill depreciation rates, which are closely related to growth in knowledge, are measured by the real value of average annual federal expenditures on basic research within a field in the two-year period prior to possible exit (National Science Foundation, 1959–1986). Because the change in skill depreciation rate since the time of occupational choice may also affect exit, I also include the average annual change in real federal basic research expenses from the time of the schooling investment decision until the time immediately prior to possible exit. I include a dummy variable representing federal financing of the individual's job. Finally, the covariates representing sectoral employment are dummy variables representing government and nonprofit employment in the period preceding potential exit.

The effects of sectoral employment on probability of exit for the two different types of exit are presented in Table 6.4. The table gives the ratio of the probability of exit of nonprofit employees to the probability of exit of for-profit employees for the total sample, for employees with five years or less of work experience, and for employees with more than five years of work experience. When this ratio is less than one, the probability of exit is lower for nonprofit than for-profit employees; when it is greater than one, the probability of exit is larger for nonprofit employees. For all three samples, the nonprofit scientist or engineer is less likely to become unemployed than the for-profit scientist or engineer after controlling for other possible determinants of employment exit. In addition, while there is no difference in the probability of leaving the labor force for experienced employees, nonprofit employees with five years or less of professional experience are two and a half times as likely to leave the labor force as for-profit employees with five years or less of professional experience.

The table also gives the ratio of the probability of exit of nonprofit employees to the probability of exit of government

Table 6.4. Effects of Sectoral Location on Probability of Exit.

	Unemployed	Out of labor force
Nonprofit/for-profit		
1. Total sample	0.305[a]	1.188
2. Five years or less of experience	0.478[a]	2.490[a]
3. More than five years of experience	0.296[a]	0.949
Nonprofit/government		
4. Total sample	0.707[b]	2.036[a]
5. Five years or less of experience	1.386	2.846[a]
6. More than five years of experience	0.620[c]	1.695[b]

[a]Initial coefficients were significant at the .01 level.
[b]Initial coefficients were significant at the .10 level.
[c]Initial coefficients were significant at the .05 level.

Table 6.5. Percentage Change in Probability of Exit Due to Salary Level 20 Percent Below Expected Level.

	Unemployed	Out of labor force
1. Nonprofit employees	0.11[a]	0.13[b]
2. For-profit employees	0.07[b]	0.01
3. Government employees	0.22[c]	− 0.01

[a]Initial coefficients were significant at the .01 level.
[b]Initial coefficients were significant at the .05 level.
[c]Initial coefficients were significant at the .10 level.

employees. Nonprofit employees with more than five years of experience are less likely to become unemployed than their counterparts in the government sector. However, there are no significant differences in the probability of becoming unemployed for the inexperienced subsample. Nonprofit employees are significantly more likely than government employees to leave the labor force, and this difference is most extreme for employees with five years or less of labor force experience.

The employment exit equations were run separately for the three sectoral subsamples to determine whether employment exit is sensitive to lower than expected salary levels and whether that sensitivity differs across sectors. The coefficient on the salary residual in these equations was used to calculate the effect of earning a salary 20 percent below the expected level on the probability of exit. These estimates are presented in Table 6.5. In the categories of exit to unemployment, the exit behavior of nonprofit employees is more responsive to low salaries than the exit behavior of for-profit employees but not as responsive as the exit behavior of government employees. Furthermore, in the case of labor force exit, nonprofit employees are the only group whose exit behavior is affected by low salaries. According to these results, the labor market behavior of the nonprofit employee is highly sensitive to wage rates.

Conclusion 2: The nonprofit sector is losing a relatively large number of employees, especially those with low levels of experience, to labor force departures, and the probability of labor force departure of nonprofit employees is positively related to low wages.

Sectoral Exit

Sectoral exit is another force that may have led to the change in the nonprofit/for-profit salary differential between 1982 and 1989. Table 6.6 gives descriptive statistics on sectoral switching over the seven-year period for the individuals continuously employed throughout that period. Sectoral switching was by far most common for nonprofit employees; 18.6 percent of scientists and engineers employed in the nonprofit sector in 1982 had switched to other sectors by 1989, while only 10.8 percent of for-profit employees and 13.3 percent of government employees had switched sectors. Furthermore, almost 35 percent of the nonprofit employees who had five years or less of professional work experience in 1982 had switched to the for-profit, government, or self-employed sector by 1989.

Interestingly, this high level of sectoral exit is not a consequence of the large number of scientists and engineers employed in educational institutions who were either leaving postdoctoral positions or responding to tenure denials. Within the nonprofit sector, the highest degree of sectoral exit occurred among employees in generic nonprofit organizations. For this group of nonprofit scientists and engineers, 33.5 percent of the total sample and 48 percent of the inexperienced sample had left the nonprofit sector by 1989. The second highest degree of sectoral exit (25.4 percent of the total sample left by 1989) occurred among employees in hospitals or clinics, the category with the second largest percentage of nonprofit employees. The lowest degree of sectoral exit (9.6 percent of the sample left by 1989) occurred among employees of junior colleges, two-year colleges, or technical institutes, the category with the lowest percentage of nonprofit employees.

I explored the high levels of sectoral exit of nonprofit scientists and engineers by estimating a multivariate sectoral

Table 6.6. Sector Switching of Scientists and Engineers by
Sectoral Location in 1982 (in Percentage).

	All employees	Five years or less of experience	More than five years of experience
1. For-profit, 1982			
a. For-profit, 1989	89.27	89.32	89.26
b. Nonprofit, 1989	2.31	2.45	2.28
c. Government, 1989	2.80	3.43	2.69
2. Nonprofit, 1982			
a. For-profit, 1989	8.67	18.10	7.44
b. Nonprofit, 1989	81.43	65.61	83.50
c. Government, 1989	5.09	8.60	4.64
3. Government, 1982			
a. For-profit, 1989	6.90	10.07	6.47
b. Nonprofit, 1989	3.26	3.24	3.26
c. Government, 1989	86.68	84.47	86.98

Note: Percentages do not total 100 because category "other" (predominantly self-employed individuals) has been omitted.

exit equation on the sample of full-time nonprofit employees in 1982 who remained employed throughout the period. I used a Cox proportional hazard equation, and the dependent variable was time until exit from the nonprofit sector. The time-varying covariates included a measure of the expected salary differential between private sector/government work and nonprofit work. This differential is the difference between the predicted wage of the nonprofit scientist or engineer if he or she were employed outside the nonprofit sector and his or her actual wage. Personal characteristic covariates include age, years of post–high school education, a set of dummy variables representing gender, race, marital status, and the presence of children under five, and dummy variables representing social scientists and natural scientists. Job characteristic covariates include dummy variables representing work outside science and engineering, managerial work activities, participation in employer-sponsored training programs, participation in other training programs, and federal financing of the job.

The results of the sectoral exit equation are presented in Table 6.7. The significant coefficients in the sectoral exit equation generally reveal that scientists and engineers with more opportunities outside the nonprofit sector are more likely to leave that sector. In particular, engineers, who are predominantly employed in the for-profit sector, are more likely than natural and social scientists to leave the nonprofit sector. In addition, working outside science or working in management jobs increases the probability of exit from the nonprofit sector, probably because skills in these types of jobs are most transferable. Participation in employer-sponsored training programs increases the probability of exit, a pattern that may occur because the skills taught in these programs are not specific to the nonprofit sector. Finally, federal financing of the respondent's job increases the probability of sectoral exit, possibly because of increased exposure to the federal government and because this funding signals a widespread perception of the importance of the individual's work.

Most significant for the current study is that the expected wage differential and age are significant and independent determinants of sectoral exit. Higher expected wage increases due to movement to the government or private sector increase the probability of sectoral exit, and younger employees are more likely to leave the nonprofit sector. More specifically, a one standard deviation increase in the expected wage differential (0.39) from its mean of 0.07 increases the probability of exit by 10.5 percent. Similarly a one standard deviation decrease in age (9.4 years) from the average age of 44.6 years increases the probability of sectoral exit by more than 800 percent.

> *Conclusion 3:* The nonprofit sector is losing a relatively large number of employees to sectoral exit, and within the nonprofit sector, sectoral exit is highest for employees of generic nonprofit institutions and hospitals. The probability of sectoral exit, which is especially high for inexperienced employees, is positively related to the expected increase in salary resulting from exit.

Table 6.7. Determinants of Sectoral Exit of Nonprofit Employees (Coefficients and Standard Errors).

1. Expected salary differential between government or private sector work and nonprofit work	0.257[a] (0.087)
2. Age	− 0.228[a] (0.012)
3. Years of post–high school education	0.018 (0.022)
4. Female	0.047 (0.125)
5. Black	− 0.187 (0.267)
6. Hispanic	0.116 (0.412)
7. Other nonwhite	0.660[a] (0.160)
8. Married, spouse present	− 0.091 (0.120)
9. Children under five years of age	0.106 (0.123)
10. Social scientist	− 0.328[b] (0.139)
11. Natural scientist	− 0.534[a] (0.122)
12. Working outside science and engineering	0.598[c] (0.341)
13. Managerial activities	0.318[a] (0.113)
14. Participation in employer-sponsored training program	0.278[b] (0.111)
15. Participation in other training program	0.129 (0.950)
16. Federal financing of job	0.516[a] (0.094)
17. Log of the likelihood	− 3105.42

[a]Estimated coefficient is significantly different from 0 at the .01 level.
[b]Estimated coefficient is significantly different from 0 at the .05 level.
[c]Estimated coefficient is significantly different from 0 at the .10 level.

Survey Exit

Survey exit rates are comparable across the three sectors. Of the responding scientists and engineers in 1982, 49 percent of the for-profit, 48 percent of the nonprofit, and 45 percent of the government scientists and engineers did not respond to the survey by 1989. In Cox proportional hazard models of survey exit, similar to those estimated for employment exit, nonprofit scientists and engineers are slightly more likely than government or for-profit scientists and engineers to exit the survey. However, survey exit equations run on the separate sectoral samples reveal that survey exit by nonprofit scientists and engineers was unrelated to salaries. On the other hand, for-profit scientists and engineers with higher than expected wages were more likely to exit the survey by 1989. Therefore, this pattern of survey exit by for-profit employees may contribute to the estimated reduction in the nonprofit/for-profit salary differential over the seven-year period.

Effects of Exit and Entry on Salary Differentials

In order to determine how exit affects the change in the estimated nonprofit salary differentials, the cross-sectional salary equation for 1982 was reestimated, deleting all respondents who had exited the survey, employment, or the sector of origin by 1989. The new estimates of the 1982 cross-sectional nonprofit salary differentials are presented in Table 6.8. Similarly, to control for the effects of sectoral entry on the estimated salary changes, I reestimated the 1989 nonprofit salary equation excluding all respondents who had changed sector of employment over the seven-year period. The new estimates of the 1989 nonprofit salary differentials are also presented in Table 6.8.

Eliminating survey and employment leavers and sector switchers does reduce the change in the nonprofit/government salary differential over the seven-year period by approximately four percentage points for the inexperienced sample and three percentage points for the experienced sample. The change in

Table 6.8. Sectoral Salary Differentials in 1982 and 1989,
Excluding All Survey, Sectoral, or Employment Leavers.

	1982	1989
1. Nonprofit/government	− 0.009	0.086[a]
	(0.011)	(0.011)
2. Nonprofit/for-profit	− 0.148[a]	− 0.134[a]
	(0.010)	(0.009)
N	14,253	14,334
Five years or less of experience		
3. Nonprofit/government	− 0.069[a]	0.080[a]
	(0.029)	(0.076)
4. Nonprofit/for-profit	− 0.202[a]	− 0.185[a]
	(0.027)	(0.026)
N	2,006	2,490
More than five years of experience		
5. Nonprofit/government	0.0003	0.091[a]
	(0.012)	(0.011)
6. Nonprofit/for-profit	− 0.143[a]	− 0.128[a]
	(0.012)	(0.010)
N	12,247	14,334

[a]The coefficient is significant at the .01 level.

the nonprofit/government salary differential, however, remains above nine percentage points for both samples.

Once leavers and switchers are omitted from the 1982 and 1989 samples, the change in the estimated nonprofit/for-profit salary differential between 1982 and 1989 estimated in Table 6.2 falls by more than 70 percent. According to Table 6.8, the recalculated differential is only 1.7 percentage points for the inexperienced sample and 1.5 percentage points for the experienced sample.

Conclusion 4: The relative increase in nonprofit salaries compared to for-profit salaries between 1982 and 1989 is to a large extent due to relatively high levels of labor force, survey, and sectoral exit of low-salary nonprofit employees.

Sectoral Differences in Wage Growth in the 1980s

Salary growth equations were estimated to determine whether the changes in the nonprofit salary differentials were due to high relative salary growth in the nonprofit sector. These equations were estimated for the pooled cross sections of respondents to the 1984, 1986, and 1989 surveys. The dependent variable is the natural logarithm of the current salary less the natural logarithm of the salary given in the previous survey. Independent variables are changes in the independent variables included in the cross-sectional salary level equations estimated above and dummy variables representing year of response. The sectoral change variables include dummy variables for every possible sectoral location combination over any two survey periods.

Estimated sectoral differences in salary growth are presented in Table 6.9. The table gives estimates of the difference in salary growth between individuals who remained employed in the nonprofit sector and individuals who remained employed in the for-profit sector. In all three samples, the point estimates of the nonprofit/for-profit salary growth differential are positive yet insignificant at conventional levels. In the inexperienced sample, however, the differential of 0.02 is marginally significant at the .15 level, possibly reflecting a modest increase in relative salaries of inexperienced nonprofit scientists and engineers.

According to the results presented next in the table, over the period between 1982 and 1989, scientists and engineers employed in the nonprofit sector experienced roughly 4 percent higher salary growth than scientists and engineers in the government sector over a two-year period. This nonprofit/government salary growth differential was slightly higher for the inexperienced employees (5.8 percent) than for the more experienced employees (3.8 percent).

> *Conclusion 5:* The large change in the cross-sectional estimates of the nonprofit/government salary differential for scientists and engineers is largely due to higher salary growth for nonprofit scientists and

Table 6.9. Percentage Differences in Salary Growth of Nonprofit,
For-Profit, and Government Scientists and Engineers, 1982–1989
(with Standard Errors).

	Total sample	Five years or less of experience	More than five years of experience
1. Nonprofit/for-profit	0.007	0.020	0.007
	(0.005)	(0.013)	(0.005)
2. Nonprofit/government	0.042[a]	0.058[a]	0.038[a]
	(0.005)	(0.015)	(0.006)
N	54,805	8,002	46,803

Note: The estimated annual growth is for two-year periods between 1982 and 1989.

[a]Coefficients are significant at the .01 level.

engineers during the 1980s. During this period, salaries of scientists and engineers employed in the nonprofit sector caught up with and surpassed salaries of scientists and engineers employed in the government sector.

Conclusion

Empirical analyses of the career paths of scientists and engineers in the 1980s reveal some interesting sectoral patterns. Nonprofit scientists and engineers earned salaries roughly 14 percent lower than their private for-profit sector counterparts during the period from 1982 to 1989. Generally, the salaries of nonprofit scientists and engineers did not gain ground relative to the salaries of the for-profit scientists and engineers. However, there is modest evidence that salary growth rates of nonprofit employees with five years or less of professional work experience may have been roughly 2 percent higher over a two-year period than salary growth rates of inexperienced for-profit employees. The reduction in the magnitude of the negative nonprofit salary differential estimated with these data between 1982 and 1989 was largely due to high sectoral and employment exit rates of nonprofit employees who were receiving relatively low wages.

The salaries of nonprofit scientists and engineers who remained employed in the sector, however, caught up to and surpassed salaries of their government counterparts. In 1982, salaries of nonprofit scientists and engineers were approximately 3 percent below the salaries of their government counterparts. During the period from 1982 to 1989, when governments at all levels were working to balance budgets, the salary growth rate of nonprofit scientists and engineers was approximately 4 percent higher than the growth rate of scientists and engineers employed by the government. By 1989, nonprofit employees earned salaries roughly 9 percent higher than salaries of comparable government employees. Probably the most striking results document the high degree of mobility that nonprofit employees exercised in response to low salaries. Nonprofit employees had the highest rate of labor force exit, and they were the only group of employees who left the labor force in response to lower than expected wages. In addition, sectoral exit was higher for nonprofit scientists and engineers than for employees in either of the other two sectors, and sectoral exit for inexperienced employees was double the sectoral exit rate for any other group of scientists and engineers. Within the broad nonprofit sector, sectoral exit was highest for employees of generic nonprofit institutions and lowest for employees of junior colleges and technical institutes, the category most heavily contaminated by the inclusion of government employees. Finally, sectoral exit is significantly related to the expected wage gain resulting from exit.

The pattern in which young nonprofit employees who earn relatively low wages leave the sector for higher-paying government or for-profit jobs supports the hypothesis that young scientists and engineers are using the nonprofit sector as a training ground. These scientists and engineers working in the nonprofit sector may intentionally give up wages in return for the opportunity to learn valuable skills that they can use in all three sectors.

Clearly, the nonprofit scientist and engineer of the 1980s

stands in stark contrast to the traditional view of the immobile nonprofit employee who sacrifices lifetime salary gains for the intrinsic rewards of the job. The marketability of skills outside the nonprofit sector may distinguish nonprofit scientists and engineers from other nonprofit professionals in their ability to switch sectors without changing occupations. However, it remains a fact that low nonprofit salaries are also leading to high labor force exit rates, a pattern that could also be evident in nonprofit occupations that do not have obvious for-profit or government counterparts. Furthermore, as the nonprofit sector faces increased competition from government and private industry, the relevance of the mobility patterns of this group of employees to the entire nonprofit labor force may be increasing.

References

Hodgkinson, V. A., and Weitzman, M. S. *Dimensions of the Independent Sector: A Statistical Profile*. Washington, D.C.: INDEPENDENT SECTOR, 1989.

Mirvis, P. H., and Hackett, E. J. "Work and Work Force Characteristics in the Nonprofit Sector." *Monthly Labor Review*, Apr. 1983, pp. 3–12.

National Science Foundation. *Federal Funds for Basic Research and Development*. Surveys of Science Resource Series. Washington, D.C.: National Science Foundation, 1959–1986.

National Science Foundation. *Survey of Doctoral Recipients*. Surveys of Science Resource Series. Washington, D.C.: National Science Foundation, 1977–1986.

Preston, A. "The Nonprofit Sector in a For-Profit World." *Journal of Labor Economics*, Fall 1989, pp. 438–463.

Preston, A. "Changing Labor Market Patterns in the Nonprofit and For-Profit Sectors: Implications for Nonprofit Management." *Nonprofit Management and Leadership*, Fall 1990, pp. 15–28.

Preston, A. "Selectivity Corrected Wage Differentials When Human Capital Is Sector Specific: The Case of the Male Nonprofit Wage Differential." Unpublished manuscript, 1991.

Preston, A. "Why Have All the Women Gone? A Study of Exit of Women from the Science and Engineering Occupations." Unpublished manuscript, 1992.

U.S. Bureau of the Census. "Current Population Survey," unpublished data, Washington, D.C., 1983.

U.S. Bureau of the Census. "Survey of Natural and Social Scientists and Engineers," unpublished data, Washington, D.C., 1989.

Weisbrod, B. "Nonprofit and Proprietary Sector Behavior: Wage Differentials Among Lawyers." *Journal of Labor Economics*, July 1983, pp. 246–263.

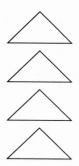

CHAPTER 7

How and Why Nonprofit Organizations Obtain Capital

Howard P. Tuckman

This chapter explores the reasons why nonprofits want capital, why they find it difficult to obtain, and how they can improve their chances for obtaining capital funds externally. Section 1 discusses the reasons for the growth of the nonprofit sector and its continued need for capital. Section 2 describes the critical role that capital plays in production. Section 3 identifies three levels of capital access—internal funding, funding from non-lending institutions, and funding from capital markets—and identifies the criteria that are required to acquire capital at each

Note: The author benefited from discussions and correspondence with Carol Babb, Cyril Chang, Chip Dudley, Katherine Moy, Alex Oliver, M. Ross, Richard Rogers, R. E. Smith, J. Tuckman, Gid Smith, Steven Ulm, Michael Vollman, and Lucas Yancey III. He also acknowledges helpful comments of David Hammack, B. Harvey, Dennis R. Young, and the participants in the Case Western Reserve conference on Nonprofit Organizations in a Market Economy. The responsibility for the ideas expressed here is his own.

level. Section 4 examines the consequences of borrowing for a nonprofit, while section 5 sets forth the criteria that lending institutions ordinarily use in deciding whether to lend to a nonprofit. Section 6 considers the factors that determine when a nonprofit may enter capital markets, and section 7 offers a profile of the nonprofits most likely to be successful in obtaining a loan. The chapter concludes with a brief summary of the analysis.

Reasons for the Growth of the Nonprofit Sector

The nonprofit sector in the United States enjoyed considerable growth during the 1980s, although there were differences in growth rates among the industries and markets that the sector comprises (Ben-Ner and Van Hoomissen, 1990; Hodgkinson and Weitzman, 1989, pp. 4–5). Several trends are responsible for this growth. Nonprofits benefited from a widespread structural shift in the economy, away from manufacturing and toward greater demand for services. The shift was particularly strong in the health area, but expansion also occurred in the number of educational institutions, nonprofit libraries, and social science agencies. The nation's apparent willingness to direct its funding toward health led to a substantial growth of this sector, from 7.4 percent of gross national product in 1980 to more than 12 percent in 1990. This benefited the nonprofit sector because of the large percentage of nonprofit health organizations dispensing health care services (U.S. Bureau of the Census, 1990).

The demand for nonprofit services was enhanced by growth in the number of two-wage-earner families. This left a vacuum in the home that led to increased market demand for day care, nursing homes, and other care providers. It also affected the demand for alcohol and drug treatment centers, counseling, and other services that address the problems created by reduced provision of services in the home. Not surprisingly, the demand for the services of religious institutions also increased (Hodgkinson and Weitzman, 1989, p. 73).

Further accounting for the expansion of the nonprofit sector was the movement away from federal government finance and provision of services under the Reagan and Bush administrations. This policy change increased the demands on nonprofits to provide services (Salamon, 1987, p. 110). The Bush-Reagan decision to deemphasize federal funding of social services was accelerated by the revenue-reducing impact of the recession of 1990 and its effects on federal, state, and local budgets (U.S. Office of Management and Budget, 1992). The resulting crunch on public revenues caused substantial cutbacks in government-provided social services and created an impetus toward "third-party government" (Salamon, 1987).

In addition, many services that the public has sought in the last decade are of a complex nature. Nonprofits enjoy an advantage in the delivery of complex services. Consumers may be unable to judge their quality or may finance them on behalf of a third party, such as a parent entering a nursing home. For these reasons, private donors and governments are reluctant to entrust provision of these services to the for-profit sector, because the profit motive gives for-profits an incentive to cheat, and monitoring their performance is costly.

Hansmann (1987) has suggested that the nonprofit is a preferred provider in these situations because it has less incentive to cheat and hence is less costly to monitor. In essence, the consumer places a trust in this entity that is not extended to for-profit providers. The increased need for complex social services—ranging from environmental studies to drug treatment programs to shelters for the homeless to training for inner-city youths—fuels the demand for the services of nonprofits. This trust is apparently extended to nonprofit provision of private goods as well as public goods. The evidence indicates that a majority of nonprofits produce a mix of both private and public goods and that the public patronizes nonprofits for both types of goods, even when for-profits are available from which to purchase the private goods (Tuckman, Chang, and Seenprachawong, 1992).

As a consequence of these trends, the number of nonprofits rose from 1.1 million in 1977 to 1.3 million in 1987, total employment in the sector rose from 9.6 million to 13.9 million, and the sector's share of national income increased from $93.6

billion to $247 billion (Hodgkinson and Weitzman, 1989). Given this impressive growth record, the nonprofit sector has had and will continue to have a strong need for capital to enable it to survive and grow. The effects on individual incomes of the recession that began in 1990, a tight federal budget, rising state and local deficits, increased worldwide demand for capital, and the large number of organizations competing for funds create an environment in which nonprofits must learn to compete for capital with governments, for-profits, and individuals. In the sections that follow, we discuss what the administrators and managers of nonprofit organizations should know if they wish · to compete for capital.

The Role of Capital

Economists distinguish between the investment and consumption of financial resources (Hyman, 1989, p. 25). A nonprofit's financial resources provide it with the purchasing power that it needs to acquire either capital or operating resources. When a nonprofit invests in equipment, machinery, structures, tools, vehicles, or the skills of its labor force, it engages in capital investment. Alternatively, when it uses funds to pay for salaries or fringe benefits, to purchase advertising, to maintain a building, or to pay for utilities, it is consuming its resources. Both types of expenditures are critical for the operation of a nonprofit, but only expenditures that involve purchase of items with a life-span beyond a year or two and that contribute to production are capital investment.

Because capital is needed for production, nonprofits that are unable to accumulate resources for this purpose have difficulty producing goods and services efficiently. Firms that produce goods and services using only labor inputs are at a distinct disadvantage to those that combine capital and labor in production. As the number of units of labor employed in production increases, limits are reached on how much additional labor can contribute. Because of what economists call "diminishing returns to production," at some point, without the addition of further units of capital, adding one more unit of labor leads to a negative increase in a firm's output (Hyman, 1989, p. 189). At that point, a firm cannot produce additional units of goods or services without additional infusions of capital. Thus, access to capital is strongly related to growth in the productivity of labor.

Because capital investment helps to augment labor productivity, it is essential for ensuring the growth and survival of a firm. Inadequate access to capital can mean that an organization is unable to obtain the technology needed to become more efficient. Financial resources are also necessary for capital investment for a nonprofit to respond to increases in the demand for its services, to replace obsolete or spent equipment, to acquire new technologies, to diversify program offerings, or to increase its efficiency or enhance the quality of its offerings (Chang and Tuckman, 1990).

In practice, lending institutions are reluctant to provide organizations with loans to meet their operational needs because loans are made with the expectation that they will be repaid. Ordinarily, both the interest and the loan principal are paid back out of revenues. Because a firm's revenue is subject to random forces, however, lenders also require the availability of collateral to secure a loan. Collateral is something of value that can be pledged by the nonprofit as security for a loan. Buildings and equipment have value as collateral because they can be sold if an organization is unable to repay its loan or if it defaults on its interest payments. Similarly, pledges of the property of the members of a board of directors may also be used for the purposes of securing a loan. Sale of the asset for which funds were borrowed or of assets pledged by board members does not guarantee a lender full recovery of the value of a loan, but it is preferable to the case where no assets can be reclaimed. Where loans are used to meet operational needs, no assets are available for reclamation and, hence, most lenders are reluctant to make these types of loans.

Capital Sources of Nonprofits

This section discusses three levels of access to capital: internal funding, funding from nonlending institutions, and funding from capital markets.

Internal Funds

Internal funds are an important source of the financial resources used by nonprofits for capital investment (Chang and
Tuckman, 1990). This source has several advantages. Funds can
be made available for investment relatively quickly, information
on the operation of the nonprofit does not have to be divulged
to external parties, and accountability for the use of the funds is
primarily to the board of directors. The amount of funds available for investment is known in advance, and internal reserves
can serve as collateral in the event that the nonprofit chooses to
seek external funding. Whether nonprofits draw down equity
when they need funds depends on the terms under which funds
can be obtained from other sources, the liquidity of their assets,
the restrictions placed on disposition of their holdings, their
financial position, and the preferences of their management. At
present, surprisingly little information is available on the uses of
nonprofit equity.

    For these reasons, many nonprofits consciously strive to
accumulate internal surpluses. In a study of 4,730 charitable
nonprofits that filed a Form 990 tax return with the IRS in 1983,
for example, Chang and Tuckman (1990) found that more than
86 percent of them reported a surplus of revenues over expenditures. This surplus increased the value of these organizations
and provided financial resources for present and future capital
investment. While there are differences by organizational type
in the average surplus and margin of earnings of nonprofits, the
vast majority of nonprofits in the sample earned surpluses, the
average operating margin (surplus divided by revenues) for
these nonprofits was 10 percent, and most of these organizations accumulated equity over several years. Tuckman and
Chang's analysis (1992b) of 1985 tax data for 6,168 nonprofits
confirmed the validity of these findings.

    The cash flow of nonprofits represents an important
source of capital, especially for organizations lacking either
endowment funds or the ability to borrow. Cash flow differs
from surplus in that it includes depreciation while surplus
excludes it. Data are not available by financial source on the

percentage of capital investments funded by nonprofits, but funds accumulated out of cash flow are almost certainly a major source of capital funds. To accumulate internal funds, the management of a nonprofit must be willing to trade off expenditures on current program needs in favor of the achievement of future program goals.

A nonprofit generates surplus by holding its expenditures below revenues. This means that it must spend fewer dollars on current programs than it might otherwise desire in order to generate surpluses. Some theories of the behavior of nonprofit managers imply that they use all their revenue pursuing market share, their own well-being, and/or improvement of program quality. To a large extent these theories ignore nonprofits' need to accumulate capital, beguiled by the fact that nonprofits do not have to earn profits for shareholders. Tuckman and Chang (1992b) provide a model of nonprofit behavior based on the assumption that accumulation of financial resources is a goal of administrators. Their empirical findings provide evidence that nonprofit administrators value equity accumulation along with other goals.

Funds can also be obtained for capital investment from a nonprofit's endowments or from its general or working capital funds. Most nonprofits account for accumulated funds in one of two ways. One approach reports surpluses using bookkeeping entries such as "working capital" or "retained earnings." This method is similar to the one used by for-profit organizations. The alternative approach creates separate endowment funds for building, maintenance, and so on. Each fund reports its income, expenditures, assets, and liabilities and balances these entries at the end of the accounting period to arrive at a surplus or deficit for the account. An advantage of the second method is that it provides assurance to donors that their gifts and bequests will be restricted to specific purposes. It also allows nonprofits to set funds aside for specific purposes. While nonprofit boards can restrict the use of financial resources without setting up separate funds for this purpose, and they can also use unrestricted funds for capital investment, the segregated funds approach provides additional guarantees that funds will be used for explicit purposes. To date, research has not been available as to whether the accounting system that a nonprofit uses affects the amount of resources that it has available for capital investment. Nor are there accurate data to show the dollar value of nonprofit endowment funds in the United States and the division of nonprofit funds between restricted and unrestricted uses.

It is possible to compute the average net worth of nonprofits from IRS tax data, bearing in mind that this measure is limited by its use of book rather than market value. Chang and Tuckman (1990, p. 123) report that the average equity of the 6,168 nonprofits in their sample was $3.4 million at the beginning of the 1985 taxable year. Even when the largest nonprofits are removed from their sample, a majority of remaining nonprofits have a positive equity position, and a similar conclusion is reached when the data are weighted to reflect the population of charitable nonprofits.

Data from the religious sector provide some insight into the capital expenditure share of total expenditures. A study reported in Hodgkinson and Weitzman (1989, pp. 191–192) showed that in 1986, 294,271 congregations spent more than $4 billion dollars for construction, capital improvements, and acquisition of new property. This represented 8.4 percent of the total expenditures made by these organizations in 1986. Capital expenditures represented 6.3 percent of total expenditures for congregations of fewer than 100 members, 7.6 percent of the total for those with between 100 and 300 members, and 8.9 percent of the total for those with 400 or more members. The largest source of revenue for congregations was individual giving (81.5 percent), while revenues from endowment and investment funds represented only 1.9 percent of the total. Unfortunately, these data do not specify the funding sources for capital investment projects, and it is not possible to determine the extent to which congregations finance capital expenditures from internal funds.

Loans and Grants from Nonlending Institutions

When nonprofits seek capital externally, they enter a realm where the financial behavior of other nonprofit organizations must be explicitly taken into account. The major nonlending sources of capital are individuals, other nonprofits, governments, foundations, and corporations. (Owner finance of real property acquisition is also important, as are various leasing strategies, but these are complex and will not be dealt with in this chapter.) Successful access to the capital funds provided by these sources depends, among other things, on the availability of information as to which entities are willing to support a nonprofit's mission, ability to frame requests that respond to donor expectations, evidence of successful service delivery in the past, and a mission that donors perceive as valuable.

Individuals. Individual giving is an important source of capital for nonprofit organizations. Data are not available on the amounts that individuals give to finance capital acquisitions, but the American Association of Fund-Raising Counsel (1990) reports that charitable giving by individuals exceeded $96.4 billion in 1989 and that bequests provided another $6.6 billion for charitable uses. Not all of these funds went to charitable nonprofits, but the data indicate that individuals favored education, health, and religious organizations in their giving. The contribution of individuals is substantially greater when the value of volunteer time is added to the total. As reported by Hodgkinson and Weitzman (1989), the value of the time that volunteers contributed to charitable nonprofits in 1987 was $149.8 billion. To the extent that volunteers provided labor that would otherwise have been paid, they increased nonprofits' surpluses.

Dove (1988, p. 1) defines a capital campaign as an "organized intensive fundraising effort on the part of the third-sector institution or organization to secure extraordinary gifts and pledges for a specific purpose or purposes." When the purpose is to raise funds for new facilities and equipment, to increase the size of an endowment fund, to renovate, or to secure equipment, the capital campaign is a means of securing access to capital. When the funds are used to offset revenue shortfalls, to raise salaries, or to add staff, they represent a temporary augmentation of revenues. From a banker's or economist's perspective, campaigns that raise funds for these purposes do not create capital. The important point to remember is that the uses to which the funds obtained from a capital campaign are put are relevant in evaluating whether the campaign produced "capital."

Donors are influenced by whether the funds they contribute are applied to capital acquisition or to operational uses, and a number of fundraisers suggest that it is easier to obtain funds when a clearly perceived need exists (see, for example, Dove, 1988, p. 19). Contributions for capital investment provide comfort to a donor that his or her contribution will benefit the organization over a period of years. Expenditures on equipment or "bricks and mortar" offer assurance that a contribution will be spent for a concrete and observable purpose. They also provide an opportunity for quid pro quo arrangements that explicitly recognize the donor's contribution—for example, a plaque or a name on a building.

Capital campaigns give rise to both collaborative and competitive behavior among nonprofits. When run through the United Way, an arts council, or some other umbrella community organization, these campaigns can facilitate capital investment for the common good, as in the case of a theater housing a number of arts groups or a piece of equipment shared by several health providers. In contrast, capital campaigns run by individual nonprofits usually enrich only those organizations. Competition for charity dollars among several nonprofits is not unusual. Such competition takes place not only among nonprofits of the same type (such as two nonprofit dance groups) but among different types (such as a cancer hospital and a nonprofit art gallery or a symphony orchestra and a nonprofit that feeds the poor). Quantitative research is lacking on whether the presence of many fundraising nonprofits in a market cuts the amount of funds flowing to each organization, leaving the aggregate given to charity the same, or whether it raises the percentage of personal income devoted to charity.

Other Nonprofit Institutions. Institutional funding is sometimes available to charitable nonprofits from other nonprofit organizations, including private, public, and community foundations, the United Way, and so on. The American Association of Fund-

Raising Counsel (1990) estimates that in 1989, $6.7 billion in grants were made to nonprofits by independent and community foundations. Nonprofits concerned with welfare received the largest share (26 percent), followed by health (21.5 percent) and education (16.5 percent). For a discussion of the rationale for this, see Tuckman and Chang (1992a).

Foundations provide funds to encourage new program initiatives, to upgrade quality, to meet the needs of groups not previously served by nonprofit organizations, and to improve the efficiency of nonprofits. However, some foundations are set up to support specific nonprofits, and this makes the distinction between internal and external funding somewhat ambiguous. Funds are usually granted for a limited number of years, with the intention that they will provide a nonprofit with time to establish its programmatic offerings. In most cases, these funds are in the form of grants, and repayment is not required. Nonprofits are required to furnish a proposal as to how funds will be used and an accounting of how funds are spent. In the late 1960s, however, some foundations began to finance projects through program-related investments (PRIs). PRIs are a middle ground between grants and loans. These loans, which must be repaid, are made for philanthropic purposes at below-market interest rates. Foundations pay close attention to social goals in deciding which nonprofits to lend to, and nonprofits must provide evidence of cash flow sufficient to cover the costs of loan repayment, as well as collateral to help guarantee the loan. The experience of these programs suggests that the criteria for collateral are "softer" than those ordinarily required by lending institutions and that projects unable to repay a loan are often refinanced (Waldhorn, Gollub, and Klein, 1989, p. 289).

Foundation funding can be particularly important for nonprofits that are new, small, or in areas that do not draw donor interest. Review of the grants made to nonprofits by foundations reveals that a large proportion are made for operational purposes, mainly for new program creation. However, some foundations focus specifically on granting funds to meet capital needs. For example, the F. W. Olin Foundation has a program to finance capital improvements to the decaying infrastructure of U.S. colleges and universities. Similarly, the Robert Wood Johnson Foundation has a multimillion-dollar public-private project in conjunction with the U.S. Department of Housing and Urban Development to improve social services and add housing units for homeless families (American Association of Fund-Raising Counsel, 1990, p. 146). The selection of projects for funding depends in large part on the priorities of the foundation, and these change through time. In the 1950s, many foundations allocated funds in support of voter registration activities. Funding for this activity diminished in the 1980s, while funding for AIDS-related support services grew dramatically.

Ylvisaker (1987, p. 361) lists five types of foundations— company-sponsored, independent, operating, community, and public— and notes that competition among nonprofits for their support takes several forms. The first two types exist primarily to make charitable grants to nonprofits. Not only do charitable nonprofits compete for funds from these sources, but they also compete with community foundations, United Way organizations, and operating foundations. Operating foundations perform a significant amount of their work internally and grant only a small proportion of their funds to other nonprofits. Hence, they both fund nonprofits and, to some extent, compete with them. In some cases, they accept funds from other foundations to provide services. Community foundations, such as the Cleveland Foundation, and public foundations make grants primarily to charitable nonprofits in the regions that they serve. Competition for funding from these foundations is largely but not entirely among operating charitable nonprofits. However, because federal law requires community and public foundations to raise a designated fraction of their total revenues from public funding or lose their status as public foundations, these organizations compete with charitable nonprofits for funds from the public.

Independent foundations are a majority of all foundations and hold the bulk of foundation assets. These entities decide which nonprofits to fund and which programmatic areas to emphasize. Foundations have sufficient resources to influence the choice of goals by nonprofits, but their resources are inadequate to provide nonprofits with general support. This forces them to be selective and to use devices such as collaboration with community foundations, matching grants, and commissioned studies and conferences to alter nonprofit behavior (Ylvisaker, 1987). Shepard's 1981 study of foundation grants made between 1955 and 1979 indicates that the bulk of their funds have gone to education, health, and cultural activities. The share devoted to education has diminished over time, while that devoted to welfare has increased.

Governments. Grants are made to nonprofits by local, special district, county, regional, state, and federal governments. In some cases, these grants support projects that would not otherwise be funded (legal aid for the poor); in others, they subsidize charitable activities already supported by the community (hospitals); and in still others, they enable nonprofits to finance services that might otherwise be provided by government (nonprofit primary care clinics). Grants can be one-time or annual, and the form of competition for these determines to some extent who a nonprofit's competitors are. For example, when nonprofits receive line-item appropriations in a state budget, this places them in direct competition with government agencies for funding. When grants are made from a pot of funds directed to nonprofits, the competition is among nonprofits.

The diversity of government sources and of nonprofit activities makes it difficult to determine the total amount that governments pay, which nonprofits get the largest share of grant funding, and the proportion of funds allocated to capital investment. Revenue data from the tax filings of charitable nonprofits in 1985 indicate that these organizations received $25.3 billion in government grants, or 9.4 percent of their revenues from this source (Hodgkinson and Weitzman, 1989, p. 45). The share of revenue represented by this category equaled direct public contributions in importance. However, researchers have found that government grants represent more than 50 percent of the total revenues of some types of nonprofits (Salamon, 1987). More recent data indicate that the percentage of nonprofits receiving government grants differs by mission (Tuckman, Chang, and Seenprachawong, 1992).

The impact of government on the cash flow of nonprofits is understated by data solely on grants. Government purchases a substantial proportion of the services provided by nonprofits, particularly in the health area, and this affects cash flow both through its effects on patient revenues and through the extent to which it covers current and operating costs. In addition, government subsidies to nonprofits lower their costs of doing business. For example, Simon (1987, p. 67) estimates that in 1985, "nonprofits received $50 billion in federally deductible contributions, generating roughly $110 billion in fee, sales, and investment revenue exempt from federal income tax, and holding an estimated $300 billion in real estate exempt from state and local property taxes." Moreover, nonprofits use government lending programs as a source of capital. A 1981 study of the sources of hospital finance found, for example, that 4 percent of the debt of hospitals in that year was financed through government lending programs (Committee on Implications of For-Profit Enterprise in Health Care, 1986, p. 55).

It is difficult to quantify the aggregate impact of these policies on capital investment, but examples of the effects of specific policies are available, particularly for health care institutions. The Committee on Implications of For-Profit Enterprise in Health Care (1986, p. 64) concluded that the tax exemption offered for hospital bonds "has been a key source of outside capital for the not-for-profit sector and that it provides a vehicle for making capital available to many institutions that otherwise would have no chance to obtain it." Similarly, Eastaugh (1987, p. 643) argues that Medicare policies favor leasing over purchase and that they create a disincentive for capital leasing over "true" leasing. Government funding affects nonprofit institutions in many ways. Consider, for example, the effects of National Science Foundation policies on the ability of research universities to acquire funding for capital expansion, the effects of overhead payments from the National Institutes of Health and the National Institute of Mental Health on loans for the construction of research laboratories, and the effects of payments by the Department of Defense for nonprofit research on defense issues on new building construction.

Corporations. The American Association of Fund-Raising Counsel (1990, p. 78) estimates that corporations and corporate foundations gave an estimated $5 billion to nonprofits in 1989, up from $4.47 billion in 1985. Educational institutions received well over one-third of the total funds, with health and human service agencies the next largest recipients. While many of the expenditures in this category were to fund programs to increase literacy, improve public education, or increase minority access, funds were also allocated for acquisition of computer equipment, construction of medical facilities, and improvement of libraries. Review of the projects funded by corporations and their foundations suggests that while these are a source of funds for programmatic development and expansion, funding of capital projects by these entities is relatively infrequent. In most cases, corporations fund nonprofits located in their own communities or regions rather than distant ones, because this increases the rewards that they receive from allocating dollars for charitable purposes, such as public recognition of their good works, publicity, and a benign image, as well as the satisfaction that comes from charitable giving. These rewards are usually greatest if they are attained in areas where the public can reward a corporation by purchasing its product.

Competition for corporate dollars exists at several levels. Charitable nonprofits with different missions compete among each other, while public and community foundations, arts councils, and United Ways compete with charitable nonprofits. The priorities of corporate donors and the heads of corporate foundations are affected by the views of their management and stockholders, their own perception of social needs, tax laws, the priorities of other foundations, and the regulatory environment.

Funding in Capital Markets

Some nonprofits seeking funds for capital acquisition can acquire them in capital markets. The primary institutional players in these markets are banks, insurance companies, investment companies, pension funds, and issuers of bonds. Nonprofits wishing to borrow in these markets must compete with for-profits and governments for funds. This competition puts pressure on nonprofits to behave in a more businesslike fashion than they might if their main source of capital was internal funds or other institutions.

Banks. In 1988, commercial banks held more than $184 billion in outstanding debt. Banks make loans for the purpose of earning a profit. In this role, they provide funds to enterprises that meet their criteria for financial soundness. Data are not available on the percentage of total loans made to nonprofits, but conversations with a number of bank officials suggest that between 2 and 10 percent of all commercial loans fall into this category.

Bank officers are reluctant to lend to nonprofits for several reasons. (1) Many bankers are not familiar with the non-profit corporate form. Because nonprofits do not have to make a profit, some bankers are confused and uncertain as to their motivations. This makes them reluctant to lend because they see these entities as risky investments. (2) Banks fear the adverse publicity that accompanies foreclosure on nonprofit property. It is easier to avoid loans to nonprofits than to face the public outcry that might accompany the sale of property devoted to charitable uses in the event of default. (3) The finances of non-profits can confuse bankers. Some nonprofits use fund accounting, and the existence of several self-balancing funds can increase banks' difficulty in analyzing nonprofit finances. Rather than incur costs training their personnel, they may instead refuse to fund projects from nonprofits with complex finances. (4) The assets of nonprofits may be constructed for specialized uses, which makes them difficult to sell. It is not easy to find an alternative use for a church building or a rural hospital. Moreover, lenders must guess as to the value of the asset at sale, and this may cause them to discount the value of the property as collateral. (5) Because of legal restrictions on a bank's ability to claim a nonprofit's assets, it is not as easy for nonprofits to pledge their assets as collateral for loans as it is for for-profits. (6) Banks prefer to lend to institutions that bank with them and that have clients that bank with them. Nonprofits that serve low-income people are not in a good position to promise new business to a bank.

In recognition of these difficulties, nonprofit enterprises may attempt to improve their access to bank and private funding through joint ventures with for-profit enterprises. Such ventures increase the likelihood that a bank will finance a loan by providing access to collateral that would not otherwise be available. For example, a bank may make a loan to a group of doctors and a small rural nonprofit hospital to jointly purchase a diagnostic machine. Because the doctors are signatories to the loan, the bank can lay claim to their assets in the event of default. Other things being equal, this gives a lending institution more security than if it lent funds solely to the nonprofit.

The enactment of the Community Reinvestment Act (PL 95-128) in 1977 created an additional incentive for banks to be responsive to the credit needs of their communities and to encourage loan applications from organizations that serve low- and/or moderate-income people. Many banks responded to this incentive by making loans and grants to local and neighborhood organizations and to individual entrepreneurs. In some cases, loans were made with "softer" criteria than are ordinarily imposed on borrowers, and, to some extent, this increased the funds available to those who would not otherwise have had access to bank finance. However, the criteria that regulators use in evaluating whether banks are fulfilling their obligations under this program have been vague, and there have not been well-developed criteria to measure its effectiveness.

Insurance Companies and Pension Funds. Life insurance and other insurance companies in the United States held more than $1.56 billion in financial assets in 1988 (U.S. Bureau of the Census, 1990, p. 492). A large proportion of this was in the form of long-term real estate loans to for-profits. Nonprofits that seek capital from insurance companies must compete with for-profits, and this requires them to have strong finances to qualify for a loan. Insurance company capital is accessible to small nonprofits on a limited basis, but the primary beneficiaries are large, well-financed nonprofits located in cities where insurance companies have operations.

Insurance companies look for safety, quality, and a high rate return, and it is difficult for many nonprofits to provide a competitive return that will cause these institutions to lend to them. Some insurance companies allocate a portion of their investments for social investment projects funded under less restrictive criteria than are ordinarily used, and encouragement for this activity is provided by the Center for Public Corporate Involvement (CPCI) in Washington, D.C. The CPCI is jointly sponsored by the American Council of Life Insurance and the Health Insurance Association of America. However, the insurance companies that belong to these organizations make their own decisions as to how much to allocate for social investment. While the insurance companies require borrowers to demonstrate economic viability, adequate debt service coverage, and adequate collateralization, the CPCI reports that most social investing companies are willing to accept below-market returns and to bear higher risks than the ordinary insurance company (Center for Public Corporate Involvement, 1990).

In 1990, the average insurance company involved in social investing had 41 percent of its dollars in housing, 19 percent in economic development and job creation, and 16 percent in commercial revitalization. Of these dollars, 64 percent went into projects serving areas in which the companies were located, 21 percent into projects national in scope, and 14 percent into projects serving cities and regions where the companies had a strong presence. These companies invested 37 percent of their funds in for-profits, 34 percent in nonprofits, and 15 percent in so-called intermediary organizations that provided funds to other users (Center for Public Corporate Involvement, 1990, p. 15).

It is useful to look at the types of financial instruments employed to provide capital funding. Roughly 75 percent of the social investment companies in the CPCI study used permanent mortgages, 51 percent secured and unsecured loans, 42 percent stock purchases, 15 percent limited partnership interests in the organization, 12 percent loan guarantees, and 12 percent construction loans. According to the American Council of Life Insurance and Health Insurance Association of America (1990, p. 5), the total contributions of the 172 member companies reached a 1989 industry high of $154.6 million. While this is a large amount in dollar terms, it represents a small percentage of the total investments of insurance companies. The investments made by companies ranged from $15,000 to $5 million, with the average for all companies at slightly over $1 million (Center for Public Corporate Involvement, 1990, p. 25).

The financial assets of private company and state and local pension funds were $1.09 billion in 1988. These organizations exist to earn a profit for their investors. As do the insurance companies, they make loans to diversify their portfolios and to raise the returns for their investors. Because of the tax-exempt status of the state and local pension funds, they gain no benefit by investing in nonprofit tax-exempt bonds and thus prefer to hold the bonds of for-profit enterprises. Investment companies can offer mortgages to nonprofits, but they cannot share in the profits of these organizations through stock holdings. Since they are more likely to seek equity positions that increase their returns than to write mortgages, their participation in nonprofit finance is limited. Data are not available on the dollar value of the loans that they make to nonprofits, but interviews with people in these enterprises suggest that the figure is probably less than half of 1 percent of total investments.

Investment Companies. Investment companies had $78 billion in outstanding debt in 1988. These organizations exist primarily to earn a profit, and they invest primarily in real estate. As in the case of insurance companies, national data are not available on the nonprofit holdings of this group. Because of the lack of opportunity to participate in profits, the problematic nature of nonprofit collateral, and the other problems involved in lending to nonprofits, it is unlikely that these companies hold more than half of 1 percent of their investments in the form of nonprofit loans.

Stock Issuances. More than $57.8 billion of new securities were issued by corporations in 1988. While nonprofits issue stocks to establish themselves as corporate entities, stock sales do not represent an important source of capital for these organizations (Hansmann, 1987). Federal and state tax laws preclude owners of nonprofits from participating in the growth of corporate earnings through time. Since the primary motivation of most stockholders is to earn profits, their inability to participate in the earnings growth of nonprofits means that they have little incentive to purchase shares of nonprofit corporations. The inability to tap stock markets for capital funds puts nonprofits at a disadvantage relative to for-profits. In addition to the fact that these markets are a large source of capital for corporations, borrowing in these markets offers certain other advantages for borrowers. The fact that stock markets capitalize earnings allows for larger capital infusions. For example, if a for-profit hospital has earnings of $1 million a year and these are capitalized at fifteen times earnings, it can issue stock worth $15 million. The same earnings will usually support a bond issue of less than $2 million. Stocks can be issued and repurchased at any time, while bonds are normally redeemed at specific times under predetermined terms. Stock issuance does not preclude access to other sources of financing, while bond finance goes on the balance sheet as debt and thus limits an organization's future borrowing chances. Hence, lack of access to the stock market can be a distinct disadvantage to a growing enterprise.

Nonprofit Bonds. Bond sales are also a major source of capital for corporations. In 1988, more than $351 billion worth of new bonds were issued. About $200.1 billion of these were sold on public markets, while $150.9 billion of them were marketed as private domestic or foreign placements (U.S. Bureau of the Census, 1990, p. 512). The dollar volume of new bond sales exceeded that of new stock sales by six to one, indicating the prominent role that bonds play as a source of capital. Bonds differ from stocks in that bonds represent promissory debts of corporations to their creditors, while stocks represent an ownership claim on profits. The interest that corporations pay to bondholders is an expense of doing business, while dividends are a distribution of profits. Nonprofits can pay interest on debt largely without concern that this will imperil their legal standing, while dividends are a distribution of profit and hence can cause a violation of their nonprofit status, which rests on non-distribution of profits. (There are, however, cases where the IRS might question bond issues, as when a private placement is sold entirely to one member of the board of directors at a higher than market interest rate). Moreover, bonds can be used to finance nonprofit capital projects with less concern for the implications of negative publicity, since if assets must be repossessed, those who reclaim them are anonymous.

Bond finance has several other advantages. Because bond markets are national in scope, borrowed funds can often be obtained in these markets at interest rates below those charged by local banks, particularly when the debt is tax exempt. Large amounts of funds can be borrowed, often far in excess of those available at local or regional banks. Companies that float bonds can provide useful input not only as to how to structure a debt issue but also as to ways to improve nonprofit financial performance. In addition, bonds can be called at designated times, allowing the issuing organization an opportunity to refinance at lower rates.

This form of finance also has several disadvantages. Long delays can accompany the floating of a bond issue, because time is required to provide the information required by the lenders, complete the paper work, and secure underwriters. Hence, this is not a good source of short-term (or quickly needed) funds. Moreover, because of relatively high fixed costs, it is not worthwhile for nonprofits to use bond finance for small loans. In addition, bonds require interest and debt repayment on fixed dates. Failure to pay on schedule can result not only in embarrassment but also in impairment of the nonprofit's credit rating. Loans from banks and other institutions may allow for greater repayment flexibility. Finally, the bond houses are not likely to issue bonds in many of the areas in which nonprofits might wish to borrow because of the effort involved in developing loan criteria and in learning the intricacies of a new industry.

Government policies generally facilitate borrowing in national bond markets for certain types of nonprofits. For example, the tax exemption granted to the bonds of nonprofit hospitals and educational institutions produces interest rates below those available to for-profits in the bond markets. These rates are also appreciably lower than those that nonprofits would pay for bank loans. Government payments for the provision of medical services also increase the cash flow of hospitals and make loans less risky than they would otherwise be. (Recent changes in the way that Medicare handles capital investment may reverse this in the future, however.) Similarly, government contracts and grants for research create a revenue base that can justify loans for construction of research facilities. From 1973 to 1984, the percentage of hospital construction funded by debt rose from 38 percent to over 70 percent, while the share funded by philanthropy fell from 21 percent to less than 4 percent (Kinkhead, 1984). Moreover, changes in the tax laws affect both the cost of borrowing to nonprofits and their attractiveness as borrowers. The 1980s reforms lowered the top rate on income and reduced the value of the tax exemption for high-income investors. This change in tax policy may have reduced bondholders' willingness to hold bonds issued by nonprofits, but research is not available to support or refute this claim.

The shift from philanthropic to bond market finance put hospitals in competition with for-profit enterprises in the national markets for capital funds. Access to these markets was limited by the criteria that the investment banking houses and rating agencies used to evaluate nonprofits. Successful institutions tend to have a large asset base, substantial revenues, well-developed financial accounting systems, and a history of growth within their industry. It is extremely rare that a nonprofit with donations as a primary revenue source succeeds in floating a bond issue. Small nonprofit hospitals, with limited revenues, also have difficulty finding bond finance. In many cases, these institutions merge with larger systems to acquire the financial resources needed to support bond issues. Nonprofit art galleries, museums, music groups, and cultural organizations also find it very difficult to obtain bond finance.

Consequences of Entry into Capital Markets

A nonprofit's decision to borrow in capital markets can affect both its current operations and its future goals. Lending institutions require management and financial data that many nonprofit managers are not accustomed to compiling. Records must be kept in a form acceptable to the lender and must provide a historical picture of the organization's finances. In most cases, a nonprofit must show evidence of a sound balance sheet, growing revenues, control over costs, and positive cash flows over time. To demonstrate acceptability in these areas, it is often necessary to trade off program goals in favor of financial ones, and this may require adjustment of the thinking of a nonprofit's management and board of directors.

Strict lender requirements can cause adaptation problems in organizations whose selection process attracts idealistic and/or traditional types of entrepreneurs (Young, 1986). In addition, many nonprofits may not be prepared for the external scrutiny that capital markets impose. For example, it is not uncommon for lenders to hospitals to require data on the average age of doctors, number and kinds of patients, loyalty of doctors and staff to the hospital, and key parties involved in decision making. Not surprisingly, some administrators find it disconcerting to share such sensitive data with third parties. Even in the case of PRIs, which represent a middle ground between grants and loans, informational requirements arise. Waldhorn, Gollub, and Klein (1989, p. 292) report that while competitive pressures improve management and design among human service agencies, the program does not always work. Some agencies fail to earn enough to repay their loans, while others have a culture that does not accommodate the notion of borrowing.

A second consequence of the decision to seek capital market funding is that the basis for competition for funds changes. Particularly in the bond market, where borrowers of many different types compete for funds, the criteria used in deciding whom to lend to are well defined and largely unrelated to judgments as to the social value of what organizations do.

Instead, the amount of risk that lenders perceive in providing funds determines both whether an entity will be funded and how much will be lent. This situation is very different from that which prevails when nonprofits compete for grants or foundation funding. Nonprofits that wish to obtain funds in capital markets must demonstrate a high degree of stability and produce evidence that they can pay interest rates equal to those prevailing in capital markets. Those with precarious finances must either pay a rate of interest sufficient to compensate lenders for the risk that they take or seek funding elsewhere. Some nonprofits will be unable to meet the criteria set down by lenders no matter what they do, particularly those in unprofitable areas of social service delivery.

Criteria Used by Lending Institutions

An important goal of lenders is to ensure that borrowed capital is returned, along with a reasonable return for the use of the funds. For this reason, most are less interested in a borrower's mission than in his or her creditworthiness and past financial performance. Screening criteria are designed to ensure that funds are lent only to those that meet the appropriate tests, a primary one being the financial history of the nonprofit. Lenders look for a minimum of five to ten years of experience in business. They also seek evidence of survivability during a recession. Consideration is given to how revenues and expenditures have changed over time (they should rise), diversity of revenue sources (there should be several), and sources of revenue (government funds are sometimes judged to be less desirable than sales to a growing customer population).

If an organization is financed primarily by donations, lenders may look at the people who donate to it, the stability of its donor base, and the extent to which its contributions have grown through time. If revenues are growing but the number of donors or customers is falling, this can raise a red flag. Attention is paid to quality of management and to the backgrounds of the members of the board of directors (people with experience running a business are preferred). Lenders look for ability to follow through on promised activities and for evidence of financial discipline. A history of rising cash flow is important, as is evidence of a reasonable ratio of debt to assets and of adequate collateral to ensure that the loan will be repaid. Industry-specific criteria such as location, competitors, market share, expectations for the future, and the regulatory environment also play a role. In industries where debt is rated by Standard and Poor or Moody, past ratings are also considered.

Nonprofits that wish to develop new sources of capital funding can do several things to improve their chances of funding by lending institutions:

- Make a goal of creating and accumulating cash reserves
- Keep well-documented financial records for at least five but preferably ten years
- Focus on financial as well as programmatic growth
- Maintain consistent cash flow whenever possible
- Resist the temptation to expand programs too quickly
- Diversify revenue sources whenever possible
- Appoint board members who have experience running a business
- Hire a key financial person who can gain the confidence of the financial community

When Nonprofits Enter Capital Markets

Most nonprofits would like to expand the amount of capital that they have available, but only a limited number seek funds from lending institutions. Conversations with the management of nonprofits and with lenders suggest that nonprofits are most likely to borrow under the following circumstances:

1. When large (relative to normal needs) sums must be borrowed. Borrowers seek bank funding for short-term and intermediate loans and lines of credit. Other lending institutions are preferred for very large loans and when long periods of time are envisioned for payback.
2. When funding is available at low interest rates. Such rates

are most likely to be found during a recession, when government guarantees the loan or provides a stable revenue
source, when the service that the organization provides is
expected to grow through time, when bonds can be issued
with tax-exempt status, and when an organization has had
an excellent credit rating in the past.

3.   To increase productivity and/or lower operating costs. Capital expansion can create economies of scale and scope, and
this provides an incentive to increase the amount used in
production.

4.   To provide competitive advantage. This may occur where
capital plant is part of the basis of competition, diversification offers advantage, marketing economies exist, and/or
acquisitions lower costs or increase the number of people
using the service.

5.   To stabilize cash flow. Particularly where revenues are sea-
sonal (for example, in educational institutions) or where
capital campaigns involve multiyear pledges, loans or lines
of credit improve cash position.

6.   To achieve intergenerational equity. Cash outlays require
the present generation to pay for items that benefit future
generations. Borrowing enables future generations to share
in the cost of constructing facilities or purchasing
machinery.

Which Nonprofits Are Most Likely to Obtain Loans?

In certain cases, the mission of a nonprofit is such that it is
highly unlikely that it can meet the criteria set forth above. In
others, the nonprofit is unwilling to sacrifice current program
expenditures to build capital for use in the future. In still others,
the management of the nonprofit is unwilling to assume debt
obligations that place a claim on revenues for a period of years.
Thus, the expectation is that some nonprofits will not borrow at
all.

There are a number of reasons for believing that commercial nonprofits (those that get a majority of their revenues from
sales) are more likely to borrow than donative nonprofits. These

organizations are business-oriented, and their finances tend to be organized in a manner that lenders understand. They are also in a position where, if a for-profit competitor borrows, they may find it necessary to borrow as well to maintain their competitive position. In addition, because commercial nonprofits earn a large part of their revenues from sales, lenders may find their finances easier to evaluate, since they are similar to those of for-profits. Moreover, a solid sales base may be perceived as offering greater assurance than a donations base that a loan will be repaid. Interestingly, the validity of these arguments has not been addressed by the research community.

Several other factors are important in determining which nonprofits will enter the capital markets. Older and larger nonprofits are more likely to qualify for funding than younger and smaller ones. Similarly, nonprofits with large asset accumulations, a strong community reputation, a popular mission, and growing revenues are also in a better position to qualify for loans. Small organizations with uncertain prospects, limited assets, unstable revenues, boards of directors that lack business experience and/or social standing, and no government guarantees find it difficult to borrow. The fact that more nonprofits fall into the latter category than in the former has consequences for the nonprofit sector. The evidence suggests that (1) nonprofits fail to keep pace with for-profits in sectors where demand is growing rapidly (Hansmann, 1987); (2) nonprofits find it difficult to grow without substantial government support (Salamon, 1987); and (3) nonprofits are very unevenly distributed among regions and between urban areas (favored) and rural areas.

Conclusion

Access to capital is fundamental for any organization that wishes to survive and grow. The above analysis suggests that there are a variety of sources through which nonprofits can acquire financial resources for capital growth. Which source is most appropriate depends on the managerial judgments of the administrators of a nonprofit, its financial and social circumstances, and its ability to gain access to external sources of capital. At a minimum, all nonprofits have a potential ability to gain access to capital through their ability to budget a positive surplus and to accumulate funds through time. Such surpluses provide both an internal source of funds and evidence of financial strength and fiscal soundness that increase the chance of obtaining external funding. It is not easy for some nonprofits to embrace the idea that they should hold some of their scarce funds in reserve rather than spending them to meet immediate programmatic needs. Nonetheless, the accumulation of equity through prudent financial management should be a goal for any organization that wishes to retain the confidence of those it serves.

References

American Association of Fund-Raising Counsel. *Giving USA*. New York: AAFRC Trust for Philanthropy, 1990.

American Council of Life Insurance and Health Insurance Association of America. *1990 Social Report of the Life and Health Insurance Business*. Washington, D.C.: American Council of Life Insurance and Health Insurance Association of America, 1990.

Ben-Ner, A., and Van Hoomissen, T. "The Growth of the Nonprofit Sector in the 1980s: Facts and Interpretation." *Nonprofit Management and Leadership*, *1*(2), 1990, 99–116.

Center for Public Corporate Involvement. *Social Investing in the Life and Health Insurance Industry*. Report prepared under a grant from the Ford Foundation. Washington, D.C.: American Council of Life Insurance and Health Insurance Association of America, 1990.

Chang, C. F., and Tuckman, H. P. "Why Do Nonprofit Managers Accumulate Surpluses and How Much Do They Accumulate?" *Nonprofit Management and Leadership*, *1*(2), 1990, pp. 117–136.

Committee on Implications of For-Profit Enterprise in Health Care. "Financial Capital and Health Care Growth Trends." In B. H. Gray (ed.), *For-Profit Enterprise in Health Care*. Washington, D.C.: National Academy Press, 1986.

Dove, K. E. *Conducting a Successful Capital Campaign.* San Francisco: Jossey-Bass, 1988.

Eastaugh, S. R. *Financing Health Care: Economic Efficiency and Equity.* Dover, Mass.: Auburn, 1987.

Hansmann, H. "Economic Theories of Nonprofit Organizations." In W. W. Powell (ed.), *The Nonprofit Sector: A Research Handbook.* New Haven, Conn.: Yale University Press, 1987.

Hodgkinson, V. A., and Weitzman, M. S. *Dimensions of the Independent Sector: A Statistical Profile.* Washington, D.C.: INDEPENDENT SECTOR, 1989.

Hyman, D. N. *Economics.* Homewood, Ill.: Irwin, 1989.

Kinkhead, B. *Historical Trends in Hospital Construction.* Washington, D.C.: U.S. Department of Health and Human Services, 1984.

Salamon, L. M. "Partners in Public Service: The Scope and Theory of Government-Nonprofit Relations." In W. W. Powell (ed.), *The Nonprofit Sector: A Research Handbook.* New Haven, Conn.: Yale University Press, 1987.

Shepard, K. "The Nation's Largest Foundations, 1959–1979." Unpublished manuscript, Twentieth Century Fund, 1981.

Simon, J. G. "The Tax Treatment of Nonprofit Organizations: A Review of Federal and State Policies." In W. W. Powell (ed.), *The Nonprofit Sector: A Research Handbook.* New Haven, Conn.: Yale University Press, 1987.

Tuckman, H. P., and Chang, C. F. "Economic Costs and the Structural Form of Charitable Nonprofits." Unpublished paper, Memphis State University, 1992a.

Tuckman, H. P., and Chang, C. F. "Nonprofit Equity: A Behavioral Model and Its Policy Implications." *Journal of Policy Analysis and Management,* 1992b, *92*(1), 76–87.

Tuckman, H. P., Chang, C. F., and Seenprachawong, U. "The Goods Produced by Nonprofit Organizations." Unpublished paper, Memphis State University, 1992.

U.S. Bureau of the Census. *Statistical Abstract of the United States, 1990.* Washington, D.C.: U.S. Government Printing Office, 1990.

U.S. Office of Management and Budget. *Budget of the United States,*

1993. Washington, D.C.: U.S. Government Printing Office, 1992.

Waldhorn, S. A., Gollub, J. O., and Klein, J. A. "New Approaches to Financing Nonprofit Organizations: The Role of Lending." In V. A. Hodgkinson, R. W. Lyman, and Associates, *The Future of the Nonprofit Sector: Challenges, Changes, and Policy Considerations.* San Francisco: Jossey-Bass, 1989.

Ylvisaker, P. N. "Foundations and Nonprofit Organizations." In W. W. Powell (ed.), *The Nonprofit Sector: A Research Handbook.* New Haven, Conn.: Yale University Press, 1987.

Young, D. R. "Entrepreneurship and the Behavior of Nonprofit Organizations: Elements of a Theory." In S. Rose-Ackerman (ed.), *The Economics of Nonprofit Institutions.* New York: Oxford University Press, 1986.

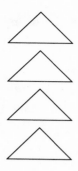

CHAPTER 8

Investment Management in the Nonprofit Sector: Studying the Performance of Private Foundations

Lester M. Salamon

Nonprofit organizations are best known for their roles as service providers and advocates of change. Yet many types of nonprofit organizations also manage substantial amounts of investment capital in the form of endowment funds. One recent estimate put the total value of the assets of U.S. tax-exempt organizations at close to $670 billion as of 1988 (see Table 8.1). Of this total, 31

Note: This chapter draws on a body of research conducted for the Council on Foundations and reported in two previous publications (Salamon and Voytek, 1989; Salamon, 1991) and is used with permission from *Managing Foundation Assets: An Analysis of Foundation Investment and Payout Prodcedures and Performance*, published by the Foundation Center, copyright © 1989 by the Council on Foundations, 1828 L Street, NW, Washington, D.C. 20036, 202/466-6512. The author wishes to express his appreciation to the Council on Foundations and especially its former vice president for research, Elizabeth Boris; to an advisory committee that the council recruited to oversee this work; to Kenneth Voytek and Jaana Myllyluoma, who provided crucial research assistance; and to the funders of this project, including the Edna

233

Table 8.1. Assets of U.S. Nonprofit Organizations, 1988.

	Assets	
Type	Amount ($ billion)	Percentage of total
Foundations	122.0	18
Hospitals and health	210.1	31
Education	154.7	23
Other	183.2	28
	$670.0	100

Note: Mutual benefit organizations and foreign foundations are excluded.

Source: Foundation data from Renz (1991, p. 2); all other data from Hodgkinson, Weitzman, Toppe, and Noga, 1992, p. 195.

percent belongs to hospitals, 23 percent to schools, 18 percent to foundations, and 28 percent to a variety of other types of institutions (for example, art galleries, museums). Although not all of these assets represent capital available for investment (for example, the works of art in galleries), it is clear that nonprofit organizations are active players in the nation's investment markets whatever their other activities.

The purpose of this chapter is to examine how one crucial class of nonprofit organizations — private foundations — handle this investment function. Although foundations have some special features that make their investment activities different from those of other nonprofits (chiefly because of a tighter set of regulatory restrictions and because they are much more overtly

---

McConnell Clark Foundation, the Geraldine R. Dodge Foundation, the Dyer-Ives Foundation, the Equitable Foundation, the Ford Foundation, the Edward W. Hazen Foundation, the William Randolph Hearst Foundation, the Conrad N. Hilton Foundation, the John & Mary Markle Foundation, the Richard King Mellon Foundation, the Eugene & Agnes E. Meyer Foundation, the Charles Stewart Mott Foundation, the New York Community Trust, the Powell Family Foundation, the Charles H. Revson Foundation, the Russell Sage Foundation, and the St. Paul Community Foundation. Needless to say, the views and opinions expressed here are those of the author and may or may not correspond to those of other individuals or organizations with which he is affiliated or that have been associated with or involved in this work.

financial in their basic mission), it seems reasonable to suppose that their experience is likely to have much in common with that of other endowed charities.

Most importantly, foundations, like other nonprofit organizations, are principally engaged in their charitable mission, which is grant making—the distribution of charitable resources. Yet their ability to perform this grant-making function depends critically on their success in handling another crucial management function: the management of foundation assets and investments. Although some American foundations are pass-through organizations that collect resources and pay them out in the same year, most are called on to manage sizable pools of investment capital that have been set aside for charitable purposes. As of 1989, these resources amounted to $138 billion (Renz, 1991, p. 2).

In a sense, foundations, like other endowed nonprofits, are required to balance two potentially competing goals: first, the promotion of their charitable mission (which for foundations is the distribution of grants) and, second, the preservation, enlargement, and stewardship of the assets that can support that mission into the future. Even foundations that intend to go out of business at some definable point in the future face the problem of effectively managing the assets under their control in the interim.

How do foundations perform this asset management function? To what extent have they adopted reasonable management practices? What has their record of investment performance been? To what extent do they consciously weigh the relationship between investment decisions and payout decisions? How are these decisions made, and by whom?

The answers to these questions are not only of academic interest. Suspicious that the foundation device has too often been used as a tax dodge on the part of wealthy individuals who want to gain the tax advantages that result from leaving one's wealth to a foundation while keeping effective control of one's business in family hands, Congress has enacted measures to prohibit "self-dealing" on the part of foundation boards and to ensure that a reasonable share of the foundation's earnings finds its way to beneficiaries. These measures culminated with the inclusion in the Tax Reform Act of 1969 of the so-called payout requirement, which stipulated that foundations must pay out each year as grants or other "qualifying distributions" the higher of a minimum proportion (initially 6 percent; later reduced to 5 percent) of their assets or the total value of their investment earnings and that imposed various taxes on foundations if they engaged in a variety of undesirable investment practices (for further detail, see Council on Foundations, 1981). This was then liberalized slightly in 1981 with the elimination of the requirement for foundations to pay out investment earnings if they exceeded 5 percent of the foundation's asset value. Henceforth, foundations could retain such earnings and reinvest them.

Despite their importance to the functioning of foundations and the attention that they have attracted in Congress, foundation investment and payout practice and performance have attracted precious little research attention. As a consequence, little is known in solid empirical terms about how foundations manage their investments, what return rates they achieve, or how they balance their investment and payout decisions. What limited work has been done on this topic has focused on too narrow a range of foundations, too limited a definition of investment performance, or too restricted a time frame to give much confidence in the results.

A major study of foundation investment practices conducted by Ralph Nelson in the mid 1960s, for example, focused chiefly on the *composition* of investment portfolios and the process of diversification. Although Nelson (1967) attempted some computation of total investment return, he covered only 45 very large foundations. Similarly, in the late 1960s, the Commission on Foundations and Private Philanthropy (the Peterson Commission) computed the return rate for some 180 foundations, but the analysis covered only one year (1968), and it is difficult to determine what methodology the commission used (Commission on Foundations and Private Philanthropy, 1970). Indeed, the commission acknowledged in its report that it made "no claims that it has exhaustively reviewed the investment performance of foundations" (p. 75).

Thus, when the Tax Reform Act of 1969 imposed its minimum payout requirement on foundations, it did not do so on the basis of any systematic data about the consequences that it would have for foundation operations. The ink was no sooner dry on the legislation, therefore, than foundation officials began to complain that it would stifle foundation investment management and lead to the dissolution of foundation assets, a contention that investment analyst Peter Williamson supported through simulation analyses that he carried out in the mid to late 1970s but for which there were no solid empirical findings (Williamson, 1976).

Three more recent studies have shed additional, useful light on foundation investment activities, but none of these provides the kind of broad-gauged empirical picture that is needed. The first of these, completed by researchers at the University of Michigan Graduate School of Business Administration, covers only thirty-nine foundations and focuses primarily on investment management policy and how it was affected by the 1981 change in the payout requirement, with no attempt to calculate actual foundation investment return rates (Reilly and Skadden, 1981). A far more ambitious analysis of the investment activities of a large sample of 1,309 foundations was completed by the Statistics of Income Division of the Internal Revenue Service in 1985, but this study focused only on income yield rather than total rate of return, examined only a single year, and made no adjustment for the widely different fiscal years of foundations (Riley, 1989). Finally, Nelson (1987) completed an analysis of the growth of private foundation assets between 1962 and 1982, but this analysis develops rate-of-return figures on only the fifty-four largest foundations for which detailed financial profiles could be developed over this twenty-year period.

Nor do the commercial investment reporting services provide much help. Although some foundations are included in the data generated by some of these services, such as Colonial Consulting and Hamilton and Johnson, the coverage is spotty. In addition, foundations essentially self-select themselves into the services, making the resulting data suspect as a basis for generalizing about the foundation universe as a whole. What is more, the number of foundations covered is small — fewer than fifty for Colonial Consulting and not many more for Hamilton and Johnson.[1]

Background of the Study

The purpose of the study on which this chapter draws was to fill these gross gaps in knowledge about the operation of the foundation investment function and about the investment and payout performance of foundations. To do so, we surveyed a stratified random sample of private foundations and collected a detailed body of financial data on a broad cross section of foundations from the 990-PF forms that foundations are required to file with the Internal Revenue Service. Altogether, 478 foundations responded to the survey, and we were able to develop full financial data spanning the period 1979–1986 on 351 foundations, including 173 that also responded to the survey (for additional detail, see Salamon, 1991, pp. 27–33).

Data from both the survey and the 990-PF data collection were then "blown up" to the total population using two weighting schemes — one to represent the universe of *foundations* ("foundation-weighted" results) and the other to approximate the universe of foundation *assets* ("asset-weighted" results).

The balance of this chapter reports what these data reveal about both the process and content of foundation investment management and about the recent record of foundation investment and payout performance. To set the stage for this discussion, however, we first look briefly at the nature of investment management and at the consensus view of what good practice in this field entails as a conceptual framework for interpreting the results.

Investment Management in Concept

Conceptually, modern investment management practice can be described in two parts: the process through which investments are made and the principles for determining the content of investment portfolios.

The Process

Investment management essentially involves three interrelated activities: the setting of overall investment objectives, the formation of an investment strategy for achieving those objectives, and the actual day-to-day management of the investment portfolio (Ellis, 1971).

Investment objectives establish the "game plan," or the overall guidance for the investment function, specifying the long-term goals of the institution, its tolerance for risk, and the time frame over which performance is evaluated. Objectives, however, must be translated into concrete action terms. To do this, an *investment strategy* is commonly needed. The role of an investment strategy is to specify the broad route that is to be taken to achieve the objectives—the types of assets to hold, the proportion of each type to include in the portfolio at any point in time, the style of management to use (active or passive), the division between internal and external management, and so forth. Finally, strategies must be implemented on a day-to-day basis. Stocks, bonds, real estate, and other assets must be bought and sold. Decisions must be made about particular stocks or bonds to buy or sell at a given time. This is the task of *portfolio management*.

Experts on investment management generally agree that certain aspects of this process are necessarily responsibilities of an organization's board but that others can be delegated to internal or external staff. More precisely, there is general agreement that the board must be involved in setting investment objectives and investment strategy but that once this is done, the day-to-day management of the portfolio—the selection of particular stocks or bonds—can be left to specialized internal or external staff, though with some regular mechanism for oversight and evaluation (Murray, 1971; Nason, 1977; Cary and Bright, 1969; Young and Moore, 1969; McDonald, 1973).[2]

The Content: Modern Portfolio Theory

With regard to the *content* of investment objectives and strategies, a consensus view is harder to discern for the obvious reason that foundations have different goals. Some foundations fully intend to go out of existence at some point in the future. For such foundations, retaining earnings and maximizing asset growth over the long run makes little sense. Other foundations expect to operate essentially in perpetuity. Such foundations can therefore afford to take greater risks in the hope of future growth, even if this means smaller short-term earnings.

While foundations obviously may fall at different points along this continuum, there is widespread agreement about the basic trade-offs that exist. This agreement has come to be embodied in what is known as "modern portfolio theory," or "capital-asset pricing theory." The central notion of modern portfolio theory is that there is a fundamental link between the level of risk associated with an investment and the return likely from it. Assets with the greatest long-term growth potential are likely to be those with the greatest risk. A foundation aiming at a high rate of total return must therefore usually accept a higher level of risk than one content with a lower rate of return. This naturally affects the kinds of assets that a foundation holds. No one expects to earn as much from an insured savings account as one might earn from wildcatting for oil. At the same time, the risk of loss is much less on the savings account as well. The markets tend to price assets accordingly: assets with the greatest certainty of returns have the highest current prices and those with the greatest risk the lowest current prices.

The challenge, however, is to define risk with clarity. This is where modern portfolio theory comes in. According to this theory, there are two basic types of risk associated with any investment: "systematic risk," which is the degree of sensitivity of an investment to overall market movements, and "unsystematic risk," which is the variability or volatility of a particular investment associated with factors peculiar to that investment rather than with overall market trends.

Modern portfolio theory holds that unsystematic risk can

be reduced through diversification but that systematic risk cannot. Investors must therefore choose the level of systematic risk that they can tolerate. To help them, a measure of the systematic risk associated with a security — known as Beta — has been developed. Beta essentially measures the historical relationship between the movements of a particular stock (or portfolio) and the movements of the market as a whole. A security with a Beta of 2 has thus on average moved up or down twice as much as the market averages — for example, going up by 10 percent when the market rises 5 percent (Malkiel, 1985; Modigliani and Pogue, 1974; Markowitz, 1959).

According to modern portfolio theory, markets tend to price assets so that the expected rewards bear some kind of systematic relationship to their perceived risks of loss. Investors that have the luxury of taking a long time horizon, which allows them to absorb some risk, therefore have the greatest opportunities for gain. To take advantage of their situation, however, such investors should pursue a "total-return" objective (focusing on capital gains as well as income growth), focus on the long term, and be willing to take some risks in order to maximize their return.

The extent to which foundations can follow these standards of investment management is somewhat limited, of course, by the special constraints under which foundations operate, such as the payout requirement, which limits the extent to which earnings can be retained and reinvested; the absence of systematic cash inflows such as those enjoyed by pension funds; penalties associated with "jeopardy investments" — those involving donor property; and an asset base that often includes large blocks of stock in the donor's company.

The Practice of Foundation Investment Management

Despite these constraints, it is still reasonable to inquire how fully foundation investment management adheres to the tenets of accepted practice identified above. To answer this question, let us look first at the investment management *process*, then at the *content* of investment objectives and strategies, and finally at the *composition* of foundation investment portfolios, which represent the tangible manifestation of investment decisions.

Process

According to the tenets of modern investment theory identified above, we would expect the boards of foundations to be actively involved in the setting of investment objectives and in the approval of investment strategies, with considerable discretion left to internal and external staff to manage the portfolio day to day in accord with these guidelines. Unfortunately, the record of foundation investment management deviates from this model in a number of important respects.

Limited Board Role in Setting Objectives and Strategies. While foundation boards are clearly the dominant players in the setting of investment objectives and strategies, as much of the literature in the field would recommend, fewer than half of the foundations represented in our survey sample indicated that the full foundation board was "extremely important" in setting investment objectives, and fewer than 40 percent indicated that they were "extremely important" in setting investment strategies (see Table 8.2).

To be sure, almost two-thirds of the foundations (64 percent) indicated that either the full board, the board chair, or an investment committee of the board plays an "extremely important" part in setting the foundation's overall investment objectives. Significantly, however, for more than a third of the foundations, not even a portion of the board is taking an active hand in this most basic investment function. And the fact that, in most foundations, board involvement is either limited overall or delegated to a subgroup or individual suggests that boards qua boards are playing less of a role in setting the broad contours of foundation investment policy than is recommended. What is more, a similar pattern holds with respect to investment strategies.

As Table 8.2 also shows, this pattern of somewhat limited board involvement in foundation objective and strategy setting

Table 8.2. Key Participants in Foundation Investment Management.

Function	Percentage of foundations identifying actor as playing "extremely important" role			
	Full board	Board Chair or committee	Staff or managers	Total
Setting objectives				
All foundations ($n = 22,214$)[a]	45.8	18.1	36.1	100.0
Large foundations[b] ($n = 73$)	48.6	40.3	11.1	100.0
Mid-sized foundations[c] ($n = 124$)	52.4	26.6	17.7	100.0
Small foundations[d] ($n = 279$)	45.7	17.7	36.6	100.0
Setting strategies				
All foundations ($n = 22,214$)[a]	37.3	23.0	39.7	100.0
Large foundations[b] ($n = 73$)	35.6	45.2	19.2	100.0
Mid-sized foundations[c] ($n = 124$)	42.8	27.4	29.8	100.0
Small foundations[d] ($n = 279$)	37.2	22.7	40.1	100.0
Portfolio management				
All foundations ($n = 22,214$)[a]	22.6	18.0	59.4	100.0
Large foundations[b] ($n = 73$)	5.6	9.7	84.7	100.0
Mid-sized foundations[c] ($n = 124$)	11.4	22.0	66.6	100.0
Small foundations[d] ($n = 279$)	23.9	17.9	59.0	100.0

[a]Foundation-weighted results, adjusted for nonrespondents to this question.
[b]Foundations with assets of $50 million or more.
[c]Foundations with assets of $10–$49.9 million.
[d]Foundations with assets under $10 million.
Source: Salamon and Voytek, 1989.

was considerably more evident among the smaller foundations (those with assets of less than $10 million) than among the larger ones. Among the large foundations, only 11 percent credited staff or outside managers with the dominant role in setting investment objectives, whereas among the small foundations, 37 percent did. In the case of investment strategies, the comparable figures were 19 percent and 40 percent.

Lack of Formal Guidelines or Procedures. Not only did a relatively small proportion of the foundations record a major role for the full foundation board in setting investment strategies, but also most foundations do not really appear to develop formal invest-

Table 8.3. Formal Investment Strategy Guidelines.

	Percentage of foundations with restriction		
Type of guideline	All foundations (n = 22,214)	Large and mid-sized foundations[a] (n = 197)	Small foundations[b] (n = 279)
Maximum stock holdings	22.0	39.6	21.5
Minimum stock holdings	11.7	20.9	11.5
Maximum fixed-income holdings	17.2	30.6	16.9
Minimum fixed-income holdings	12.4	21.8	12.2

[a]Assets of $10 million or more.
[b]Assets of less than $10 million.
Source: Salamon and Voytek, 1989.

ment strategies. Thus, as shown in Table 8.3, fewer than a quarter of the foundations reported having a formal guideline spelling out the maximum portion of their assets that could be held in common stock, perhaps the most basic kind of guideline that might be expected. Other kinds of restrictions — for example, on trading in commodities or holdings of real estate — were even less common. Here again, the larger foundations seem to have more formal guidelines than the smaller ones, as might be expected, but even among the large foundations, no more than 40 percent indicated any formal guidelines even on the share of assets that could be held in common stock. Consistent with this, only about 40 percent of the foundations surveyed reported having any formal procedure for reviewing their investment strategies. The conclusion that seems inescapable is that most foundations do not develop formal strategies to guide their investment operations, preferring to operate in a more ad hoc fashion or to leave it to outsiders to make the necessary choices.

Limited Board Involvement in Portfolio Management. An ad hoc management style, in which investment strategy is left loose and unspecified, would make sense if those with ultimate responsibility for the foundation—the trustees or senior executives—played a significant role in the third aspect of the investment process, day-to-day portfolio management. Under this scenario, the trustees would develop their strategies and objectives in the course of making specific investment decisions. Guidelines might still be desirable for rational investment decisions, but the formality of the process could be greatly curtailed.

As it turns out, however, fewer than a quarter of the foundations we surveyed credited their full boards of trustees with an "extremely important" role in the day-to-day management of foundation assets (see Table 8.2). To be sure, the smaller foundations, which less commonly had formal guidelines or strategies, were somewhat more likely than the larger foundations to involve boards in actual investment management, although for many of these, bank trust departments may function as both the board and the asset managers. But only about a quarter of the smaller foundations reported that their full boards of trustees play an extremely important part at this stage of the process, and only 41 percent indicated that either the full board, the board chair, or a board committee played such a role.

Extensive Reliance on Outside Portfolio Managers. At least as important as board members and senior staff in the actual business of managing foundation portfolios are bank trust departments and other outside managers. In fact, as reflected in Table 8.4, just over 40 percent of the foundations vest day-to-day portfolio management in outside managers of some sort, and most of these rely on such managers to handle two-thirds or more of the foundation's assets.

This reliance on outside managers is particularly evident among the largest foundations, those with assets exceeding $50 million. Close to 90 percent of these foundations rely on outsiders to handle at least some of their assets, and nearly three out of four use outside managers for two-thirds or more of their assets. Such delegation may make sense for these foundations, since they are the ones whose trustees most often define explicit investment objectives and set investment strategy. Here, in other

Table 8.4. Share of Foundation Assets Managed Outside,
by Size of Foundation.

| | Percentage of foundations recording given share of assets managed outside | | | | |
Size of foundation	None	1–33%	33.1%– 67%	Over 67%	Total
All foundations (n = 22,214)	58.2	2.0	2.0	37.8	100.0
Large foundations (n = 73)	12.5	8.3	6.9	72.2	100.0
Mid-sized foundations (n = 124)	24.6	5.9	8.5	61.0	100.0
Small foundations (n = 279)	59.4	1.8	1.8	37.0	100.0

Source: Salamon and Voytek, 1989.

words, guidelines exist to give direction to outside managers in carrying out their day-to-day activities.

In addition to placing a substantial share of their assets in the hands of outside managers, large foundations also tend to utilize more than just one manager. Fifty-eight percent of the large foundations use two or more managers, and 44 percent use four or more. By contrast, only 40 percent of the small foundations make any use of outside managers. In addition, smaller foundations that make use of outside managers tend to rely on only one manager, usually a bank trust department. The preference for inside management may simply be the result of the modest size of the foundation and the larger role of the trustees relative to professionals in the running of the whole operation. In addition, as noted earlier, for many of these foundations, the roles of trustee and outside manager may be merged in the form of a bank trust department that plays both roles. Finally, small foundations may use mutual funds as a substitute for outside managers.

Extensive Discretion for Outside Managers. One final point about outside managers has to do with the degree of discretion granted to them by their foundation clients. Generally speaking, foundations vest a substantial degree of discretion in outside managers. More than half of the foundations that utilize outside managers indicate that they give their managers "complete autonomy and discretion" in day-to-day portfolio management, and another 30 percent indicate that their managers enjoy a "high degree of autonomy and discretion." Clearly, outside managers, where they are used, are significant shapers of foundation investment behavior.

Summary: Limited Management of the Investment Function. What emerges from this overview of the management of the investment function of foundations is that most foundations do not appear to manage this process very systematically. Most do not involve their full boards in the setting of investment objectives or the specification of investment strategies. The investment function is therefore allowed to float, picking up its cues from the professional managers inside and out. This is understandable, since the vast majority of these foundations (82 percent) report having no staff, and some have no separate boards of directors as such, vesting this function instead in bank-appointed trustees. The one countervailing consideration is that the more structured approach appears to be much more common among the larger foundations, so that the larger part of foundation assets may be handled in the recommended way even though most of the foundations manage the function far less directly and formally.

Content

To what extent do these features of foundation investment management affect the actual *content* of foundation investment goals and strategies?

To answer this question, it is necessary to look at four key facets of foundation investment operations: the rate-of-return goal, the degree of risk tolerance, the time frame over which performance is judged, and, finally, the nature of the management style used. As noted earlier, modern portfolio theory would lead us to expect that foundations, by virtue of their stable funding base and long-term perspective, could afford to take a long-term approach to investment, absorbing a relatively high level of risk and therefore aiming at fairly substantial long-term total returns (income plus appreciation). To what extent do foundation investment objectives and strategy adhere to these expectations? Our survey offers some very important clues.

Lack of Focus on Total Return as Investment Goal. Given the nature of investment markets, foundations must explicitly or implicitly choose to maximize either their current income, the long-term value of their assets, or some combination of the two. In other words, they must decide whether their rate-of-return goal is income maximization, capital appreciation, or total return.

Modern portfolio management encourages a balanced total-return approach as the one most likely to maximize long-term success. One of the major criticisms of the tax act of 1969 was that it discouraged such a balanced approach because it required foundations to pay out the full amount of their investment income each year and thus penalized them for investing in high-yielding bonds (Williamson, 1981, pp. 20–24).

As Table 8.5 shows, although total return — a combination of appreciation and investment income — was by far the most popular investment objective of the foundations that we surveyed, fewer than half of the foundations in our survey reported pursuing such a total-return objective as of 1984, when our survey was completed.

Total return was far more common among the large foundations than the small ones, however. More than 80 percent of the larger foundations identified the maximization of total return as their investment objective. By contrast, only 45 percent of the small foundations did; larger proportions of the small foundations focused on income maximization, maintaining asset value, and achieving program spending levels.

This disparity seems to suggest a greater degree of investment sophistication on the part of the larger foundations, which is consistent with findings reported above about the lack of coherence and structure in the investment processes of many

Table 8.5. Investment Objective, by Size of Foundation, 1984.

Objective	Percentage of foundations with indicated objective			
	All foundations (n = 22,135)	Large foundations (n = 72)	Mid-sized foundations (n = 124)	Small foundations (n = 278)
Total return	46.0	80.6	64.5	45.3
Income maximization	5.0	—	11.3	25.5
Capital appreciation	5.4	1.4	8.1	5.4
Maintaining asset value	11.1	12.5	8.1	11.2
Achieving spending goal	6.7	2.8	3.2	6.8
Other	5.8	2.8	4.8	5.8
Total	100.0	100.0	100.0	100.0

Source: Salamon and Voytek, 1989.

smaller foundations. Many small foundations may, in fact, not be pursuing a coherent investment strategy at all but rather trying to minimize their risk of loss by placing their assets in highly secure bonds or other relatively conservative investments and accepting whatever return rate and payout level result.[3]

Interestingly, the share of foundations pursuing a total-return objective increased significantly after 1981, when the payout requirement was liberalized. While a total-return objective still characterized fewer than half of all foundations as of 1984, this was an increase over the 35 percent of all foundations that were pursuing a total-return goal prior to 1982. This is consistent with one of the arguments put forward in support of the 1981 change: that eliminating the requirement that foundations must pay out all their investment income would free foundations to maximize their total return without worrying about whether the return took the form of appreciation or income.

How important the change in the payout requirement was to this shift toward a total-return objective among foundations is difficult to say, however. Of those that had shifted their investment objective since 1981, about 50 percent reported that the payout requirement change was "not too important" or "not important at all." It may be that the exciting rates of capital appreciation in both the stock market and the bond market after 1981 just changed investor perceptions of what investing was all about.

Relatively Conservative Rate-of-Return Goals. Not only were most foundations not pursuing a total-return objective, but also our survey revealed a relatively conservative set of investment expectations on the part of foundations as of the mid 1980s (see Table 8.6).

At a time when the Standard and Poor's 500 had generated a rate of return over the prior three years of 16.5 percent, and the Salomon Brothers long-term corporate bond index had returned 20.6 percent, 92 percent of the foundations in our sample reported a three-year rate-of-return goal of less than 13 percent. The rate-of-return goals among the larger foundations were more aggressive, but even here, well over a third reported total three-year rate-of-return goals of less than 10 percent, and only a quarter reported rate-of-return goals of 13 percent or more. Evidently, the majority of foundation investment manag-

Table 8.6. Foundation Rate-of-Return Goals.

	Percentage of foundations seeking given total rate-of-return goal		
Three-year rate of return	*All foundations* (n = 21,195)	*Larger foundations[a]* (n = 192)	*Smaller foundations[b]* (n = 266)
3–5 percent	2.3	3.1	2.3
6–9 percent	48.1	33.7	48.5
10–12 percent	41.6	36.8	41.7
13 percent or more	8.1	25.9	7.5
Total	100.0	100.0	100.0

[a]Assets of $10 million or more.
[b]Assets under $10 million.
Source: Salamon and Voytek, 1989.

Table 8.7. Risk Tolerance of Foundations.

Risk level	Percentage of foundations with given risk tolerance			
	All foundations (n = 21,188)	Large foundations (n = 68)	Mid-sized foundations (n = 122)	Small foundations (n = 266)
Very low[a]	31.7	5.9	13.1	32.3
Moderately low[b]	40.6	29.4	45.1	40.6
Moderately high[c]	24.2	57.4	37.7	23.7
Very high[d]	3.4	7.4	4.1	3.4
Total	100.0	100.0	100.0	100.0

[a]Less than popular bond market averages.
[b]About equal to popular bond market averages.
[c]About equal to popular stock market averages.
[d]Greater than popular stock market averages.
Source: Salamon and Voytek, 1989.

ers were skeptical that recent market trends would continue and were therefore hedging their expectations.

Limited Risk Tolerance Overall. Similarly, although modern portfolio theory could be expected to recommend relatively expansive risk tolerance for foundations, fully 70 percent of the foundations that we surveyed reported risk tolerances at or below those associated with popular fixed-income bond market averages (see Table 8.7). Only about a quarter of them were comfortable with the risks associated with owning the common stocks listed on the popular stock averages (such as the Dow Jones). These results are consistent with the fairly low rate-of-return goals identified by these foundations. In other words, the majority of foundations appeared willing to accept lower rates of return as the price of avoiding greater risks.

Greater Risk Tolerance Among Large Foundations. Table 8.7 also shows that risk tolerance was much higher among the larger foundations than among the smaller ones. Only about one-third of the largest foundations classified themselves in the very low or moderately low risk-tolerance groups, while almost 75 percent of the small foundations reported low risk tolerance. This, too, is consistent with earlier findings. In fact, it provides further evidence of a "bimodal" distribution of foundations, with one group operating in a more aggressive and activist mode characterized by active board involvement in the setting of priorities, an aggressive rate-of-return goal, and a relatively high risk tolerance, while the other group is operating in a more conservative and less aggressive fashion. Moreover, while the fit is far from perfect, the first group tends to contain a disproportionate number of the largest foundations and the latter group a disproportionate number of the smallest foundations. Perhaps their smaller size leaves the smaller foundations feeling that they have less capacity to absorb losses and therefore inclines them against taking the risk of incurring such losses. In the process, however, it also necessarily lowers their expectation of gain.

Relatively Limited Time Horizon. A third key element in investment decision making is the time horizon over which investments are managed. Although security markets are volatile, they do exhibit clearly defined long-term trends. Therefore, the longer the time horizon over which a manager can operate, the more that manager can assume short-term risks in the expectation of earning higher long-run rewards. This is so because there will be time to recover from temporary setbacks and thus a greater willingness to enter markets where the prospects for above-average gains are more favorable but where the chances of short-term setbacks are also greater.

The investment time horizon that a foundation uses is also affected by the grants strategy that it pursues. Foundations that are interested in giving money away sooner rather than later are likely to place more emphasis on current income and less emphasis on long-term growth than would foundations interested in giving away more money in the future than in the present.

In view of the data presented earlier, it should come as no surprise that the largest concentration of foundations in our sample reported investment time horizons of only one year. Table 8.8 shows that 46 percent of the respondents reported that

Table 8.8. Foundation Investment Time Horizon.

	Percentage of foundations			
Time horizon	All foundations (n = 21,827)	Large foundations (n = 73)	Mid-sized foundations (n = 124)	Small foundations (n = 274)
One year	46.3	27.4	34.7	46.7
Three years	14.4	17.8	18.6	14.2
Five years	15.4	41.1	27.4	15.0
Other or don't know	14.4	13.7	19.4	24.0
Total	100.0	100.0	100.0	100.0

Source: Salamon and Voytek, 1989.

horizon, while only 15 percent reported an investment time horizon of five years or more. Here again, however, the designated time horizon is much shorter among small foundations than among large ones. Among the large foundations, 41 percent reported a time horizon of five years or more, compared to 15 percent of the small foundations. These findings are consistent with the evidence reported earlier that large foundations have risk tolerances and investment policies that are more aggressive than the approaches taken by small foundations. The larger foundations can afford to take more risk because they are managing their investments over a longer time span and therefore can afford more short-term volatility.

Many Foundations with No Clearly Specified Time Horizon. Table 8.8 also shows that almost 15 percent of the foundations failed to specify their investment time horizon, with nearly one out of four of the small foundations falling into this group. This suggests that many foundations may be giving inadequate attention to a critical variable in the management of their assets.

Few Foundations with Active Management Style. As shown in Table 8.9, most foundations not only pursue relatively modest investment goals and have limited risk tolerance but also have relatively passive investment management styles. In particular, only

Table 8.9. Foundation Investment Style.

	Percentage of foundations			
Style	All foundations (n = 21,188)	Large foundations (n = 68)	Mid-sized foundations (n = 122)	Small foundations (n = 266)
Passive	50.3	6.9	14.6	51.5
Moderately active	37.7	51.4	61.8	37.0
Very active	12.0	41.7	23.6	11.5
Total	100.0	100.0	100.0	100.0

Source: Salamon and Voytek, 1989.

12 percent of all foundations represented in the sample identified their management style as very active, that is, involving "considerable turnover and activity, weekly or monthly review of performance, constant reevaluation of investment strategies in light of market conditions, and heavy use of outside data and analysis." By contrast, 50 percent identified their style as passive, that is, involving little turnover in the investment portfolio, review by foundation officials or board members of investment performance on only a quarterly basis or less, and little use of outside data and analysis on the part of foundation officials.

A dramatic contrast exists, however, between the management styles of the large and small foundations. Almost all (93 percent) of the large foundations consider themselves either moderately active or very active investment managers. By contrast, fewer than half (48 percent) of the small foundations put themselves in these two categories.

Limited Use of Investment Reporting Services. Further evidence of the generally passive management style used by the bulk of foundations is provided by foundation responses to a question about outside investment performance reporting services. Despite shortcomings in coverage, such services offer foundation managers a benchmark against which to compare the performance of their own foundations. They are therefore a potentially important management tool. Nevertheless, only about one in ten of the foundations that we surveyed indicated that they subscribe to such a service.

One reason for this lack of interest in performance reporting services may be evident in foundation responses to a question that asked how important comparisons to other foundations are in their own decision making. Only about 12 percent of the foundations indicated that comparisons between their own foundation and other foundations or investment pools were important in their own investment decision making, while close to 80 percent indicated that they were "not too important" or "not important at all."

Summary: The Two Worlds of Foundation Investment Management.
Taken together, the results reported here lend credence to the notion that there are several different worlds of foundation investment management in operation. One of these worlds, characterized by a generally inactive and risk-averse style, is populated by most of the small foundations, a third of the mid-sized foundations, and one in ten of the large foundations. Another, characterized by a much more aggressive and activist style, is the domain of about half of the large foundations, one in five of the mid-sized foundations, and only a small share of the smaller ones. A sizable middle ground is occupied by between 40 and 50 percent of the large and mid-sized foundations and about 30 percent of the small ones.

These findings underline the dangers involved in making broad generalizations about foundation investment management. Indeed, even the division between large and small foundations that has emerged from our data requires significant qualification. Not all large foundations fall into the active and aggressive group, and not all small foundations fall into the inactive and risk-averse group. Indeed, because of the disproportionate number of small foundations, there are actually a greater number of small foundations in the active category than there are large foundations.[4] Therefore, while the fit between management approach and size is statistically significant, it is by no means complete.

Portfolio Composition

Ultimately, investment objectives and strategies find tangible manifestation in decisions about asset composition (the shares of assets to be invested in stocks, bonds, land, commodities futures, and so forth). Although the data available to examine foundation asset composition have serious flaws,[5] they nevertheless provide some revealing insight into this aspect of foundation investment operations. In particular these data suggest the following conclusions.

Most Foundation Assets Are in Equities. The common rule of thumb for institutional investment pools such as foundations is to diversify investments so that roughly 60 percent are in common stock, 30 percent in fixed-income securities (bonds), and 10 percent in cash (Williamson, 1976). As Table 8.10 indicates, this is roughly how foundation assets are in fact distributed. As of 1980, about 61 percent of foundation assets were in common stocks, and about 29 percent were in bonds—11 percent in government bonds and 18 percent in corporate bonds.

Most Foundations Are Primarily Invested in Bonds. While 60 percent of all foundation assets were invested in stocks as of 1980, this was due in substantial measure to the investment practices

Table 8.10. Composition of Foundation Investment Portfolios, 1980.

Asset type		*Percentage of assets*
Corporate stock (equities)		60.7
Government bonds	11.0	
Corporate bonds	17.6	
Subtotal, bonds		28.6
Cash, savings, temporary investments		2.8
Land, depreciable assets, mortgages[a]		1.8
Other		6.1
Total		100.0

[a]Some assets may be recorded at book value.
Source: Salamon and Voytek, 1989.

Table 8.11. Share of Foundation Assets in Common Stock,
by Foundation Size, 1980.

| Share of assets in stock | Percentage of foundations with given share of assets in stock | | | |
	60 percent or more	40–59.9 percent	Less than 40 percent	Total
All foundations (n = 22,294)	13.0	8.6	78.4	100
Large foundations (n = 88)	60.0	22.5	17.5	100
Mid-sized foundations (n = 252)	33.9	28.7	37.4	100
Small foundations (n = 119)	12.1	8.1	79.9	100

Source: Salamon and Voytek, 1989.

of the larger foundations, which control the vast majority of all assets. As Table 8.11 shows, three out of five of these large foundations had 60 percent or more of their assets in stock. By contrast, only one out of eight of all foundations were 60 percent or more invested in stocks as of 1980. On the other hand, four out of five of all foundations—but only one out of five of the large foundations—had less than 40 percent of their assets invested in stocks. In short, the conventional wisdom about how foundations invest their assets may apply to most foundation *assets*, but it does not accurately characterize most *foundations*. The bulk of the small foundations, which comprise most foundations, are more heavily invested in fixed-income securities.

Conclusions: Foundation Investment Management Practice

Given the data reviewed so far, *Institutional Investor's* 1968 characterization of the world of foundation investment management as "a place untouched by the revolution in money management" (Wells, 1968, p. 31), whatever its validity at the time, seems much less valid today. From all indications, a sizable share of the larger foundations, a proportion of the medium-sized foundations, and substantial numbers—if not proportions—of the small foundations seem to have adopted an approach to investment management that is in reasonable accord with the more sophis-

ticated thinking in the field, involving trustees in setting specified investment objectives, focusing on total return, pursuing
ambitious rate-of-return goals, tolerating a significant level of
risk and higher rates of portfolio turnover, conducting frequent
investment reviews, and maintaining a balanced portfolio
weighted toward equities.

At the same time, the data also make clear that the vast
majority of foundations, most of them small, continue to operate their investment function in a fashion close to what *Institutional Investor* described in 1968—with only minimal trustee
involvement, a variety of "satisficing" objectives, limited rate-of-
return goals, low risk tolerance, a narrow time horizon, a less
involved management style, and heavy reliance on fixed-income
securities.

Arriving at judgments about the desirability of one approach compared to the other is no simple matter, of course.
The jury is out on whether more frequent changes in portfolios
provide better returns at lower risk than less frequent changes
would achieve. Furthermore, the appropriate approach depends heavily on the particular characteristics of any given
foundation. A small foundation with a relatively short time
horizon and a sense of limited longevity may be acting rationally in settling on a policy of maximizing income and not
attempting to maximize capital over the long run, even though
this might be unwise for a large foundation run by a professional staff and planning to operate in perpetuity.

Yet, despite some evidence of considerable sophistication, the data presented here provide reason to suspect that, in
fact, many foundations are giving insufficient attention to preserving and enhancing the available philanthropic resources
under their control. The ultimate test of these suspicions, however, lies in the record of actual investment performance. It is to
this record that we therefore now turn.

Foundation Investment Performance

The Approach

To assess the investment performance of foundations, we uti-
lized the unique body of data that foundations are required to

make available annually to the Internal Revenue Service on their 990-PF forms. Although these forms do not include a rate-of-return measure, they do contain enough information on the aggregate value of assets at the beginning and end of each year and on gifts and expenditures to make it possible to develop a reasonable approximation of each foundation's total rate of return after taking account of the inflow and outflow of funds (for further detail on the methodology used, see Salamon, 1991, pp. 27–33). Total return was chosen because it is the recommended measure of investment performance at the present time, combining as it does both current income on investments (dividends and interest) and appreciation or depreciation in the basic value of the assets.

Form 990-PF data were sought on all 699 foundations with 1981 assets of $10 million or more, as well as on all 304 foundations with assets of less than $10 million that responded to a mail survey on foundation investment policies and practices that we distributed (Salamon, 1991, pp. 27–33). Altogether, we were able to compile complete 1979–1986 data on 351 foundations, of which 173 also responded to the survey. These 351 foundations form the basis of the discussion that follows.

To put foundation performance into context and hold constant the impact of market conditions on the results, we constructed an imaginary "control portfolio" composed of 60 percent common stock, 30 percent fixed-income securities, and 10 percent cash or cash equivalents (for example, treasury bills), which we assumed to perform the way standard stock, bond, and treasury bill indexes, respectively, performed during this time period.

As reflected in Table 8.12, the performance of these market indexes during the 1979–1986 period was extraordinarily good by historical standards. Stocks, bonds, and treasury bills all registered average annual rates of return well above their historical averages. Thus, for example, the average annual rate of return on the Standard and Poor's 500 stock index was 17.7 percent during this period, compared to only 4.3 percent during the immediately prior 1974–1978 period and 10.6 percent over the longer 1950–1978 period. Similarly, corporate bonds registered an average annual rate of growth of 12.4 percent

Table 8.12. Performance of Market Indexes, 1979–1986 Versus Earlier Periods.

| | Average annual rate of change (percentage) | | | | | |
| | Study period | | | | Prior periods | |
	1979–1986	1979–1981	1982–1986	1974–1978	1950–1978
Stocks[a]	17.7	14.1	19.9	4.3	10.6
Bonds[b]	12.4	− 2.6	22.4	6.0	3.2
Cash[c]	9.9	12.0	8.6	6.2	3.8
Consumer Price Index	6.3	11.4	3.3	7.9	3.7
Composite Market Index[d]					
Nominal	15.3	8.9	19.5	5.1	7.7
Real	9.0	− 2.5	16.2	− 2.8	4.0

[a]Standard and Poor's 500 Stock Index.
[b]Salomon Brothers Bond Index.
[c]Treasury bill rate.
[d]Assumes a portfolio composed 60 percent of stocks, 30 percent of bonds, and 10 percent of cash performing the same as the respective stock, bond, and cash indexes.

during 1979–1986, compared to only 6.0 percent in 1974–1978 and 3.2 percent during 1950–1978. Reflecting this, our composite "control portfolio" would have yielded 15.3 percent over the 1970–1986 period, compared to 5.1 percent during 1974–1978 and 7.7 percent during 1950–1978.

While return rates were unusually high during 1979–1986, so was the rate of inflation. The Consumer Price Index rose at an annual rate of 6.3 percent during 1979–1986, compared to 3.7 percent over the 1950–1978 period. This had the effect of cutting into the real value of returns, though even in real, inflation-adjusted terms, our study period registered higher returns than either earlier period. As Table 8.12 makes clear, however, this was more true of the latter part of the period, 1982–1986, than of the earlier one, 1979–1981. Perhaps more significantly, our study period was a time of great volatility in return rates. Thus, while corporate bonds registered an average annual increase of 12.4 percent during 1979–1986, this was the result of three years of declines followed by one year of tremendous growth (44 percent in 1982), followed by another slow year (4.7 percent in 1983) and then by three years of high returns (16.4 percent, 30.9 percent, and 19.8 percent in 1984, 1985, and 1986, respectively). Obviously, this kind of volatility can play havoc with investment planning.

The Results

How, then, did foundations perform in relation to this market index? Several conclusions emerge from our data.

Most Foundations Performed Worse Than the Market Index. The median annual foundation rate of total return averaged 15.1 percent during 1979–1986, compared to 15.3 percent for our market index (see Table 8.13). In other words, slightly more than half of the foundations performed below what could have been achieved by investing in the basic market indexes during this period. In inflation-adjusted terms, the median foundation achieved a real growth rate of 8.8 percent, just enough to meet the minimum payout level and still have a small margin of error.

Table 8.13. Foundation Investment Performance, 1979–1986.

| | Average annual rate of total return (percentage) | | |
	1979–1986	1979–1981	1982–1986
Actual			
Median foundation	15.1	10.9	17.0
Large foundations[a]	17.6	14.0	20.0
Mid-sized foundations[b]	16.5	12.3	18.9
Small foundations[c]	15.1	10.4	17.0
Asset-weighted	17.0	11.9	20.1
Market index	15.3	8.9	19.5
Median as percentage of index	99.0	122.0	87.0
Inflation-adjusted			
Median foundation	8.8	– 0.5	13.7
Large foundations	11.3	2.7	16.7
Mid-sized foundations	10.2	0.9	15.6
Small foundations	8.8	– 1.0	13.7
Asset-weighted	10.7	0.5	16.8
Market index	9.0	– 2.5	16.2

[a]Foundations with assets of $50 million or more.
[b]Foundations with assets of $10–49.9 million.
[c]Foundations with assets under $10 million.

The Overall Rate of Return on Foundation Assets Exceeded the Market Index. While most foundations performed worse than the market index, the larger foundations performed better than the index. As Table 8.13 also shows, these foundations achieved an average annual rate of return of 17.6 percent during this period, compared to 15.1 percent for the smaller foundations. As a result, the asset-weighted average annual rate of total return for foundations during 1979–1986 exceeded the rate of our control portfolio (17.0 percent versus 15.3 percent). After adjusting for inflation, the rate of return on foundation assets was close to 11 percent a year during 1979–1986, which was more than enough to support a 5 percent payout rate without eating into the real value of the asset base.

Foundations Had Higher Return Rates Following the Change in the Payout Requirement, but This Was Due Largely to Market Developments. Foundations had higher return rates in the latter part of this period, after the change in the payout requirement in 1981, than during the earlier part (1979–1981). Thus, as shown in Table 8.13, the average annual rate of return for the median foundation during 1982–1986 was 17.0 percent, compared to only 10.9 percent in 1979–1981.

Although this improved performance may be due in part to the 1981 change in the payout requirement, which allowed foundations to retain earnings in excess of 5 percent of their assets, it is probably due in even greater part to a change in market conditions between these two periods. Relative to the market index, in fact, foundations actually did better in the earlier period than they did in the later one, achieving a return rate of 122 percent of the market index versus 87 percent in the later period (see Table 8.13). What this suggests is that foundations tend to do better than the market during weak market periods and worse than the market during strong market periods. This is consistent with our earlier finding that foundations tend to be somewhat conservative investors that hedge against downside risks but in the process limit their participation in upside gains. While the payout change may have encouraged foundations to take more advantage of the changed market conditions than they might have done otherwise, it did not alter this basic characteristic of foundation investment management.

Although foundations performed better than the market average during the 1979–1981 period, however, inflation ate away most of the gains. Adjusted for inflation, the median foundation had a real rate of return during the 1979–1981 period of − 0.5 percent, as shown in Table 8.13. In other words, most foundations lost ground in real terms yet were still obligated to pay out a minimum of 5 percent of their assets in grants. This experience helps to explain the pressure that emerged in the late 1970s for a change in the foundation payout requirement. During the more recent period, with inflation slowed and return rates high, foundations did much better. Adjusted for inflation, the median real rate of return for foundations during this period was 13.7 percent.

Foundations That Adhered to the Modern Portfolio Management Generally Perform Better Than Those That Did Not. According to modern investment management theory, investors that focus on total return rather than simply income yield, have relatively long investment time horizons, pursue fairly high rate-of-return goals, and accept relatively high risk tolerance are likely to achieve high return rates. As noted earlier, most foundations do not adhere to this approach. To what extent did this affect their rates of return? The answer, it turns out, is quite substantially, and in the direction that the theory predicted. The findings are shown in Table 8.14.

Foundations with longer time horizons tended to perform better than those with short time horizons. Thus, foundations reporting a time horizon of five years or more had a median annual rate of total return during the 1979–1986 period of 15.9 percent, compared to 15.5 percent for foundations with a one-year time horizon and 15.3 percent for those with a three-year time horizon. Although these differences are not great, they do suggest that foundations that invest for the long run perform better than those that focus on shorter-term returns.

Foundations consciously pursuing a higher rate-of-return goal, which typically involves a willingness to assume greater risk, also performed better than those with more limited rate-of-return goals. In particular, foundations reporting a three-year rate-of-return goal of 13 percent or more had a median rate of return of 17.6 percent per year, compared to only 14.8 percent for the foundations with low (3–9 percent) rate-of-return goals. It should be noted that even the ambitious three-year return goal of 13 + percent was well below what the markets were delivering during this period.

Foundations with moderately or very high risk tolerance also outperformed those with low risk tolerance. Thus, the foundations with "very high" risk tolerance, which we defined as a willingness to absorb risks greater than those associated with popular stock averages (for example, the Standard and Poor 500

Table 8.14. Foundation Investment Management and Return Rates, 1979–1986 ($n = 166$).

Investment management dimension	Median annual rate of return, 1979–1986 (percentage)
Time horizon	
1 year	15.5
3 years	15.3
5 + years	15.9
Rate-of-return goal	
Low (3–9%)	14.8
Moderate (10–12%)	15.7
High (13 + %)	17.6
Risk tolerance	
Very low	14.8
Moderately low	14.5
Moderately high	16.5
Very high	16.9
Management style	
Passive	15.6
Moderately active	16.1
Very active	16.7
Asset composition (percentage in stocks)	
Low (0–29%)	16.0
Medium (30–59%)	16.3
High (60 + %)	17.5

Source: Salamon and Voytek, 1989.

or the Dow Jones average), recorded a median return rate of 16.9 percent. Foundations with "moderately high" risk tolerance, which we defined as equivalent to the risk associated with the popular stock market averages, recorded a median return rate of 16.5 percent. By contrast, foundations with "moderately low" or "very low" risk tolerance, which we defined as a level of risk equivalent to or less than the popular bond market averages, recorded return rates of 14.5 and 14.8 percent, respectively. Once again, it should be noted that the risk levels used here were all well within a fairly narrow and generally conservative band of options, yet the differences still seem to have translated into real differences in performance.

Foundations pursuing an "active" investment management style recorded a higher median annual rate of return (16.7 percent) than those that followed a more "passive" approach (15.6 percent).

Foundations with more of their assets in stocks had higher return rates than those with more of their assets in fixed-income securities. Thus, as Table 8.13 shows, foundations with 0–29 percent of their assets in stocks had a median annual return rate of 16.0 percent over the 1979–1986 period, compared to 16.3 percent for those with 30–59 percent of their assets in stocks and 17.5 percent for those with 60 percent or more of their assets in stocks.

Interestingly, most of the relationships summarized above held during both the early part of the period that we studied (1979–1981), when markets were relatively weak, and the later part (1982–1986), when markets were more robust. Indeed, some of the key relationships — for example, that between risk tolerance and return rate — held more powerfully during the early period than the later one. This suggests that the so-called modern portfolio management approach to investment, which emphasizes total return, long time horizons, and moderately high risk tolerance, is not one that works only during boom times. Whether it would hold in a true down market, however, is not possible to determine from these data.

Payout Policies and Performance

The Issues

Foundation investment management is not an end in itself. Rather, it is a means to enable foundations to carry out their charitable missions — to distribute the resources under their control for charitable purposes. But critical choices have to be made about how to balance current and future beneficiaries of foundation largesse. Other things being equal, the higher the current level of payout, the smaller the pool of assets left to support future distributions. On the other hand, the more investment earnings are retained and plowed back into the asset base, the more questionable the foundation's claim to tax-exempt status as a charitable institution. The task of foundation financial management therefore goes beyond merely earning a high rate of return. It involves striking a meaningful balance between these competing concerns.

Prior to 1969, as we have seen, foundations were left essentially on their own in making these decisions, albeit with some general congressional guidance after 1950 about the need to avoid excessive accumulations of resources. In response to concerns that at least some foundations were abusing this freedom and neglecting to distribute sufficient funds for charitable purposes, however, Congress changed this situation fundamentally in 1969, enacting a payout requirement that established a mandatory floor for foundation charitable distributions.

In 1981, Congress agreed to liberalize this payout requirement by eliminating the requirement that foundations must pay out 5 percent of their assets. One of the key congressional concerns in making this change, however, was that it might lead to a significant decline in payout rates. To what extent has this concern proved warranted? What has the record of foundation payout been, and how is the relationship between return rate and payout rate managed?

The Results

Several conclusions emerge from our survey and 990-PF data analysis on these points.

Foundations Pay Out More Than Required by Law. The median payout rate for the foundations in our sample averaged 7.7 percent a year during the period that we studied (1979–1986), or more than 50 percent above the minimum 5 percent rate set by law (see Table 8.15).

The Payout Rate Was Higher for Small Foundations Than for Large Ones. This relatively high payout rate essentially reflects the payout performance of the numerous small foundations. As Table 8.15 shows, these foundations had a median annual aver-

Table 8.15. Foundation Payout Rates, by Size of Foundations, 1979–1986.

	Median average annual payout rate (percentage)			
	Small foundations	Mid-sized foundations	Large foundations	All foundations[a]
1979–1986	7.7	6.1	6.0	7.7
1979–1981	7.7	6.5	6.6	7.7
1982–1986	7.7	5.8	5.5	7.7

[a]Foundation-weighted median.

age payout rate of 7.7 percent during this period. By contrast, the payout rates for the medium-sized and large foundations were considerably lower (6.1 percent and 6.0 percent, respectively). This is somewhat paradoxical, since the larger foundations, as noted above, had higher overall return rates. In other words, the foundations with the highest rates of return had the lowest payout rates, and those with the lowest rates of return had the highest payout rates.

Most Foundations, Particularly Small Ones, Pay Out All Investment Income. An important part of the explanation for this paradoxical relationship lies in the payout policies and practices of foundations. As Table 8.16 shows, foundations pursued a variety of different approaches in setting their payout rates. The most common approach, reported by close to 40 percent of the foundations, was to set payout equal to investment income. Another 30 percent of the foundations reported that payout decisions are shaped by overall investment performance, including appreciation, rather than merely the amount of investment income. A much smaller 14 percent of the foundations reported paying out only what the law requires. And, strikingly, a mere 7 percent indicated that the primary determinant of payout levels is programmatic goals.

Significantly, the proportions of foundations that fell into these different categories varied considerably by the size of the foundation. For example, only 14 percent of all foundations reported that they pay out only the minimum that the law

Table 8.16. Foundation Payout Policy by Size of Foundation.

	Percentage of foundations			
Payout policy	All (n = 8,684)	Large (n = 44)	Mid-sized (n = 70)	Small (n = 108)
Pay out all investment income	37.5	9.1	8.6	37.0
Payout shaped by investment performance	30.8	6.8	31.4	28.7
Pay out what law requires	14.1	36.4	28.6	16.7
Payout shaped by program goals	7.4	13.6	8.6	5.6
Payout determined by gifts	4.8	—	—	1.9
Payout slightly more than required	2.9	34.1	21.4	1.9
Other	2.5	—	1.4	8.2
Total	100.0	100.0	100.0	100.0

Source: Salamon and Voytek, 1989.

requires and another 3 percent that they pay out just slightly more than the law requires, but about 70 percent of the largest foundations reported one of these two responses. By contrast, among the small foundations, investment performance, particularly investment income, plays the dominant role in determining payout levels.

This suggests that at least two very different approaches to payout decision making are evident among foundations and that size is an important factor in explaining how foundations are distributed between them. In particular, among the smaller foundations, investment decisions are most likely to determine payout levels. By contrast, among the larger foundations, payout considerations seem more likely to shape investment decisions. Put somewhat differently, the small foundations tend to pursue a conservative investment approach focusing on fixed-income securities and then, whether by choice or necessity, pay out all the earnings that this investment approach generates. By contrast, the larger foundations are more likely to devise an investment strategy that takes account of the payout requirement and to arrange their investments in such a way as to minimize the impact of the payout requirement on the long-term asset base of the foundation.

This finding is consistent with the earlier finding that larger foundations tend to have more formalized and coherent investment strategies. What becomes clear is that these formalized investment strategies embrace payout decision making as well: investment decisions are made with the payout requirement in mind. This may help to explain why the payout rates of the larger foundations are generally lower than those of the small foundations.[6]

Some Foundations Relaxed Their Payout Policies After the Change in the Payout Requirement. An examination of early reactions to the 1981 change in the payout requirement indicates that about 15 percent of all foundations made a change in their payout policies after 1981, and most of these credited the change in the legal payout requirement with major responsibility for the change. Significantly, the most frequently cited change was away from setting payout at what the law required and toward having payout shaped by investment income or overall investment performance. Thus, the proportion of foundations reporting that their policy was to pay out what the law requires went from 4 percent prior to 1982 to 14 percent afterward, and the proportion that reported that their payout decisions were shaped by investment performance went from 12 percent to 31 percent. In other words, foundations expressed greater freedom to adjust payout rates to investment conditions and performance, as advocates of the change in the law had sought.

The Median Foundation Payout Rate Remained Remarkably Stable, but This Was Due Mostly to the Performance of the Small Foundations. Despite the change in the payout requirement and in foundation payout policies in 1981, payout rates remained virtually unchanged at 7.7 percent in the two subperiods that we examined, one before the payout requirement change (1979–1981) and one following this change (1982–1986) (see Table 8.15). This is consistent with the finding that most foundations gear their payout policies not to the requirements of the law but to their income yield. And the income yield for the median foundation was fairly constant during this period at around 7 to 7.5 percent.

As Table 8.15 shows, however, this record of relatively unchanged payout rates between these two periods essentially reflects the behavior of the numerous small foundations. By contrast, the mid-sized and large foundations pursued a very different course. Their payout rates declined noticeably between the two subperiods. Thus, the payout rate for the mid-sized foundations declined from 6.5 percent in the 1979–1981 period to 5.8 percent in the 1982–1986 period. For the large foundations, the corresponding change was from 6.6 percent to 5.5 percent.

Implications

Several explanations for this pattern of foundation payout performance seem possible. In the first place, small foundations are more likely to be influenced by the original donors or their immediate families and to be more interested in maximizing current grant making than in holding the foundation's assets for the longer term. This would lead them to favor low-risk/high-current-yield investments and to give away all of their earnings in a given year, even if this eats into the asset base over time. By contrast, the larger foundations, run by professional staffs, are more likely to be committed to operating in perpetuity and therefore to selecting investment and payout policies that encourage this.

Another explanation of these results may be that the smaller foundations are not pursuing coherent investment and payout strategies at all but rather are placing their assets in "safe" investments regardless of the impact on either return rates or payout. Their high payout rates may therefore reflect the unusually high yields on fixed-income securities during the period of this study. By contrast, the larger, professionally staffed foundations may treat the payout provisions as a systematic part of their investment decision making and arrange their investments in a way that minimizes the impact of the payout requirement on their long-term asset base. Although these foundations may have lower payout *rates*, this approach may still allow them to have higher payout *amounts*, since the rates are applied against a growing, or at least not declining, asset base.

In all likelihood, both explanations have an element of truth in them. Under any circumstances, it seems clear that the larger foundations have taken far more advantage of the flexibility afforded them by the change in the foundation payout requirement. Since these foundations control the bulk of the foundation assets, there is evidence here that the payout requirement change has achieved some of its major objectives, especially in light of the strong investment performance that these larger foundations achieved.

At the same time, it seems clear from these results that the foundations that stand to benefit the most from the 1981 change in the payout requirement are paradoxically the ones with the lowest rates of total return (income plus appreciation). By virtue of their high income yield, these are the foundations that generally had payout levels in excess of the 5 percent minimum prior to 1981. Therefore, they are the ones that have the option since 1981 of not paying out this "surplus." It thus becomes especially important for the foundation community to encourage these foundations to make sensible and effective decisions about how to utilize the savings that may result.

Conclusions and Recommendations

As this chapter has made clear, foundations are not simply financiers of charitable activities. They are also institutional investors charged with maintaining and enhancing the charitable resources within their control. Yet this facet of foundation activities has not received the attention it deserves.

At a time when investment management is becoming increasingly complex and competitive, it is imperative that foundations give as much attention to the management of their assets as they do to the management of their grants and that those who regulate foundations recognize the dilemmas inherent in this task.

By demonstrating that a significant number of foundations are performing quite well while many others still have some distance to go, the data presented here suggest the importance both of protecting the gains that have been made and of stimulating further change. More specifically, several possible recommendations find support in the data presented here.

Extend the 1981 Payout Requirement

Perhaps most fundamentally, the data in this chapter provide some confirmation of the wisdom of the liberalization of the payout requirement in 1981. This change has allowed some greater flexibility for foundations in designing their investment strategies without evident negative side effects in terms of foundation payout rates. The 1981 change should therefore be sustained.

Use a Multiyear Payout Computation

While the 1981 change in the payout requirement was a step in the right direction, it may not have gone far enough. A useful next step would be to replace the current one-year base for computing the payout rate with a three- or five-year floating average. While the current system's provision for carryovers from one year to another provides some flexibility, it still exposes foundations to considerable year-to-year fluctuations in their payout levels, which impede effective grant making. An explicit multiyear formula would allow foundations to lengthen their investment time horizons and also reduce the year-to-year fluctuations in required distributions.

Create a Common Fund for Foundations

To equip the smaller foundations in particular to operate as successfully as possible in today's highly specialized capital markets, the foundation community should seriously consider borrowing a page from the higher education field and organizing a "common fund" for foundations. Such a fund could pool the investment resources of a number of foundations and manage them centrally, permitting small and mid-sized foundations to benefit from expert management at lower cost than is now possible.[7]

Give More Attention to Foundation Investment Management

In view of the fact that most foundations seem to be pursuing rather ad hoc investment approaches and achieving rates of return below market averages for a comparable portfolio, more attention needs to be focused on the investment function of foundations. This could take the form of training sessions and educational materials as well as a more systematic and permanent mechanism for tracking foundation investment behavior. Beyond this, there is a need for improvement in the basic data systems for tracking foundation investment performance. Limitations in the basic 990-PF form for tracking investment activity coupled with shortcomings in foundation responses to these forms and in IRS handling of them make this potentially invaluable source of information far less useful than it needs to be.

In the wake of government budget cuts and continued constraints on government spending, private foundations have gained unexpected prominence in American life. Naturally enough, this prominence has attracted considerable attention to the grant-making activities of foundations. The message of this chapter, however, is that as important as the grant-making activity of foundations may be, there is an equally important management function — the supervision of foundation assets. This function has received far less attention, both within the foundation community and without. Given the vital importance of this function, it is time that it received the greatly increased attention that it deserves.

This conclusion very likely holds not only for foundations, moreover, but for other nonprofit organizations as well. Foundations, after all, are the most financial of charitable institutions. But, as we have seen, they are hardly the only type of nonprofit organization managing substantial assets. Indeed, the practice of seeking endowment funds is spreading throughout the nonprofit sector. If significant numbers of foundations are managing their assets in a rather lackadaisical way and achieving far less than optimal returns, therefore, it seems highly likely that even larger proportions of other types of nonprofits are exhibiting similar shortcomings. Under these circumstances, it becomes increasingly important to ensure that investment management is improved not only among foundations but throughout the nonprofit sector more generally.

Notes

1. A third investment reporting service, InData, covers 157 institutions in its endowment fund universe, but many of these are universities and other nonfoundation endowments, and the 157 had total assets of only $5.3 billion in 1985, compared to $92.6 billion in foundation assets.

2. For a forceful statement of the position that foundation boards should retain an active voice not only in the setting of foundation investment objectives but also in the day-to-day management of foundation investments, see Frazer (1985).

3. An alternative explanation may be that small foundations, in contrast to large ones, are more interested in spending money in the short run than over the longer run, perhaps because the dominant influence in a small foundation is more likely to be the original donor interested in spending "his" or "her" money, in contrast to a large foundation run by a professional staff. Either way, this would lead us to expect a more conservative investment approach on the part of the smaller foundations.

4. Thus, the 46 percent of large foundations scoring high on an "investment approach index" that we constructed represent 78 foundations. By comparison, the 4 percent of small foundations scoring high on this index represent 842 foundations.

5. Prior to 1982, foundations were regularly asked to report on their 990-PF forms the share of their investment portfolios that they held in each of seven classes of assets: cash, savings

and temporary investments, government obligations, corporate bonds, corporate stocks, land and depreciable assets, and other. However, the forms did not specify that asset values were to be recorded at "market value," that is, at their current value on the market, as opposed to their purchase price or "book value." There is thus reason to doubt the accuracy of the data as a measure of actual portfolio composition. Since 1982, foundations have been specifically asked to report the market value of the different components of their investment portfolios. However, the categories were significantly reduced, and the three main categories of assets—corporate stocks, corporate bonds, and government bonds—were merged into one on the form. As a consequence, we cannot determine from the 990-PF forms since 1981 what share of foundation assets are held in fixed-income securities and what share in equities or stock holdings.

6.   For an alternative explanation, see note 3.
7.   Fortunately, following the introduction of this recommendation in the initial report on which this chapter draws, efforts have gone forward to put this suggestion into effect, and the needed legislation is now pending in Congress.

References

Cary, W., and Bright, C. B. *The Law and Lore of Endowment Funds*. New York: Ford Foundation, 1969.

Commission on Foundations and Private Philanthropy. *Foundations, Private Giving, and Public Policy*. Chicago: University of Chicago Press, 1970.

Council on Foundations. *The Handbook on Private Foundations*. Washington, D.C.: Council on Foundations, 1981.

Ellis, C. D. *Institutional Investing*. Homewood, Ill.: Dow Jones–Irwin, 1971.

Frazer, D. R. "Investing Your Foundation's Assets." *Foundation News*, Jan.–Feb. 1985, pp. 46–49.

Hodgkinson, V. A., Weitzman, M. S., Toppe, C. M., and Noga, S. M. *Nonprofit Almanac 1992–1993: Dimensions of the Independent Sector*. San Francisco: Jossey-Bass, 1992.

McDonald, J. G. "Setting Investment Objectives." Research Paper no. 136, Graduate School of Business, Stanford University, 1973.

Malkiel, B. G. *A Random Walk Down Wall Street*. New York: W.W. Norton, 1985.

Markowitz, H. *Portfolio Selection: Efficient Diversification of Investments*. New York: Wiley, 1959.

Modigliani, F., and Pogue, G. "An Introduction to Risk and Return." *Financial Analysts Journal*, 1974, *30*, 68–80.

Murray, R. "Foundation Investments: Problems of Investment Policy." In H. Sellin (ed.), *Tenth Biennial Conference on Charitable Foundations*. New York: New York University, 1971.

Nason, J. W. *Trustees and the Future of Foundations*. New York: Council on Foundations, 1977.

Nelson, R. *The Investment Policies of Private Foundations*. New York: Russell Sage Foundation, 1967.

Nelson, R. "An Economic History of Large Foundations." In T. Odendahl (ed.), *America's Wealthy and the Future of Foundations*. New York: Foundation Center, 1987.

Reilly, R. R., and Skadden, D. H. *Private Foundations: The Payout Requirement and Its Effect on Investment Spending Policy*. Ann Arbor: Graduate School of Business Administration, University of Michigan, 1981.

Renz, L. *Foundation Trends*. New York: Foundation Center, 1991.

Riley, M. "Private Foundation Returns, 1985." *SOI Bulletin*, 1989, *9*(1), 27–43.

Salamon, L. M. *Foundation Investment and Payout Performance: An Update*. New York: Council on Foundations, 1991.

Salamon, L. M., and Voytek, K. P. *Managing Foundation Assets: An Analysis of Foundation Investment and Payout Procedures and Performance*. New York: Foundation Center, 1989.

Wells, C. "Foundations: The Quiet 20 Billion." *The Institutional Investor*, 1968, *2*(11), 31–90.

Williamson, J. P. "Investment Expectations and the Foundation Payout Rate." *Foundation News*, Jan.–Feb. 1976, pp. 13–18.

Williamson, J. P. "Inflation and the Foundation Payout Requirement." *Foundation News*, Mar.–Apr. 1981, pp. 18–24.

Young, D., and Moore, W. *Trusteeship and the Management of Foundations*. New York: Russell Sage Foundation, 1969.

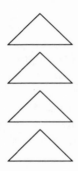

CHAPTER 9

Obtaining Resources
Using Barter Trade:
Benefits and Drawbacks

Avner Ben-Ner

Barter is an exchange of goods or services for other goods or services. Partners to both barter and monetized trade need to engage in similar activities: they need to search for sellers of products of interest to them and find buyers for their own products, evaluate the products, evaluate their own costs of production, compare the terms of trade that others offer or demand, and establish the terms of trade for the transaction in which they engage. In addition, however, barter also entails establishing a "double coincidence of wants," wherein one individual's desire for apples and possession of excess tomatoes is matched with somebody else's desire for tomatoes and possession of excess apples. Multilateral exchange (*A* exchanges tomatoes for potatoes with *B*, then *A* exchanges potatoes for

Note: The helpful comments of Egon Neuberger, Theresa Van Hoomissen, and Dennis R. Young are gratefully acknowledged.

apples, B exchanges tomatoes for clothes with C, and so on) ameliorates but does not totally eliminate the problem of establishing a double coincidence of wants. Multilateral exchange requires that each individual seek out multiple trading partners and maintain stocks of goods that he or she does not care about.[1]

Monetized trade, however, entails an additional exchange relative to barter, because each good needs to be traded for money (tomatoes for money, money for apples). Nonetheless, the cost of establishing a double coincidence of wants for each good that an individual wishes to consume is generally likely to be much greater than the cost of exchanging goods for money and then money for desired goods. In fact, it is easy to imagine a situation in which barter trade entails many more exchanges than monetized trade (holding constant some notion of volume of trade). It is for this reason that when exchange, specialization, and division of labor developed, it was useful to establish a medium of exchange, whether it was salt bars, precious metals, credit, or paper notes — various forms of *money*.[2] Indeed, a fully barter economy has hardly ever existed, though barter has played a significant role in traditional societies (Humphrey, 1985). Despite the prevalence of monetized trade, however, barter persists even in developed market economies. While government-to-government barter ("countertrade") attracts most attention and accounts for a significant volume of world international trade, for-profit, nonprofit, and government organizations engage in barter trade as well (Banks, 1985; Magenheim and Murrell, 1988; Reisman, 1991a, 1991b).

The existence of barter in economies where markets and monetary instruments are well established presents a puzzle, since the transaction costs of barter trade appear to be so much higher than those of monetized trade. The objective of this chapter is to understand part of this puzzle: barter among nonprofit organizations. Several examples put forth by Reisman (1991a, pp. 11–13) illustrate the nature of this practice: (1) a recreational center loans computer programmers to a rehabilitation center in return for a recreational training program; (2) a nonprofit executive explains the barter exchanges in which his organization engages (trading preparation of annual reports, creation of mailing lists, and procedures for strategic planning), saying "why use valuable dollars for consultants when we share the same goals?"; (3) an orchestra performs for the dedication of a new hospital facility in exchange for the use of a hospital hall for an orchestra event; (4) a hospital allows a museum's employees to use its meeting rooms occasionally, receiving in exchange free access to the museum for hospital patients; and (5) a nonprofit organization trades printing services for staff training services from another nonprofit organization.

The following section revisits the barter puzzle in general, comparing both the benefits and transaction costs of monetized and barter trade. Barter is likely to occur among organizations that are familiar with their respective productive services and needs and can trust each other. The subsequent section examines why nonprofit organizations engage in barter trade, concluding that the conditions for barter are met more easily in nonprofit organizations than in for-profit firms. The last section concludes the chapter with some policy recommendations.

Why Barter in a Monetized Market Economy?

The existence of barter trade suggests that either some traders are irrational or there are circumstances that induce rational parties to prefer barter over monetized trade. Barter is rationally preferable when monetary transactions are costlier than barter transactions and/or when the benefits of barter are greater than those of monetized trade.[3] This section examines the circumstances in which the costs and benefits of barter differ from those of monetized trade.

Humphrey (1985), Clower (1969), Goodhart (1989), Niehans (1971), and Ulph and Ulph (1975) suggest that low money supply or low-quality money may induce barter, since money is exactly the stuff that makes monetized trade possible. Barter nonetheless occurs when money is plentiful (in the sense that there is enough of it to satisfy transaction needs without recourse to credit or other less abundant or riskier monetary instruments), safe (nobody suspects that counterfeit money is being peddled around), and steady in value (there is no inflation).

Purported Benefits

What is it that barter can do that monetized trade cannot under these conditions? Below I consider nine answers to this question, most of which appear elsewhere in the literature. As subsequent discussion indicates, several of these answers are not logically consistent, and several constitute neither sufficient nor necessary conditions for barter trade but rather serve as facilitating factors.

Resource Enhancement. The argument is that because certain goods and services cannot be sold on the market for various reasons, bartering them gets some return, hence enhancing the organization's resources (Reisman, 1991a). Although intuitively appealing, this argument by itself does not make sense: if a product is not wanted, nobody will give up anything valuable for it (there are two parties to a trade), and if there is demand for the good, it will be backed up by a price. In this case, barter only imposes the additional burden of establishing a double coincidence of wants.

Excess Capacity. The argument here is that it is advantageous to barter away some excess service capacity (Reisman, 1991a), perhaps at marginal rather than average cost. The previous counterargument applies here as well.

Price Discrimination. The argument for this answer is that barter allows products to be unloaded at lower implicit prices, so that firms can surreptitiously price discriminate (that is, sell the same product to different customers at different prices). This argument makes sense if the terms of trade in barter are less transparent than those in monetized trade, as Magenheim and Murrell (1988) argue (see also Banks, 1985).

Avoidance of Price Restrictions. If the government mandates non-market-clearing prices, this argument runs, barter may develop to circumvent these prices (Banks, 1985). This argument is sound only as long as the barter terms of trade are tolerated by the government.

Exploitation. Barter, it is argued, is a tool that can be used by a sophisticated party to exploit a more naive party. In this case, the sophisticated party manages to get better terms of trade than would have been obtained in monetized trade. This argument is similar to the previous two in that someone with an interest in the terms of trade (tax authorities, potential or actual traders) is fooled by the different appearance of barter relative to monetized trade (Banks, 1985).

Lack of Marketing Expertise. This argument posits that a firm that lacks the requisite expertise to market a particular good will seek to barter it to a firm with established marketing capabilities. Presumably, the terms of trade are set such that there is an implicit charge for the marketing services. For example, the Soviet Union is said to have bartered its vodka for soda from Pepsi Cola for this reason. The argument is not compelling, however, because such transactions do not require barter (Banks, 1985); the Soviet Union, for example, could have contracted for marketing services with a third party rather than barter its vodka. Although the barter arrangement reduces uncertainty for the partner lacking marketing ability, it is hardly the only (or best) device for that.

Reciprocity and Trust. Delayed barter may enhance reciprocity among parties, thus enhancing trust and preserving the social relationship among them. This argument has two components. First, it is argued that delayed barter fosters reciprocal social obligations (regardless of whether the barter is informal, a formal commercial exchange, or ritual gift giving), and that helps to develop trust relationships. (Trust has many economic and social uses and functions; see, for example, Gambetta, 1988.) Second, it is argued that some individuals or groups prefer to partially insulate some of their economic relationships from the market and its implications. Barter, in which no money is exchanged and which typically requires face-to-face interaction, is more akin to "social exchange," in which the norm of reciprocity based on moral obligations replaces the closely linked exchanges in market monetary relations. In sum, barter trade is regarded in some circumstances as an exchange among friends who do not want to "infect" their relationship with monetary trades. (See Lane's 1991 discussion of this issue, relying on the work of Blau, 1964; Homans, 1961; Gouldner, 1960; and others; see also Malinowski, 1922; Polanyi, [1944] 1957; and Humphrey, 1985).

Inexpensive Barter. Barter, it is argued, occurs among traders who know each other's production facilities and find it relatively costly to seek partners for monetized trade. This claim asserts that a double coincidence of wants can sometimes be established at lower cost than engaging in monetary transactions. For example, if A has product x and wants product y, and B has y and wants x, direct trade will be cheaper than selling their respective products on the market and purchasing each other's products with money.

Expensive Monetized Trade. This argument, which is an extension of the previous one, suggests that barter occurs among traders who know each other's production facilities and find the terms of monetized trade relatively unattractive. The transaction costs of monetized trade may be high for a number of reasons. For example, if buyers are imperfectly informed about the qualities of products x and y, the market will generate a situation in which high-quality products can be traded at only average-quality prices (this is an Akerlof, 1970, "market for lemons" situation). Similarly, transportation, marketing, storage, or disposal costs may be significant, or the traders may have little cash on hand. In these situations, barter (when delayed) can substitute for credit, lead to savings in storage and disposal costs, or be conducted on terms that reflect a recognition of the "lemons" problem. Likewise, when it is expensive for two traders to seek market outlets each time an unexpected surplus occurs, if each is ac-quainted with the other's needs and trusts the other, they may economize on transaction costs by simply exchanging these products *over time*. This is the kind of deployment of excess capacity that occurs within firms and even across firms that belong to a loose umbrella organization, such as the Japanese keiretsu (in keiretsus, it is apparently common to lend equip-ment and employees among member firms).

Merits of the Claims

The claims examined above, as we see, have different degrees of merit. The resource-enhancement, excess-capacity, and expensive-monetized-trade explanations describe conditions that provide incentives for barter but do not constitute sufficient conditions for it, whereas the explanations that cite price dis-crimination, avoidance of price restrictions, exploitation, and lack of marketing expertise present sufficient conditions for barter but assume bounded rationality or outright irrationality of some participants in the market. The reciprocity-and-trust and inexpensive-barter explanations present sufficient condi-tions for (rational) barter trade. As the discussion of the inex-pensive-barter and expensive-monetized-trade explanations suggests, situations that provide incentives for barter (because the relative transaction costs of monetized trade are higher than usual) can become cases of barter only if the potential traders are familiar with each other's productive services.

An example may collectively illustrate some of the points made above. Suppose individual A has a parking garage but no car. This individual could advertise the availability of the garage, but the cost of advertising and screening applicants may be considerable if there are few potential customers. Moreover, it may be expensive to write and enforce a contract that covers possible damages to both the garage and the car, as well as to regulate the behavior of the car owner in a way that does not discomfort the garage owner. Suppose that A has a friend, individual B, who has a car but no garage. The two individuals may engage in a barter trade whereby A lets B use the garage in

exchange for occasional use of the car. The regulating mechanism may be their mutual trust, thanks to their friendship. It is
likely that the terms of trade that they establish (how often A can
use the car and when B can use the garage) will be affected
explicitly or implicitly by the known costs of garage and car
rental and by the relative bargaining powers of the two parties
(how much trouble it would be to rent the garage, A's needs for a
car, B's parking alternatives, and so on), as well as by the possible
desire of both individuals to make "gifts" to each other to
strengthen their friendship.

In sum, an examination of different claims regarding the
beneficial aspects of barter reveals that there are three classes of
circumstances that directly lead rational individuals and organizations to engage in this kind of trade: (1) the absence of
reliable money, (2) the existence of direct economic benefits
from barter trade (lower transaction costs, tax avoidance, or
price discrimination), and (3) the existence of noneconomic
benefits derived from the barter process itself. In low-inflation,
stable developed economies, the first factor cannot contribute
toward barter trade. The economic benefits of barter can be
derived only if the traders are familiar with each other and often
only if they trust each other (for example, with delayed barter or
with tax avoidance). The noneconomic benefits can be derived
only if traders already know each other and seek to preserve or
enhance their relationship. Hence, the necessary conditions for
the occurrence of barter in a developed market economy are
two: familiarity with potential traders' productive services and
needs (so that the double coincidence of wants is easily established and traders can engage in cost-saving direct exchange)
and the existence of trust among them (which permits open-
ended deals). Finally, it is possible that barter occurs because of
the irrationality of some agents, whether those who engage in
the bartering or those who try to affect the terms of trade
through supervised prices or taxes.

Why Barter Among Nonprofit Organizations?

To address this question, I first characterize nonprofit organizations as a distinct form of organization (summarizing the theory

developed in Ben-Ner and Van Hoomissen, 1991) and then examine their possible benefits from barter as compared to monetized trade.

Nonprofit organizations are founded and controlled primarily by "demand-side stakeholders" interested in the provision of some services for themselves as consumers and/or for the benefit of others, as donors or sponsors. (This contrasts with for-profit firms, which are founded and controlled by suppliers of capital who are interested in returns to their investment rather than in the product as such.) Nonprofit organizations are controlled by these high-demand stakeholders (who have the greatest interest in the organizations' products), who have the time, expertise, and so on to engage in controlling them. The willingness of high-demand stakeholders to engage in these functions (participation in the board of directors, making and acquiring donations, and so on) is enhanced by their belonging to common groups and networks that exercise social pressure against free riders (people who do not carry out their obligations, assuming that they will partake in the benefits of others' contributions), as well as providing help with the provision of start-up capital and other inputs.

High-demand stakeholders prefer the nonprofit form in situations in which for-profit firms either fail to provide products that stakeholders can trust or provide insufficient quantity or quality and when government provision fails to compensate for this market failure. Such market and government supply failures, if they occur, tend to occur in the provison of nonrival goods[4] that are difficult for stakeholders to evaluate (trust goods) and in public goods, charitable goods, and certain mixed goods where high-demand stakeholders may be quantity or quality constrained; that is, for collective goods where a fixed quantity and quality of service is provided to all citizens by public or nonprofit agencies, and consumers cannot choose how much they individually obtain. The individuals who would like to have greater quantity or better quality than that which is provided at the prevailing price or tax rate are quantity or quality constrained. Services are far more likely to fall into one or more of these categories than are consumer goods. Indeed, as

Ben-Ner and Van Hoomissen (1993) show, essentially all non-profit organizations provide services, particularly in local markets.

Nonprofit organizations are more likely to engage in barter trade among themselves than are for-profit firms, both because of the identity of their controllers and because of the nature of their products. The controlling stakeholders of non-profit organizations (mainly members of boards of directors) often belong to the same social, religious, or cultural groups and other local networks, often referred to as community or urban elites (see, for example, Ratcliff, Gallagher, and Ratcliff, 1979; Hall, 1982; Galaskiewicz, 1985; Middleton, 1987; DiMaggio and Anheier, 1990). Members of a social network who interact with each other tend to trust each other more than they trust others (see Ben-Ner, 1993). If members of the same network control different nonprofit organizations, then their mutual trust facilitates barter trade among those organizations. Moreover, these individuals are likely to be familiar with the productive capacities and needs of nonprofit organizations in addition to those with which they are directly involved.

Controlling stakeholders may have an interest in the products of more than one nonprofit organization; for example, a museum and several social welfare organizations. This further reinforces the links among nonprofit organizations and breeds familiarity and trust. Moreover, individuals who sit on several boards may seek to operate the organizations that they control as economically as possible by using temporary and unanticipated excess capacity in the network of organizations with which they are associated.

Importantly, it is not only controlling stakeholders who belong to networks. The management and professional staffs of nonprofit organizations often belong to associations that promote the common interests of their organizations (DiMaggio and Anheier, 1990). For example, development officers belong to local fundraising associations, interact with each other in organizations such as the United Way, and participate in other local nonprofit sector umbrella organizations.

Controllers in for-profit firms may also be drawn from

similar social circles and be members of the same organizations (often nonprofit organizations), and professionals in these firms also belong to common professional associations. However, competition among for-profit firms engenders a degree of conflict that is uncommon among nonprofit organizations. (Of course, the stronger the social and other links among for-profit firms' controllers, the more likely it is that barter will take place among them, as is the case in the keiretsu groups in Japan.)

An exchange of services that are not ordinarily traded and that are available only irregularly takes place on terms of trade that must be bargained separately in each situation. The costs of haggling in such a situation may be considerable, unless each party regards the other's objectives sympathetically, rejecting the notion that the other's gain is its loss. As the discussion above suggests, controllers of nonprofit organizations may care simultaneously about several organizations, so that a dollar lost by organization A in favor of organization B counts as less than a dollar. Such an attitude must be quite rare in relations among for-profit firms.

The affiliation of members of nonprofit organizations with similar networks fosters familiarity with the needs of various organizations, increasing the probability that a double coincidence of needs can be established at a low cost. This is aided by the fact that nonprofit organizations' financial information is largely open to the public under legal requirements. Thus, the relationships between members of nonprofit organizations create a situation that resembles the Japanese keiretsu, in which the needs of individual organizations are internalized in the broader community of nonprofit organizations. This encourages the barter transfer of excess resources among organizations as needs arise, reducing the need for complicated contingent contracts.

The nature of nonprofit organizations' products also contributes toward barter. Because they provide mainly local collective services, the markets for the outputs of many nonprofit organizations and for some of their specialized inputs are "thin"; that is, there are few sellers and/or buyers. In thin markets, prices are not competitively determined, and there are occasional temporary and unanticipated excess demands or supplies. Excess supply causes excess capacity. Weisbrod and Lee (1977) and Holtmann (1983) suggest that the need to maintain some excess capacity in the face of uncertain demand is an important attribute of nonprofit organizations. The excess capacity of an organization is reflected not only at the point of production of the marketed service (such as the heart transplant facility of a hospital) but also throughout the rest of the organization (such as meeting rooms). And while some facilities of an organization (for example, a transplant facility) are too specialized for use by other organizations, other facilities (the meeting rooms) have greater flexibility of use. Instead of "dumping" services at low prices, nonprofit organizations with excess capacity engage in price discrimination, favoring other nonprofit organizations but continuing to charge "full" monetary price to others. Alternatively, instead of searching for potential customers interested in a service on a short notice and for a limited time, members of nonprofit organizations may rely on their superior information about other nonprofit organizations to pass on such services in return for other services (which may be provided on a similarly temporary and unanticipated basis or on a more scheduled one). For similar reasons, nonprofit traders may barter in a way that avoids the problems associated with the "market for lemons."

Barter among nonprofit organizations is also a way to avoid paying sales taxes (nonprofit organizations are exempt from most other taxes). Since some measure of trust is required among partners to actions that are not entirely legal, the relationship among members of nonprofit organizations is helpful in this case as well.

The explanations for barter among nonprofit organizations adduced in this chapter may be evaluated for their ability to interpret the examples presented at the beginning of the chapter. What appears to be common to all five examples is the possibility of some unanticipated excess capacity; bartering among nonprofit organizations on flexible terms (according to need rather than on a specified schedule) is probably more beneficial than attempting to market these services on an irregular basis. Further, a certain sympathy with the goals of the trading partners may help in establishing a barter relationship. However, in addition to these moderating influences, the over-arching explanation for these examples of barter, if it is rational, must be the ease of establishment of the double coincidence of needs among the traders, which makes the transaction costs of barter low. As the previous section indicated, familiarity with the needs and resources of other organizations is necessary to make barter feasible; nonprofit organizations within one locality, with members who belong to similar social networks, probably satisfy the familiarity and trust condition better than for-profit firms. Sympathy with each other's goals, along with mutual trust, allows for the formation of barter relations in which disparities between market prices and the barter terms of trade (often resulting from the indivisibility of facilities) are tolerated, often with the expectation that they will be redressed in the future. This may also fulfill the trust- and social-exchange-enhancing role of barter.

    Barter may also occur between nonprofit organizations and for-profit firms. As noted earlier, the controllers of non-profit organizations often come from the "urban elite," which is composed of controllers (owners and managers) of for-profit firms. The cozy relationships that develop among nonprofit organizations may also develop between some nonprofit organizations and for-profit firms controlled by the same individuals. In such circumstances, one may expect barter, for reasons similar to those described above, or even self-dealing, for purposes of tax-evasion, price discrimination, or exploitation.

Conclusions and Policy Recommendations

The key attributes of nonprofit organizations—the identity of their controllers and the nature of their products—are such that they are more likely to engage in barter among themselves than is the case with for-profit firms. Of the general circumstances that may lead an organization to choose barter over monetized trade, in all but one (price discrimination), nonprofit organizations seem to have at least as strong incentives or as conducive conditions for engaging in barter as for-profit firms.

However, barter trade may often appear more attractive than it actually is. For example, barter has high transaction costs that may not be apparent to decision makers who do not account correctly for the time involved in seeking barter partners or do not compare the costs and benefits of barter with its alternative, monetized trade. As the examination of the nine claims for barter indicates, the circumstances that favor barter are rather specific, and it is necessary to examine the actual circumstances of an organization before deciding to embark on a barter deal. In particular, long-term or repeated barter trades may be indicative of chronic excess capacity (which must be eliminated) or an outright erroneous commercial strategy.

Notes

1. Trade agreements, which are de facto barter of *bundles* of goods, further ameliorate the double-coincidence-of-wants constraint, but only large firms or governments have the ability to engage in them.

2. This is, with some variations, the standard explanation in economics. See Clower (1969), Goodhart (1989, pp. 32–33), Niehans (1971), and Ulph and Ulph (1975).

3. As Reisman (1991b) suggests, barter is preferred when its marginal benefit minus the transaction costs incurred in this type of trade exceeds the marginal benefit from monetized trade net of transaction costs related to this form of trade (assuming that the costs of production are independent of the form of trade).

4. Nonrival goods have the property that the consumption of one unit of a good by one individual does not detract from the consumption of that same unit by other individuals. An example of a nonrival good is physical space, such as a theater hall in which all spectators may enjoy the same show, within the seating limits of the hall. Another example is the quality of a service that must be provided at the same

level to all consumers, such as a theatrical production or the educational program of a day-care center.

References

Akerlof, G. "The Market for 'Lemons': Quality, Uncertainty and the Market Mechanism." *Quarterly Journal of Economics*, 1970, *84*, 487–500.

Banks, G. "Constrained Markets, 'Surplus' Commodities and International Trade." *Kyklos*, 1985, *38*, 249–266.

Ben-Ner, A. "Cooperation, Conflict, and Control in Organizations." In S. Bowles, H. Gintis, and B. Gustafsson (eds.), *Democracy and Markets: Participation, Accountability, and Efficiency*. Cambridge, England: Cambridge University Press, 1993.

Ben-Ner, A., and Van Hoomissen, T. "Nonprofit Organizations in the Mixed Economy: A Demand and Supply Analysis." *Annals of Public and Cooperative Economics*, 1991, *62*(4), 469–500.

Ben-Ner, A., and Van Hoomissen, T. "A Portrait of the Nonprofit Sector in the Mixed Economy: New York 1981–1987." In A. Ben-Ner and B. Gui (eds.), *The Nonprofit Sector in the Mixed Economy*. Ann Arbor: University of Michigan Press, 1993.

Blau, P. *Exchange and Power in Social Life*. New York: Wiley, 1964.

Clower, R. W. (ed.). *Introduction to Monetary Theory: Selected Readings*. Harmondsworth, England: Penguin Books, 1969.

DiMaggio, P. J., and Anheier, H. K. "The Sociology of Nonprofit Organizations and Sectors." *Annual Review of Sociology*, 1990, *16*, 137–159.

Galaskiewicz, J. *Social Organization of an Urban Grants Economy: A Study of Business Philanthropy and Nonprofit Organizations*. Orlando, Fla.: Academic Press, 1985.

Gambetta, D. (ed.). *Trust: Making and Breaking Cooperative Relations*. Oxford, England: Blackwell, 1988.

Goodhart, C.A.E. *Money, Information and Uncertainty*. Cambridge, Mass.: MIT Press, 1989.

Gouldner, A. W. "The Norm of Reciprocity." *American Sociological Review*, 1960, *25*, 161–178.

Hall, P. D. "Philanthropy as Investment." *History of Education Quarterly*, 1982, *22*, 185–203.

Holtmann, A. "A Theory of Non-Profit Firms." *Economics*, 1983, *50*, 439–449.

Homans, G. *Social Behavior: Its Elementary Forms*. New York: Harcourt Brace Jovanovich, 1961.

Humphrey, C. "Barter and Economic Disintegration." *Man*, 1985, *20*, 48–72.

Lane, R. *The Market Experience*. Cambridge, England: Cambridge University Press, 1991.

Magenheim, E., and Murrell, P. "How to Haggle and Stay Firm: Barter as Hidden Price Discrimination." *Economic Inquiry*, 1988, *26*, 449–459.

Malinowski, B. *Argonauts of the Western Pacific*. London: Routledge, 1922.

Middleton, M. "Nonprofit Boards of Directors: Beyond the Governance Function." In W. W. Powell (ed.), *The Nonprofit Sector: A Research Handbook*. New Haven, Conn.: Yale University Press, 1987.

Niehans, J. "Money and Barter in General Equilibrium with Transaction Costs." *American Economic Review*, 1971, *61*, 773–783.

Polanyi, K. *The Great Transformation*. Boston: Beacon Press, 1957. (Originally published in 1944.)

Ratcliff, R., Gallagher, M. E., and Ratcliff, K. S. "The Civic Involvement of Bankers: An Analysis of the Influence of Economic Power and Social Prominence in the Command of Civic Policy Positions." *Social Problems*, 1979, *26*, 298–303.

Reisman, A. "Countertrade (Barter) and Enterprises: Direct and Indirect Means of Enhancing Resources." Paper presented at the conference on Nonprofit Organizations in a Market Economy, Case Western Reserve University, Nov. 1991a.

Reisman, A. "Enhancing Nonprofit Resources Through Barter." *Nonprofit Management and Leadership*, 1991b, *1*(Spring), 253–265.

Ulph, A. M., and Ulph, D. T. "Transaction Costs in General Equilibrium Theory: A Survey." *Economica*, 1975, *42*, 355–372.

Weisbrod, B., and Lee, A. J. "Collective Goods and the Voluntary Sector: The Case of the Hospital Industry." In B. Weisbrod (ed.), *The Voluntary Nonprofit Sector*. Lexington, Mass.: Lexington Books, 1977.

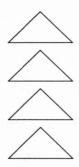

CHAPTER 10

Marketplace Practices and Fundraising Ethics

Robert F. Carbone

President Calvin Coolidge once proclaimed that the business of America *is* business. It would be as difficult to refute that assertion today as it was then, even though much of American business is experiencing serious difficulties. Now, however, there is another major actor on the stage of America's marketplace — nonprofit organizations.

What has come to be called America's third or independent or nonprofit sector, though only one-tenth the size of the nation's business world, is still impressively large. Citing an array of earlier studies, O'Neill (1989, pp. 5–9), a leading scholar who studies nonprofits, describes its dimensions. He asserts that its continued growth is so vigorous that we do not really know how many nonprofit organizations there are in the United States. The most recent attempt to measure the dimensions of the independent sector (Hodgkinson, Weitzman, Toppe, and Noga, 1992) estimates that there are 1.4 million nonprofit organizations in the nation, including the 489,882 that the Internal Revenue Service (IRS) classified in 1990 as charitable nonprofit organizations.

With a growth rate said to be faster than that of either the business or the government sector, nonprofits are clearly an important factor in the nation's economy. According to Hodgkinson, Weitzman, Toppe, and Noga (1992), in 1990 nonprofits generated 6.2 percent ($289 billion) of the $4.6 trillion total national income. This compares to 15 percent generated by government and 78.2 percent generated by the for-profit sector, and it reflects a rate of increase for nonprofits that was substantially greater than increases in the other two sectors.

Of course, these figures attributed to the nonprofit sector include the "assigned or imputed value for volunteer time or unpaid family workers" (p. 51). This is a significant point, since estimates suggest that half of all adult Americans spend some time doing volunteer work for nonprofit organizations (Hodgkinson and Weitzman, 1986). Yet most Americans are likely to agree that the marketplace still rules. Assuming that this view is warranted, it follows that nonprofit organizations cannot help but be influenced by practices and values inherent in the marketplace. As a matter of fact, only 27 percent of nonprofit organizations' revenues come from private gifts (O'Neill, 1989, p. 2), so their relationships with the world of business are extensive. It is generally accepted that about half of all funds garnered by nonprofit organizations come in the form of payments for services or memberships. Thus, it can be said that a substantial portion of the business of nonprofits *is* business.

Since nonprofits are involved in business activities and since at least some of their private gift income is derived from businesses and recipients of business income, it is not surprising that marketplace practices have been adopted and adapted by the nonprofit sector. Some of these practices are among the tools used by nonprofit organization fundraisers. This chapter explores ethical issues associated with fundraising techniques of this type. A context for the discussion of these issues is presented in the paragraphs that follow.

Ethics and Professionalism

According to a report published by the Josephson Institute for the Advancement of Ethics (1989, p. 1), "Organized philanthropy is intrinsically an ethical undertaking." Philanthropic behavior, including the gathering and dispensing of charitable resources, enjoys a moral foundation derived from a wide spectrum of religious and philosophical thought.

In return for public trust, nonprofit organizations and the people associated with them are expected to behave in ethically responsible ways. As in other sectors of the economy, nonprofits face ethical issues in virtually every facet of their activities. Ethical choices are part of deciding what social needs will be addressed, what will be done to address those needs, who will be responsible for carrying out the activities, what will be required to fulfill the mission, and how the needed resources will be accumulated and expended.

When nonprofit organizations or their employees and boards fail to act ethically, public trust and thus financial support diminish. Even the perception of questionable behavior — inflated salaries, perquisites for executives, conventions at plush resorts — pose serious problems. Moreover, the manner in which resources are raised is a particularly sensitive matter that can compromise the integrity of any nonprofit.

Another way of viewing this situation is in the context of professionalism. Because they are, to some extent at least, separate from the allegedly crass environment of profit-driven enterprises, nonprofits generally hold themselves to be professional organizations. And it appears that they are regarded as such by both expert observers and the general public.

If so, the expectation of ethical behavior is reinforced. One scholar agrees but then cites a serious problem: "Professionalism should be conceived in such a way that it is limited to moral conduct and elicits moral conduct, and . . . morality should be conceived in such a way as to require professionalism . . . [but] some of the practices of the professions are defective from the moral point of view, despite the impression conveyed by their codes of ethics. . . . Major deficiencies in professional morality are due to the structure of the profession rather than defects of character in professionals" (Kultgen, 1988, p. 4).

This notion that flaws in organizations, rather than in the people who operate them, account for moral lapses is one that most fundraisers might well find appealing. An interesting if unscientific survey conducted by fundraising letter expert Jerry Huntsinger (1989, p. 42) led him to conclude that "fund raisers have exceptionally high ethical standards [but] many of them appear to feel trapped in situations where their own private standard of ethics is sometimes different from the techniques they must use to hold their jobs and raise the necessary money."

Whether such clean separations can be made among charitable organizations, fundraising practitioners, and the profession to which they belong is a debatable point. The view on which the remainder of this chapter rests is that these three elements are one and the same thing.

If nonprofits are professional organizations, and if fundraisers for nonprofit organizations are professionals, and if fundraising is indeed a profession, then the responsibility for ethical behavior of the organization and its employees is evenly distributed. As a consequence, influence of the marketplace aside, ethical lapses cannot be assigned to any one of the three. Collectively, they either warrant public trust or suffer the consequences of diminished esteem and lack of support.

It is necessary to make clear, however, that expecting fundraisers (or any other occupational group, for that matter) to behave ethically is not a simple either-or, open-shut affair. The very nature of their work creates for fundraisers a constant stream of dilemmas that raise ethical issues. Even the most routine aspects of their work are often subject to changing circumstances and unexpected conditions. Codes of ethics, while admittedly valuable guides to behavior, cannot possibly anticipate all the vicissitudes encountered by fundraisers.

Ethics in Market-Oriented Fundraising

In this section, we examine the application of ethical principles in a number of market-oriented fundraising techniques. We begin by presenting some ethical guidelines that appear especially relevant to these techniques. These guidelines are derived in large measure from ethical codes promulgated by several national associations of fundraisers: the National Society of Fund Raising Executives, the Council for Advancement and Support of Education, the Association for Healthcare Philanthropy, the American Prospect Research Association, the American Association of Fund-Raising Counsel, the National Committee on Planned Giving, and the Committee on Gift Annuities. While stated in rather general terms, these guidelines address the thoughts and behaviors of fundraisers who apply market-oriented techniques in seeking support for charitable organizations. These statements admonish fundraisers to:

- Employ, and encourage charitable organizations to employ, sound management, fiduciary, and accounting practices to ensure that gifts are managed for the sole and maximum benefit of intended recipients and that the purposes of giving are being honestly fulfilled
- Observe accepted standards of accuracy, truth, integrity, and good faith in personal and professional conduct associated with promotion of charitable organizations and causes
- Stress to donors the primacy of their desire to aid charitable causes but also explain implications of available giving incentives and the importance of seeking competent legal and financial advice
- Safeguard privacy of donors and confidential information associated with gifts to avoid damaging reputations of donors, charitable organizations, and the profession
- Leave intact all information about donors and gifts acquired in service to current or former employing organizations
- Accept compensation that is reasonable and proportionate to services rendered, in accordance with the employing organization's customary guidelines and antitrust laws
- Comply with all applicable laws and regulations, respect standards of professional ethics, and adhere to policies and procedures of employing organizations
- Protect and enhance the reputation and public image of

charitable organizations as worthy of support from donors and volunteers

The use of these guidelines in the following discussion of market-oriented fundraising techniques is not exhaustive; rather, it is intended to stimulate a more wide-ranging analysis of the dilemmas that fundraisers encounter. These statements are didactic, in the true sense of that word — intended to teach. They are not offered as absolutes, in one of the less happy meanings of that word — indubitable, unquestionable, and arbitrary standards of measurement.

Cause-Related Marketing

Perhaps the fundraising technique most closely associated with commercial enterprises is cause-related marketing, a concept said to be originated by American Express Corporation. In actuality, it is a three-way venture involving a business, a non-profit organization or cause, and consumers. Consumers purchase a product or service that they want from a firm that makes a profit on the transaction and also makes a donation to the charitable entity. Since the term *cause-related marketing* is protected by copyright, an alternative and perhaps more descriptive term is *joint venture*. Whatever term is used, it is an idea that generates strong differences of opinion. Called "phony philanthropy" by one critic (Gurin, 1989, p. 32), it is described as "productive partnership" by a supporter (Webster, 1989, p. 30).

Krentler (1989), distinguishes between the image-oriented direct giving of corporations that seek to be socially responsible and the bottom-line profit motives that drive commercial enterprises. Joint ventures, she asserts, are profit-oriented and thus not inherently philanthropic in nature. The evidence about the profitability of joint ventures is mixed, but Krentler concludes that they are probably here to stay.

One joint venture often cited raised funds for restoring the Statue of Liberty through the use of American Express services. Special Olympics is a charitable cause that reportedly realizes significant funding from joint venture arrangements.

Other examples are Coca-Cola and the "Hands Across America" project and General Foods' efforts to benefit the Muscular Dystrophy Association.

In all such ventures, charitable organizations receive funding while their corporate partners derive publicity (maybe even image enhancement), often the assistance of volunteers to promote the venture, and increased sales. The question most often raised about joint ventures, however, is whether companies unduly profit from association with socially sanctioned causes. It is fair to explore ethical considerations that derive from these outwardly synergistic relationships.

The reputation of nonprofits is a fundamental concern. Is the philanthropic nature of a nonprofit organization diminished or changed by its association with a for-profit organization? Are the values that motivate its executives and fundraisers somehow contravened in a relationship where maximization of profit is the prevailing consideration? Answers to these questions are not readily found, possibly because experience with joint ventures is rather recent and not widespread. If the answers are positive, evidence of an ethical lapse must be acknowledged.

If fundraisers are expected to remind donors that the philanthropic impulse is uppermost, then combining this value with acquisition of a product or service may dilute the philanthropic impulse. For example, nonprofits involved in joint ventures may be viewed as benefiting from unrelated business dealings or competing unfairly with other companies in the same business as the joint venture partner.

Two thoughtful observers, both heavily involved in the nonprofit sector, provide insights that clearly illustrate the dilemmas that fundraisers encounter in cause-related marketing activities. The first, a fundraising consultant (Levis, 1991), suggests that this technique can utilize corporate advertising budgets to generate charitable gifts, acquire new donors, educate potential donors about a cause, stimulate business and nonprofits to cooperate, and increase corporate social consciousness and corporate giving. He concludes that "Businesses that employ cause-related marketing techniques *appear* to be socially responsible, [but] it is important that they be encouraged – if not prodded – to translate the appearance into reality."

The second observer, an industrialist and veteran nonprofit organization board member, sees "no real ethical problems with cause-related marketing. . . as long as the business partner is a good one and an ethical one." He cautions, however, against "getting hooked up with a sponsor who is a competitor of one of your major contributors," and he worries about companies that use advertising dollars to supplant dollars in their corporate contributions budgets (Gelb, 1991).

In the final analysis, fundraisers and the nonprofit organizations for which they work will have to make critical judgments about the balance between benefits and liabilities inherent in joint ventures. If philanthropic qualities of a nonprofit can be preserved, if its mission remains unchanged, if no laws are violated, ethical issues may be considered moot.

Affinity Cards

A variation on cause-related marketing is use of credit cards that produce income for nonprofits or encourage customer support of designated charitable causes. Widespread use of credit cards in modern society presents fundraisers with a technique for generating donations that is virtually free of cost and staff time. When issued as so-called affinity cards, these ubiquitous instruments of commerce return a small percentage – typically 0.5 percent – of each transaction to the nonprofit identified on the card.

As early as 1988, an estimated fifteen million Visa cards, 10 percent of all Visa cards in circulation, issued by 200 banks were generating contributions to 1,200 nonprofits (Sterne, 1988, p. 6). It is thought that each card has potential for generating $10 to $20 a year for the designated nonprofit. One company created a "donation pool" of thirty nonprofits that share contributions raised from purchases of affinity card holders.

Nonprofit organizations that have an arrangement with a credit card company encourage members and other donors to apply for an affinity card. Some charitable causes have even mounted door-to-door solicitations to identify prospective card holders, using canvassers from their regional and local chapters. As an incentive to stimulate membership, some credit card companies waive the annual membership fee for a period of time, typically one year.

Contributions may be generated in other ways as well. One firm does not forward a commission to the nonprofit but charges its members a lower interest rate and encourages them to contribute that savings. A card company that provides a cash-back bonus to members offers them an option of having the bonus forwarded to a charity that serves seriously ill children.

Still other variations on this form of "partnership marketing" are in use. Some financial institutions make charitable donations on the basis of other financial products—home equity lines of credit, checking accounts, or money market accounts. A midwestern supermarket chain permits customers to add a donation to their grocery receipts. The chain combines these donations into vouchers that are used by local Salvation Army units to obtain food for soup kitchens. A New York–based bank simply puts promotions for nonprofit organizations on receipts issued by its automatic teller machines.

It is not easy to conceive of ethical problems arising from the use of affinity cards and similar devices that promote charitable causes. While these arrangements are not totally unlike cause-related marketing agreements discussed earlier, the relationship between commercial and nonprofit interest appears to be more benign in their case. The appeal is more indirect, and the pressure of hard-sell advertising is absent. If credit card companies, financial institutions, or other business enterprises involved in these relationships are reputable, it is hard to see how reputations of nonprofits can be harmed. If nonprofits report such contributions to monitoring agencies, their ethical obligations are fulfilled. The same is true if donor intent is satisfied and if funds are managed responsibly by recipient organizations.

Perhaps the only obvious downside of these relationships is their effect on a corporation's existing charitable giving program. Does the affinity relationship restrain fundraisers from vigorously seeking significant and regular grants from corporate contributions officers? Are these corporations substituting the modest commissions generated by card users for the larger percentage of corporate profits that nonprofits hope to attract? If so, nonprofits and their fundraisers may have an ethical obligation to carefully evaluate existing affinity relationships to ensure that they are maximizing the potential benefits to the causes that they serve.

Pay-per-Call Donations

Telefund appeals have long been a staple fundraising technique. A recent variation pioneered by commercial enterprises involves using 900 telephone numbers and what telemarketers call "inbound calling." Donors respond to a mail or media appeal by placing a telephone call and are automatically billed by the telephone company for both the call and a donation.

Unfortunately, some commercial pioneers of this technique peddled pornographic conversations or operated dating services. It has also been used by the National Rifle Association to oppose gun control legislation before Congress or state legislatures. Despite this image, however, the technique has produced substantial income for some nonprofits.

A New York City public television station is reported to have received more than a quarter million dollars in this manner. A Boston station did well by broadcasting quiz questions that yielded a modest prize for callers who provided correct answers. Another variation involved cooperation between a health-related foundation and a cosmetic manufacturer. When callers purchased several dollars' worth of merchandise, a portion of the purchase price—albeit a very small portion—accrued to the foundation (Gurfield, 1990, pp. 1, 15–16).

An enterprising Florida evangelist combined his 900 numbers with a full-page ad in USA Today that carried the bold-print, upper-case question "WILL SEX SPLIT THE CHURCH?" Readers, urged to call whether they agreed or disagreed, were informed (in small print) of the charge that they would incur by doing so. Regardless of the caller's view, the evangelist was in a position to realize some revenue.

Securing the names and addresses of callers appears to be an important element of this technique. While nonprofits may realize relatively little in direct income, they expand prospect lists for future direct-mail appeals or for sale, rental, or exchange with commercial firms or other nonprofits.

Another negative factor associated with this technique is cost. Telephone companies extract a set-up fee as well as a per-minute charge for the call, usually between twenty-five and thirty cents. In addition, a "service bureau" or broker is usually employed, generating further cost. What remains constitutes the charitable donation, and in some cases that could be a relatively small portion of the amount that donors find listed on their monthly telephone bills.

Ethical implications associated with using 900 numbers to garner donations are not hard to identify. One issue is whether donors know that they are actually making a charitable contribution. On the other hand, donors may be unaware that a portion of the charge that they incur goes to the telephone company and the broker, thinking instead that their gift is being managed for the sole and maximum benefit of intended recipients. Also, most donors would probably be shocked to learn that making the call could result in their names and addresses appearing on prospect lists of commercial firms as well as other nonprofit organizations.

In all these ways, the charitable intent of donors can be perverted and the good-faith obligation of fundraisers and charitable organizations tarnished, if not completely violated. It is not likely, then, that widespread misuse of 900 number techniques can bring much credit to nonprofit organizations or the fundraising profession.

Donor Lists

It is not uncommon in the world of commerce for business concerns to make available, at a price, names and other relevant information about customers or clients. This information is exchanged with or sold or leased to other businesses, including telemarketing firms, as well as to nonprofit organizations inter-ested in identifying gift prospects.

The need to expand donor lists makes this an appealing venture for many nonprofit organization fundraisers. The cost of acquiring information on potential donors can be offset by increased contributions. In addition, the nonprofits can gener-ate funds by selling or leasing their own donor lists. It is obvious, of course, that doing either of these things creates another ethical dilemma with which fundraisers must grapple.

"All you need are the right names," proclaims the adver-tisement by the Dallas-based up-scale department store Neiman Marcus, placed periodically in *NonProfit Times*. The "right names" in this case are "550,000 catalog shoppers in a uniquely affluent and proven mail responsive market." They are "a list of well-educated people who respond . . . to medical associa-tions . . . educational offers . . . to any worthy cause" [*NonProfit Times*, Oct. 1990, p. 7.] In the same newspaper, nonprofits are invited to "increase donations with targeted lists" offered by Consumers Marketing Research, Inc., of South Hackensack, New Jersey. Unlike Neiman Marcus, it is not clear where this firm obtains its "ethnic, religious . . . minority group . . . high income [and] current donors" lists.

Unfortunately, some names on these lists undoubtedly originate with nonprofit organizations that realize revenue from their sale. The chairperson of an ethics committee con-cerned with nonprofits estimates that 75 percent of nonprofit organizations rent or exchange donor lists and asserts that they have a "sad" record of disclosing this fact to donors ("Direct Mail Group . . . 1990, p. 1).

The Direct Marketing Association, which numbers only 100 nonprofits among its 3,500 members, urges organizations to inform consumers and donors that their names may be sold or exchanged and that they can opt out of the process. Some observers predict that legislative action could result if non-profits do not improve their disclosure practices. Legalities aside, the relevant issue here is ethical implications of nonprofit organizations' selling, renting, or exchanging lists of donors or prospective donors.

Nonprofits are admonished to safeguard the privacy of donors and protect confidential information about them. There can be no doubt, then, that making donor lists available to any outside group—commercial or nonprofit, for a fee or in exchange for any consideration—is an unethical practice. Failure to disclose this practice to donors appears to be an equally reprehensible action. At the very least, however, nonprofits that trade in donor lists should inform donors of that fact and afford them a convenient way to choose not to have their names used in this manner.

Fundraisers who make frequent job changes could be tempted to carry with them donor information for sale to commercial list firms or for use in another fundraising office. A survey by the American Prospect Research Association found that only 30 percent of its members said that they would not take information with them when changing jobs; 58 percent would take some information, and 12 percent would take *all* donor information if they moved to another position (Nichols, 1990, pp. 235–239). This clearly violates a widely accepted ethical tenet: donor information is to remain with the organization that developed it, not pirated away when an employee leaves the organization.

Nonprofits that do not safeguard donor names and other information run a high risk of alienating donors who learn of this ethical lapse. If, however, confidentiality is maintained and donors are assured of this fact, the public image of nonprofits that do so is likely to be measurably enhanced.

Sweepstakes and Games of Chance

Increased use of sweepstakes in fundraising by some charitable organizations during the 1980s prompted a report advising the philanthropic community about this technique, which is most often associated with for-profit ventures (Council of Better Business Bureaus, 1988, pp. 1–2). The report assigns this increased use to growing competition for charitable contributions and a desire to provide added donor incentive and thereby increase contributions.

Sweepstakes, unlike lotteries, are legal but are regulated by state laws and to some extent by rules of the U.S. Postal Service, the Federal Communications Commission (when broadcast advertising is used), and the Federal Trade Commission. Lotteries, on the other hand, are illegal nationwide, except for those operated by government programs sanctioned under state laws. The difference between lotteries and sweepstakes is made clear in a set of guidelines on ethical business practices (Direct Marketing Association, 1990, p. 7).

Lotteries require that participants render something of value — what is called a "consideration" — to become eligible to win a prize. Sweepstakes do not ask participants to purchase anything or make a contribution, although subtle and sometimes slightly deceptive cues are given that may indeed elicit a donation. Providing information about the good work of the charity constitutes the soft sell. A harder sell asks recipients to return a blank check marked "void" with a hole punched to obliterate their checking account number. It is hoped, of course, that the prospects will in fact enclose a modest contribution instead.

In another variation of this theme, recipients of the appeal are informed that they are preselected winners and urged to make a donation when they return a form claiming their prize. The value of the prize, it often turns out, amounts to only a small fraction of the donation, and the organization keeps the balance.

Charitable gambling — bingo, pull tabs, raffles, and what are often called Las Vegas Nights — is yet another fundraising gambit. While such activities are closely regulated by state laws throughout the nation, in certain states charitable organizations are exempt from such laws, or the use of games of chance by nonprofits is ignored, because these organizations serve eleemosynary purposes. Bingo is legal in forty-four states, and it is estimated that charity bingo games nationwide generate more than $2 million annually (Hall, 1989, p. 1).

Law enforcement agencies have expressed considerable

concern over what outwardly may appear to be innocent games of chance such as bingo. Critics of such games charge that oversight is lax, stealing by both volunteer and paid workers is rampant, and there is evidence of skimming, profiteering, and involvement of organized crime syndicates.

Fundraising techniques such as these raise clear ethical issues. In each case, they hold out hope of some quid pro quo and thus downplay charitable intent, compromising fundraisers' obligation to stress charitable intent above all else. Appeals of this nature often appear to be (or, in fact, are) crass and deceptive. Clearly, this tarnishes a charitable organization's image and fuels negative feelings about fundraising and fundraisers. Worse yet, associating gambling activity with nonprofits is hardly designed to emphasize the philanthropic qualities of nonprofits or suggest that they are managed under sound fiduciary and accounting practices.

Furthermore, an ethical lapse occurs when nonprofits are not held to antigambling laws. And even in states where games of chance are legal, the history of corruption associated with these activities discredits the entire nonprofit sector and raises doubts about the truthfulness, integrity, and good faith of fundraisers and the work that they do.

Other Business-Oriented Techniques

In addition to the five fundraising techniques discussed thus far, several other techniques based on practices of commercial enterprises deserve mention. Their somewhat shorter treatment here does not suggest that they are unimportant matters. Rather, they appear to be artifacts of fundraising rather than major techniques for use in actual solicitation of charitable contributions. Of interest here are premiums, advertising, telemarketing, and commission fundraising.

Not uncommon among nonprofit organizations is a practice of granting recognition awards—lapel pins and paperweights are two examples—to donors whose gifts are deemed significant. More commercial in character are premiums, usually associated with smaller donations that are sought through an appeal to the general public. T-shirts, tote bags, and audio tapes offered during public television station marathon broadcasts are relevant examples. Sometimes these premiums are more expensive (television sets), unorthodox (food), or even very specialized (greens fees).

These techniques pose a number of ethical issues for fundraisers. Some experts think that younger donors are most likely to find premiums appealing. More experienced contributors are more likely to be alienated by such offers. For one thing, they may not need or want the premium. Of more importance, however, is realization among donors that some part of their gift pays for the premium and does not go directly to a cause that they wish to support. Fundraisers, it should be recalled, are admonished to focus on charitable intent, not rewards. Another relevant ethical issue is the responsibility of fundraisers to inform donors of the specific charitable portion of their gift and the related responsibility of donors to declare only that amount as a tax deduction.

Advertising, long a staple of the marketplace, is carried out by nonprofits primarily through public service announcements broadcast by radio or television statements and donated advertising space in newspapers and magazines. When used appropriately, advertising of this type assists nonprofits in informing the public of their good work as well as their continuing need for support. There are, however, at least two somewhat negative considerations that raise minor ethical concerns.

A media expert contends that nonprofits are frequently "looking for publicity to solve their fund raising problems, instead of building a lasting image that will . . . draw support over the years" (Johnston, 1988, p. 14). Moreover, he suggests that ad agencies that produce these appeals may be more interested in showing off their creativity than in portraying the nonprofit accurately. "A catchy campaign that miscasts a nonprofit in the public mind," he asserts, "can create problems that remain for years" (p. 16). Ethical strictures regarding protecting a nonprofit's image and philanthropic quality appear to apply directly to this adaptation of a business-related practice to charitable organizations.

Employing paid telemarketing firms is another market-place practice used by some nonprofits. Practitioners of what is called "outbound calling" often receive a percentage of contributions and use random or automated calling methods directed at prospective donors who have no prior relationship with the nonprofit. More than likely, these telemarketing firms are retained by what O'Neill (1989, p. 8) refers to as "nonphilanthropic nonprofits" that concentrate on special events. The annual "won't you help us take disadvantaged kids to the circus" call from the local fraternal order of police or fire fighters is a prime example.

There is considerable agreement among fundraisers that these campaigns yield more income to telemarketing companies than they do to nonprofits. A case in Connecticut revealed that in seventeen campaigns, one telemarketing firm grossed more than $230,000, of which only $26,000 went to nonprofits. David Ormstedt, Connecticut's assistant attorney general who monitors philanthropic activity, commented that "donors are getting the shaft" and do not suspect that they are supporting the telemarketer more than the charitable cause (Blumenthal, 1988, pp. 1, 8).

Ethical issues associated with this practice include protection of a nonprofit's reputation and its responsibility for maximizing assistance to intended beneficiaries. Ethical questions can also be raised about methods of compensation, appropriateness of fiduciary and accounting practices, and the integrity of fundraising personnel.

Methods of compensation are the final business-related practice to be included in this chapter. Compensation based on commissions—indeed, sometimes only on commissions, with no salary—have long been employed in the world of business. This practice has probably also existed in fundraising for as long as philanthropic appeals have been made, despite long-standing opposition by membership associations in the field. Recent legal actions, however, prompted removal of tenets against "percentage fund raising" from ethical codes promulgated by these groups. Fear of litigation based on violation of antitrust laws motivated these ethical code amendments.

While the legality of paying or accepting a percentage of philanthropic contributions is clear, there remains widespread distaste for the practice in the philanthropic community. A predetermined retainer or salary (normally calculated on an annual basis) based on services rendered is generally thought to be the most appropriate compensation arrangement. But, as in all things, there is some middle ground between percentage fundraising and straight retainer or salary.

Many nonprofits offer compensation plans that recognize productivity by providing end-of-the-year bonuses or other rewards for fundraising personnel. In a free-enterprise, marketplace-oriented economy, few observers raise objections to basing compensation packages, in part at least, on fundraising success. The one reservation often heard is fear that this may focus undue attention on short-term gains at the expense of developing long-range relationships with donors, which may yield far greater benefits to nonprofits over time.

Since there is not likely to be closure on ethical implications of compensation methods in the near future, if ever, avoiding specific conclusions on the issue of percentage fundraising appears to be warranted.

Conclusion

There appears to be renewed concern about matters of ethics among fundraisers and nonprofit organization executives. An informative monograph published by the Chicago chapter of the National Society of Fund Raising Executives asserts that "Board members, executives, and development officers of nonprofit organizations today face complex ethical and legal questions in their fund raising activities. . . . This booklet summarizes issues and facts that affect fund raising today . . . [and] . . . is designed to . . . stimulate thinking about potential conflicts of responsibility in fund raising" (National Society of Fund Raising Executives, 1991, p. 1).

Concern about ethical issues involved in garnering philanthropic support for worthy causes is not new, however. Curti and Nash (1965, pp. 33–35) note that the problem was present in colonial America. As they recount, Moor's Charity School in Lebanon, Connecticut, sent an Indian preacher named Occom to England to raise money so that the school could educate Indian youth; the funds raised, however, helped create Dartmouth College, which educated young white men.

Perhaps the renewed focus on fundraising ethics is best explained by Boris and Odendahl (1990, p. 188), who assert that "many decisions made on a daily basis in this field have ethical dimensions that are not recognized as such." Illustrations of many such ethically tinged decisions, including some made at the institution where she was employed as a fundraiser, are provided by Kelly (1991), in a book based on her award-winning doctoral dissertation.

Current concern about ethical issues is voiced in a statement by INDEPENDENT SECTOR (1991, p. 1) that reads, in part: "While all institutions are under scrutiny, violations of legal as well as commonly held ethical standards in voluntary and philanthropic organizations are particularly troublesome because of the special trust the public has vested in our community." This theme underlies a useful set of case studies published by the Institute for Nonprofit Organization Management at the University of San Francisco (O'Neill, 1990). In his introduction to the collection, O'Neill asserts that "ethics is just as much a part of nonprofit management as it is of business or government management. . . . If nonprofits are to be characterized by ethical management, they should not take such qualities for granted but should instead highlight and support ethical concerns. The fact that many nonprofit organizations are value-oriented is more, not less, reason to take ethics seriously" (p. i).

These admonitions must indeed be taken seriously, especially by fundraisers and nonprofit organizations that employ income-generating techniques such as those discussed in this chapter. But the responsibility for doing so has to be shared by many other segments of our society as well. Lawmakers and public officials, including jurists and prosecutors, have a major role to play in giving these ethical matters high priority. National, regional, and local membership organizations of fundraisers, nonprofit organizations, and grant makers are important actors, as are institutions of higher education, even those that do not claim to prepare nonprofit organization personnel. In like manner, the press and electronic media owe nonprofits and their employees the same critical attention now focused on businesses and government agencies. Finally, donors themselves have an obligation to discourage unethical fundraising practices by directing their philanthropy to organizations and causes that disdain gimmicks, hucksterism, and get-rich-quick schemes.

As in all other aspects of public and private morality, ethical fundraising depends, in the final analysis, on the watchful eyes of many people as much as it does on codes of ethics created by practitioners or scholars. Such broad-gauge scrutiny is likely the only effort that will make "obedience to the unenforceable" a greater reality.

References

Blumenthal, L. "Special Event Telemarketers Often Raise Little for Clients." *NonProfit Times,* June 1988, p. 1.

Boris, E. T., and Odendahl, T. J. "Ethical Issues in Fund Raising and Philanthropy." In J. Van Til and Associates, *Critical Issues in American Philanthropy: Strengthening Theory and Practice.* San Francisco: Jossey-Bass, 1990.

Council of Better Business Bureaus. *Direct Mail Sweepstakes and Charities.* Arlington, Va.: Philanthropic Advisory Service, Council of Better Business Bureaus, 1988.

Curti, M., and Nash, R. *Philanthropy in the Shaping of American Higher Education.* New Brunswick, N.J.: Rutgers University Press, 1965.

"Direct Mail Group Toughens List-Rental Rules." *NonProfit Times,* Jan. 1990.

Direct Marketing Association. *Direct Marketing Association Guidelines For Ethical Business Practice.*

Gelb, V. "Discussant Remarks." Presented at the conference on Nonprofit Organizations in a Market Economy, Case Western Reserve University: November 1991.

Gurfield, S. "Charities Get Mixed Results on 900 Numbers." *NonProfit Times*, Aug. 1990, p. 8.

Gurin, M. "Phony Philanthropy." *Foundation News*, May–June 1989, pp. 32–35.

Hall, H. "$2 Billion-a-Year Charity Bingo Game Market Gets Closer." *Chronicle of Philanthropy*, Apr. 18, 1989.

Hodgkinson, V. A., and Lyman, R. W. (eds.). *The Future of the Nonprofit Sector*. Washington, D.C.: INDEPENDENT SECTOR, 1989.

Hodgkinson, V. A., and Weitzman; M. S. *Dimensions of the Independent Sector: A Statistical Profile*. Washington, D.C.: INDEPENDENT SECTOR, 1986.

Hodgkinson, V. A., Weitzman, M. S., Toppe, C. M., and Noga, S. M. *Nonprofit Almanac 1992–93: Dimensions of the Independent Sector*. San Francisco: Jossey-Bass, 1992.

Huntsinger, J. "More on Ethics and Fundraising Letters." *NonProfit Times*, Oct. 1989, p. 42.

INDEPENDENT SECTOR. *Obedience to the Unenforceable: Ethics and the Nation's Voluntary and Philanthropic Community*. Washington, D.C.: INDEPENDENT SECTOR, 1991.

Johnston, D. "PSAs Are Powerful Promotional Tools, but Experts Warn of Potential Pitfalls." *NonProfit Times*, June 1988, p. 14.

Josephson Institute for the Advancement of Ethics. *Ethical Obligations and Opportunities in Philanthropy and Fund Raising*. Marina del Rey, Calif.: Josephson Institute for the Advancement of Ethics, 1989.

Kelly, K. S. *Fund Raising and Public Relations: A Critical Analysis*. Hillsdale, N. J.: Erlbaum, 1991.

Krentler, K. A. "Cause-Related Marketing: Advantages and Pitfalls for Nonprofits." In V. A. Hodgkinson and R. W. Lyman (eds.), *The Future of the Nonprofit Sector*. Washington, D.C: INDEPENDENT SECTOR, 1989.

Kultgen, J. *Ethics and Professionalism*. Philadelphia: University of Pennsylvania Press, 1988.

Levis, W. "Discussant Remarks." Presented at the conference on Nonprofit Organizations in a Market Economy, Case Western Reserve University, November 1991.

National Society of Fund Raising Executives, Chicago Chapter. *Honorable Matters: A Guide to Ethics and Law in Fund Raising*.

Chicago: National Society of Fund Raising Executives, Chicago Chapter, 1991.

Nichols, J. E. *Changing Demographics: Fund Raising in the 1990's.* Chicago: Bonus Books, 1990.

O'Neill, M. *The Third America: The Emergence of the Nonprofit Sector in the United States.* San Francisco: Jossey-Bass, 1989.

O'Neill, M. (ed.). *Ethics in Nonprofit Management: A Collection of Cases.* San Francisco: Institute for Nonprofit Organization Management, University of San Francisco, 1990.

Sterne, L. "Boom in Affinity Credit Cards Bring New Profits and Problems." *NonProfit Times,* Sept. 1988, p. 6.

Webster, P. J. "The Case for Cause Related Marketing." *Foundation News,* Feb. 1989, p. 30.

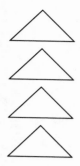

PART THREE

Interfaces Between Nonprofit Organizations and Business

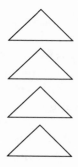

CHAPTER 11

What Can Nonprofits and Businesses Learn from Each Other?

David Billis

Recent years have witnessed the international rise in prominence of the "voluntary," "nonprofit," or "nongovernmental" sector and the associated growth of nonprofit studies. Despite this
growth, both the nonprofit sector and its academic study remain
dwarfed by the business enterprise and its long history of scholarly investigation. It is not surprising, therefore, that the exchange of practical expertise and management theory has been
essentially a one-way street. Only a handful of writers have
ventured to suggest that we have reached the stage at which the
movement of knowledge between the two sectors might be a two-
way process, although it should be noted that the nonprofit
literature now includes a substantial body of writings that touch

Note: I am grateful for the suggestions made by the discussants of this chapter
(Melissa Stone and David Mason) and the editors of the book (David C.
Hammack and Dennis R. Young) for their comments on the chapter and their
suggestions regarding possible further avenues of investigation.

on the subject, for example, the alternative explanations for the existence of the sector (such as Hansmann, 1980; Lohmann, 1989; Weisbrod, 1977, 1988). And other works deal with key aspects of nonprofits and for-profits (for example, Kanter and Summers, 1987).

In 1984, David Mason made a powerful case for the distinctiveness of the nonprofit sector and "identified 14 major characteristic differences between voluntary not-for-profit enterprises and profit-seeking businesses" (p. 21). These included the absence of precise market value, volunteerism, distinct resource and service systems, special constituencies, legal status, distinctive social character, and, importantly for this chapter, the claim that "voluntary enterprises are characteristically more complex than their business counterparts" (p. 22). At about the same time, Dennis Young (1986) suggested that "business can learn from nonprofits," a phrase that was later repeated by Peter Drucker (1989). Young (1986, p. 6) suggested that there were at least "six aspects of organizational structure and operations that were especially germane to the management of nonprofits": small size, organizational youth, service production, service experience of managers, sensitivity to self-motivating personnel, and the need to articulate organizational purpose. He thus took the argument one stage further by proposing not only that nonprofits are distinctive but that their areas of distinctiveness reflect important needs that have not been sufficiently addressed by the traditional business management or administration schools. Some of these themes are also taken up by Drucker (1989, 1990b), who maintains that, unlike many businesses, nonprofits have clarity of mission, a functioning board, and a motivated work force.

As befits the early stage of development of nonprofit management studies and the continued absence of comparative sectoral research, all three writers relied heavily on their personal research, consultancy, and work experience in their presentations. I, too, have drawn heavily on my own personal research in business and nonprofits over the past twenty-five years in the United Kingdom and other European countries and in

India, Kenya, and Israel. This chapter is, therefore, inevitably broad-brush and speculative.

After outlining the approach to be adopted, I present a summary of some of the most frequent management problems faced by each sector. I continue by offering a theoretical explanation for the distinctive sectoral problems that are seen to arise from basic structural differences and argue that it is hazardous for one side to learn from the other without an understanding of those structural differences, which give rise to both distinctive advantages and problems. Finally, taking these into account, I offer some concluding speculations regarding possible hazards and benefits of the exchange of knowledge.

The Approach

In examining the management of the two sectors, I have taken an approach that is rather different from that of my predecessors. First, the focus here is on not only the possible benefits but also the *hazards* of exchange of knowledge between the two sectors. Second, I have decided to explore what we might learn if we began with an examination of the distinctive *problems* of the sectors.

The original reason for including the possible hazards in the exchange of knowledge was a growing sense of discomfort with the imbalance in the transfer of knowledge between the sectors in the United Kingdom. The traffic has been coming from the business sector—sometimes stopping at the seats of government on the way—toward the nonprofit sector. Funders, particularly governmental, increasingly look to nonprofits for the introduction of "good business practices" and familiar organizational structures. The voluntary sector has been invaded by large consultancy firms (often paid by the funders) and primarily familiar with the workings of the business sector. This has accelerated the implicit acceptance of the virtues of what will later be identified as the traditional bureaucratic model.

My concern about the hazards of the exchange of knowledge was reinforced by recent experiences in companies on three different continents. In each, the ubiquitous "span of control" (suggested by Graicunas in 1933 and emphasized by Gulick and Urwick in 1937) had a deep-seated and fond place in the corporate psyche and caused much damage to the decision-making structures. The resilience of this concept is quite remarkable, despite the powerful criticism of numerous commentators since its original formulation (for an analysis of the span-of-control debate, see Hammond, 1990). I will return to this later; the point here is that the nonprofit world does not need worn-out panaceas drawn from other sectors.

The second, and main, feature of the approach adopted in this chapter is a belief that in exploring what each side might learn from the other, it will be helpful to understand how they handle their distinctive management problems. At first glance, this may seem a little perverse, but there are sound methodological and practical reasons for taking this route. From a methodological standpoint, Popper (1974) argues that theoretical development often starts from practical problems, "that those problems arise because something has gone wrong," which in turn means that a previous adjustment has been made—and that adjustments to the environment are "a preconscious form of developing a theory." He concludes by stating that "problems, even practical problems, are always theoretical. Theories, on the other hand, can only be understood as tentative solutions of problems, and in relation to problem situations" (p. 135).

The problem-oriented approach that underpins much of the research on which this chapter draws is different from that of the "bureaupathologist," who "investigates diseases and factors detracting from cooperation" (Caiden, 1969, p. 29). The emphasis on organizational problems is merely the starting point in an attempt to develop "usable theory" (Billis, 1984).

At a more practical level, it makes sense that if there are distinctive problems—and this remains to be established—then the true experts, like experts in other fields, will be found among those who have the most experience with grappling with those problems. Furthermore, both business and nonprofits have attracted their own myths—all too often, today's "good practice" can turn out to be tomorrow's disaster. A problem-based approach can help to get beneath the myths and might avoid reinforcing unfounded stereotypes of each sector.

This chapter assumes that an exchange of knowledge and ideas between the sectors is in itself worthwhile, an assumption that is far from self-evident and presumably requires a number of preconditions. For example, each side must at least believe that it has something to learn and must be open to new ideas. This is not always easy. Insights into the barriers promoted by sectoral stereotyping are provided by a project undertaken in the United Kingdom, not with nonprofits but with public and private sector managers (Brousinne, 1990). Not the least of the differences was each side's view of the other's style and attitude. For example, private sector managers were seen as "ruthless," "opportunist," and "arrogant"; public sector managers were seen as "pedantic," "conservative," and "stolid." A similar exercise with nonprofit and private sector managers might produce a not dissimilar gulf in perceptions.

Nevertheless, despite the one-way traffic, hazards, and barriers, I shall take the traditional optimistic stance of the researcher and assume that a genuine exchange is possible and fruitful.

Problems of the For-Profit Enterprise

What are some of the problems that regularly arise in the for-profit sector? In an earlier publication (Rowbottom and Billis, 1987), we listed typical complaints that we had heard from management, frontline workers, and middle managers in twenty years' work in a wide variety of for-profit organizations in the United Kingdom: difficulties in getting clear decisions, lack of proper direction or policy, absence of systematic planning or development, lack of scope for individual initiative, insufficient personal support and guidance, poor communication, and lack of meaningful consultation. Many of these complaints could be summed up as "too much bureaucracy." Mason (1991) has suggested a number of additional problems faced by for-profits, including the waste of energy caused by internal competition and the obsession with uniformity among employees. In their search for corrective models, both Mason (1991) and Stone (1991) have drawn attention to the importance of the study of family-owned, family-managed firms for the analysis of for-profits and nonprofits.

Little appears to have changed in the past few years. Thus, the chairman of Ford of Europe recently ordered that two management tiers be removed to try to end the "huge bureaucracy" in which "seven management layers was too weighty, time-consuming. . . (and) too slow to report" (Eason, 1991, p. 1). The managing director of Marks and Spencer, responding to criticism of the firm's layoffs, explained that they were necessary to prune "management layers which had become over extended" (Silver, 1991, p. 9). Cutting management layers was also seen as an essential part of IBM's reorganization (Davidson, 1991, p. 3). In *Thriving on Chaos*, Peters (1989, p. 359) suggests that much of the problem of sluggishness "comes from the sheer excess of staff and layers of staff." "Flatter" organization is at the top of the list of characteristics of what he calls the "winning look" and the "successful firm in the 1990s and beyond" (p. 27).

A phenomenon that I have encountered frequently is the tendency of business organizations to rest on their laurels. If they are making an acceptable level of profit, they may be unwilling to consider improvements to their organizations. This leads to the thought that we may need to look again at one of the most cherished beliefs—"the discipline of the bottom line." A senior personnel director with whom I have worked for many years, and who has vast international experience, is fond of describing this phenomenon as "the arrogance of profit." Attacks on the sovereignty of the bottom line have come from many other sources as well. For example, comparing private and government organizations, Bozeman (1987, p. 148) argues that "managing publicness" is more important than the essentially short-term considerations of the bottom line.

In a recent project with a major private sector research laboratory, I found it difficult not to be impressed with the conditions of work, the large salaries, and the intellectual ability of the new recruits. Yet the overwhelming message was that convoluted decision-making structures and excess layers of management that had grown "like Topsy" were depressing the initial enthusiasm of the new recruits and stifling creativity throughout the laboratory. I could not help feeling that the much criticized U.K. universities might not stand up too badly by comparison.

I suggest, therefore, that a useful first step in achieving the "winning look" would be the abandonment of one of the few entrenched business "concepts" — the belief in a maximum span of control of say five or six subordinates, which leads inevitably to elongated hierarchies.

Problems of Nonprofits

This discussion of the management problems of nonprofits draws heavily on research, consultancy, and training under-taken in the United Kingdom with several hundred voluntary organizations, primarily in the fields of social welfare, health, and housing, during the past thirteen years. The vast majority of these agencies had at least some paid staff.

When discussing their management problems, nonprofit workers use many words and phrases similar to those used in the business world. And it must be emphasized that, particularly in the larger agencies, familiar bureaucratic problems of role rela-tionships can be significant. However, closer investigation re-veals that it is really a different language that nonprofit workers are speaking. When, for example, they mention problems of *governance*, what they are talking about does not turn out either to be quite the same problem or to occupy the same place in their realm as what employees of for-profit companies mean by that word. It is far more intense, personal, and immediate. As Drucker (1990a, p. 8) put it, "No subject provides more heated debate in the nonprofit world than that of governance."

This is not just a British phenomenon but is a subject of debate in many countries. Harris (1989) reviews the literature on board-staff tensions and discusses the implications of "the self-fulfilling cycles of expectations" between the two groups. Sum-ming up the experience of helping twenty-seven U.K. organiza-tions, Dartington and Garner (1990) diplomatically note that "becoming a member of a management committee [board of directors] is getting more and more challenging" (p. 7). From Australia, Lyons (1990, p. 4) notes that while there has been little research on the management of nonprofit organizations in his country, "A popular theme in writing about community organisations is the tension between the volunteer board and their (few) paid staff."

When nonprofit personnel talk about *accountability*, it is likely to be a rather broader concept than commonly employed in business circles. They are apt to challenge the concept itself. This is very different from the "straightforward" managerial accountability that is a central concern of private sector organizations. In a study of accountability in voluntary organizations in the United Kingdom, Leat (1988, p. 85) concludes that the "problem identified was that of the different meanings of accountability and the multiple groups to which voluntary organisations may be perceived as accountable."

When they raise problems about relationships between *headquarters* and *local groups*, nonprofits are rarely referring just to the problems of teasing out accountable staff roles. More fundamental constitutional questions about "autonomy" and "membership" form part of the dialogue. As Young (1989, p. 104) points out in a discussion of national associations, "Power struggles take place between national and regional or local offices. Indeed vast differences in perception may exist within an association as to what its structure really is."

So, too, when nonprofit personnel talk about *clients* or *users*, the discussion is certain to range well beyond questions of quality of service to customers and into debates over participation in decision making. And when they talk of managing *volunteers*, they enter a realm of discourse unknown to the for-profit sector. Finally, in this brief excursion into the way in which even the use of the same word differs in importance as an expression of a managerial problem in the two sectors, we might note the far-reaching and complex nature of *organizational change* for the nonprofit when compared with what is usually encountered in the business sector (Powell and Friedkin, 1987). Although there are some immediate and fairly obvious explanations for a few of these differences, such as the more complex funding relationships in nonprofits, these fall well short of providing anything that could be called a usable theory of nonprofit organization. Indeed, in a review of the nonprofit sociological literature, DiMaggio and Anheier (1990) confess to being "skeptical about the plausibility of any *general* theory of nonprofit organizations (p. 154). They begin their review by suggesting that "For social scientists, the origins and behavior of sectors that stand outside market and state are tantalizing puzzles" (p. 138).

Whether or not such pessimism is justified, we might sum up by suggesting that the management agenda of nonprofits is dominated by problems of "stakeholder relationships": relationships between board and paid staff, between members and staff, between volunteers and staff, between headquarters and local groups, between funders and agency leaders, and so on (see McCauley and Hughes, 1991). These might not be the most obvious problems — for example, they do not include funding — but most of our work with numerous nonprofits in financial difficulties over the past decade has invariably led to the revelation of deeper problems, such as confusion among the stakeholders over who is or should be making policy. Even where it appears that the problem is entirely external to the agency, such as the sudden withdrawal of government funding, it may be asked whether the governing body of the agency was wise to be so dependent. It is precisely this sort of question that is beginning to concern the U.K. voluntary sector as it contemplates the growth of contracting (Chanan, 1991).

An exploration of possible reasons for the existence of distinctive problems in the two sectors is the subject of the following sections.

The *ABCs* of Organizations: Business Bureaucracies, Associations, and Nonprofits

Mason (1984) has suggested that whereas the operations of business resemble checkers (or what in the United Kingdom we call "draughts"), nonprofits are playing a different kind of game — chess — where "complexity and ambiguity are endemic [to] the multiple purposes of voluntary enterprises, their dual internal systems, their achievement of objectives by both volunteer and paid personnel, the lack of measurability, and other variables" (p. 178). Since the position may be even more complex than the chess-checkers example suggests, I propose to continue the sporting metaphor but with games that do not so immediately imply a substantial difference in complexity. Thus, we shall for the moment submit that business is playing the healthy game of tennis.

The business game, whatever it is, is based on clear-cut rules. The paid staff, who, following Jaques (1976), will be called the bureaucracy, are organized into hierarchical roles and are bound together by concepts such as accountability and authority. Managers are not elected by their subordinates but appointed by superior authorities. The hierarchical chain of command is the cornerstone of bureaucratic organization. Bureaucracies, according to Jaques, are dependent on the employing body that decided to establish the bureaucracy in the first place and whose existence is essential to the continued existence of the bureaucracy.

I propose to refer to the employing body or association as A, the bureaucrats as B, and, finally and most importantly, the customers, consumers, or clients as C. The customers are outside the organization and have their own motivations and demands. Although there are numerous definitions of bureaucracy (see, for example, Lane, 1987), the ABC separation of ownership from paid staff and customers is the traditional view of organizations held by most management theorists. For example, Bertram Gross's magnum opus, *Organizations and Their Managing* (1968), shares the traditional ABC division and suggests that the "hierarchic structure has been traditionally described in terms of a simple pyramid" (p. 223) and produces a diagram remarkably similar to that of Jaques (1976, p. 50).

There may be some blurring between A and B (the ownership and staff, or "management," roles), particularly in small firms. Stone (1991, p. 3) has drawn attention to the fact that in "family-owned, family-managed firms . . . the person-organization overlap is high." However, Birley (1989, p. 79) suggests that even here, "As time passes and the firm continues to survive. . . ownership and management become more separate." At the other end of the scale, we hear from the former chair of the large U.K. multinational ICI that the board was often "quite unclear as to whether they are merely a coordinating committee. . . or whether their primary responsibility is to the group as a whole" (p. 188). Although many boards of large companies recruit primarily from their own executives, Harvey-Jones (1988, p. 191) is quite clear that, whatever the reality, the "director's first duty is, clearly, to the shareholders for the maintenance of their investment."

Business tennis is not the only game in town. (We know that nonprofits with paid staff are playing something, but let us return to consider that later.) There is another set of organizations in the wider nonprofit universe that also have their own rules; let us call their game badminton. They also have their own distinctive problems. These are the voluntary associations, whose defining characteristic (unlike that of nonprofits) is membership. In his discussion of "collective action" organizations, Knoke (1990, p. 6) argues that they "maintain their formal boundaries by designating specific criteria for membership status and by controlling the movement of persons across these boundaries. . . the mass membership has at least formal rights to select leaders." Knoke includes in his discussion national associations with paid staff, although he emphasizes that the staff members work under authority granted by the membership and usually delegated through elected officers. I believe that some of these may be better understood as nonprofits (Billis, 1989).

I define associations in which the overwhelming mass of the "operational" work (the work that the association was set up to undertake) is carried out by the membership rather than by paid staff as "pure" voluntary associations. These associations, which may be mutual-benefit and/or service-providing organizations, are playing their own game with its own clear-cut rules. They also have special problems and a distinct body of literature. (For a critical review of the literature on functional and occupational groups, including the works of Olson, 1965, see Dunleavy and O'Leary, 1987.) The primary associational rules of the game are those of representative democracy—a system of elections, majority voting, committees, and chairpersons.

In voluntary associations, there is by definition no B, and there may or may not be a distinct category of C. The owners (A) are the members, the dominant and core group of the association. The characteristic problems of mutual-benefit associations have been summarized by Blau and Scott (1963, p. 45) as "maintaining membership control, that is, internal democracy." We might note here that the well known Blau and Scott typology [mutual-benefit associations, business concerns, service organizations, commonweal organizations] does not comfortably deal with the volunteer associations that deliver services to others, such as the Samaritans: "This involves coping with two main problems: membership apathy and oligarchical control." These authors, who draw on Lipset's work on trade unions (Lipset, Trow, and Coleman, 1956; Lipset, 1960) and Michels's work on political parties and the famous "iron law of oligarchy" (Michels, 1949) for their summary, also take note of Gouldner's counteracting "iron law of democracy" (1955, p. 506). Picking up the threads of this debate, Knoke (1990) bluntly declares: "Michels was wrong." Knoke continues by arguing that "American collective action organizations are not oligarchies nor even rigid bureaucracies . . . members retain sufficient control through meetings, committees, and elections to assure that majority sentiments prevail. . . the vulnerability of the organization to members' withholding of commitment ensures that leaders' interests align with the members" (pp. 229–230).

A detailed review of the problems of "pure" associations, lies well outside the boundaries of this chapter. Indeed, using my definition of membership groups that do not employ paid staff to undertake operational work, it is not at all certain that the task can be easily undertaken. It seems that most of the research into associations outside the new nonprofit literature does not regard paid employment as a major definitional boundary. This is evident from Knoke's work, in which he accepts that large associations have certain advantages but argues that size in turn requires "coordination that can be more readily achieved by the use of a paid staff" (p. 230). So despite his doughty defense of

democratic processes in U. S. associations, "The persisting dilemma is the inherent tension between the legitimacy of constitutional democracy and the efficiency of administrative bureaucracy" (p. 230). I believe that the tension may be better
understood as arising from the failure to differentiate nonprofits from pure associations and to identify what games are
really being played.

The argument is therefore that business bureaucracies
and pure associations have their own distinct rules of the game.
Business tennis is built on the divorce of ownership (A) from the
majority of paid staff (B) and the customers (C) and follows the
rules of managerial accountability and authority. This can be
compared with association badminton, in which the ABC division is scarcely relevant (save for the existence in some cases of a
distinct category of client) and which follows the rules of election and majority voting.

We are left with the dilemma of understanding nonprofits. Their key problems (stakeholder tensions) have been
identified earlier, but if any transfer of knowledge is to take
place, some plausible explanation will be necessary. Following a
line of research reported elsewhere (Billis, 1991), I suggest that
nonprofits play a mixture of tennis and badminton.

The contention is that from a structural standpoint, nonprofits contain elements of both bureaucracies and pure associations and that this gives rise to both their distinctive problems
and their distinctive competence. Thus, they employ frontline
operational staff who may be engaged in straightforward routine tasks or who may be more skilled professionals or semi-
professionals—the "street-level bureaucrats" (Lipsky, 1980).
However, if they are to be considered genuine nonprofits, they
must also possess real associational roots. Somewhere it must be
possible to identify a group of people who, although they might
not be formally called members of the association, are deeply
committed to the mission and future of the agency. This "membership" may be barely visible, perhaps surfacing only at times
of crisis. It will be drawn from the organization's stakeholders,
possibly including funders, board members, staff, volunteers,
and present and past clients and users. This discussion raises the

question of whether nonprofits in which only one group of stakeholders is really committed to the mission of the agency — for example, where a group of paid staff are effectively running the agency and appointing the management committee or board and there are no volunteers or membership — are really nonprofits or are better seen as crypto for-profit or governmental agencies.

This exposition of nonprofit organization provides an explanation for one of its most puzzling aspects for the observer more familiar with the traditional bureaucratic organizational forms of business — or, for that matter, governmental organization. There is no standard *ABC* division of roles in nonprofits. Many roles are ambiguous, combining several elements. For example, in some cases, board members may consider themselves members of the association, committed to its long-term mission, perhaps even engaging in operational activity as volunteers. In other cases, board members may be paid staff members or clients or users of the agency. Volunteer service-delivery workers may or may not be part of the formal membership, and we have found cases where members of the board are clients of the agency or where the clients include staff members. The permutations go well beyond the *ABC* formulation employed for simplicity in this chapter. Many different combinations can be discovered as an intrinsic part of the nonprofit agency. This is very different from the relatively simple structure of bureaucracies or pure associations.

Nonprofit managers must consequently understand both bureaucratic tennis and associational badminton and be capable of playing a continuing and changing mixture of both games, depending on the particular mix of stakeholders at any given time. (In fact, the same manager may have to play yet another game — that of the governmental bureaucracy — but that takes us into even deeper water and does not alter the main thrust of this chapter.) They must be capable of managing all the combinations of boundaries between the stakeholders and must understand their ambiguous nature and the connections between them. For example, we have encountered several striking examples where directors fresh from a business or military setting have arrived to run a large nonprofit, only to be completely overwhelmed by the reality of a board whose members are also clients. The case of St. Paul's Cathedral and "a city banker's attempt to introduce the ways of Mammon into the church" makes salutary reading. The former banker, who had run his own insurance company, was a lifetime communicant of the Church of England and believed that the job "was similar to that of a managing director" (Gledhill, 1990, p. 9). He was sacked after five months as chief executive.

Of crucial importance for nonprofit management is the pivotal boundary between board and staff (Heimovics and Herman, 1990). But there are many other vital boundaries, which are ignored at the manager's peril. Who are the funders, and are they part of the real membership or fly-by-nights? What happens to the boundaries between management and board and between management and membership if fly-by-night funding is accepted? How should the boundary between the board and government, often a major funder, be negotiated? And for those agencies with substantial support from the general public, there arises a question that is causing much anxiety: how should the balance be struck between public image and the membership's views of mission? How is the boundary between volunteers and paid staff to be managed? What happens, for example, to the original volunteers when some volunteers start receiving "expenses"?

This view of nonprofits as containing elements of both bureaucracy and association also provides an explanation for the earlier assertion that the great skill of nonprofit management must lie in managing the relationships with and among stakeholders.

Conclusion: Avoiding the Hazards and Appreciating the Benefits

We have so far identified key problem areas of business and nonprofit organizations and offered a possible structural explanation for their existence. The absence of comparative sectoral research, noted at the beginning of this chapter, leaves a rich agenda of unexplored issues. For example, is the transfer of knowledge more likely between business and nonprofits of similar organizational size? Elsewhere (Billis, 1992) I have suggested that, as far as nonprofits and government agencies are concerned, the structural *ABC* differences are more significant than similarity of size. However, the position with respect to nonprofits and business remains to be examined.

Another question that awaits resolution is the extent to which knowledge can usefully be transferred across the sectors in organizations in the same field. The key contention of this chapter is that distinctive problems—and, indeed, distinctive attributes—flow from basic structural differences: from different *ABC* structures. Crudely put, the challenge of business management is to organize paid workers into an effective and efficient machine and conquer the forces that push toward excessive bureaucratic layers and cumbersome decision making. This can be compared with the position of nonprofit managers, whose main challenge is to handle the changing demands of multiple stakeholder roles and the forces that push toward separating out *A*, *B*, and *C*—the forces that reduce boards to ciphers, drive out volunteers, discourage client involvement, and discourage staff from behaving like volunteers or funders from behaving like members.

The logic of this argument intimates that business can teach nonprofits much in the area of intra-staff relationships and the crucial place of managerial accountability. This is particularly decisive for pure associations that are taking on their first operational paid staff and are unwilling to accept that they are now dealing with a new organizational animal with different characteristics and demands. A powerful indictment (Landry, Morley, Southwood, and Wright, 1985) of the failure of numerous "radical" voluntary organizations—made all the more powerful since it came from the inside—saw the roots of failure in "the determination to reject formal structure" (p. 12). A focus on organizational accountability can help nonprofits to avoid the endless meetings and the "analysis paralysis" syndrome of pseudodemocratic decision making often widespread in the early stages of agency development. It can help, too, in concentrating the minds of nonprofit staff members who see the agency as "theirs" and fail to realize the public responsibilities of a bureaucratic organization.

But the main lessons are likely to be gained from the vast experience that business has accrued in systems and techniques and in supporting functions such as financial management, logistics, marketing, and sales. The higher profile that U.K. nonprofits now have in the welfare state has been accompanied by several critical governmental reviews of their financial management. The wider introduction of suitable systems, especially in the area of financial accountability, would seem to be uncontroversial and wholly beneficial. I believe that business has less to offer in the management of mainline operational functions, or what has been called the "service-providing system," whose objectives "are the purposes for which the organization exists" (Mason, 1984, p. 64).

Nonprofits can teach business for-profits much about "stakeholder management": how to ensure that the bureaucracy maintains responsive relationships with shareholders, governmental departments, the local community, all levels of staff, and customers. Although managers must manage, remoteness from their main stakeholders is a sure path to business problems. Some examples from my own recent experience may illustrate the point. Compare, for example, two large electronics companies, in one of which meals are served in "messes" strictly divided into different levels of management (reflecting the military background of many senior staff) and in the other of which there is one large dining room with directors and workers eating together the same food. Or consider the example of the marketing and sales director who failed even occasionally to visit the market and find out what his customers really thought of his products. Yet another recent case is of the senior manager of a large company who decided to buy a small business and found that his remote style of management, tolerable in a large organization, was unsuitable for an owner-manager; it alienated his new work force, with disastrous effects. Nonprofit managers cannot afford to be divorced from their stakeholders.

Both business and nonprofits face hazards if they try to

ape each other. In view of the power of business concepts, it is the nonprofit that faces the greatest danger. As noted above, nonprofits have to be aware of the hazards of diminishing the place of stakeholders. Thus, Steinberg (1990, p. 149), noting that "nonprofit firms have long been criticized for their failure to adopt modern management techniques," cautions against the introduction of the popular business method of incentive contracts, since they "may discourage donations. . . [and] may alter the long-run character of the work force." Similar warning signals have also been raised by Lipsky and Smith (1990). There is clear evidence that increased contracting diminishes the roles of volunteers and boards (Billis and Harris, 1991).

Nonprofits must also avoid the characteristic problem of business — building in excessive layers of decision making and bureaucratization, partly because of a slavish adherence to rigid notions of span of control. That this is a real danger is clear from Kramer (1990, p. 40), who points out that changes in the national organizations that he studied in the United Kingdom were "almost invariably" the result of the intervention of management consultants and that the chief executive's span of control was cut, "in several instances from twenty to seven."

The hazards for business lie in the inappropriate introduction of structural ambiguity. In the British context, this can be seen where powerful trade unions have moved into the sphere of management, perhaps assuming that the bureaucratic rules of the game are those of an association based on democracy. Perhaps a bigger danger is the failure to establish a distinction between boards and senior management. Although we have argued that businesses must be *sensitive* to stakeholders, we have not suggested that they can follow the nonprofit route and have overlapping roles. According to the line of argument of this chapter, they must play business tennis well, appreciating the skills of badminton but not trying to graft its rules onto the handbook of tennis. Some support for this thesis is to be found in a recent research report that analyzed forty-five deceased companies for symptoms of collapse (Waller, 1991, p. IV). One of the key symptoms was the presence in more than 60 percent of the failures of "a combined chairman and chief executive or

executive chairman with no separate chief executive or managing director."

It seems self-evident that business studies, as the big
brother or sister, must have an enormous amount to offer the
fledgling study of nonprofit management. It would seem equally
self-evident that the experienced businessperson must naturally
and with good reason have much to teach the nonprofit manager. However, the argument here suggests that the exchange of
knowledge between the two sectors ought to be regarded as a
more complex relationship. If the barriers of insularity and
entrenched interests could be overcome, we might speculate on
developments in the coming decade.

For example, the analysis provides an additional explanation of why nonprofit management is so complex, exciting,
challenging and, often, attractive to people who have chosen
unconventional careeer paths. It might not be surprising, therefore, if the smart business enterprise — if it has not already done
so — decided to turn its attention to the best of the nonprofit
managers, who will know a great deal about staff management,
about keeping in touch with "customers" and the community,
about negotiating with politicians, and about managing in very
stressful conditions. The process of secondment (temporary
assignment of a person to another organization), now seen as a
way of transferring business skills to the nonprofit sector, will be
matched by much valued nonprofit secondments to the business sector.

Further, the study of nonprofit management will challenge much of the received wisdom of the past decades of management writing. The sector dimension — far from becoming
submerged under some new "iron law" of the blurring of sector
boundaries — will be seen as a crucial determinant (Fottler,
1981) in the study of management. Thus, ideas about organizational change and development, leadership, and motivation
may all need to be reconsidered.

It may seem far-fetched to imagine the very junior nonprofit partner having a dramatic impact on the wider management scene. Yet the progress of just the past few years has been
quite startling, and those studying the field a decade or more

ago would probably have found it difficult to envisage the present vibrant state of study. Whatever happens in the next decade, at the very least a more balanced approach toward the exchange of knowledge would be beneficial to both sectors. The traffic should start moving in two directions.

References

Billis, D. *Welfare Bureaucracies: Their Design and Change in Response to Social Problems.* London: Heinemann, 1984.

Billis, D. *A Theory of the Voluntary Sector: Implications for Policy and Practice.* London: Centre for Voluntary Organisation, London School of Economics, 1989.

Billis, D. "The Roots of Voluntary Agencies: A Question of Choice." *Nonprofit and Voluntary Sector Quarterly,* 1991, *20* (1), 57–69.

Billis, D. "Planned Change in Voluntary and Government Social Service Agencies." *Administration in Social Work,* 1992, *16,* 1–2.

Billis, D., and Harris, M. "Taking the Strain of Change: UK Voluntary Agencies Enter the Post-Thatcher Period." Chicago: Association for Research on Nonprofit Organizations and Voluntary Action, 1991.

Birley, S. "Corporate Strategy and the Small Firm." In E. Asch and C. Bowman (eds.), *Readings in Strategic Management.* London: Macmillan, 1989.

Blau, P. M., and Scott, W. R. *Formal Organizations.* London: Routledge, 1963.

Bozeman, B. *All Organizations Are Public: Bridging Public and Private Organizational Theories.* San Francisco: Jossey-Bass, 1987.

Brousinne, M. "Across the Sectoral Divide: How Managers See Each Other." *Public Money and Management, 1990, 10* (1), 51–55.

Caiden, G. E. *The Dynamics of Public Administration: Guidelines to Current Transformations in Theory and Practice.* New York: Holt, Rinehart & Winston, 1969.

Chanan, M. G. *Taken for Granted.* London: Community Development Foundation, 1991.

Dartington, T., and Garner, J. "Managing Change." *National Council of Voluntary Organizations News* (London), Sept. 1990.

Davidson, A. "Compac Surges Ahead at IBM's Expense." *The Sunday Times,* Jun. 16, 1991, Sec. 4, p. 3.

DiMaggio, P. J., and Anheier, H. K. "The Sociology of Nonprofit Organizations and Sectors." *Annual Review of Sociology,* 1990, *16,* 137–159.

Drucker, P. F. "What Business Can Learn from Nonprofits." *Harvard Business Review,* July–Aug., 1989, pp. 88–93.

Drucker, P. F. "Lessons For Successful Nonprofit Governance." *Nonprofit Management and Leadership,* 1990a, *1*(1), 7–14.

Drucker, P. F. *Managing the Non-Profit Organization.* Oxford, England: Butterworth-Heinemann, 1990b.

Dunleavy, P., and O'Leary, B. *Theories of the State: The Politics of Liberal Democracy.* London: Macmillan, 1987.

Eason, K. "Top Men Must Go as Ford Cuts the Red Tape." *The Times,* May 8, 1991, pp. 1, 20.

Fottler, M. D. "Is Management Really Generic?" *Academy of Management Review,* 1981, *6,* 1–12.

Gledhill, R. "St. Paul's Sacks Banker with Commercial Ideas." *The Times,* Oct. 12, 1990, p. 9.

Gouldner, A. W. "Metaphysical Pathos and the Theory of Bureaucracy." *American Political Science Review,* 1955, *49,* 496–507.

Graicunas, V. A. "Relationship in Organization." *Bulletin of the International Management Institute,* 1933.

Gross, B. M. *Organizations and Their Managing.* New York: Free Press, 1968.

Gulick, L., and Urwick, L. (eds.). *Papers on the Science of Administration.* New York: Columbia University Press, 1937.

Hammond, T. H. "In Defence of Gulick's 'Notes on the Theory of Organization.'" *Public Administration,* 1990, *68,* 2.

Hansmann, H. B. "The Role of Nonprofit Enterprise." *Yale Law Review,* 1980, *89,* 835–901.

Harris, M. "The Governing Body Role: Problems and Perceptions in Implementation." *Nonprofit and Voluntary Sector Quarterly,* 1989, *18*(4), 317–335.

Harvey-Jones, J. *Making it Happen.* Glasgow: Fontana/Collins, 1988.

Heimovics, R. D., and Herman, R. D. "Responsibility for Critical

Events in Nonprofit Organizations." *Nonprofit and Voluntary Sector Quarterly*, 1990, *19*(1), 59–73.

Jaques, E. *A General Theory of Bureaucracy*. London: Heinemann, 1976.

Kanter, R. M., and Summers, D. V. "Doing Well While Doing Good: Dilemmas of Performance Measurement in Nonprofit Organizations and the Need for a Multiple-Constituency Approach." In W. W. Powell (ed.) *The Nonprofit Sector: A Research Handbook*. New Haven, Conn.: Yale University Press, 1987.

Knoke, D. *Organizing for Collective Action: The Political Economies of Associations*. New York: Aldine de Gruyter, 1990.

Kramer, R. M. "Change and Continuity in British Voluntary Organisations." *Voluntas*, 1990, *1*(2), 33–61.

Landry, C., Morley, D., Southwood, R., and Wright, W., *What a Way to Run a Railroad: An Analysis of Radical Failure*. London: Comedia, 1985.

Lane, J. E. *Bureaucracy and Public Choice*. Newbury Park, Calif.: Sage, 1987.

Leat, D. *Voluntary Organisations and Accountability*. London: National Council of Voluntary Organizations, 1988.

Lipset, S. M., *Political Man: The Social Basis of Politics*. New York: Doubleday, 1960.

Lipset, S. M., Trow, A., and Coleman, A. S. *Union Democracy*. New York: Free Press, 1956.

Lipsky, M. *Street-Level Bureaucracy*. New York: Russell Sage Foundation, 1980.

Lipsky, M., and Smith, S. R., "Nonprofit Organizations, Government and the Welfare State." *Political Science Quarterly*, 1990, *104*(4), 625–648.

Lohmann, R. A. "And Lettuce Is Nonanimal: Toward a Positive Economics of Voluntary Action." *Nonprofit and Voluntary Sector Quarterly*, 1989, *18*(4), 367–383.

Lyons, M., "Government and the Non-Profit Sector in Australia: An Overview." Paper presented at the INDEPENDENT SECTOR Research Forum, Boston, March 1990.

McCauley, C. D., and Hughes, M. W. "Leadership Challenges for Human Service Administrators." *Nonprofit Management and Leadership*, 1991, *1*(3), 267–281.

Mason, D. E. *Voluntary Nonprofit Enterprise Management*. New York: Plenum Press, 1984.

Mason, D. E. "Discussant Remarks." Presented at the conference on Nonprofit Organizations in a Market Economy, Case Western Reserve University, November 1991.

Michels, R. *Political Parties*. New York: Free Press, 1949.

Olson, M. *The Logic of Collective Action: Public Goods and the Theory of Groups*. Cambridge, Mass.: Harvard University Press, 1965.

Peters, T. *Thriving on Chaos*. London: Pan Books, 1989.

Popper, K. R. *Objective Knowledge*. London: Routledge & Kegan Paul, 1974.

Powell, W. W., and Friedkin, R., "Organizational Change in Nonprofit Organizations." In W. W. Powell (ed.), *The Nonprofit Sector: A Research Handbook*. New Haven, Conn.: Yale University Press, 1987.

Rowbottom, R., and Billis, D. *Organisational Design*. Aldershot, England: Gower, 1987.

Silver, C. V. "Recession Not Behind Restructuring" [Letter to the editor]. *Financial Times*, May 11, 1991, p. 9.

Steinberg, R. "Profits and Incentive Compensation in Nonprofit Firms." *Nonprofit Management and Leadership*, 1990, *1*(2), 137–151.

Stone, M. M. "Discussant Remarks." Presented at the conference on Nonprofit Organizations in a Market Economy, Case Western Reserve University, November 1991.

Waller, D. "Clues that Warn of a Collapse." *Financial Times*, May 25–26, 1991, p. Weekend IV.

Weisbrod, B. A. *The Voluntary Nonprofit Sector*. Lexington, Mass.: Lexington Books, 1977.

Weisbrod, B. A. *The Nonprofit Economy*. Cambridge, Mass.: Harvard University Press, 1988.

Young, D. R. "What Business Can Learn from Nonprofits." In *Models of Health and Human Services in the Nonprofit Sector*. Proceedings of the 14th annual meeting of the Association of Voluntary Action Scholars, October 1986, pp. 103–119.

Young, D. R. "Local Autonomy in a Franchise Age: Structural Change in National Voluntary Associations." *Nonprofit and Voluntary Sector Quarterly*. 1989, *18*(2), 101–117.

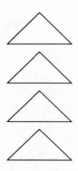

CHAPTER 12

Business Involvement in Education: The Nonprofit Route

P. Michael Timpane

During the past decade, the American business community, with the help of nonprofit entities, has become progressively more deeply involved in efforts to assist and reform public education. At local, state, and national levels, business round-tables, chambers of commerce, and similar groups have been giving education greater priority and providing the initial focus and initiative for the emergence of new roles in education for business. These groups, however, are often inadequate or inappropriate for intensive and targeted activities in the area of education. Thus we see, at every level, the development of new nonprofit institutions explicitly designed to promote business

Note: Much of the material in this chapter is adapted from *Business Impact on Education and Child Development Reform*, by P. Michael Timpane and Laurie Miller McNeill, a study prepared for the Committee for Economic Development, New York, 1991.

interests in education, such as local and state education funds and Boston-style education compacts.

The new American Schools Development Corporation is the most dramatic example of the implications of this new type of institution. Inasmuch as it overshadows or even replaces established public functions (for example, funding of educational research and development), it raises questions of public accountability. And because of its scale, it competes with other nonprofits for scarce corporate philanthropic resources. The coming decades will test the effectiveness and benefits of these efforts and of the long-term commitment of business to educational improvement in the nation.

Business in Education Reform

The 1980s were years of stunning change in the nation's perception of public education and of equally remarkable changes in the attitude and behavior of the American business community toward the schools. A once aloof, deeply skeptical, and frequently hostile business community has, in hundreds of localities and, most recently, at the national level, moved swiftly to a posture of engagement, programmatic initiative, and political support for education (Timpane, 1984). This about-face has been the single most significant factor in a growing political focus on education, helping to raise the issue from virtual obscurity to the top of the domestic social policy agenda. How did this happen? Our answer must begin with where education as a policy issue stood in 1980.

The 1970s were a time of great disappointment and discouragement in American education, a decade in which the turmoil of desegregation and busing produced great political conflict surrounding the schools. A "youth culture" flourished and produced a generation gap—remember that? New curricula and notions of open education sprang up and just as quickly withered. In the courts and legislatures, school finance equalization had improved financing schemes in almost thirty states by the end of the decade but in the process had put new strain on available resources and contributed to the backlash of the tax-limitation movements that emerged in California, Massachusetts, and many other states and localities.

The decade of the 1970s was a particularly difficult one for the teaching profession. By the end of the decade, collective bargaining agreements governed the working arrangements of most American teachers. Because of the "baby bust," however, the number of job openings plummeted and, predictably, pay levels sank — by almost 15 percent in real terms. The teaching profession became the lowest-paid college-trained profession in the nation. At the same time, the status of teaching diminished as the reforms of the day concentrated on bypassing the perceived shortcomings of teachers through the use of such schemes as "teacher-proof" curricula and alternative schools, rather than building on their strengths (Darling-Hammond, 1984).

By the end of the 1970s, American public schools had become bureaucratized. They were governed by a highly elaborated set of rules and procedures, many of them the result of new federal and state legislation. The proportion of dollars and employees devoted to administration and support services, as opposed to classrooms, was expanding steadily. In both administration and teaching, there was a relentless press for specialization, the effect of which was to narrow the professional responsibilities of most educators, but especially of classroom teachers.

These developments were accompanied, moreover, by perceived and real declines in the outcomes of education. Test scores, notably on the SAT, declined markedly during the decade. Analyses suggested that changes in the nature of the test-taking population accounted for some of the decline, but there was a real residual that could not be explained away (College Entrance Examination Board, 1977). There was also little gain in attainment: the dropout rate had remained relatively constant, with 25 percent of each age cohort failing to complete high school. A larger proportion of high school graduates did go on to college, but their arrival there was soon followed by widespread reports of the inability of many college students to do college-level work and by high rates of attrition.

All of these adverse developments led to a growing disillusionment with public education. The Gallup poll recorded a steadily diminishing number of Americans willing to give a satisfactory grade to the public schools (Timpane, 1984). This decline in public favor coincided with a diminishing proportion of parents and other directly concerned voters who were active in the local and state electorate, leaving education weaker and more vulnerable politically than it had been at any time during the postwar period. Policy makers concerned with education were uniformly pessimistic about its prospects for improvement, and, significantly, nowhere in the nation could one find a prominent politician ready to make education his or her signature concern.

Remarkably, just ten years later, in October of 1989, the president of the United States and the governors of the states assembled in Charlottesville, Virginia, for an education summit. The president had promised during his campaign to be an "education president" and had been strongly and continually urged by a powerful and vocal business leadership to come to this summit. Governors in virtually every state had reformed and refinanced education, with a strong and consistent ally in the business community (Doyle, Cooper, and Trachman, 1991). The education summit proposed for the nation's consideration a series of national goals in education — an inconceivable outcome ten years earlier.

This auspicious meeting signified the end of a decade in which a new educational agenda had been developed. That agenda consisted of higher standards, requirements, and outcomes in education; radical restructuring of the schools; and new proposals for comprehensive action to help at-risk children. And a new coalition of politicians and business leaders had helped bring it to pass.

Why Business Is Interested in Education

The involvement of business in education is not new. For the first half of the twentieth century, U.S. industry was a strong force behind the movement for universal schooling and vocational education. Most school board members were business or professional people, and public school management came to be modeled on business management. Business and educational leaders agreed that the preparation of students for a productive work life was an important objective of education. Curricula, testing, counseling, and placement programs were all developed within this comfortable consensus.

During the mid to late 1960s, the context of educational policy making changed swiftly, as new issues of educational equity, due process, and political power came to the fore. And with those new issues came new actors: organized parent and community groups, organized teachers, advocates of previously neglected groups of students, lawyers and judges, and federal and state program managers. These new issues and groups were unfamiliar and frustrating to the businesspeople, who thought themselves stewards of the schools. For the first time, in issues such as desegregation, busing, and school violence, business leaders confronted the possibility that their participation in educational policy would involve real costs, and they began to shy away from service related to education (on local school boards, for example). Over the period of only a few years, business influence was eclipsed. Its representatives were less and less prominent in deliberations about local educational policy and rarely involved in the development of important new state and federal educational roles (Timpane, 1984).

In these critical years, business interest shifted toward the universities. The children of business leaders often attended private elementary and secondary schools or public schools in elite suburbs. Lacking contact with the public schools, many business leaders found it easy to believe the stereotypes about public education that were circulating during these years: test scores falling and school systems failing because of unruly students, untested innovation, militant and uncooperative teachers, and ineffectual administrators.

Also during these years, an ample supply of qualified entry-level workers was to be found among the large numbers of young people born during the postwar baby boom and women reentering the labor market. Business could ignore or postpone its concerns about the quality of the schools and concentrate instead on their cost in taxes. These were the days of strong business support for state tax-limitation statutes in California, Massachusetts, and elsewhere and for local school bond issues. Business dealt with schools through its public affairs or personnel offices, which had little authority, small budgets, and, as a result, little or no credibility with or influence on educators.

In the late 1970s and early 1980s, this picture began to change. In cities such as Chicago, Minneapolis, and Dallas, and in states such as California, Florida, and Mississippi, business leaders began to reestablish connections with public education through the intermediary efforts of such nonprofits as business roundtables, public industry councils, and chambers of commerce. This phenomenon spread quickly to many other cities and states. And the business community found unexpected allies among the ranks of education reformers, who were drawing new and far-reaching conclusions from their own failures and frustrations in the 1960s and 1970s, and among a new generation of political leaders, state governors in particular, eager to make economic development through educational improvement a centerpiece of their programs.

It seems clear that changes in labor supply and demand have been the most significant spur to the renewal of business interest in education. Neither an abstract devotion to the importance of schools in society (to prepare employees, citizens, and consumers) nor local interest in communities that were "good places to do business" nor even contemporary theorizing about corporate social responsibility had been sufficient to rekindle that interest—but a growing concern about the quantity and quality of labor provided this incentive.

There would be a shortage of young people entering the labor market during the remainder of the century. The number of annual high school graduates would decline by 20 percent between 1980 and 1990 and would not grow throughout the 1990s. The proportion of women in the labor market would never again rise as swiftly as it had in the recent past. Spot shortages of labor were beginning to occur, and many industries began to contemplate the need for painful choices: raising entry-level wages, substituting technology for labor, or exporting jobs to new locales, domestic or overseas.

The quantitative issue was quickly joined by concerns about quality and the economy's failure to maintain historical annual advances in productivity. There were many macroeconomic and managerial explanations for this lag, but there was also a legitimate, if unproven, concern that the observed declines in educational performance were being translated into lower productivity in the workplace. This was heightened by the decline in the U.S. international competitive position during the 1980s compared with Japan and Germany (for instance), whose education systems were efficiently geared to serve vigorous economies.

Yet another factor was the rapidity of technological change, led by computers and telecommunication technologies. There were indications, again unproven, that as the new technologies became more pervasive in the workplace, workers would require different and often more complex skills.

These basic concerns about quantity and quality grew throughout the decade, reinforced by other changes in the labor market: increasing mobility of the work force; increasing heterogeneity of the work force, with the proportions of African-Americans, Latinos, and recent immigrants growing steadily and presenting new educational and performance problems; and evidence that success in the world economy would increasingly depend more on the quality of workers than on financial or natural resources. All in all, during the 1980s, human development and performance rose to first place among the issues troubling corporate leaders throughout the nation.

The dominant themes of the renewed business interest in education were historical and familiar: management, accountability, and education for employment (Education Commission of the States, 1983). And yet their specific meaning had changed dramatically. Education for employment no longer meant job-specific preparation primarily through vocational education, as it had in the past; it now meant general knowledge and skills that would enable workers to be productive in a variety of situations, adapting to a rapidly changing workplace. And it implied special concern for the youngest children in poverty, who would need a great deal of help before and after their schooling for them to attain the necessary levels of literacy and skill (Committee for Economic Development, 1987).

Similarly, the admonition to education to be "businesslike" had acquired radically different implications. Rather than being asked to be factorylike organizations run by a managerial hierarchy, schools were being asked to restructure themselves, as many of the most successful businesses had, to give operating sites (that is, individual schools) clear expectations, incentives, resources, authority, and, ultimately, responsibility for producing greater educational outcomes, such as measurably improved student performance (Committee for Economic Development, 1987).

Patterns of Business Involvement

The most visible expression of the new business interest in education during the 1980s and into the 1990s was the remarkable growth in the number and strength of new alliances among business, schools, and communities, almost always in the form of new, sometimes novel nonprofit enterprises. New relationships were formed at every level of government and in almost every area of educational policy. An entirely new context for educational policy making emerged, as well as a new set of expectations for the role of schools in the society. Business leaders began to play a new and vital part in deciding the very purposes of public education.

To be sure, not every instance of business activity in education has been substantial and productive. Many so-called partnerships are superficial and will likely remain so. But there is a clear pattern of successful business involvement in education, a pattern that often moves from the more superficial forms of partnership to forms that are progressively more significant for educational reform and improvement; from a few projects to many; from marginal programs of assistance to participation in efforts to change schools and school districts; from local to state-level involvement to emerging efforts to shape national attitudes and federal policies.

Helping-Hand Relationships

By all indications, the most widespread and popular type of relationship between business and the schools is the "helping-hand" relationship. Helping-hand relationships are usually suggested by educators and provided by businesses to supplement or enhance existing school programs. They provide schools with resources that the schools could not secure on their own, such as guest speakers, equipment and computers, and minigrants to teachers. Many adopt-a-school programs, especially those that respond primarily to a wish list of donations developed by schools, begin as helping-hand relationships.

These local partnerships are far and away the most numerous and popular form of connection between schools and business. They occurred in 17 percent of the nation's schools in 1984; they occur in 40 percent of the schools today. There are now more than 140,000 partnerships in 30,000 public elementary and secondary schools, and more than half of these relationships (52 percent) are between business organizations and schools. Small business firms sponsor about 40 percent of the partnerships, while medium-sized and larger firms support roughly 30 percent (National Center for Education Statistics, 1989).

IBM's extensive local partnership programs are prominent examples. IBM involves more than 10,000 employee-volunteers in more than 750 partnerships between its local offices and community schools. These helping-hand relationships include local partnerships supporting individual schools, Junior Achievement programs, loaned executives, and mentoring programs, as well as support for programs promoting literacy and education in mathematics, science, and engineering. Support comes in the form of guest instructors and speakers, teacher training, tutoring, equipment, software, participation on special education committees, and advice on curriculum and instruction, management, and school governance issues.

The expansion of helping-hand relationships has been accompanied and stimulated by a decided shift in corporate contribution programs, with corporate giving to precollegiate education growing almost 50 percent between 1987 and 1988 alone (Council for Aid to Education, 1989). Many companies report new long-term commitments to precollegiate education, including a new philanthropic focus and direct involvement in schools. Several of the nation's largest corporations have recently dramatized this shift: General Electric has set aside $20 million to double the number of disadvantaged college-bound youth in communities where its manufacturing activities are concentrated; IBM has designated $25 million for innovative computer use in schools; and R.J.R. Nabisco recently promised $30 million for local educational improvement projects.

How successful are helping-hand relationships in promoting school reform or improvement? They are highly successful at achieving peripheral goals, but they do not "reform" education. Branded as "feel-good" partnerships by some critics, these relationships do not set out to challenge the ways in which schools go about the business of education or the ways in which business goes about its involvement with schools. Nor do they attempt to redesign a specific program or school or challenge the basic assumptions that underlie the way schools work or the priorities educators set. In a worst-case scenario, they are a union of opportunists, both seeking public relations gains.

At their best, though, helping-hand relationships have substantial benefits. Enterprising educators can put the resources that helping hands provide to excellent use to enhance ongoing school programs. Since school people are often accustomed to scarce resources and being creative with what they have, a single donation can often make a significant difference in the day-to-day business of teaching and learning.

Moreover, helping-hand partnerships often provide a first, safe step toward greater business involvement and allow business and the schools to get acquainted and form a relationship for the future. When helping-hand relationships succeed, the business interest clearly evolves from "how can we support this school?" to "how can we support more substantial, long-lasting change in education?"

Programmatic Initiatives

Programmatic initiatives, the next stage of business involvement, are intensive efforts to improve one particular program or one particular school by concentrating on it a variety of special resources from both school and business partners to create enhanced learning opportunities for students. These initiatives are larger in scale and more expensive and complex than helping-hand relationships. They require greater commitment from both business and the schools and a shared vision of the desired outcome of the relationships. They are also the projects producing the greatest gains.

There are many varieties of programmatic initiatives, from ambitious science and technology courses in elementary and secondary schools to career preparation, mentoring, and job readiness programs in high schools to reorganized school curricula.

Programmatic initiatives differ from helping-hand projects in that they use business resources to change existing practice rather than to enhance existing school programs. Because of their careful design and the close and sustained relationship between business and the schools, programmatic initiatives tend to produce substantial educational outcomes.

Compacts and Collaboration

Compacts and collaborative ventures differ significantly from programmatic initiatives and helping-hand relationships. They involve joint efforts between several businesses and one or more school districts. Rather than investing in one program or one school, compacts and collaborative efforts coordinate a variety of efforts serving a number of programs and schools, as well as fostering districtwide policies geared to school improvement and reform. Civic and community organizations, higher education institutions, and local government are often included in the efforts. By organizing under one umbrella, business and community leaders become an important force for districtwide school improvement and reform. A unified coalition supporting an agenda for educational improvement and reform dramatically alters the context of educational decision making in a community. It creates new forums for debates about goals and performance and new expectations that district education officials cannot ignore.

The compacts and collaborative efforts established over the past decade have varied greatly. Some coordinate existing activities, while others challenge district and board policy on school improvement and reform issues. Both are important demonstrations of business and community involvement in the schools, but they embody two different strategies for change. Compacts and collaborative efforts that are primarily coordinating mechanisms provide community and business support for *internally* driven school improvement efforts. The relationship is primarily supportive: it fosters school improvement by supporting programmatic initiatives and helping-hand relationships with the district.

Local education funds (LEFs) created in several dozen communities are prominent examples of this type of collaboration. They bring together business executives, community leaders, and school managers to develop and provide resources for an array of supportive projects. Minigrants for teachers and community public relations assistance for the school system have been the projects most frequently launched. Where they have conducted larger efforts, such as San Francisco, Los Angeles, and New York, LEFs have also provided extensive professional support for teachers in the arts, sciences, mathematics, and humanities; dropout prevention programs; and local models of educational reorganization and improvement.

Compacts and collaborative ventures that are oriented toward political action create effective *external* pressure groups to drive school reform efforts. The relationship can be adversarial, at least to the extent of forcing the scope and pace of change.

Implicit in these two strategies are competing philoso-
phies about what is wrong with schools and what should be
done to fix them. Compacts and collaborative ventures that
emphasize supportive strategies (programmatic initiatives and
helping-hand relationships) advance the view that school programs need *improvement*, something that can be brought about,
in part, by extra resources and moral support provided by
business and community leaders. In supportive relationships,
business and community groups work cooperatively with school
officials on targeted areas to bring about improvement.

In contrast, some compacts and collaborative ventures
engage in political action to bring about *reform* in school policy
and practice. School improvement is too modest a goal for
troubled districts that will require deep structural changes in
teaching, learning, and educational decision making. In these
communities, business leaders are willing to commit extra resources and provide moral support to their local districts, but
only for the quid pro quo of change and improvement. They set
their own expectations and agendas for school reform.

The Boston Compact is the most prominent and fascinating example of this mode (Farrar and Cipollone, 1987). Begun
in 1982, the compact promised extra resources to the school
district but, at the same time, established clear goals for school
improvement as part of the deal. In a formal agreement signed
by the business community and the school district, business
guaranteed high school graduates jobs and college aid in return
for systemwide improvements in student performance, particularly improvements in Boston's high dropout rate.

But the Boston Compact revealed that the *expectation* of
change and the *reality* of change are quite different. After six
years, even though local firms exceeded hiring goals, only marginal gains had been made in the reading ability of graduates,
and the dropout rate in the district had actually increased.
Business leaders refused to renew the agreement with the
Boston public schools until they received assurances that the
pace of reform would pick up.

The National Alliance of Business has used the Boston
Compact's strategy for promoting educational reform in its

efforts to organize business involvement in education in other cities, including Cincinnati, Detroit, Indianapolis, Louisville, Memphis, Miami, Pittsburgh, Providence, Rochester, San Diego, and Seattle. It derived several principles from the experience of the Boston Compact:

- Develop long-term, measurable goals
- Designate a business intermediary
- Develop a planning structure
- Establish base-line data
- Secure financial resources
- Organize collaboration

This model establishes an alternative forum for setting district goals and evaluating district performance *outside* the realm of the school board and the district's central administration, and enables compacts to take a firm stance on reform goals that are not met. The challenge for the compacts in each of these cities will be creating effective pressure for districtwide improvement and reform.

The strategy of business leaders in Chicago was even more radical and ambitious (Bednarek, 1989). Convinced that the Chicago public schools were too disorganized and ineffective for conventional improvement tactics to succeed, business and community leaders demanded major structural reforms. Together they lobbied the Illinois state legislature to enact the nation's most dramatic effort to restructure urban education. School decision making and governance moved from the central office and city school board to individual schools and included parents, teachers, and administrators. Local school councils, made up of several thousand parents elected by the community, have authority to adopt school improvement efforts, hire and fire principals, and allocate school budgets.

Most compacts and collaborative efforts do not challenge districtwide practices, as those of Boston and Chicago have. Instead, they provide a coordinating mechanism for a variety of efforts to support changes and programmatic improvements identified by educators. To some, this strategy is too "soft"; to others, it is "empowerment." However, the increasing number of instances in which more critical demands are being placed on school systems suggests that simply supporting schools and school districts will not be sufficient; business leaders will be able to foster systemwide changes only if they remain extensively involved and take political risks.

Policy Change

The 1980s were years of intensive educational policy making in almost every state in the Union, producing new laws and regulations of unprecedented scope and number. The business community was quickly drawn into this activity, both by its own growing engagement in local educational affairs and by the strong invitation of state political leadership.

Thus, the origin and organization of business activity at the state level differ greatly from the local experience and involve political action, not supportive services. Moreover, business leadership (especially from state business roundtables) was often included in a new coalition for education reform spearheaded by governors and state legislators rather than educators.

This new coalition, dedicated to reform, often challenged existing policy as well as the policy-making authority of state school boards, state school superintendents, and other traditional education interests. In fact, in many states, it amounted to an alternative system for educational policy making.

During the 1960s and 1970s, business was not a prominent participant in state educational politics. Education was considered a political backwater under the control of a few traditional professional, legislative, and bureaucratic interests. During the 1970s, in fact, business involvement in many states was anything but supportive of public education and concentrated on support of tax-limitation measures, by referendum, as in California and Massachusetts, or by legislation.

Contemporary business involvement in state educational policy reform emerged when governors and state legislators began to engage corporate leaders in their new economic development and employment policy efforts. The fiscal condition of the states was extremely tenuous a decade ago; many states experienced their worst budget crises since the Great Depression. Intense international and interstate economic competition for high-growth, high-technology industry made it increasingly clear that state policy on economic development, employment, and education needed to change. Economic development no longer meant simply tax abatements to lure industry, because that strategy attracted businesses that had little long-term commitment and were easily lured away by more generous tax benefits or cost savings in other states and nations. More and more, investment in *human* capital became the focus of both economic development and employment policies.

It was inevitable that this theme of economic development would extend to educational reform in the states, since state governments devote more resources to public education than to any other public service. It was also inevitable, given the new view of economic and human resource development emerging in the states, that business leaders would become prominently involved in efforts to reform education.

The first wave of state reform activity concentrated on creating and raising standards for public schools and encouraging accountability for student achievement, teacher effectiveness, and administrative performance. These were congenial goals for business participants, reflecting their own operating style and (sometimes simplified) view of the way organizations should perform. In pursuing this agenda, the governor and legislators, with business participation and support, were not hesitant to override the traditional policy-making responsibilities of state boards and superintendents. Between 1983 and 1985 alone, they created more than 300 special state task forces and commissions to "reform" education through new standards and procedures, from the top down. Business played an important role. Its representatives constituted almost 25 percent of the membership of these task forces—9 percent of the participants on task forces sponsored by educators but 31 percent on task forces sponsored by governors and state legislators. And in many key instances, a business leader was the designated chair (Miller McNeill, 1989).

Once standards and accountability schemes were established, business involvement in state educational policy took the new form of representation on newly mandated special councils that oversee implementation of reform, superseding wholly or in part the responsibilities of state boards and agencies.

In the vast majority of cases, businesses became involved in policy making by invitation rather than by initiating reform itself. In response to gubernatorial and legislative calls to action, business leaders participated in special task forces and commissions to set education agendas, lobbied for special causes, gave testimony before state legislatures, and, mirabile dictu, supported tax increases to pay for the new reforms. Such involvement was particularly notable in the mid 1980s in Mississippi, Florida, South Carolina, and throughout the South—where the most remarkable changes in policies and budgets took place (Peterson, 1989). Later in the decade, as state economic conditions worsened, such willingness to support new taxes became rare, and business support for education funding was far less secure. (The 1990s have begun with another set of state reforms—notably in Texas and Kentucky—driven by state court decisions that threw out entire school financing schemes.)

Less frequently, though most visibly, the business community furnished the principal impetus for state education reforms. Business roundtables in California, Washington, and Minnesota—and Ross Perot in Texas—established their own agendas and coalitions for reform early in the decade. More recently, business leaders and councils in Arkansas and Texas have similarly tried to be "out in front," with varying persistence and effect. Very few of these out-front efforts have been successfully sustained. In California, for instance, the Business Roundtable's ambitious agendas for higher standards and accountability and expanded programs for teacher and school improvement were swiftly enacted along with new education funding in the early 1980s, but since then the state's business community has not sustained a leadership role in the development of educational policy in the state (Kirst, 1983).

Whatever the mode of intervention, in most states the new reforms would not have passed without business support. In some cases, business is credited with creating a positive climate for educational reform; in other cases, business has garnered the political support necessary to pass specific proposals in state legislatures, especially bills related to funding.

The most recent and remarkable business-related developments in educational policy making have occurred on the national scene. As the president and governors met in an education summit and struggled to produce national goals and objectives, they were cheered on by an impressive array of the nation's leading nonprofit business organizations: the National Alliance of Business, the Committee for Economic Development, the Business Roundtable, the U.S. Chamber of Commerce, the National Association of Manufacturers, the Conference Board, the American Business Conference, and the U.S. Hispanic Chamber of Commerce joined together in yet another new nonprofit organization, the Business Coalition for Education Reform. And the agenda of the president and governors strongly reflects the business agenda for higher standards, accountability for outcomes, restructured schools, and greater concentration on early intervention for at-risk children and youth (Business Roundtable, 1988; Committee for Economic Development, 1987, 1991).

A few months later, the Bush administration's America 2000 initiative — touted as a joint enterprise with governors and business leadership — included a further development in business involvement: the New American Schools Development Corporation (NASDC) was announced as a $250 million privately funded nonprofit corporation to promote the design and implementation of "new American schools" that will "break the mold" and "jump-start the system." The NASDC, with a board composed almost entirely of business leaders, is now raising the money from corporate sources. It issued its first requests for proposals in October 1992 and planned to start funding thirty first-round winners later in the year.

Conclusion

As we look back on a decade of renewed corporate interest in education, it is difficult to make generalizations about its nature or impact, given the varied and complex character of events and of the business community. Different parts of the business sector have entered the picture at different times in different places at different levels of government, and significant parts of the business sector have not participated at all. The manner of participation has varied, too, ranging from hostile or uninterested inaction to shallow contacts to profound involvement combining a good measure of social responsibility with an essential self-interest. The actual policies promoted and projects launched have also varied greatly. The tendency has been toward more well-informed, appropriate, and effective action at the higher levels of both corporate management and public policy. There seem to be few second thoughts among the business leaders who have been involved in the educational reform movement about the continuing importance and necessity of their efforts. Sober assessments, yes; second thoughts, no.

Looking over the range of initiatives spawned in the last decade, the business sector should take pride and satisfaction in its work, most of which has been advanced through creative use of nonprofit instrumentalities. There are many thousands of new business-sponsored projects in up to half the nation's schools, with notable concentrations in areas of urban poverty. Some entail only modest donations of time and equipment, but growing numbers are programmatic and political partnerships of considerable duration. The limitations of the initial efforts have become increasingly clear: they are unlikely to affect educational achievement directly or to solve the problems of policy, resources, and management that all school systems face. At the same time, they have had no adverse side effects. They have introduced many thousands of managers and employees to the realities of the public schools and motivated them to become involved in further partnerships with those schools. The more extensive and programmatic partnerships in a few communities have shown some gains in student and schooling outcomes. The communitywide councils and compacts that today characterize business support in the large cities have stimulated far-reaching policy changes in Boston, Chicago, and other cities.

Business's access to and involvement in the policy councils

of education seems ensured. Business-education compacts and collaborations are active in most urban communities. The processes of state policy making in education have changed substantially with business participation and approval. A number of states — South Carolina, Ohio, Florida, Indiana, Maryland, Minnesota, and New Jersey, for example — have institutionalized a business role in state educational policy making by creating state-level business advisory councils and officially encouraged the creation of school-business partnerships at the local level.

The auspicious collaboration between the president and the governors at the national level builds on the emerging business agenda with remarkable fidelity. The quest for national goals carries forward an emphasis on outcomes, while acknowledging the diversity of appropriate standards and measures in states and localities, and promotes the nation's continuing focus on the issues. The call for easing federal program requirements is clearly tied to restructuring efforts. And the pleas for immediate expansion of federal early-childhood programs such as Head Start give a clear priority to the problems of poverty and disadvantage and the strategy of early intervention. The influence of the business community through the Business Roundtable and the Business Coalition for Education Reform was critical — indeed, decisive — in persuading the president to put forward a substantive agenda for education in the United States.

References

Bednarek, D. *Chicago Business Leadership and School Reform.* Occasional Paper no. 3. Washington, D.C.: Institute for Educational Leadership and the Edna McConnell Clark Foundation, 1989.

Business Roundtable. *The Role of Business in Education Reform: Blueprint for Action.* New York: Business Roundtable, 1988.

College Entrance Examination Board. *On Further Examination: Report of the Advisory Panel on the Scholastic Aptitude Test Score Decline.* New York: College Entrance Examination Board, 1977.

Committee for Economic Development. *Children in Need: Invest-*

ment Strategies for the Educationally Disadvantaged. New York: Committee for Economic Development, 1987.

Committee for Economic Development. *The Unfinished Agenda: A New Vision for Child Development and Education.* New York: Committee for Economic Development, 1991.

Council for Aid to Education. *Business and the Schools: A Guide to Effective Programs.* New York: Council for Aid to Education, 1989.

Darling-Hammond, L. *Beyond the Commission Reports: The Coming Crisis in Teaching.* Santa Monica, Calif.: Rand Corporation, 1984.

Doyle, D. P., Cooper, B. S., and Trachman, R. *Taking Charge: State Action in School Reform in the 1980s.* Indianapolis, Ind.: Hudson Institute, 1991.

Education Commission of the States. *Action for Excellence: A Comprehensive Plan to Improve Our Nation's Schools.* Denver, Colo.: Education Commission of the States, 1983.

Farrar, E., and Cipollone, A. *The Business Community and School Reform: The Boston Compact at Five Years.* Buffalo: State University of New York, 1987.

Kirst, M. W. "The California Business Roundtable: Their Strategy and Impact on State Education Policy." Paper prepared for the Committee for Economic Development, New York, 1983.

Miller McNeill, L. "The State Education Reform Movement and the Reform of the State Politics of Education." Unpublished doctoral dissertation, Columbia University, 1989.

National Center for Education Statistics. *Education Partnerships in Public Elementary and Secondary Schools.* Survey Report CS 89-060. Washington, D.C.: Office of Educational Research and Improvement, U.S. Department of Education, 1989.

Peterson, T. *Sustained Business Involvement in State School Reform: The South Carolina Story.* Occasional Paper no. 11. Washington, D.C.: Institute for Educational Leadership and the Edna McConnell Clark Foundation, 1989.

Timpane, P. M. "Business Has Rediscovered the Public Schools." *Phi Delta Kappan,* 1984, *6*(65), 389–392.

Timpane, P. M., and Miller McNeill, L. *Business Impact on Education and Child Development Reform.* New York: Committee for Economic Development, 1991.

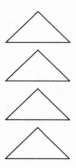

CHAPTER 13

Technological Innovation: The Role of Nonprofit Organizations

Richard R. Nelson

This chapter is not an essay focused tightly on the role of not-for-profit organizations in a particular arena of activity, in this case industrial innovation. Rather, it is an essay on the organizational ecology of that arena, the diversity of organizations involved, the roles played by nonprofits in that ecology, and the reasons not-for-profits play those roles and not others. In the arena of industrial innovation in the United States, nonprofit organizations find niches in different places, as complements to and substitutes for private for-profit and governmental organizations.

An important question that I pose is why one finds nonprofits where one does and not in other places. I find two alternative explanations for this phenomenon. In some cases, nonprofits show up where they have strong "efficiency" or "governance" advantages over other legal forms and not where other forms are clearly superior. In other cases, the context does not strongly select for or against nonprofits, and their presence or absence is largely a matter of historical happenstance or preferences that have little to do with "advantage" of one legal form or another, in any well-defined sense. In these cases, what matters is the details of how an activity is governed, which may not be tightly determined by legal form.

In the first section of the chapter, I describe some salient aspects of industrial innovation in today's modern capitalist economies and the institutional actors involved in industrial innovation in the United States. Then I ask "Why do you find nonprofits where you do, and what other organizations could do the trick?" Finally, I offer a reprise of my conclusions.

Technology as a Private Good and a Public Good

I hinted above that a quite complex and varied set of activities and institutions are involved in industrial innovation. In this section, I lay out the basics of what is going on and who is doing what.

Virtually all contemporary accounts of technical advance in modern capitalist economies start with the one provided by Schumpeter (1950) in *Capitalism, Socialism, and Democracy*. For-profit business firms in rivalrous competition with each other are the featured actors. Firms innovate in order to gain an edge over their rivals or to catch up with them. A firm that successfully innovates can profit handsomely. On the other hand, in an industry where competitors are innovating, a firm is virtually forced to do so too, or fall farther and farther behind. While it does not fit the facts in all industries, Schumpeter's picture is a good first-cut approximation for a large number of them. In the United States and all other advanced capitalist economies, for-profit industrial firms are the locus of the lion's share of research and development and employ the largest share of a nation's scientists and engineers engaged in research and development (see, for example, National Science Board, 1991).

The key firms in Schumpeter's *Capitalism, Socialism, and Democracy* are sizeable, with research and development laboratories attached to them. In his *Theory of Economic Development*

([1911] 1934), written approximately forty years earlier, Schumpeter also stressed the key role of innovation, but in that earlier work, the key actors were "entrepreneurs" rather than large established business firms. Schumpeter was a perceptive observer of the scene around him. The forty years between two books saw the rise of the industrial research and development laboratory attached to business firms, first in the chemical and electrical industries and then much more widely (see, for example, Mowery, 1984). The laboratories proved profitable for the firms that established them, because they served to link the increasingly powerful generic knowledge and methods of modern science to the problems and opportunities of industrial technology, in an environment where both kinds of knowledge could be brought to bear on project selection and execution.

However, for a modern industrial research laboratory to be profitable, it was not sufficient that organized, focused scientific research be able to push forward industrial technology in directions that the market would pay well for. The firm also had to be able to appropriate a nontrivial share of those benefits. In particular, a for-profit firm undertaking expensive R&D had to have assurance that its competitors would not reap on the cheap what they did not sow.

Historians and economists studying technological change in capitalist countries have recognized a wide variety of means by which firms appropriate returns to their investments in innovation. A recent survey (Levin, Klevorick, Nelson, and Winter, 1987) undertaken by my colleagues and me has provided valuable information regarding the means that are most effective in different industries. What we found yields important insights into the factors behind the dominant role played by industrial R&D labs in industrial "inventing."

To oversimplify somewhat, we distinguished three broad classes of means by which firms can appropriate returns from their innovations — the patent system, secrecy, and various advantages associated with exploiting a head start — and asked our respondents to rate their effectiveness. Contrary to widespread impressions, patents were not rated as particularly effective in most industries, nor was secrecy. On the other hand, in most industries where industrial R&D is significant, our respondents reported that a firm could profit from its innovation if it tailored it to customer needs and its own capabilities, got it on the market ahead of its rivals, and backed it up with strong production and marketing.

Note that the general weakness of patents and the advantages of a head start tend to give strong advantages to companies with their own research and development laboratories over freestanding laboratories. Weakness of patent protection and the ineffectiveness of mechanisms to guard secrecy put freestanding laboratories at a significant disadvantage in trying to bargain with existing firms for the production and marketing of their innovations. At the same time, since starting up de novo a production and marketing organization is time-consuming as well as costly, any head-start advantages of an independent laboratory likely would erode. These reasons explain why the industrial research laboratory attached to firms has become the dominant source of industrial innovation in most fields. (I will consider some areas of exception later.)

The mechanisms that firms have for protecting their innovations are leaky, however. The advantages that a firm wins from a particular innovation tend to be transient. Sooner or later, competitors are able to catch on and imitate or come up with an equivalent — or even with something that is an advance over the original innovation. While new industrial technology starts out proprietary in many cases, much of it becomes largely "public."

The weakness of patent protection and the inability of companies to keep technology secret for very long mean that much of the technological knowledge won in industrial R&D goes public even if companies try to protect that knowledge. In many cases, in fact, companies do not try very hard to protect technological understandings won through their R&D efforts. When a company comes up with a superior new product, describing that product and its advantages usually is an essential part of sales promotion. And it knows full well that once it starts to market the product, its competitors will obtain it and "reverse engineer" it. In addition, a new product or production process often requires specialized materials and other inputs that will have to be made known to the company's suppliers. Again, there is little stopping that information from getting into the hands of rivals.

In most industries, as noted above, a company gains profit from its innovation by getting it out into the market ahead of its competitors, moving rapidly down the learning curve, and supporting the product and improvements to it through sales and service efforts. To keep its competitive edge, a company will want to keep certain aspects of its technology secret, but it can be pretty open about much of it.

It is useful to think of technology at any time as having two different aspects. On the one hand, technology consists of a set of specific product designs and industrial practices that are sources of competitive advantage and that companies try to keep secret. On the other hand, technology at any time consists of a body of generic knowledge that surrounds particular products and industrial processes and provides understanding of how things work, key variables affecting performance, the nature of limitations on development of the technology, and promising approaches to overcoming them. This kind of technological knowledge is difficult to keep secret, even if won in industrial R&D (see the discussion in Nelson, 1990).

And there are considerable advantages to firms if such knowledge is shared. This kind of knowledge must be imparted to scientists and engineers if they are to be effective in industrial R&D. To the extent that formal schooling is an important vehicle for training scientists and engineers, it is to the advantage of the companies in an industry that university faculty know enough about that industry's generic technology to be able to teach it. Further, all firms using a particular broad technology can have an advantage over firms competing with them but using another broad technology if they can share generic technological knowledge among themselves rather than each company having to develop it on its own. Thus, academic disciplines and scientific and technical societies tend to grow up around bodies of generic technological knowledge.

There is nothing inherently "scientific" about generic

technological understanding. In many fields even today, a considerable portion of it stems from operating or design experience with products and machines and their components. Consider, for example, a mechanic's guide, the general knowledge of potters or steel makers, or the shared savvy of aircraft designers. However, over the last century, bodies of generic technological knowledge have become increasingly sciencelike. This is largely the consequence of the birth and development of scientific fields such as electrical engineering, aerodynamics, metallurgy, and pathology. These fields of study basically deal with generic technological understanding and reflect attempts to make it more scientific (see Nelson, 1990, and Rosenberg, 1985, for general discussions; Thackray, 1982, provides a detailed analysis regarding the field of chemistry). All of these have become recognized fields of university teaching and research.

I suggested earlier that the rise of the industrial research laboratory was associated with the increasing relevance of science to industrial technology. The links were forged largely through the kinds of disciplines listed above. And the rise of these disciplines and the industrial research laboratories employing people skilled in them naturally led to a new importance of universities as part of the industrial innovation system. Universities are, first of all, the places where future industrial scientists and engineers get their academic training. A good deal of that training, beyond the basic introductory courses, is in the applied sciences and engineering disciplines that I have been talking about. And the rise of these disciplines significantly increased the importance of academic research to industrial innovation. The precise role of academic research varies from field to field. In a few fields, university researchers are direct creators of new product designs or solvers of particular practical problems, but this role is not widespread. Thus, universities account for only about 1.5 percent of the total patents granted to all individuals and institutions.

There are interesting exceptions, fields where one finds universities playing a large role in "inventing." This occurs, first of all, in recently opened fields of science that are rich in potential applications, where the industrial laboratories have not yet staffed or organized to develop those applications. Biotechnology has been such an area. Second, academic work in some of the applied sciences and engineering disciplines is inherently close to practical problem solving. Thus, academic electrical engineers are often in the business of building and experimenting with radically new devices; this is what their "research" is about. Third, in some fields, such as agriculture and health, the federal and state governments expressly fund academic institutions to solve practical problems. I shall elaborate these (obviously overlapping) categories shortly.

As I have stressed, however, freestanding laboratories and university laboratories are not major direct sources of new products or processes or practical problem solving in most fields. Even in the cases that I have described, university research for the most part provides understandings, findings, techniques, and ideas that in turn are used in industrial R&D. While university patents are important in only a few areas, university-authored articles account for a large share of the articles cited in patents in a large number of fields.

The above description of interactions of industrial and academic research suggests that the industrial-academic connections are close where academic research is an important input to industrial R&D. There are many ways in which those links are institutionalized. Scientific and technical societies are one of them. While students of technical advance have only begun to study and to understand the role of scientific and technical societies, preliminary findings suggest that they are important in a number of technological fields. Their journals and meetings are the vehicles through which technical people in the field, from industry as well as academia, share new developments. Industry scientists and engineers, as well as academics, write for their publications and give talks at their meetings (see Nelson, 1990). In a study currently under way, my colleagues and I are finding that a very significant share of the references cited in patents on semiconductor process equipment are to papers that have been presented at technical society meetings.

Industry associations, while in most cases not nearly as important in industrial innovation as scientific and technical societies, also play a variety of roles. One important one is the setting of standards. In a wide range of technologies, there are strong pressures and incentives for members of an industry to agree on certain standards, particularly if the products of the industry are part of a system involving other products as well. In some cases, these standards are imposed by government. In most cases, however, appropriate standards are hammered out in industry associations, which may also fund research and study regarding the standards.

Private foundations used to play a significant role in the innovation system, principally as funders of research undertaken in universities and specialized nonprofit laboratories. During the 1920s and 1930s, foundations were a major influence on and support for academic research, and even after the federal government took on the role of principal funder of academic research, foundations continued to play a leading role in some areas, particularly medicine and the biological sciences (see Geiger, 1986). Since World War II, however, the federal government has taken on the role of principal supporter of basic research in most fields.

I began this discussion of the institutions supporting industrial innovation with Schumpeter's account. While Schumpeter was rather weak on many of the institutions that complement and support industrial R&D, he was virtually mute on the role of government. That is largely a result of the times in which he was writing. As of 1940, when Schumpeter was doing the thinking and observation that went into *Capitalism, Socialism, and Democracy*, the government's role in the innovation system was indeed limited. In the 1930s, the largest government research support program was for agriculture.

With the close of World War II, all this changed. Since that time, the government has been a major funder of research and development, and government laboratories have been an important locus of R&D activity in a number of fields. The bulk of government R&D funding goes to areas such as national security, for which government agencies have primary responsibility; the development of new technology is an important part of that responsibility. However, after the close of World War II, the federal government also took on the responsibility for funding the nation's university research enterprise. A small fraction of government monies in support of R&D goes to projects and institutions largely concerned with technological advances for a civilian industry. While the largest of these areas now is health, government continues to fund a significant portion of the total R&D concerned with agriculture.

The Role of Private Nonprofit Organizations

It is interesting to reflect on where private nonprofit organizations show up in this system of institutions and where they do not. In the first place, they rarely show up in activities aimed directly at creating a marketable new product or a more effective industrial production process. I have noted that this kind of activity is conducted overwhelmingly in the industrial research and development laboratories of the for-profit firms that will produce and market the product and employ the processes. Business firms have the advantage of knowing their market and the strengths and weaknesses of existing products and manufacturing processes. And their ability to control the operations of affiliated laboratories enables them not only to allocate R&D where it is likely to be profitable but also to coordinate R&D with the other investments and activities needed to enable them to profit from that R&D. One does, of course, often see "invasion" of an industry by firms from outside it. But for the most part, these firms also are for-profit, and their inventive work is largely done in house.

As noted earlier, there are some cases in which university laboratories and other laboratories not tied to particular firms play an important role in inventing. This occurs, for instance, with new technologies with which for-profit firms have too little experience to put them in an advantaged position. In some cases, for-profit firms directly support the work of independent laboratories in exchange for patent rights. In a few fields, such as biotechnology, independent inventors may obtain patents so that that their work is rewarded by royalties, sale of rights to the technology, and so on. Of course, in fields such as biotechnology, researchers in university and other freestanding laboratories are not dependent on "buyers" of their inventions for their research funding, which is largely provided through government grants. The "royalty" money is gravy.

Biotechnology is one example of a field where public R&D subsidy keeps separate laboratories — often but not always associated with universities — active in inventing and practical problem solving. The otherwise limited role of nonprofit labs in inventing at least partly reflects the absence of public funds to support them in such activities. Where public funds are provided, as in health, agriculture, and national security, university and other nonprofit labs can be drawn into the "inventing" business.

Funding, however, is not the only factor. A strong case can be made that, in most industrial fields, freestanding labs are not as effective at "inventing" as labs tied to firms. While R&D subsidies can partially offset the economic advantages of industry laboratories, the informational advantages that industry laboratories enjoy by virtue of their close ties with marketing and production may still limit the effectiveness of subsidized freestanding labs if their work is closely directed to specific products and processes. Offsetting this problem may require special circumstances or arrangements.

In the field of medicine, these informational limits on the "demand side" are not severe, because the community of physicians and hospitals (as contrasted with a company's marketing people) are the principal source of "demand" information and because new substances developed in university labs have the same access to clinical trials as substances developed in industry labs. In agriculture, university or government agricultural research laboratories have developed a variety of mechanisms for reading the needs of farmers and of industries tied to agriculture. But these mechanisms by which freestanding labs get tuned to markets are not cheap. And the difficulties involved in linking into "production" and "marketing" expertise are often even more formidable.

Again, the case of biotechnology is a nice illustration. Many university professors active in the field of biotechnology have set up their own companies to provide some distance between their "invention" work and their university-related work. These for-profit labs, which are freestanding in the sense that they are not part of a firm that actually produces products, although they are often funded by such firms, have been quite successful in the early stages of "inventing," since their market is not difficult to fathom. However, almost all the "development" work has been done by firms with established production operations. Further, even when lab firms have managed to get into production, they have usually found marketing very difficult. (For a good analysis, see Pisano, 1990.)

Thus, universities and other freestanding labs have played only a limited role in product and process development. Since many of these are nonprofit organizations, this might be interpreted as indicating that the nonprofit legal form is not suitable for inventing. But I believe that this argument misses the point. The point is that production and marketing are usually undertaken, in a capitalist economy, by for-profit firms, and effective product and process innovation generally requires tight organizational ties to production and marketing. It is the "freestanding lab" that is disadvantaged in this role, whatever its legal form. The limited success of the for-profit lab firms supports this position. Several observers have suggested that, now that integrated companies have set up their own biotech labs, the for-profit lab firm is doomed in this field.

Universities do play essential roles in innovation systems, in teaching and research, and in advancing generic technological knowledge, if not in product and process invention and innovation. In the United States, many of these are private nonprofit organizations. A reasonably good argument can be made that organizing universities and university research in a for-profit mode would cause some difficulties. That argument is largely based on the expectation that university scientists will publish the results of their research in open journals and the fact that that research now is financed primarily by government agencies (and, to a lesser extent, by foundations) that are interested in creating public knowledge. This is why the "commercial inventing" aspects of university research cause tensions within universities and between them and their research funders. But the fact that many of the great American universities are private nonprofits, rather than public organizations, seems mostly the result of history.

In the United States at present, it is hard to find much difference between the operations of private universities and comparable public ones. In both, the bulk of funding for research now comes from government. In both, the institutions themselves and the individual faculty members have considerable autonomy regarding what they do. In both, open publication is not only expected but required for promotion or tenure. If it is argued that a special advantage of the private nonprofit form of organization is that it can at once draw in grant money from the outside, avoid heavy top-to-bottom hierarchial control, and stay relatively secure from the winds of national or state politics, the major state research universities show that nominally public organizations can achieve this as well.

I propose that the American university research system would continue to operate more or less as it currently does even if all presently private universities were made public. Indeed, this has been basically the pattern in England and Germany, where, over the last quarter century, the formally private parts of the university research system have almost entirely been taken over by government.

I suspect that it is another matter with the scientific and technical societies and the industry associations. Clearly, it makes little sense for these groups to be formed as for-profit organizations. They are not organized to make money for anyone, and much of their input is volunteered. These are essentially voluntary associations of people and organizations that expect to gain from their involvement and are willing to contribute funds and labor to keep the association going effectively. To make them official "governmental" bodies, therefore, would at best be very awkward.

Conclusion

I have long been impressed by the diversity of the organizational forms that we use to accomplish various tasks and by the variety of organizations that one often finds in a cluster of related activities, such as industrial innovation, health care, transportation, or child care. One of my intentions in writing this chapter was to develop that theme, using the cluster of activities associated with industrial innovation as a case study. I trust that the endeavor has been a useful one and that I have been persuasive that it is often valuable to view nonprofits in the context of an ecology of organizations, interacting with for-profits and governmental organizations and filling various niches in the system for which the other forms are not well suited.

I have also long been impressed by the diversity of actual structures that one finds under a particular legal organizational form and by the wide range of substitutability among forms. Thus, one finds private nonprofit universities and public sector ones looking very much alike and in some activities acting very like for-profit organizations. I have always doubted that stylized models comparing the character of organizations with different legal forms and predicting their behavior and performance were very helpful analytical devices, except as vehicles to stir thought.

If my analysis of how institutions with different legal forms behave is on the mark, context matters very much, and so do the details of the activities being undertaken and governed. Thus, the fact that we do not see much industrial inventing going on in nonprofit laboratories has nothing to do with the nonprofit form of the laboratories. It has to do with the facts that production and marketing are carried on by for-profit firms and that there are strong informational and proprietary advantages for an R&D organization that is tied in with these other functions of a firm.

On the other hand, we find universities performing a range of other important functions. In the United States, universities are a mix of private nonprofit and public. Which they are does not seem to matter much. Given what universities do and their constituencies and the fact that public monies are now important to all universities, I think it inevitable that private and public universities will behave and be governed in quite similar ways. Differences could, of course, be imposed by differential outside treatment — for example, if legislators or departments of education felt more free to dictate admission rules or curricula to public institutions than to private ones—but the universities have held out pretty well against this, and if there is a trend, it seems to be toward government treating private and public universities as basically alike. New York State, for example, provides budget support to private universities as well as public ones.

In other contexts and in other activities, things seem at first glance to be different. Public primary and secondary schools are in fact under very different constraints than private ones—regarding rules of admission and expulsion, curricula, and salary schedules, for example. But it seems to me that the differences here are best viewed as the result of different contexts rather than different legal forms. In this case, much of the context is provided by who pays. If private schools became largely financed by public funds, as they would under various voucher proposals, I think it a good bet that they would be regulated quite tightly and that the differences between private and public schools would be greatly diminished.

References

Geiger, T. *To Advance Knowledge*. New York: Oxford University Press, 1986.

Levin, R., Klevorick, A., Nelson, R., and Winter, S. *Appropriating the Returns to R and D*. Brookings Papers in Economic Activity. Washington, D.C.: Brookings Institution, 1987.

Mowery, D. "Firm Structure, Government Policy, and the Organization of Industrial Research." *Business History Review*, 1985, *58*(4), 504–531.

National Science Board. *Science and Engineering Indicators*. Washington, D.C.: National Science Board, 1991.

Nelson, R. "Capitalism as an Engine of Progress." *Research Policy*, 1990, *19*(3), 193–214.

Pisano, G. P. "The R and D Boundaries of the Firm: An Empirical Analysis." *Administrative Science Quarterly*, Mar. 1990, *35*(1), 153–176.

Rosenberg, N. "The Commercial Exploitation of Science by

American Industry." In K. B. Clark, R. H. Hayas, and C. Lorenz (eds.), *The Uneasy Alliance: Managing the Productivity and Technology Dilemma*. Boston: Harvard Business School Press, 1985.

Schumpeter, J. *The Theory of Economic Development*. Cambridge, Mass.: Harvard University Press, 1934. (Originally published 1911.)

Schumpeter, J. *Capitalism, Socialism, and Democracy*. New York: HarperCollins, 1950.

Thackray, A. "University-Industry Connections and Chemical Research: An Historical Perspective." In National Science Board, *University-Industry Research Relationship*. Washington, D.C.: National Science Board, 1982.

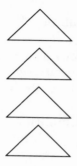

CHAPTER 14

User-Oriented Marketing for Nonprofit Organizations

Jagdish N. Sheth

This chapter proposes a user-oriented marketing approach for private nonprofit organizations as they compete and cooperate with private for-profit organizations in an increasingly market-economy-oriented society. The first section of the chapter defines the nonprofit sector; the second section suggests why it is becoming less ideology-driven and more market-driven. The third section discusses the basic dilemma that nonprofit organizations are likely to face in trying to increase their market orientation and, at the same time, preserve the public interest. The success or failure of a private nonprofit organization in the future will depend on how it manages this dilemma. I suggest that the best way to do this is to adopt a user-oriented marketing

Note: I am grateful to Atul Parvatiyar for his comments and suggestions on an earlier draft of this chapter. My thanks also to the editors and conference discussants Arthur Blum and Mohan Reddy for their constructive comments.

philosophy and practice. The fourth section of the chapter proposes a ten-point user-oriented approach, the first five points designed to improve the market orientation of nonprofit organizations and the next five to preserve and enhance the public interest.

Definition of the Nonprofit Organization

Textbooks and scholarly papers have provided numerous definitions of a nonprofit organization (Oleck, 1972; Wyszomirski, 1990; Kotler, 1982; Rados, 1981; Rao and Tagat, 1989). From an analysis of these sources, it is obvious that governmental policy, rules, and regulations play a major role in defining a nonprofit organization. For example, areas of the economy where the public interest is presumed to be paramount are defined as exclusively public, in which the private sector is not allowed to participate. Similarly, certain tax exemptions are granted only to organizations that the government defines as nonprofit (Oleck, 1988; Webster, 1992). Where private nonprofit organizations are permitted to engage in activities ordinarily assigned to the public sector, there is a strong symmetrical interdependent relationship and sharing of responsibilities between nonprofit and state agencies (Saidel, 1991; Rainey, 1991). On the other hand, in economic activities where the self-interest of suppliers is likely to enhance market efficiency, for-profit organizations are allowed to own and operate businesses. Furthermore, if there are no barriers to entry and there is potential for full competition, governments generally impose very few market rules and regulations, especially avoiding the area of setting prices.

Figure 14.1 provides a matrix of different types of nonprofit and for-profit organizations. While this chapter focuses primarily on private nonprofit organizations, the underlying dilemma of preserving the public interest while embracing market-efficient practices extends to all entities in boxes A, B, and C in Figure 14.1. Box A includes private nonprofit organizations that pursue a public mission but are independent of governmental support and administrative control. Public organizations (those in boxes B and C), managed and supported by the government, are considered nonprofit organizations because, in addition to their having a public mission, none of the surplus that they may generate is passed on to individuals (Clarkson, 1973; Hunter, 1980; Kotler, 1982). Bryce (1987) describes nonprofits as all organizations that have a mission to improve public or community welfare.

Forces Shaping the Market Orientation of Nonprofit Organizations

The current trend in nonprofit organizations, or the "third sector" (Drucker, 1988), is to become more market-economy-

Figure 14.1. Organizational Matrix.

	Private	Public
Nonprofit	**A** Private museums Charities Universities Schools Hospitals Associations	**B** Government agencies Public schools Public hospitals Railroads
For-profit	**D** Private corporations Partnerships Owner-managed businesses	**C** State-owned airlines Telephone companies Utilities Postal services

Figure 14.2. External Forces Encouraging a Market Orientation.

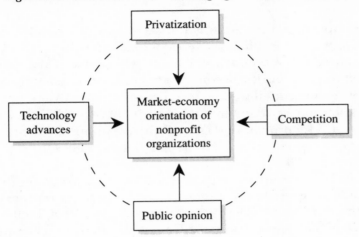

oriented by adopting a businesslike approach and bottom-line orientation (Giunipero, Crittendon, and Crittendon, 1990). Several academic and industry observers have also recommended that nonprofit organizations adopt a marketing approach to successfully meet the challenges of maintaining and increasing their base of clients, members, funds, and other resources (Kotler, 1982; Rados, 1981; Shapiro, 1973; Conlan, 1988).

Four major external forces have encouraged the "third sector" to become increasingly more market-economy-oriented: privatization, competition, public opinion, and technological advances. These forces are depicted in Figure 14.2. These external forces are interdependent and therefore correlated. It is not, however, possible to hypothesize or model the directional causality of these four forces. In other words, I will not focus on which force triggers the change or creates the domino effect and how it affects other forces to shape the market-economy orientation of nonprofit organizations. Instead, I will try to assess why these forces are leading nonprofit organizations to become more market-economy-oriented and what changes they must make in their philosophy and practice to be successful.

Privatization

The force of privatization is indicated by three trends in the nonprofit sector. First, many public organizations are being privatized all over the world, including the developed as well as developing countries. Second, there has been an emergence of joint ventures linking a for-profit organization with a nonprofit organization for their mutual benefit (Barnes, 1991a, 1991b; Carty, 1991; Ensman, 1991). Third, private nonprofit businesses are growing in numbers and strength (Oleck, 1988; Olson, 1989; Zaltman, 1979).

       The antecedents of these trends are easily traceable to the inability of governments to generate funds to support programs of the third sector. Most governments of the world, including those of the United States, the United Kingdom, and Germany, are finding themselves in financial difficulties. Recently, for example, the city of Los Angeles announced that Los Angeles International Airport will be privatized in a manner similar to what the United Kingdom did with Heathrow Airport, and the government of Australia announced that its national airline, Quantas, will be sold to private investors.

       Governments these days are unable to generate revenues by direct tax increases because of citizen revolt or by indirect taxes (sales tax, property tax, and so on) because of slow economic growth. At the same time, costs have continued to rise, at least at the rate of inflation, resulting in wider gaps. Mortgaging the future through bonds does not seem feasible as the investment community's confidence about the government's ability to repay the principal or even the accrued interest is shaken. While exports may help out in the short run, they are highly unpredictable given currency exchange fluctuations and the vagaries of international trade. Often, the only way for a government to raise capital is to sell its assets to private investors. It is less important to debate whether privatization is good or bad for nonprofit organizations than to recognize that it is here to stay (Moe, 1987; Wolch, 1990; Mosher, 1980; Kettl, 1987; Seidman and Gilmour, 1986; Weidenbaum, 1969). With privatization comes the necessity to reorganize the public sector, eliminate cross-subsidies, and improve productivity. As governments privatize the public sector, it is likely to set new benchmarks for the existing private nonprofit organizations. For example, several state universities and colleges have become innovative in their programs and processes as a consequence of significant reductions in their state-supported budgets and have become a major threat to private universities and colleges.

Competition

In some industries, government is unable or unwilling to sell public assets and at the same time is under pressure to improve productivity and cost efficiency. One approach is to liberalize the markets, abandon the concept of a natural monopoly, and encourage competition from private for-profit organizations (Barnekov and Raffel, 1990). This happened to the U.S. Postal Service with successful entries from many firms, such as UPS and Federal Express; it happened in the airline, railroad, trucking, and other infrastructure industries through deregulation. It is a major global movement and is likely to happen in such nonprofit private sectors as hospitals and schools.

The hope and the expectations are that when a private for-profit organization starts to compete with a nonprofit organization, the latter will be forced to adopt a market-economy orientation in which prices will be set by the external marketplace, rather than by inefficient internal cost structures. Hence, improvements in productivity, modernization, reorganization, and streamlining will occur.

Federal cutbacks have also forced private nonprofit organizations to compete for funding by acquiring a share of the private contributor's dollar (Cotton, 1991). This competition has led to a dramatic increase in mailbox clutter and has seriously affected the resource attraction and allocation efforts of nonprofit organizations (Smith, 1990). They realize that charitable donations are relatively elastic and that there is positive elasticity of demand to fundraising efforts (Posnett and Sandler, 1989). Therefore, in order to differentiate themselves from their competitors, private nonprofit organizations are embracing a marketing approach so that they can harness the power of intimate relationships with current and prospective donors and clients.

Public Opinion

Interestingly, negative public opinion and public image have become a significant impetus for at least some private nonprofit organizations to become more market-economy-oriented. This is evident in health care, education, and religious and charitable institutions. Public opinion, especially as expressed through broadcast media or debated in Congress (Zimmerman, 1991), seems to be a powerful motivator for nonprofit organizations to concede that operations and expertise-driven policies and procedures need to be supplemented by an orientation toward users, donors, watchdogs, and social critics. The recent forced resignation of the head of the national United Way is a good example of this. In search of answers to criticism and improved facility utilization, managers and policy makers are interested in learning from private for-profit organizations how to become more market-economy-oriented.

Technological Advances

Perhaps a less understood force in shaping the future expectations of nonprofit organizations is advances in information technologies, such as computers, telecommunications, and task automation. Nonprofit organizations have generally been reluctant to deploy information technology for a variety of reasons, including limited operating budgets, labor unions' resistance, and reliance on a volunteer work force. Indeed, if there is one area where for-profit and nonprofit organizations tend to differ significantly, it is in the deployment of office, factory, and work automation. But information technologies do offer significant advantages (Birnbaum, 1990; Cohen and Perreault, 1991; Lant, 1991; Keefe, 1991; Craver, 1991). Probably the most important is quality assurance. For example, both Federal Express and UPS gained significant competitive advantage over the U.S. Postal

Service by deploying information technologies and promising more reliable delivery of overnight packages. Second, information technology enables the nonprofit organization to move from one-time transaction-oriented marketing to relationship-oriented marketing. Obviously, the possibility of generating lifetime revenues from the same stakeholders allows greater cost efficiency and productivity in selling and service. Third, information technologies break down time and place barriers between the providers and the users of products and services. Indeed, they make it possible for a nonprofit organization to increase its market scope from local to national to global (Nelson, 1991). For example, the use of the 800 number service, voice mail, and fax mail has amply demonstrated that the global village is a reality for most charities. The most significant impact of information technology advances is visible in the broadcast of religious services through cable television. Finally, information technologies increase productivity and cost efficiency by reducing cycle time, consolidating overlapping functions, and enabling frontline workers to do their jobs faster, better, and more reliably.

The Marketing Dilemma of Nonprofit Organizations

As nonprofit organizations become market-economy-oriented, they are likely to experience the classic dilemma of fulfilling their public interest mandate while enhancing their market orientation (Holmes and Grieco, 1991; Wood, 1991; Gallagher and Weinberg, 1991). Each dimension offers certain benefits but also requires some fundamental trade-offs.

A market orientation improves productivity and cost efficiency by eliminating or at least minimizing some social and other nonbusiness missions of the nonprofit organization, such as providing employment, subsidizing costs for those who cannot afford to pay full price, and contracting with minority suppliers. It creates a positive public image that minimizes the problems of customers who have little choice among suppliers. It also generates innovation and change, since markets offer more dynamism than reliance on supplier expertise. Finally, market orientation tends to create greater user satisfaction and, indeed, stakeholder satisfaction in general (Friedman, 1962).

On the other hand, a market orientation has a number of aspects that often conflict with the public interest. For example, it tends to ignore disadvantaged users who cannot afford to buy market-priced products and services. Similarly, given the diversity of users, the greater the market orientation, the greater the segmentation of the market, resulting in open discrimination and inequity in provision of services (Levin, 1968). Third, a market orientation has the tendency to offer what the users want, as opposed to what they need. Indeed, in many nonprofit sectors of the economy (for example, health care, higher education), enhancing the provision of services by providing for users' wants as well as their needs may be desirable, but substituting one for the other is often socially unacceptable. Finally, a market orientation tends to place a strong emphasis on the opinions of users and donors. Unfortunately, we are all familiar with numerous situations in which users or donors do not really know what they need or want.

Unfortunately, most public policy research and debate has tended to be value-laden: scholars and professionals either take the side of market efficiency and, therefore, strongly believe in Adam Smith's theory of value creation through self-interest (Shapiro, 1973, used the argument of consumer self-interest as the driving force for nonprofit organizations as they become more market-oriented) or advocate the preservation of the public interest through other processes than the market economy, largely because of their belief that self-interest and the public interest are in conflict with each other. In my judgment, this conflict between market efficiency through self-interest and pursuit of the public interest through nonprofit organizations needs to be resolved and managed rather than debated and discussed. In the following section, I propose a user-oriented approach that seems capable of resolving the marketing dilemma.

User-Oriented Marketing for Nonprofit Organizations

It would appear that the common denominator in both market efficiency and public interest is end users. This is obvious for the public interest dimension, except, perhaps, regarding the issue of offering what the public wants as opposed to what it needs. It is not so obvious, however, how the end-user focus can generate market efficiency. There are at least four ways in which an end-user orientation leads to market efficiency. First, it reduces the cost of doing business. For example, one dissatisfied user is often five times as costly as five satisfied users. Indeed, in many areas where nonprofit organizations operate, the users have no choice. A dissatisfied user with no choice often becomes a terrorist! (Hirschman, 1970, articulates this as the "voice option" of the customer, as opposed to the "exit option"—a favorite concept of economists convinced of the power of the invisible hand.) Second, an end-user orientation can increase revenues: satisfied users not only use more of a product or service but also use other products and services of the organization. This has been found to be true in private nonprofit higher education and health care services, for example. When a user continues to patronize an organization over his or her lifetime and uses more than one service or product of that organization, significant market efficiency is realized through economies of scale and scope. Third, satisfied users tend to mean satisfied employees, especially in the nonprofit sector, where a significant percentage of employees are volunteers or are driven by nonmonetary rewards. Of course, satisfied employees lead to cost efficiency through reduction in employee turnover and increases in productivity. Finally, and probably most importantly, satisfied users are the best antidote to competition, especially from the private for-profit sector. Most users would prefer to do business with nonprofit organizations because of their distrust of for-profit suppliers, especially in critical services. Indeed, it is only when the nonprofit organization begins to become less user-oriented and more procedurally oriented that users look for alternatives. In short, user orientation generates a win-win situation for balancing public interest and market efficiency.

The ten-point approach described here is an integration and modified application of extensive research in total quality management, customer service excellence, and customer satisfaction (Davidow and Uttal, 1989; Lele and Sheth, 1987). Most of

Figure 14.3. Ten-Point Approach for User-Oriented Marketing.

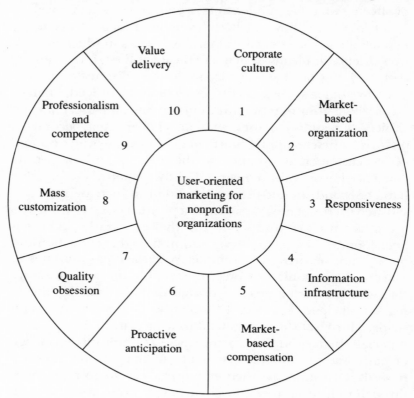

this research has concerned private for-profit service providers, and care needs to be taken with its application to private nonprofit organizations, such as hospitals and educational institutions. Figure 14.3 is an effort to selectively and carefully apply this knowledge, especially to balance the dilemma between public interest and market efficiency. It is, of course, possible that there are some trade-offs that cannot be fully addressed by the ten-point approach.

The first five elements of the approach are designed to enhance the market orientation of private nonprofit organizations and therefore draw on the experiences of the private for-profit sector. The second five elements are designed to preserve and enhance the public interest mission of the nonprofit organization. Below I describe each element and provide some examples to illustrate the concept of user-oriented marketing.

Enhancing Market Orientation

The following five elements of the approach are likely to further a market orientation and, therefore, improve market efficiency in nonprofit organizations. Most of the differences that users perceive between nonprofit and for-profit organizations seem to be related to these five process dimensions.

Corporate Culture. Does the culture of the nonprofit organization put the user's viewpoint first? The more expertise-driven the organization, the less likely it will have a corporate culture that puts the user first. The legendary examples in this area are found mostly among for-profit organizations, such as Nordstrom's and Federal Express, with a few among nonprofit organizations that have changed from a production-driven to a market-driven philosophy as a consequence of competition from private for-profit suppliers.

Market-Based Organization. Nonprofit organizations tend to organize their departmental structure around geographical service areas and functional specializations of work, such as lab services, counseling, fund development, or human resources administration, because it is easy to implement the public interest objective. This functional-territorial organization design also helps to ensure that all users are treated equally. Unfortunately, the greater the diversity of users, the less likely the organization is to satisfy any one of them by some common, standardized way of dealing with them. It becomes increasingly necessary to reorganize the nonprofit entity around its markets, as defined by user groups and the specific products or services that they want to obtain. For example, higher education can switch its organizational focus from the functional (academic) disciplines to its bachelor's, master's, and doctoral programs, and hospitals can switch their focus from general practice and functional specializations to treatment of particular illnesses such as cancer, heart, lung and other diseases.

Responsiveness. Responsiveness concerns the time that elapses between an initial user request and delivery of a product or service and the manner in which it is delivered. It sometimes requires giving frontline people the discretion to bend standard operating procedures (Shelton, 1991; Maier, Thompson, and Thomas, 1991). For example, it should not take months for a client to schedule a routine physical examination at an HMO or for an applicant to find out whether he or she has been admitted to a university.

Information Infrastructure. The level of an organization's capital investment in information technologies (computers, telecommunications, and work automation) and how they are used by its frontline people are key aspects of the information infrastructure. Most nonprofit organizations invest less on à per capita basis than their counterparts in the for-profit sector, and most of the investment is for management systems, rather than for use by the frontline people in their thousands of interactions with users. This is particularly true in universities, hospitals, and civic and fraternal organizations. Users are most concerned that the frontline people have on-line information about who they are, what products and services the organization has in its inventory, and how quickly they can be served (Carr, 1990; Conhaim, 1991).

Market-Based Compensation. Perhaps the factor that most inhibits nonprofit organizations from developing a market orientation is that their reward system is not directly linked to user satisfaction. In at least 70 percent of nonprofit organizations, the reward system is straight salary, with no incentives for trying a little harder. This is further complicated by the fact that compensation is based on the internal hierarchy's ideas of performance excellence, rather than any measures of user satisfaction. Industry observers have suggested a number of approaches to implementing incentive plans in nonprofit organizations

(Rocco, 1991; Hildebrandt, 1991). These approaches need not be limited to the frontline people who have direct contact with users; it is possible to evaluate each job and every function on the basis of satisfaction: if you are not serving the users directly, you are serving someone who does.

Preserving the Public Interest

The remaining five elements of the approach are designed to preserve and enhance the public interest.

Proactive Anticipation. Anticipating users' needs and desires is extremely important in the nonprofit sector, for several reasons (Gwin, 1990). First, users neither know nor can anticipate their own needs and wants in many markets where the public interest is of paramount importance—for example, health care, library services, education, religion, arts, and broadcasting. Second, users are totally dependent on suppliers in many areas of economic activity, because regulation precludes choices. Third, resource commitments are substantial in markets where the public interest is critical. Therefore, the efficient and universal deployment of resources requires that suppliers anticipate not only present needs but future needs and wants. This is best illustrated in art galleries, museums, hospitals, and educational programs. Unfortunately, this requires unique expertise and must involve more than simply asking users their opinions. Indeed, opinion surveys are often not as useful as observation of behavior, because users may not be able to articulate what they need or want. And interpreting the findings from observation requires investigative intelligence—it is similar to putting together a jigsaw puzzle.

Quality Obsession. It is obvious that economic activities that serve the public interest are probably critical to the individual, the community, and the society at large and hence should not be entrusted to the profit (self-interest) motive of the private sector. Quality assurance is particularly important in such activities— in fact, it should be elevated to the level of an obsession. "Zero defects" and "doing it right the first time" are not just theoretical norms but real necessities in such critical services as health care (Koska, 1991) and education (Wiggins, 1991). Furthermore, this is one area where benchmarking quality assurance to user expectations is not sufficient; it must be benchmarked to perfection.

Mass Customization. Mass customization means tailoring mass-produced products or services to the individual needs and wants of users (Davis, 1987). It requires balancing efficiencies of scale with the effectiveness of personalized delivery. Examples of mass customization are printing of personal checkbooks, self-service breakfast bars, the publishing of custom textbooks, cabbage patch dolls, computer application of software possessing customization capabilities, and cash registers with custom features as in cafeterias and fast-food restaurants. In all these instances, the basic production process is the same, but the assembly of the product is customized for each order. Mass customization is even more important for nonprofit organizations because, while there may be great demographic diversity among their users, especially in such heterogeneous nations as the United States and India, they must serve all users; for example, patients who come to an emergency room or researchers using library services and data bases.

Professionalism and Competence. The professionalism and competence of workers are very important where critical services are involved. Since users may lack the education or technical competence to take care of their own needs and wants, their trust in the nonprofit sector is vital. A single negative incident can easily destroy that trust, resulting in criticism, cynicism, or even outright revolt. In recent years, unfortunately, trust and confidence in the nonprofit sector have been shaken in such vital areas as health care and education. The only way to maintain user confidence in an institution is to ensure that providers are professional and competent in carrying out what they are expected to do (Tobias, 1990; Pearse and Fram, 1991).

Value Delivery. The nonprofit organization's ability to use its fixed resources to deliver value to all users depends on bridging the gap between user needs and wants and its internal capabilities. It also means removing any barriers to entry for users, such as price and availability. In my assessment, nonprofit organizations tend to be good at value creation but not at value delivery. For example, higher education institutions expend considerable effort in ensuring that academic curriculum and excellence are preserved but make it difficult for students to gain access to their resources, such as the library, computing services, parking, and even professors.

Summary

The ten-point approach for developing user-oriented marketing for nonprofit organizations has several unique properties. First, the strength of the total approach is equal to that of its weakest link. Therefore, the best place to improve first is the area in which the nonprofit organization is weakest. Second, consistency across business units or product or service groups is vital. Therefore, if there is significant variation in the elements of the approach across business units or functional departments, it is critical to reduce the variance. Finally, the ten-point approach is a benchmark. It encourages the organization to establish a continuous-improvement philosophy to narrow the gap between performance and benchmark.

Conclusion

In this chapter, I have outlined four forces that are driving nonprofit organizations toward a market-economy orientation: privatization, competition, public opinion, and technological advances. As nonprofit organizations try to emulate the for-profit sector, they are likely to encounter the classic conflict between preserving the public interest and becoming more market-driven. This dilemma can be substantially resolved and the trade-offs between market efficiency and the public interest minimized if nonprofit organizations take a user's perspective.

The chapter has also proposed a ten-point user-oriented marketing approach. The first five elements of the approach—corporate culture, market-based organization, responsiveness, information infrastructure, and market-based compensation—are designed to improve an organization's market orientation. The remaining five processes—proactive anticipation, quality obsession, mass customization, professionalism and competence, and value delivery—are designed to preserve the public interest in a market-economy context. It is my hope that this user-oriented marketing approach will establish a benchmark with which a nonprofit organization can assess itself and improve itself by implementing changes in its business practice.

References

Barnekov, T. K., and Raffel, J. A. "Public Management of Privatization." *Public Productivity and Management Review*, 1990, *14*(2), 135–152.

Barnes, N. G. "Joint Venture Marketing: A Strategy for the 1990s." *Health Marketing Quarterly*, 1991a, *9*(1, 2), 23–36.

Barnes, N. G. "Philanthropy, Profits and Problems: The Emergence of Joint Venture Marketing." *Akron Business and Economic Review*, 1991b, *22*(4), 78–86.

Birnbaum, S. "Information Management: For-Profits Share Insights." *Nonprofit World*, 1990, *8*(4), 11–14.

Bryce, H. *Financial and Strategic Management in Nonprofit Organizations*. Englewood Cliffs, N.J.: Prentice-Hall, 1987.

Carr, C. *Front-Line Customer Service: 15 Keys to Customer Satisfaction*. New York: Wiley, 1990.

Carty, P. "Lots of Compassion but Less Cash." *Accountancy*, 1991, *108*(1180), 66–68.

Clarkson, K. W. "Some Implications of Property Rights in Hospital Management." *Journal of Law and Economics*, 1973, *15*, 363.

Cohen, J. A., and Perreault, R. A. "Nonprofits' Most Common Computer Pitfalls—and How to Avoid Them." *Nonprofit World*, 1991, *9*(6), 8–10.

Conhaim, W. "On the Electronic Frontier." *Foundation News*, 1991, *32*(5), 20–24.

Conlan, M. "Marketing for Non-Profit Success." *Fund Raising Management*, 1988, *19*(6), 48–52.

Cotton, M. "Yes, I Would Like a Choice Where My Contribution Goes!" *Fund Raising Management*, 1991, *22*(10), 36–37, 48.

Craver, R. M. "Management: Looking Back at Tomorrow." *Fund Raising Management*, 1991, *21*(13), 32–41.

Davidow, W. H., and Uttal, B. *Total Customer Service: The Ultimate Weapon*. New York: HarperCollins, 1989.

Davis, S. M. *Future Perfect*. Reading, Mass.: Addison-Wesley, 1987.

Drucker, P. F. "The Non-Profits' Quiet Revolution." *Wall Street Journal*, Sept. 8, 1988, p. 30.

Ensman, R. G. "Private Sector Cooperation: The Challenge of the 1990s." *Fund Raising Management*, 1991, *22*(4), 62–63.

Friedman, M. "The Role of Government in Education." in M. Friedman, *Capitalism and Freedom*. Chicago: University of Chicago Press, 1962.

Gallagher, K., and Weinberg, C. B. "Coping with Success: New Challenge for Nonprofit Marketing." *Sloan Management Review*, Fall 1991, pp. 27–42.

Giunipero, L. C., Crittendon, W., and Crittendon, V. "Industrial Marketing in Non-Profit Organizations." *Industrial Marketing Management*, 1990, *19*, 279–285.

Gwin, J. M. "Constituent Analysis: A Paradigm for Marketing Effectiveness in the Not-for-Profit Organization." *European Journal of Marketing*, 1990, *24*(7), 43–48.

Hildebrandt, D. "Planning Rewards." *Association Management*, 1991, *43*(5), 97–99, 101.

Hirschman, A. O. *Exit, Voice and Loyalty*. Cambridge, Mass.: Harvard University Press, 1970.

Holmes, L., and Grieco, M. "Overt Funding, Buried Goals, and Moral Turnover: The Organizational Transformation of Radical Experiments." *Human Relations*, 1991, *44*(7), 643–664.

Hunter, R. *Not for Profit Business: Reading, Legal Documents and Commentary*. South Bend, Ind.: Icarus, 1980.

Keefe, P. "Hi Tech Helps Speed Location of Missing Children." *Computerworld*, 1991, *25*(42), 63.

Kettl, D. F. (ed.). *Third Party Government and the Public Manager:*

The Changing Forms of Government Action. Washington, D.C.: National Academy of Public Administration, 1987.

Koska, M. T. "Refocusing the JCAHO Is New Chairwoman's Goal." *Hospitals,* 1991, *65*(8), 62.

Kotler, P. *Marketing for Nonprofit Organizations.* (2nd ed.) Englewood Cliffs, N.J.: Prentice-Hall, 1982.

Lant, J. "Your Best Marketing Tool—Your Computer." *Nonprofit World,* 1991, *9*(5), 8–10.

Lele, M., and Sheth, J. N. *The Customer Is Key.* New York: Wiley, 1987.

Levin, H. M. "The Failure of the Public Schools and the Free Market Remedy." *Urban Review,* June 1968, pp. 32–37.

Maier, M., Thompson, C., and Thomas, C. "Corporate Responsiveness (and Resistance) to Work-Family Interdependence in the United States." *Equal Opportunities International,* 1991, *10*(3, 4), 25–32.

Moe, R. C. "Exploring the Limits of Privatization." *Public Administration Review,* 1987, *47*, 454–460.

Mosher, F. C. "The Changing Responsibilities and Tactics of the Federal Government." *Public Administration Review,* 1980, *40*, 541–548.

Nelson, N. M. "Networking in the U.K.: Computing in Canada." *Information Today,* 1991, *8*(9), 10–12.

Oleck, H. L. "Nature of American Non-Profit Organizations." *New York Law Forum,* 1972, *18*, 1066–1088.

Oleck, H. L. *Nonprofit Corporations, Organizations and Associations.* Englewood Cliffs, N.J.: Prentice-Hall, 1988.

Olson, S. *The Foundation Directory.* New York: Foundation Center, 1989.

Pearse, R. F., and Fram, E. H. "Are You Giving Your Professionals the Directions They Need?" *Nonprofit World,* 1991, *9*(5), 31–35.

Posnett, J., and Sandler, T. "Demand for Charity Donations in Private Non-Profit Markets: The Case of the U.K." *Journal of Public Economics (Netherlands),* 1989, *40*(2), 187–200.

Rados, D. L. *Marketing for Nonprofit Organizations.* Boston: House Publishers, 1981.

Rainey, H. G. *Understanding and Managing Public Organizations.* San Francisco: Jossey-Bass, 1991.

Rao, K.L.K., and Tagat, R. G. "Relevance of the Marketing Concept and Strategy to Public Enterprises." In J. N. Sheth and A. Eshghi (eds.), *Global Marketing Perspectives*. Cincinnati, Ohio: Southwestern, 1989.

Rocco, J. E. "Making Incentive Plans Work for Nonprofits." *Nonprofit World*, 1991, *9*(4), 13–15.

Saidel, J. R. "Resource Interdependence: The Relationship Between State Agencies and Nonprofit Organizations." *Public Administration Review*, 1991, *51*(6), 543–553.

Seidman, H., and Gilmour, R. *Politics, Position, and Power, from the Positive to the Regulatory State*. (4th ed.) New York: Oxford University Press, 1986.

Shapiro, B. "Marketing for Nonprofit Organizations." *Harvard Business Review*, Sept.–Oct. 1973, pp. 123–132.

Shelton, K. "People Power." *Executive Excellence*, 1991, *8*(12), 7–8.

Smith, R. M. "Individual Marketing for Non-Profits." *Fund Raising Management*, 1990, *21*(5), 50–51, 68.

Tobias, L. L. "Selecting for Excellence: How to Hire the Best." *Nonprofit World*, 1990, *8*(2), 23–25.

Webster, G. D. "Defining Nonprofits." *Association Management*, 1992, *44*(L), L59–L61.

Weidenbaum, M. L. *The Modern Public Sector*. New York: Basic Books, 1969.

Wiggins, G. "Standards, Not Standardization: Evolving Quality Student Work." *Educational Leadership*, Feb. 1991, pp. 18–25.

Wolch, J. R. *The Shadow State: Government and Voluntary Sector in Transition*. New York: Foundation Center, 1990.

Wood, D. J. "Corporate Social Performance Revisited." *Academy of Management Review*, 1991, *16*(4), 691–718.

Wyszomirski, M. J. "The Puzzle of Organizational Dimensions: A Trisectorial Perspective." *International Journal of Public Administration*, 1990, *13*(1, 2), 45–81.

Zaltman, G. *Management Principles for Nonprofit Agencies and Organizations*. New York: AMACOM, 1979.

Zimmerman, D. "Nonprofit Organizations, Social Benefits, and Tax Policy." *National Tax Journal*, 1991, *44*(3), 341–349.

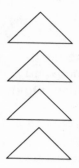

CONCLUSION

Nonprofit Organizations in a Market Economy: Common Threads And Research Issues

Dennis R. Young
David C. Hammack

What is the essential composition of the market economy? Twenty years ago, even sophisticated economists would have answered this question by pointing to two principal sectors—business and government. Business was seen as the engine of production and distribution of goods and services, and government was seen as the enforcer of laws needed for markets to function, the provider of public goods, and the protector of social justice (see, for example, Musgrave and Musgrave, 1983). A nice, neat package!

Ten years ago, the answer would have been different. Some economists, at least, would have pointed to three principal sectors—business, government, and the private, nonprofit sector—and alluded to aspects of government or market failure that required the voluntary provision of collective goods or the provision of semiprivate goods that suffered from contract failure (Hansmann, 1987). Slowly, the realization had grown among economists and others that private nonprofit organizations are a major part of the market economy and integral to its functioning. Yet the degree to which nonprofits are important and precisely how they contribute to the market economy were still to be fully appreciated. Nor was it understood how nonprofits are themselves influenced by markets or how they are affected by the declining influence of government and the increasing market orientation of the economy in the United States and other Western countries.

The chapters in this volume provide some answers and raise many questions about the role of nonprofits in a market economy. In particular, they reveal a much more intricate and subtle tapestry than has been appreciated to date. Taken together, these chapters show that a simple three-part model of the economy, in which business, government, and the nonprofit sector each have cleanly separated and delineated roles, is simply naive. Rather, these chapters consistently describe an economy in which the sectors are highly interwoven and interdependent—all part of a single piece, rather than separate worlds existing side by side. The situation is reminiscent of discussions about intergovernmental relations in the United States some thirty years ago, when public finance scholars replaced the "layer-cake" model of relationships among federal, state, and local governments with the "marble-cake" model. In the market economy, as in intergovernmental relations, where hierarchies give way to horse trading and boundaries are poorly delineated, the principal actors tend to "mix it up."

Given that this more sophisticated view of the market economy is just emerging, it is not surprising that many of the research questions suggested by the chapters in this volume involve articulating and clarifying the new picture. This exercise in reconceptualizing the market economy and the role of nonprofits within it yields five overriding research themes concerning the many market relationships that engage nonprofit organizations. Each of the themes is related to a common notion, set forth in the Introduction, that the "marble cake" of the market economy can be usefully understood as a complex ecology of

organizations (see Hannan and Freeman, 1989, for a full theoretical development of the concept of organizational ecology).

The five research themes we identify are the following:

1. Nonprofits are part of a complex ecology of for-profit, nonprofit, and governmental organizations, and we need to
   understand why different mixes of these organizations are
   found or preferred in different circumstances.
2. Nonprofits play a variety of functional roles, and we must
   understand their particular niches within this ecology.
3. Managing nonprofit organizations within the ecology of
   the market economy presents special challenges that must
   be better appreciated and addressed.
4. Recognizing the participation of nonprofits in the ecology
   of the market system presents special opportunities to advance microeconomic theory.
5. The possibilities for systematic learning by experimenting
   with new arrangements within the ecology of organizations
   in the market economy suggest that institutional reforms
   for improving public services can productively be designed
   as experiments.

In this summary chapter, we elaborate on these five themes as
the basis of an important agenda for the next decade of research
on nonprofit organizations.

Nonprofits in an Ecology of Organizations

Several of the authors in this volume describe the market economy as a complex, interactive, and interdependent mix of for-
profit, nonprofit, and government institutions. Thus, one set of
research questions has to do with why we observe a particular
overall mix of institutions in the U.S. economy as a whole and
why we observe alternative mixes in different parts of that
economy. Moreover, we may ask why we observe a particular mix
in the United States at present, why this mix is different from
that in other countries, and how the mix is likely to change in the
United States and other parts of the world.

In the Introduction, we suggested that the particular constitutional tradition of the United States helped to define the institutional mix by limiting the role of government, prohibiting the formal establishment of any particular religion, and emphasizing freedom of expression. The Constitution thus created significant niches for nonprofit organizations in religion and advocacy and in the provision of a variety of services traditionally related to the religious context, such as health care, social services, and education. However, other factors, such as the advance of technology and the secularization of U.S. society in this century, have operated within this constitutional context to shift services such as health care into the secular realm, thus altering the institutional mix over time. This experience in the United States suggests that forces and variables at the societal level—political and cultural traditions and technological change—may go far to explain a nation's overall mix of for-profit, nonprofit, and government institutions. It further suggests that an agenda of international comparative research among countries with market-based economies that have different cultural and political traditions could substantially advance our understanding of the varying compositions of market economies, the varying emphases that these economies place on nonprofit organizations, and how cultural and political factors influence the institutional mix.

A number of contributors to this volume have tried to understand the mix of for-profit, governmental, and nonprofit organizations in particular industrial or service sectors in the United States. Elinor Ostrom and Gina Davis (Chapter One) investigate this question in the case of elementary and secondary education, while Richard R. Nelson (Chapter Thirteen) considers it for the field of industrial innovation. At this level of analysis, the focus is on the particular characteristics of the services provided and how these characteristics mesh with the strengths and weaknesses of different institutional forms. Ostrom and Davis identify a number of important attributes of educational services, such as informational asymmetries, economies of scale and scope, asset specificity, and team production, that influence how well different types of organizations perform the various steps (for example, finance, delivery) in the provision of this set of services. Similarly, Nelson highlights the tight relationship between innovation and the production and marketing of advanced technological products in explaining why research and development is organized in particular ways and involves a certain mix of institutional forms.

These contributions highlight an important dimension to a future research agenda that would expand understanding of the mix of institutional forms in the ecology of a market economy. In particular, one must ask, for each different service or good, what its intrinsic attributes are and how these attributes match the comparative strengths and weaknesses of different institutional forms at various stages in the process of service provision.

The mix of institutional forms cuts even more finely within industries, including those industries characterized by a single sectoral form. For example, in his analysis of foundation investment behavior, Lester M. Salamon (Chapter Eight) discovers "two worlds" of foundations—one consisting generally of large foundations that are fairly sophisticated in their approach to investing and the other generally composed of small, less sophisticated foundations. David Knoke (Chapter Five) finds other kinds of differentiations within the world of trade associations, such as between narrowly based, smaller associations whose members are homogeneous groups of firms in a highly specialized industrial subsector and broadly based "peak" associations that span large industrial segments of the economy. In ecological terms, it is interesting to ask what niches these different groups of nonprofits occupy within their respective industries and what the relationships are between them. In the trade association case, for example, there is a tension between maintaining the leverage and power of the larger, broadly based associations and the pressure of subgroups to split off into more specialized associations that can better represent or serve their particular interests. So, too, in the case of foundations, there may be a two-way pull on the smaller foundations—to join in a common pool of funds for investment purposes or, indeed, to combine with other foundations in other ways, versus the losses of discretion and independence that joining a common effort might involve.

The sorting and survival of different subspecies within industrial subsectors of the nonprofit world and the forces influencing consolidation versus further differentiation of these subspecies are subjects worthy of considerable further investigation. In addition to the internal forces identified by Knoke, Salamon, and others in this volume, the analysis by Catherine C. Eckel and Richard Steinberg (Chapter Two) reveals how the rules of the game — in this case, the rules for competition and cooperation in the marketplace — also influence this differentiation within nonprofit subsectors. This suggests a particularly interesting subtheme for future research: how do the rules constructed to govern the behavior of for-profit firms apply to the behavior of nonprofits? Eckel and Steinberg make a strong case that such rules can have unintended and unfortunate consequences if they are crudely and thoughtlessly applied to nonprofits.

As are natural, biological ecologies, the institutional ecologies found in market economies are quite intricate and complex. Different institutional mixes are found in different countries, within different industries in a given country, and even within the nonprofit segments of particular industries. The reasons for these patterns of differentiation are as yet poorly understood. Given the insights to date, we can appreciate that global factors such as culture and political tradition, intrinsic factors such as the characteristics of particular services, public policies designed to govern market processes, and internal organizational dynamics all seem to play a role. The interaction of these factors results in the overall ecological system within which nonprofits operate. Future research will help illuminate these systems. And, as discussed below, such research can also address the particular functions and contributions of nonprofits within these systems.

Nonprofit Niches in the Ecology of the Market Economy

If market economies resemble ecologies in which various institutional forms occupy different functional niches, then what are the particular functional niches for nonprofit organizations? Taken as a whole, one of the most fascinating contributions made by the authors of this volume is the identification of many different nonprofit niches. Thus, in various circumstances, nonprofit organizations are seen to provide or produce services, advocate for causes, build consensus for change, promote innovation, broker new ideas, and contribute to the basic functioning of the constitutional and economic framework of a democracy and market economy. Ostrom and Davis especially contribute to our understanding of nonprofit niches through their admirably precise distinction between the provision of a service — that is, ensuring the supply of a service through appropriate financing and governing arrangements — and the actual production of the service. Using education to illustrate a principle applicable to many fields of service, they argue that while nonprofits can be involved in service provision, their most important role may be as producers of services in a system where government ensures the provision. In any event, Ostrom and Davis persuasively distinguish between provision and production and suggest that nonprofits may find their niches in either activity.

In Chapter Twelve, P. Michael Timpane, also focusing on education, emphasizes the role of nonprofits not as producers of this service but as advocates and intermediaries in the debate over educational policy. Timpane's interest is in the role of business in bringing about reform of the educational system in the United States. He observes how businesses have sought to work through nonprofit organizations to shape educational policy and make schools more effective. Working through nonprofits, business firms seek to advance their own interests in education, work with other businesses, and collaborate with schools and others to identify common concerns and support the provision of supplementary services to the schools.

Reform of education is, of course, a high-stakes mission with no less than fundamental changes in the functioning of democratic society and market institutions as its basic goal. That businesses may be involved largely for their own self-interested reasons does little to diminish the fact that nonprofits can facilitate social change in a market economy by assisting for-profit business in such endeavors. Timpane's analysis points to the fact that education is a key lubricant to the functioning of business. Without an educated labor force, well versed in basic reading, writing, and math skills, business will founder and lose its competitive edge. If nonprofits assist business in improving education, then this is yet another important role for nonprofits in the ecology of the market economy.

Nonprofits play still other roles in education and knowl-edge development. Nelson emphasizes the importance of uni-versities, industry associations, and professional societies in providing basic scientific knowledge and in advancing new discoveries that ultimately fuel technological advance and eco-nomic growth. Anne E. Preston's results, discussed in Chapter Six, hint that nonprofit institutions sometimes serve as trainers of young scientists and engineers who gain valuable experience at lower pay in nonprofit institutions before going on to higher-paid work in the corporate sector. More generally, as we point out in the Introduction, the wide variety of scientific, cultural, economic, religious, and other nonprofit institutions in the U.S. political context underwrites a "marketplace of ideas" from which new concepts emerge that contribute to innovation and vitality in the market economy.

Finally, and perhaps most profoundly, Louis Galambos (Chapter Three) argues that nonprofit organizations play a fundamental role in the evolution of the modern industrial state by serving as the vehicles through which key societal values are promoted and protected. Those values—he identifies equity, security, efficiency, and innovation—at one time or another each represented the gut issues that had to be faced if the modern industrial state was to progress to its next stage of development. Galambos does not argue that nonprofits are the sole guardians of these values at any given time. Rather, he makes a dynamic argument that the ability of the market econ-omy to address its pressing problems and to reform itself de-pends on nonprofits as institutional facilitators. Nonprofits were the defenders and promoters of particular values, such as equity or efficiency, when those values were critical to reform at a given stage of development. Without nonprofits, the economy might stagnate or disintegrate for its inability to self-correct.

All told, the authors here identify a rich set of possible niches that nonprofit organizations can occupy in various parts of the ecology of the market system at different stages in its evolution. While the above discussion is focused largely on education and industrial development, nonprofits play equally diverse and critical roles in many other areas, including health care, social services, and arts and culture. A full articulation of the variety of possibilities and an understanding of the circumstances under which nonprofits assume their different possible roles within different fields are the stuff of a much fuller set of research inquiries for the future.

Challenges to Nonprofit Management

Whatever their particular niches in the market economy, nonprofit organizations are fundamentally different from the prototypical inhabitants of the market environment — for-profit businesses. Markets and businesses are driven by competition and financial reward. Nonprofit organizations are mission-driven, collaborative, and propelled by a variety of public and private motivations other than money. Inevitably, tensions exist between the values underlying nonprofit organizations and the values of the marketplace. These tensions create special challenges for nonprofit managers' guidance of their organizations within the context of the market-system ecology. The chapters in this volume identify significant challenges regarding the delivery of services, the acquisition of resources, accounting, and strategic planning.

Service Delivery

Several contributors to this volume analyze the tensions between nonprofits' emphasis on mission and their need to be responsive to market forces in the delivery of services. These tensions emerge strongly in David B. Starkweather's analysis in Chapter Four of hospitals, where competition from the for-profit sector and the increased flow of funds through Medicare, Medicaid, and private insurance have led nonprofit hospitals to emulate for-profit behavior through creation of for-profit subsidiaries, reduction of charitable patient care, use of advertising and other marketing techniques, and, in general, the evaluation of performance in terms of the bottom line. In this industry, the tendency of nonprofits to emulate for-profit behavior has gone so far as to call into question the very tax-exempt status of nonprofit hospitals. Indeed, it seems no exaggeration to say that nonprofit hospitals — at least in the form that they have held since the 1920s — may be an endangered species in the ecological subsystem of the health care industry.

The tension between mission and market is by no means restricted to the hospital industry. In Chapter Fourteen, Jagdish N. Sheth demonstrates that this tension may be found in a spectrum of nonprofit fields. He suggests how a user-oriented marketing approach might be employed to reduce this tension. Eckel and Steinberg suggest how the tension between mission and market may manifest itself in nonprofits that produce both public and private goods. They show that, in managing this tension, nonprofits must find a balance between open and collusive practices and between restricting output and reducing private consumer benefits, on the one hand, and using monopoly profits to finance public benefits, on the other hand. In short, nonprofit leaders in a variety of settings face difficult pressures, trade-offs, and judgments in reconciling market pressures with fulfillment of public missions. The full panoply of these dilemmas and how they are best resolved will require considerable future inquiry.

Input Resources

A second source of tensions for nonprofits operating in the market economy is the special difficulties that these organizations face in acquiring resources — labor, capital, and operating funds. Preston, for example, demonstrates that low wages are an important cause of the early exit of talented and experienced professionals from the nonprofit sector. Lacking the monetary resources of business firms and facing intense pressures from donors or the general public to keep personnel compensation under control, nonprofits must often depend on other rewards to maintain their competitiveness within the ecologies of key labor markets. In some areas and eras, as in science and engineering in the past ten years, nonpecuniary rewards have proved insufficient to attract and retain first-class talent.

Similar observations apply to the capital markets through which nonprofits secure the long-term financial and durable resources that they need to operate effectively. As Howard P. Tuckman points out in Chapter Seven, nonprofits not only are effectively proscribed from participating in equity markets, but they suffer substantial disadvantages in many debt markets as well, particularly in borrowing from banks. Here, too, nonprofit managers face market-based pressures and dilemmas. For example, one effective way to finance capital needs is to generate and retain financial surpluses (profits). But to what extent can this be done without sacrificing attention to mission?

In the management of financial portfolios and endowments, nonprofits face other pressures and dilemmas. In the case of foundations, for example, Salamon finds that many smaller foundations are setting payout rates equal to or exceeding investment returns, effectively spending their way out of existence as inflation eats into the real value of their portfolios. He also finds some foundations to be pursuing excessively conservative risk-averse and short-term investment policies rather than embracing a long-term strategy to ensure their survival. Does this behavior represent myopia and ineptness on the part of small foundations, or are they desperately coping with the pressures of maintaining mission in the face of market forces? We know precious little about the forces pulling on foundation managers, let alone managers of other kinds of nonprofits with significant endowments, as they balance mission with market pressures.

Finally, as demonstrated by Robert F. Carbone (Chapter Ten), the field of fundraising for charitable donations is rife with tensions between mission and market. Carbone chronicles the various ethical issues that arise when nonprofits pursue a

variety of market-based strategies, such as cause-related marketing, affinity credit cards, and various telemarketing techniques,
to increase donations. A key consideration is the loss of reputation and public confidence that may result if the nonprofit
becomes associated with disreputable businesses or questionable practices, such as excessive fees paid to fundraising firms or
large commissions paid to individual fundraisers. Managing
financial affairs with maximum sophistication and effectiveness
while maintaining the public confidence that is so absolutely
essential for survival of nonprofits in the ecology of the market
system presents a constant challenge to nonprofit leaders.

Overall, mobilizing resources presents a major challenge
to nonprofit managers. More often than not, nonprofits must
compete for these resources in markets with for-profit as well as
nonprofit competitors and in contexts where they can benefit
from but must also be wary of for-profit collaborators. A complete research agenda for the future must include a fleshing out
of the challenges involved in obtaining resource inputs, including the competing pressures and ethical dilemmas associated
with gathering those resources in competitive markets.

Accounting Issues

The application of accounting practices developed in the for-
profit sector to nonprofit operations represents another challenge to nonprofit organizations operating in a market context,
as several of the chapters here show. Starkweather and Tuckman
both demonstrate that nonprofits must often generate profits if
they are to finance their capital needs. Yet, as Starkweather
notes, the accounting definition of profit is, at present, highly
contested. Standard accounting practice in the nonprofit field
values depreciated assets at historical values, leaving organizations open to challenge when they seek to accumulate sufficient
surpluses to replace those assets at current, let alone future,
market prices. Another accounting issue is the choice of fund
accounting versus conventional for-profit accounting. Tuckman
observes that "research has not been available as to whether the

accounting system that a nonprofit uses affects the amount of resources that it has available for capital investment."

A third issue arises when a nonprofit manager must decide how to allocate joint costs among "related" and "unrelated" activities of a nonprofit organization for the purpose of calculating income tax. Still another accounting issue pertains to the treatment of pledges and other types of charitable contributions. The fact that nonprofits are accountable to donors and government agencies and that they sometimes seek to borrow capital means that they must submit their operations to the scrutiny of accountants. An important part of a future research agenda should be documenting and analyzing how the accounting system affects nonprofit organizations' behavior and how it can be more effectively adapted to the nonprofit context.

Adaptive Strategies

The stresses and strains associated with the operation of nonprofit organizations in market environments require that these organizations develop adaptive strategies that permit them to survive and compete in this ecological system while maintaining their mission focus. One overall strategy is to adopt and adapt the management practices of for-profit businesses. Thus, Salamon describes how larger foundations have begun to use modern portfolio methods to maximize the total return on foundation investments, while Sheth outlines a set of marketing principles through which nonprofits may become more responsive to their customers. Tuckman points out how nonprofits generate operating surpluses (profit) to fund capital needs, while Carbone describes a variety of marketing techniques and incentive schemes applied to fundraising. However, the wholesale adoption of business methods by nonprofit organizations can be highly problematic. As David Billis (Chapter Eleven) reasons, while businesses may have much to teach nonprofits in the use of administrative systems and the management of staff, they are limited in what they can tell nonprofits about managing their overall sets of relationships. Indeed, the association roots of nonprofits leave them much more adept at managing complex multistakeholder environments than are businesses.

Clearly, the authors here have again barely scratched the surface of a significant area for future research. What managerial methods and strategies used by for-profit business are transferable to nonprofit organizations, and which management principles and techniques from the nonprofit world can be usefully adopted by the business sector? These questions are being asked by researchers and practitioners with increasing seriousness and deserve more careful and comprehensive attention than they have been given to date.

In addition to adopting business management techniques for individual organizations, nonprofits are increasingly adapting to their market environments through structural devices that are also borrowed from business. Thus, Knoke highlights the application of the business franchise system to national nonprofit associations. Starkweather describes how hospitals have created complex, interlocking networks of nonprofit and for-profit corporate units. And Eckel and Steinberg show how mergers and consolidations of nonprofit organizations may create benevolent monopolies that can exploit their power in private goods markets in order to finance the provision of public goods.

Even at the basic level of individual organizations, our current state of knowledge of nonprofit organizational structure is rudimentary. As Billis notes, the nonprofit corporation may be viewed as a hybrid between a pure, horizontally structured, egalitarian membership association and a classical, hierarchical business corporation. Along this spectrum alone — between association and corporation — the variety of nonprofit structures is substantial. Add to this the myriad of possibilities for combining nonprofits with one another and intermingling them with for-profit units, and we glimpse an enormous research task of classifying and describing the various combinations and developing an understanding of how different structural designs allow nonprofit organizations to adapt to and modify the ecologies of the market environments in which they operate.

One may argue, of course, that large-scale structural solutions — for example, mergers that create monopolies, ownership of for-profit subsidiaries, or franchising systems — apply to only a small part of the nonprofit world: large institutions such as hospitals, universities, and national social service organizations. Most nonprofit organizations are very small and easily buffeted in a turbulent market environment over which they have no control and for which large-scale structural options are not apparent. But even in this part of the nonprofit world, structural issues are important. Small agencies are constantly under pressure, by funding agencies, for example, to merge with one another to enhance efficiency and improve stability. Indeed, it is the rare nonprofit that is a completely solo operation. Most nonprofits belong, formally or informally, to networks — umbrella federations, united funding agencies, professional or trade associations, and the like. These networks are also manifestations of nonprofits' structural adaptation to the market environment. A full research agenda would examine both the structural adaptations and strategies of large nonprofits and the network-based adaptive responses of small nonprofits.

Contributions to Economic Theory

Markets are, of course, at the heart of the study of economics. And markets, on the supply side, are dominated in most cases by for-profit businesses. Thus, classical economic theory derives largely from the study of business behavior. But as this volume demonstrates, nonprofit organizations are also involved in markets and may influence the operations of those markets — often in unexpected ways. The behavior or results that we may observe when nonprofits participate in markets are unexpected because we tend to base our expectations on existing theories. And those theories are in turn built on the assumption that markets consist solely of the interaction of profit-maximizing firms. What is needed instead is a broadening of economic theory to take account of the new elements introduced into the ecology of the market system by the participation of nonprofit organizations. Thus, the introduction of nonprofit firms as market participants presents the opportunity to expand economic theory itself and to question the classical models by asking what happens when we modify the assumptions that we normally make about participating (business) firms.

Of all the chapters in this volume, the one by Eckel and Steinberg presents the clearest challenge to classical economic theory. By introducing the notion that mergers can create nonprofit organizations whose market power generates surpluses that pay for public goods, these authors question the classical understanding of the relative efficiencies of monopoly, duopoly, and competition. And with this questioning comes a skepticism about the applicability of contemporary antitrust law to the collaborative activities of nonprofit organizations.

Another example that suggests the need to stretch economic theory is Salamon's analysis of the investment behavior of foundations. One approach to this subject is to assume that all foundations should follow the tenets of modern portfolio theory, taking a long-term view to maximize their total return. Such an approach may very well apply to most foundations. But this view may also be inappropriately shaped by the classical assumption that foundations, like business firms, seek to ensure their long-term survival, growth, and wealth. Some foundations (following the example of the Rosenwald Fund) may prefer to spend themselves out of existence, doing as much good as they can as soon as possible (benevolently suicidal participants in the ecology of the market system!). Others are constrained by portfolio limitations imposed by donors. Still others may prefer to combine financial and social objectives in order to invest in socially desirable enterprises. How can modern portfolio theory account for these considerations or be adapted to serve nonprofits' diverse purposes and missions?

Preston's work on labor markets in which nonprofit workers participate provides a third example. Classical theory would have us understand that, assuming uniformity in the quality of workers, labor markets will clear, and wages for a given type of worker will be the same from one sector to another. Otherwise, workers will simply move from the low-wage to the high-wage sector until the differentials disappear. But in labor markets involving nonprofit workers, these differentials do not disappear. Typically, nonprofits pay consistently lower wages than for-profit organizations in the same labor markets for workers of the same caliber. While Preston does confirm a steady exit of non-profit workers in the scientific and technical professions, such exit does not serve to fully equilibrate these markets. More factors are at work, such as the nonpecuniary rewards of non-profit labor that workers accept in compensation for lower pay. Clearly, the study of nonprofit organizations' participation in labor markets can lead to a fuller understanding of the operation of labor markets in general by identifying factors that preclude reaching the simple, classical equilibrium solutions.

A fourth example is manifested in Avner Ben-Ner's analysis in Chapter Nine of the use of bartering practices by non-profit organizations. Apparently, nonprofits use barter rather than participating in monetized markets for goods and services more commonly than businesses do. Why is this? What are the conditions under which a monetized market is more efficient than a bartering arrangement, and vice versa? This is a very fundamental question, surprisingly neglected by economists, to which new insights can be drawn by comparing nonprofit and for-profit behavior in bartered versus monetized markets.

A fifth example concerns the operations of capital markets. How do organizations raise capital when they cannot sell ownership rights and distribute dividends to individuals who are willing to take risks in order to reap commensurate rewards? This, of course, is a particularly cogent question for nonprofits operating in a market economy. One answer, as we have seen, is to imitate business practice by generating profits and reinvesting them internally. Another answer is to participate in debt markets. Even in this realm, however, there is much that can be learned to stretch our understanding of how capital markets work. As Tuckman points out, lending institutions find it difficult to deal with nonprofits, because nonprofit finances and accounting are different from those of for-profit firms and because it is more difficult to hold nonprofit assets as collateral. These assets may be specialized and may be protected by special laws, and public sensitivities often make it difficult to foreclose on nonprofits. How do capital markets function when such regulations, uncertainties, and constraining factors interfere with market transactions? Does the contemporary theory of transaction costs adequately account for the problems associated with nonprofit borrowing (see Williamson, 1975)? What accounting conventions, informational programs, guarantee mechanisms, and regulatory policies can ameliorate these problems? How would such solutions, addressed to ameliorating the capital needs of nonprofits, help increase the efficiency of capital markets for other borrowers? All these questions are stimulated by inquiries about the special experience of nonprofit organizations in debt markets.

A final example of how studying the role of nonprofits in the ecology of the market system may stretch the bounds of economic theory concerns the operations of markets in which nonprofits and for-profits combine their energies in order to pursue separate but compatible and mutually supportive agendas. This is increasingly the case in cause-related marketing, where, as Carbone observes, businesses market their services in a manner that provides publicity benefits to the for-profit and revenues to the nonprofit. Existing economic theory deals little with such markets. We do have some understanding of how poor information can undermine markets in which there is a risk of inadvertent purchase of poor-quality goods (Akerlof, 1970). Moreover, this theory has been extended to explain how the nonprofit form can provide protection to consumers in such situations. But what happens when nonprofit and for-profit fortunes are intertwined through joint marketing arrangements? Does the for-profit firm benefit in its markets from the good reputation of the nonprofit? Does the nonprofit benefit from the wider exposure that it receives from the for-profit's marketing effort? Does it suffer if the for-profit turns out to be disreputable in some way? Do the for-profit and nonprofit organizations modify each other's behaviors in some way? For example, does the nonprofit become more profit-oriented or less sensitive to social ills in which the for-profit may be implicated (for example, drinking, smoking)? Or does the for-profit tend to become more socially aware and responsible in its market behavior as a consequence of its association with the nonprofit? These are all boundary-stretching questions for economic theory and research suggested by the study of nonprofit organizations in the marketplace.

It seems audacious to suggest that the study of nonprofits can have a major influence on the development of economic theory. Yet this claim is not terribly far-fetched. The strength of classical theory is that it is built on relatively simple assumptions about economic motivations, constraints, and information and the mobility of resources. The result is tractable models with extraordinary explanatory power. These models constitute a strong core framework for understanding economic institutions. The study of nonprofits can add substantial nuance to this framework. What happens when we add altruistic and other nonpecuniary motivations to the mix of factors driving the behavior of individuals and organizations participating in markets? What happens when participating organizations produce public as well as private goods? What happens when organizational survival is subservient to accomplishing a goal or mission? What happens when individuals value the intrinsic character of their work as well as their wages and other economic benefits? What happens when informational difficulties inhibit the functioning of output and capital markets? What happens when the success of an organization is critically dependent on reputation and public trust? What happens when laws and public policy, which undergird the operations of markets, are broadened to accommodate the full mix of nonprofit, public, and for-profit organizations that collaborate and compete within the overall ecology of the market economy? Such questions, while they have been raised specifically in the context of markets in which nonprofits participate, apply in some degree to markets in general. The focus on nonprofits merely highlights these issues and guides economists to broaden the base of existing theory in a variety of productive directions.

Reforms as Experiments

If there is one message that comes through clearly throughout the pages of this book, it is the theme set forth by Ostrom and

Davis and echoed by Timpane in their chapters highlighting the issues and institutional alternatives involved in the delivery of educational services. In a nutshell, we have barely begun to appreciate the variety of possible institutional arrangements, involving various mixes and interrelationships among for-profit, governmental, and private nonprofit organizations, that can be used for the provision and production of many different public and private services in the market economy. Only a few service areas are dealt with in depth in these pages—education, health care, foundations, research—but even this narrow slice of the nonprofit service world clearly demonstrates the limits of our understanding of the possible arrangements and their relative merits and weaknesses. We have some concepts and theories and some limited experience concerning private versus public schools and choice-based versus bureaucratic school systems, concerning independent versus in-house research and development laboratories and university-industry collaborations, concerning for-profit and nonprofit hospital systems, and so on. But documentation of experience is spotty and incomplete, and many ideas for reform are new or untested. Should foundations pool their investments in common funds? Should elementary and secondary education be offered through voucher systems? Should nonprofit mergers be judged by different standards than business mergers? Should nonprofit hospitals' tax exemption be revoked if these institutions fail to behave differently than for-profit hospitals? These are perplexing and difficult questions that defy simple answers or easy theoretical analysis.

Two principles emerge from these pages that may be helpful in guiding an agenda for future research as well as practical reform, in the face of the bewildering array of institutional possibilities. The first principle, articulated most clearly by Ostrom and Davis and by Nelson, is that there are few across-the-board answers or simple models that apply to all circumstances. In short, institutional solutions must be devised to fit the particular case at hand. History, local context, culture, and individual tastes and preferences may all influence the particular mix and combination of institutions through which a given service is best provided, and the preferred combination may very well change over time. Thus, institutional design in the

ecology of the market system becomes a matter of crafts-
manship, of molding the institutional building blocks — government, for-profit firms, and nonprofit organizations — into arrangements that fit the time and place. Theoretical principles
and experience derived elsewhere can help, but they cannot
identify solutions unequivocally.

The second, related principle is that institutional reforms
are best viewed as experiments. Underlying this idea is the
notion that changes in institutional arrangements should be
designed as societal learning experiences (for a discussion of
this idea, see Rivlin, 1971). That learning can take place in
several ways. By systematically documenting experience on how
particular arrangements function in different contexts, we can
learn what works in which circumstances. And by evaluating
new arrangements as they are implemented, we can generate the
information required to make adjustments over time — to fine
tune institutional parameters so that the arrangements fit better
and adapt as local circumstances change.

The beauty of market-based economic arrangements and
democratic systems that support market-based arrangements is
that these systems are fundamentally adaptive. When markets
falter in various ways, we devise policies to patch them up,
supplement them, or develop incentives to make them work
better. For example, in addition to the religious and constitutional roots of the nonprofit sector discussed in the Introduction, the invention of nonprofit organizations may also be
viewed in part as an adaptation to the ecology of the untram-
meled marketplace, offering services of a type or in a manner
that for-profits or government cannot adequately provide. Thus,
viewing reforms as experiments is entirely consistent with the
fundamental concept of the market economy and the adaptive
nature of participants in an organizational ecology.

Outlook

The five themes identified above encompass broad dimensions
along which the subject of nonprofit organizations in a market
economy can be productively studied. It is interesting to observe

that the formulation of this agenda resembles the way in which markets themselves function as adaptive institutions. When our knowledge base in inadequate, we look for ways to enhance it — with new information, with new theories and concepts, and with adjustments to old ways of thinking. The study of nonprofit organizations in a market economy offers this opportunity. Such study not only expands our conception of what is involved in the functioning of markets and the role of nonprofits within the ecology of market systems; it also stimulates our thinking in general — about how the economy works, about how our institutions function and how they can be reformed, and about the value systems around which we organize society as a whole. In this way, the study of nonprofits in markets truly reflects the ultimate role that nonprofit organizations can serve in a healthy market economy — a venue for the interchange of ideas. Such a functional role as the purveyor of information and ideas will certainly move nonprofits from the periphery to center stage in the markets of the information age in the twenty-first century. Present and future researchers will thus do well to draw themselves to this new focus.

References

Akerlof, G. "The Market for 'Lemons': Quality, Uncertainty and the Market Mechanism." *Quarterly Journal of Economics*, 1970, *84*, 487–500.

Hannan, M. T., and Freeman, J. *Organizational Ecology*. Cambridge, Mass.: Harvard University Press, 1989.

Hansmann, H. "Economic Theories of Nonprofit Organizations." In W. W. Powell (ed.), *The Nonprofit Sector: A Research Handbook*. New Haven, Conn.: Yale University Press, 1987.

Musgrave, R., and Musgrave, P. *Public Finance in Theory and Practice*. (4th ed.) New York: McGraw-Hill, 1983.

Rivlin, A. M. *Systematic Thinking for Social Action*. Washington, D.C.: Brookings Institution, 1971.

Williamson, O. E. *Markets and Hierarchies*. New York: Free Press, 1975.

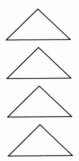

APPENDIX

Conference Participants

Nonprofit Organizations in a Market Economy:
A Research Conference

Sponsored by
the Mandel Center for Nonprofit Organizations
Case Western Reserve University
Cleveland, Ohio

November 7 through 9, 1991

Plenary Speakers

Reynold Levy, AT&T Corporation
Morton L. Mandel, Premier Industrial Corporation
Steven Minter, The Cleveland Foundation
Elinor Ostrom, Indiana University

421

Paper Presenters

David Billis, London School of Economics and Political
   Science
Robert F. Carbone, University of Maryland
Louis Galambos, Johns Hopkins University
David Knoke, University of Minnesota
Richard R. Nelson, Columbia University
Anne E. Preston, State University of New York, Stony
   Brook
Arnold Reisman, Case Western Reserve University
Lester M. Salamon, Johns Hopkins University
Jagdish N. Sheth, Emory University
David Starkweather, University of California at Berkeley
Richard Steinberg, Indiana University
P. Michael Timpane, Columbia University
Howard P. Tuckman, Memphis State University
John A. Yankey, Case Western Reserve University

Panel Chairs and Discussants

Raj Aggarwal, John Carroll University
Arthur Austin, Case Western Reserve University
Darlyne Bailey, Case Western Reserve University
Avner Ben-Ner, University of Minnesota
David Bergholz, George Gund Foundation
Arthur Blum, Case Western Reserve University
Elizabeth Boris, The Aspen Institute
Laura Chisolm, Case Western Reserve University
Okiana Christian Dark, University of Richmond
David Cooperrider, Case Western Reserve University
Rosemarie Emanuele, John Carroll University
Ted Fabyan, Vocational Guidance Services
Michael Fogarty, Case Western Reserve University
Vic Gelb, Gelb Associates
Paul Gerhart, Case Western Reserve University
Peter Gerhart, Case Western Reserve University
Benjamin Gidron, Ben Gurion University

David Gillespie, Washington University
Bradford Gray, Yale University
David C. Hammack, Case Western Reserve University
Bart Harvey, Enterprise Foundation
Susan Helper, Case Western Reserve University
Michael Krashinsky, University of Toronto
Susan Lajoie, The Cleveland Foundation
Bill Levis, United Way of America
Richard Magat, The Foundation Center
David Mason, Consultant
Robert Mason, Case Western Reserve University
Duncan Neuhauser, Case Western Reserve University
Michael O'Neill, University of San Francisco
Herbert J. Paine, Consultant
Mohan Reddy, Case Western Reserve University
Paul Salipante, Case Western Reserve University
Harvey Salkin, Case Western Reserve University
Richard Shatten, Cleveland Tomorrow
J. B. Silvers, Case Western Reserve University
Mark I. Singer, Case Western Reserve University
Melissa M. Stone, Boston University
Dennis R. Young, Case Western Reserve University

Funders

The Lilly Endowment
The W. K. Kellogg Foundation
The Cleveland Foundation
The George Gund Foundation
Anonymous Donor

Staff

Linda K. Serra, Conference Manager
Diane Felder, Julia Brown, Ramona Wright, Pat Martin,
Secretarial Assistance

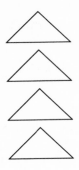

NAME INDEX

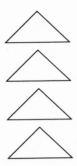

SUBJECT INDEX

American Prospect Research Association, and marketing, 298, 306

American Red Cross, as trade association, 140

American Schools Development Corporation, 343

American Symphony Orchestra League, as trade association, 167

Amherst College, and competition, 59

Anticipation, and marketing, 391

Antitrust laws, standards of, 57–58

Arkansas, education and business in, 358

Asia, sovereignty in southeast, 12

Asset specificity, in education, 41–42, 44

Associated In-Group Donors v. *United Way, Inc.*, 59, 80

Association for Documentary Editing, development of, 82–83, 98

Association for Healthcare Philanthropy, 298

Asymmetrical information: and competition, 76–77; and measurement, 35–36; and public goods, 24

AT&T, divestiture of, 99–100

Australia: management issues in, 326; privatization by, 382

Autonomy: and management, 326; for schools, 45

B

Banks, capital from, 218–219

Barter: aspects of, 278–293; background on, 278–280, 291; benefits of, 281–284; conclusions on, 290–291; merits of claims on, 284–285; among nonprofits, 285–290, 291–292; and product nature, 288–289; reasons for, 280–285, 291; and trust, 282–283, 285, 287, 289

Bituminous Coal Operators Association, as trade association, 140

Boards: in community networks, 287; and foundation invest-

ments, 242–243, 244–245; and management, 328–329, 332–333

Bonds: capital from, 222–224; foundation assets in, 256–257

Boston: education compact in, 343, 354–355, 360; telefund appeals in, 303

Boy Scouts, as trade association, 138, 168

Bureaucracy: in management, 323–325, 328–329, 331–332, 336–337; in schools, 344

Bush administration, 147, 151, 205, 345, 359

Business, attitudes toward, 149–150. *See also* For-profit sector

Business Coalition for Education Reform, 359, 361

Business History Conference, development of, 82–83, 97

Business Roundtable: and education, 358, 359, 361; as trade association, 151

C

California: education and business in, 347, 353, 355, 358; hospitals in, 115–116, 118, 119–120, 130; privatization in, 382; tax limits in, 344, 347, 356

Canada, and sovereignty, 12

Capital: aspects of, 203–232; background on, 203–204; conclusion on, 229–230; consequences of seeking, 225–226; criteria for borrowing, 226–229; from internal funds, 208–210; from loans and grants, 210–217; markets for, 217–224; need for, 204–206; role of, 206–207; sources of, 207–224

Capital-asset pricing theory, 240

Career paths: aspects of sectoral patterns for, 177–202; background on, 177–179; conclusions on, 186, 191–192, 194, 197, 198–201; data for study of, 179–184; and exit and wage differ-